DEPARTMENT OF URBAN & REGIONAL PLANNING

UNIVERSITY OF TORONTO

230 COLLEGE STREET TORONTO, M5S 1A1, ONT.

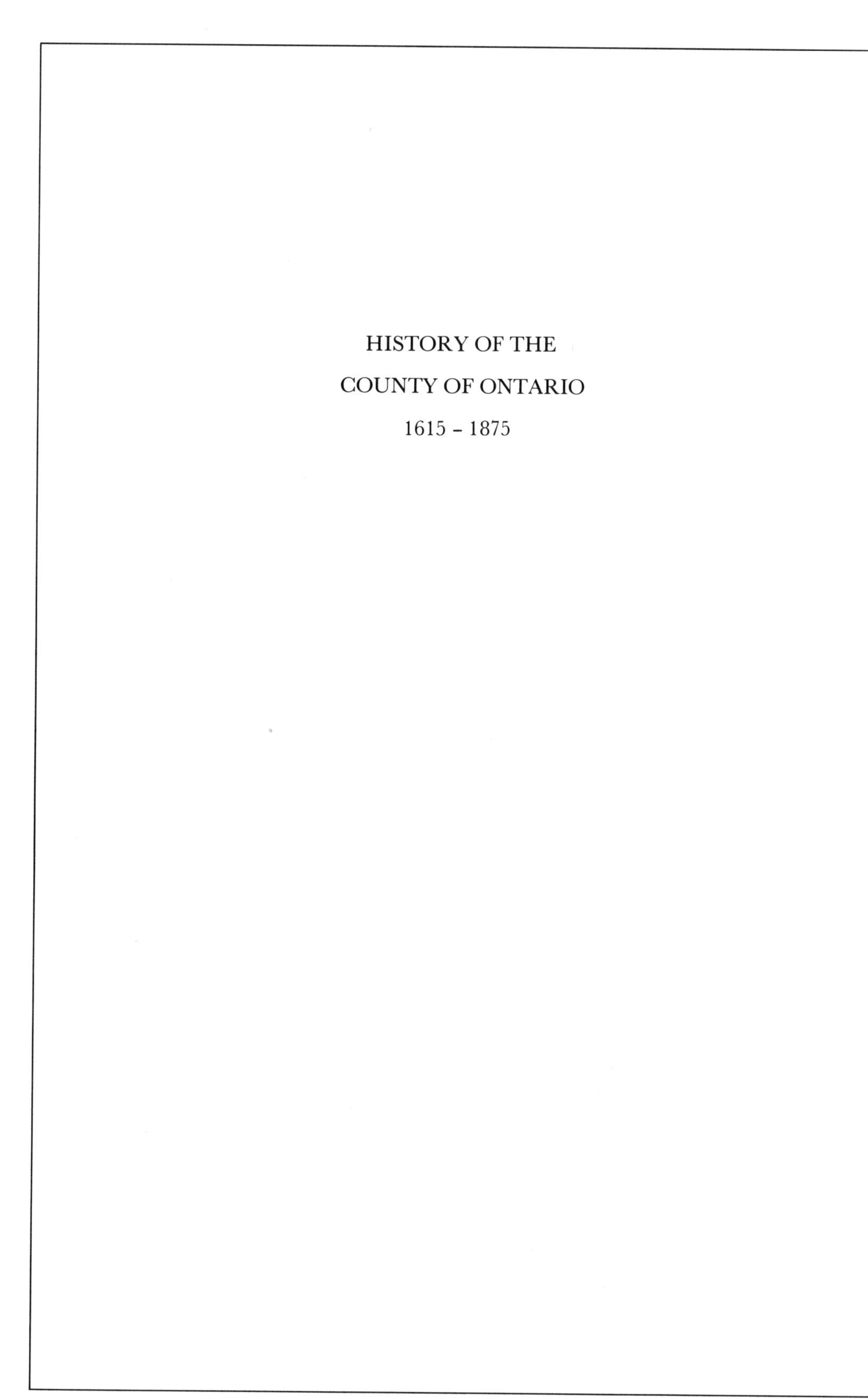

HISTORY OF THE COUNTY OF ONTARIO

1615 - 1875

HISTORY OF THE COUNTY OF ONTARIO

1615-1875

LEO A. JOHNSON

THE CORPORATION
OF THE COUNTY OF ONTARIO
WHITBY, ONTARIO

ISBN 0-9690996-0-6

Printed and bound in Canada.

Co-ordinating Editor: Helen Nolan
Designer: Sam Smart
Printing and Binding: The Hunter Rose Company
Typeface: Baskerville
Paper: Plainfield Offset
Cover: Tanalin 10

FOREWORD

I am indeed proud to be associated with the members of the 1973 council in publishing this early history of our county.

Professor Johnson's well-documented synthesis covers the period from the trading Indians of the fifteenth and sixteenth centuries through the late 1800s when the County of Ontario began to assume its modern-day profile. With fluid chronological organization he presents the elements, circumstances and events which contributed to our history in that era.

From its beginning, the record of the County of Ontario has been one of significant geographic, social, economic and cultural growth. Business, industry, commerce and agriculture have flourished within its boundaries.

People of many countries, creeds and cultures with different political beliefs – but with the common goal of development and progress – have written this meaningful history.

It is our hope that all, historian, teacher, student and general reader alike, will find our story informative and rewarding.

John a. Hawden

Warden, County of Ontario, 1973

During my life I have been
fortunate enough to have known
three great teachers:

Alicia Dorothy Abbott Johnson,
Luella Phoebe Tomlinson Barker,
Kenneth Alexander Mackirdy.

This book is offered as a small
token of the gratitude I feel for
their influence on my life.

L.A.J.

PREFACE

The writing of this history has been both a pleasure and a challenge: a pleasure because it allowed me to meet and know many of the residents of Ontario County; and a challenge because so little scholarly work has been done in Canadian local history that innumerable problems of intellectual approach, method and style remained to be attempted.

In the conception of this book four factors have been uppermost in my mind. First, I hoped to write a history that was relevant and useful to the residents of the county in understanding their own development and circumstances. Thus the themes that are studied here are those which seemed to have the greatest lasting effect on the area and contributed most centrally to the shape of local society. Secondly, I have attempted to deal with the local situation on two planes: the first at the level of an historical analysis of the various forces at work in the area and their local effects; and the other at the level of the perceptions of those forces and effects held by the residents. Thirdly, because the Ontario County area existed as an economically, politically and socially subordinate hinterland to the metropolitan areas stretching from Toronto to Montreal and to London, its internal development was frequently interrupted by decisions and actions emanating from those centres. Thus it was necessary at times to discuss both continuity and disruption and the contexts within which the external interventions originated. Finally, I have endeavoured, through the use of extensive quotations, to communicate some of the colour and flavour of life in nineteenth-century Ontario County.

In the preparation of this work I have incurred large debts to a host of people. Chief among these are: William B. Manning, Administrator and Clerk-Treasurer of Ontario County, whose patience and help have done much to smooth the way for me; the owners and editors of the Oshawa *Times*, Port Perry *Star*, Uxbridge *Times-Journal*, and Cannington *Gleaner* who allowed me the use of their files; Arleen Michael, my typist; Janet Campbell, who read the manuscript and saved me from innumerable errors; and Helen Nolan, my co-ordinating editor. To all these I offer my thanks. I hope only that the end result of my labours justifies their interest and aid.

Leo A. Johnson
August 8, 1973.

Contents

THE NATIVE PEOPLES

Ontario County's first farmers and traders were not daring French *coureurs de bois*, nor were they Loyalists fleeing the Revolutionary Wars. Instead, the first farmers and businessmen were members of a quite different civilization – that of the Indian nations of the Huron and Iroquois Confederacies.

During the fifteenth and sixteenth centuries, before Europeans had penetrated to this area, southern Ontario and New York State were inhabited by a number of Indian nations who spoke varieties of the Iroquoian language. Over the years these Iroquoian nations had gradually divided into two rival trading alliances separated by the lower Great Lakes. South of Lake Ontario resided the Iroquois Confederacy – the Mohawks, Oneidas, Onondagas, Cayugas and Senecas – who were joined about 1720 by the Tuscaroras to make up the Six Nations. North of the Lakes the Petuns (or Tobacco Indians) and the Neutrals were dominated by the vigorous Huron nations who lived in about twenty large villages between Lake Simcoe and Georgian Bay.

Among all Indian tribes who participated in trade (and almost all did), control of that trade became the basis of intertribal rivalries as each tribe strove to be the middleman. Although the Hurons were an agricultural people who grew great crops of Indian corn (maize), beans, pumpkins and tobacco, their chief occupation and source of prosperity was a trade monopoly between their neighbours to the south, the Petuns and Neutrals, and the northern Ottawas, Chippewas, and even the distant Winnebagos. So prosperous was this monopoly that by 1630 Huronia contained more than 30,000 inhabitants – a greater population than the area would again contain before 1906.[1] The

Hurons traded in three kinds of goods: foodstuffs – corn, pumpkins and beans – grown by themselves, the Neutrals and the Petuns; manufactured articles, such as flints, copper ornaments, and hemp nets and bags; and the rich furs, buffalo robes and birch bark canoes purchased from the tribes living to the north and west.

All winter the men and women of the Huron longhouses prepared for the coming summer's trade by grinding corn, weaving collars of nettles and making sacks and fishnets from the hemp grown for them by the Petuns.[2] In the summer almost every able-bodied man went on trading expeditions hundreds of miles up the rivers and across the lakes of Ontario, Quebec and the northern American States, their great birch bark canoes loaded with corn, tobacco and hemp, the bales of sacks and fishnets, and the bundles of tools and ornaments so highly prized by their northern and western neighbours. At Sault Ste. Marie, on James Bay and in northern Quebec they traded their goods for the warm buffalo robes, rich furs and dried fish that could be sold to the south. So large was this trade, and so advantageous was it to all concerned, that the Nipissings, for instance, bought their entire year's supply of corn from the Hurons and grew none themselves, concentrating instead on fishing and trapping for the next year's exchange.[3]

The Huron trading economy was naturally reflected in their government which made provision for personal, family or clan monopoly of small trading areas, and for sharing among the entire tribe any trade which was too large to be handled by a single clan.[4] Le Jeune, a Jesuit missionary to the Hurons, made a study of their civil government in 1636.

> There is . . . a certain order established as regards foreign nations . . . Several familes have their own private trades, and he is considered Master of one line of trade who was first to discover it. The children share the rights of their parents . . . as do those who bear the same name; no one goes into it without permission, which is given only in consideration of presents; he associates with him as many or as few as he wishes. If he has a good supply of merchandise, it is to his advantage to divide it with few companions, for thus he secures all he desires in the Country; it is in this that most of their riches consist. But if any one should . . . engage in a trade without permission from him who is Master, he may do a good business in secret and concealment; but if he is surprised by the way, he will not be better treated than a thief, – he will only carry back his body to his house . . . there will be some complaint about it, but no further prosecution.[5]

Under the law, since the Rock tribe of the Hurons was the first to encounter the French trade, they had a right to a monopoly, but because the trade was too great for the Rock tribe to handle alone, they shared it with other Huron tribes to the benefit of all.

All aspects of Huron government showed the same characteristics of traditional laws modified by good sense. Traditionally there existed tribal councils and a national council, a crude standing army and a police force,[6] but the government was decentralized and, when there were no active duties to perform, existed in name only. Moreover, if a tribe disagreed with the decision of the national council, it was not bound to abide by it, but could, and often did, refuse to act with the other tribes. The government did not collapse during periods of inactivity, mainly because membership in the councils and individual governmental responsibilities were passed on by a combination of inheritance and election.

The Hurons were a matriarchal society. That is, they passed the family name and property from one generation to another through the women of the tribe. When the daughter of a family married, she and her husband lived in her mother's house,[7] and the husband became a member of the wife's family. Family property was passed down through the women and so was the right to name members to the tribal and national councils. Whenever a council member died, it was the duty of the eldest grandmother of that line to name his successor from among the male members of her family. The chosen man then assumed both the name and the duties of his predecessor. So strong was this tradition that among the present-day descendants of these families, many of the hereditary titles still persist.[8] Once elected, the chief served for life.

During long periods when times were prosperous, no wars were contemplated and no questions of civil order or trade were in dispute, no active government can be said to have existed. On the other hand, the hereditary organization was always there and ready to operate when emergencies arose. Such an arrangement had some obvious drawbacks, of course. Because the chief had no overriding authority in the individualistic Huron society, projects or expeditions could be carried on only as long as his followers remained enthusiastic – as soon as things went badly (a battle was lost, trade fell off or hunting was poor) the organization fell apart and the more easily discouraged would go their way or return home. As Champlain noted in 1615, it took days of oration to persuade the warriors to attack the Iroquois, and even when the long trek down the Muskoka-Trent waterways had begun, long orations were still necessary every morning to keep up their spirits.

Domestic life among the Hurons derived from their agricultural methods and their extensive family ties. Because the Hurons had few domestic animals and no method of making fertilizer, they lacked a means of fertilizing their fields. Thus they were forced to move their villages whenever yields began to decline because of soil exhaustion. While these moves customarily occurred at ten-year intervals, reports of villages remaining in the same spot for up to twenty years are not uncommon.

Délamberville, a Jesuit missionary, described the problems such a move created for the Iroquois, whose methods were the same as the Hurons.

> On arrival, I found the Iroquois of this village occupied in transporting their corn, their effects, and their cabins to a place 2 leagues distant from their former residence, where they had dwelt for 19 years. They made this change in order to have their firewood in convenient proximity, and to secure fields more fertile than those they were abandoning. This is not done without difficulty; for inasmuch as carts are not used here, and the country is very hilly, the labour of men and women, who carry their goods on their backs, is consequently harder and of longer duration. To supply the lack of horses, the inhabitants of these forests render reciprocal aid to one another, so that a single family will hire sometimes 80 or 100 persons; and they are in turn obliged it from them, or they are freed from that obligation by giving food to those whom they have employed.[9]

Although there were meadows or open areas in the forest, the Hurons chose to build their villages in the woods "on account of the convenience of building their towns there",[10] and also because of the fertility of the deep leaf mould under the trees. When a village was moved, it was done gradually because of the difficulty of clearing new land and building new longhouses. Such a move might require two or three years, for without iron axes, clearing new land was extremely difficult. As Champlain noted:

> They clear it with great difficulty on account of not having proper tools for their purpose. A party of them will strip the trees of all their branches which they burn at the foot of the said tree to kill it. They clear the ground thoroughly between the trees and then sow their corn a pace apart, putting in each spot about ten grains, and thus continuing until they have enough for three or four years' provision, for fear lest they should have a bad year. The women have charge of sowing and gathering.[11]

Huron diet reflected their dependence upon their major crop, corn. Often the Hurons flavoured the boiled corn (called by the French "Sagamite") with herbs or a handful of waterflies in season. The Jesuit Fathers at first were dismayed with the way it was prepared. One Jesuit wrote:

> A little Indian corn boiled in water, and for the better fare of the country a little fish, rank with internal rottenness, or some powdered dried fish as the only seasoning–this is the usual food [and] drink of the country; as a little something extra, a little bread made of the same corn.... Fresh fish and game are articles so rare that they are not worth mentioning.[12]

While such food at first seemed strange and unpleasant to the missionaries, in time they grew to like it despite its strangeness. As one priest remarked, "I find the sagamite not only good, but it often tastes delicious".[13]

While the Hurons were said to hunt "only for pleasure or on extraordinary occasions", they did conduct a large-scale hunt during the late winter – "the only time of the year where they have a little meat".[15] At other times the women fished and snared rabbits and carrier pigeons to augment their diet.

When European explorers first reached the Huron and Iroquois villages, they were so impressed by their size and strong defenses that they called the villages "castles". A main feature of the more important Huron villages was the strong palisades around them which, according to Champlain, were as much as thirty feet in height. These stockades were made of trunks of trees set upright in the ground "in three tiers, interlaced into one another, on top of which they have galleries which they furnish with stones for hurling, and water to extinguish the fire that their enemies might lay against their palisades".[16] Around the bottom of the walls were great trunks of trees placed lengthwise, resting on strong short forks made from tree trunks, over which an enemy would have to clamber to reach the walls, so that he would be exposed to attack from the galleries above while he was engaged in scrambling across the barriers. These fortified villages were very large, containing up to 1,200 or 1,500 persons living in from fifty to a hundred longhouses.

The Huron longhouse, more than anything else, expressed Huron ideas about family ties. When a Huron daughter was bethrothed, at night she went to the bed of her husband, returning every morning to her mother's house. After a child was born, thus confirming the marriage, the husband moved to the house of his mother-in-law and became a member of her family. So close were family ties that, rather than build individual homes, the members built additions to the mother's home to accommodate the growing family. Some of these extended homes – longhouses – grew very large indeed, dimensions of twenty feet wide by one hundred feet long were not uncommon, although lengths of sixty to eighty feet seem about average.[17]

The longhouse was constructed by cutting poles about three inches in diameter which were pointed by fire and driven firmly into the ground. These uprights were bent together into an arched top about twenty-five feet high, and tied with leather thongs. Over this framework the Hurons placed elm bark to keep out the rain and cold.[18] Inside the longhouse, fires were placed at about ten-foot intervals. Each fire was shared by two families who lived on opposite sides of it. Thus a three-fire house held six families, and a twelve-fire house, such as Champlain describes, held twenty-four families containing perhaps a hundred or more people. Smoke from the fires was supposed to escape through a hole in the roof which also served as the "window". Pieces of bark were used to close the hole in bad weather. Doors, placed at the ends of the longhouses, were closed with a slab of bark suspended from above. In winter the door was insulated with blankets and skins. Against the walls were built platforms, about five feet wide and four feet high, running the length of the longhouse.[19] The Hurons slept on these in the summer to escape the fleas, while in the winter the cold forced them to sleep on the ground near the fire. Wood, collected by the women in March and April, was kept under the platform, and at the end of the longhouse was a space to store maize. Ears of corn were braided into bunches and hung from the rafters, while poles hanging from the roof provided a place to hang pots, clothing and provisions.[20] In other buildings of similar construction were kept the furs, trade goods and so forth belonging to the family.

The missionaries' reaction to life in the longhouse varied as radically as did their reaction to Huron food. Newcomers, especially, found it difficult to adjust to the crowded, noisy, smoky conditions. One missionary wrote:

> If you go visit them in their cabins, - and you must go there oftener than once a day, if you would perform your duty as you ought, - you will find a miniature picture of Hell, - seeing nothing, ordinarily, but fire and smoke, and on every side naked bodies, black and half-roasted, mingled pell-mell with the dogs, which are held as dear as the children of the house, and share the beds, plates, and food of their masters. Everything is a cloud of dust, and if you go within, you will not reach the end of the cabin before you are completely befouled with soot, filth, and dirt.[21]

Despite the discomfort of smoke and crowding, once they became accustomed to the strange conditions of the longhouse, the missionaries found that life there was not so uncomfortable as it had at first seemed. Another missionary explained:

> The Architects of this country build their houses, Places, and Ships much more rapidly than those of Europe; and if one be not lodged there so sumptuously, still one often dwells there in great comfort and gladness.[22]

Thus when the French arrived at Georgian Bay and Lake Simcoe in 1615, they discovered that a flourishing civilization already existed there. As the missionary, Bressani, pointed out, "because of their trade and excellent devisings" the Hurons were "hardly Barbarians, save in name".[23] Through the forests of Rama, Mara, Thorah and the southern townships the men trapped and, in the winter, hunted deer, bear and moose. Down the Holland-Rouge trail they passed with their trade goods and their war parties looking for profit or conquest. The Hurons were a happy, proud, successful people, but for them the future was dark. Although the French brought hymns of salvation and promises of riches, they brought also the seeds of despair. In 1615, for the Hurons, the end had begun. The irony of the Hurons' fall was that the same trade monopolies which had been the key to their prosperity would provide the means of their destruction.

Long before the French had actually penetrated to Huronia, the effects of the new European trade goods had already been felt by the Hurons. For at least a century there had been contacts and exchanges of goods on the Atlantic coast between cod fishermen on the Grand Banks and the coastal Indians, and these goods had quickly passed from hand to hand into the interior, creating an appetite for more as they were exchanged from one tribe to another. The primary attraction of the European goods for the Indians was the superiority of iron and steel tools over implements made of stone and bone. With a steel axe a single workman could clear land at a rate of five or even ten times faster than he could with a stone axe. Thus productivity could be raised and a higher standard of living could be gained through the use of advanced European technology.

It should be made clear, however, that the Indians possessed a unique and valuable technology of their own. In the early years the French depended for survival almost entirely on the Indians' knowledge of the life-supporting capacities of the environment of the Canadian Shield. During Jacques Cartier's first attempt to winter in North America in 1535-36, his party was almost wiped out by scurvy (the lack of vitamin C), before the Indians showed them that a life-saving tea could be made by boiling white cedar. Similarly, the birch bark canoe - one of the finest small craft ever designed because of its light weight, durability and load-carrying capacity - made possible the navigation of the rough rivers of Canada. In addition, many of the foodstuffs of the Indians - potatoes, corn, pumpkins, beans and tobacco - were quickly adopted by the Europeans. Unfortunately for the Indians, the ability of the Europeans to maintain a monopoly of their technology while acquiring a knowledge of the Indians' inventions and adaptations, soon placed the Europeans at a distinct advantage in their economic relationships.[24]

The Hurons would pay a high price for their adoption of European tools without acquiring the ability to make them themselves. As European tools became more common, old tool-making skills were abandoned and new agricultural and trading methods appeared which were based on the existence of iron and steel tools. Thus the original Huron-French alliance of mutual trade and economic advantage gradually changed to one in which the French acquired the upper hand because of their monopoly of necessary goods. This shifting economic situation underlay Huron-French relations until the fall of the Huron empire in 1649.

The first recorded direct contact between the Hurons and Europeans occurred in 1535 when Jacques Cartier sailed up the St. Lawrence to visit the Huron and Seneca villages at Stadacona (Quebec) and Hochelaga.[25] As Cartier travelled up the St. Lawrence he was impressed by the way in which the natives paddled up to the ships "with many signs of joy", bearing foods to exchange for European trinkets.[26] What Cartier did not realize was that a thousand miles to the northwest at Sault Ste. Marie or James Bay those trinkets would bring a fortune in furs or buffalo hides at the next summer's trading fair. So valuable to the Indians were such items that a few years later when French merchants began to trade regularly at Tadoussac, the Stadaconans went to war with the Hochelagans in order to maintain a monopoly.[27] In the end, this war came to nothing since the Algonquins drove both nations out of the St. Lawrence Valley and occupied their village sites. Although no records remain of the war, by 1603 the Hurons had abandoned their permanent villages in the St. Lawrence Valley, relying instead on summer voyages from Huronia to carry on the trade. Moreover, the Hurons had negotiated an alliance with the Algonquins against the Iroquois who were their rivals for the French trade.

To the French government, and to Champlain in particular, the aims of colonization in North America were threefold: to enrich France by developing trade; to increase France's power and glory by exploring and settling the new land; and to do God's and the King's work by Christianizing and "civilizing" the native races. To carry out these tasks, Champlain would carry out a lifelong struggle to explore and colonize the new land. The first effort at colonization (Port Royal in 1604) failed, and Champlain turned his attention northward. After careful consideration, he decided on a new site – the old Huron village of Stadacona on the St. Lawrence River. There, in 1608, Champlain founded Quebec thereby placing himself, unsuspectingly, in the middle of the Algonquin-Huron-Iroquois trade rivalry.

The colony at Quebec was in jeopardy not only because it was too small and weak to stand alone among rival Indian alliances, but also because its monopoly was placed under constant attack by rival trading groups from France. In fact, as early as 1609 it became clear that there was no sure method of preventing rival French traders from breaking the colony's trade monopoly. To solve these two problems Champlain decided on a daring strategy – he would ally himself with the stronger of the two alliances, that of the Hurons and Algonquins. To seal the bargain and to gain information and a knowledge of each other's languages, young men were exchanged between the French and Hurons. One of these young men, Etienne Brûlé, later became the first white man to live among the Hurons in the Ontario County area.

Champlain's efforts to cement understanding between the two peoples did not stop there. Year after year he braved dangers and hardships in leading exploration trips inland and aiding the Hurons in their attacks on the Iroquois. It was one such expedition that first brought Europeans to Ontario County. In the winter of 1614-15 Champlain had been in France arranging with the Récollet Order for missionaries to be sent to Canada. After some discussion it was agreed that four missionaries, including Father Joseph Le Caron, would go. On July 2, 1615, Champlain arrived back in Canada to find a Huron delegation asking for aid in an attack against the Iroquois, whose raids on Huron trading routes were causing serious losses. Champlain decided to combine a raid into Iroquoian territory with an exploration trip into Huronia, and sent Le Caron ahead to establish a mission while he prepared for the raid. On July 9, Champlain and a small band of French and Indians were on their way. Travelling by the Ottawa-Mattawa-Lake Nipissing route, then following the shores of Georgian Bay south to Huronia, the party arrived on August 1, 1615.

Despite the lateness of the season, which made Champlain eager to get the attack under way, the Hurons found it necessary to spend a week dancing, feasting, singing and making fiery orations to raise the warriors' spirits, and to persuade them to undertake the long and hazardous trip south. At length, the feasts and orations came to an end and preparation began. To Champlain's disgust the Huron warriors numbered only five hundred, not the twenty-five hundred he had been promised at Quebec. Further, not even a week of orations could unite such an individualistic people. Finally in early September, the expedition got under way.

The route they followed was one familiar to the present-day boater - from the Narrows, across Lake Simcoe, up the Talbot River between Mara and Thorah townships, and down the Trent River system to Lake Ontario. The expedition was a disaster. Champlain was wounded twice; the attack on the Iroquois "castle" was a dismal failure; and the retreat back to Lake Ontario, with the wounded Champlain tied to the back of a stout brave, was a "hell" of pain.[28] Despite his request for a canoe and paddlers to carry him directly down the St. Lawrence to Quebec, Champlain was forced by his hosts to return the way he had come and to spend the winter in Huronia.

Despite the failure of the attack, Champlain had, by his bravery and willingness to aid the Hurons, won the friendship and admiration of his allies, particularly the Rock tribe. During the long winter at Cahiague, a Rock village, his intelligence, kindness and character cemented this friendship into an alliance that lasted for many years and helped pave the way for more extensive relations between French missionaries and traders and the Huron.[29]

From 1615 on, Frenchmen visited and lived in Huronia. Their purpose was twofold: to encourage the Hurons to come down to Quebec to trade; and to act as interpreters and guarantees of French good faith. Many of these French traders, like the *coureurs de bois* of later days, to the displeasure of the missionaries, quickly adopted Huron customs, took Huron wives, and ranged the rivers and woods with their adopted brothers.

Missionary efforts in Huronia were also tied to the fur trade - not so much because the missionaries were involved directly in the trade, but because the Hurons tolerated the missionary efforts in order to retain the good will of the French government and traders. As Father Gabriel Sagard observed, it was hard to work among any tribe that was not engaged in the Franco-Huron trade alliance.[30] For many years missionary efforts were sporadic. The Récollet, Le Caron, spent the winter of 1615-16 in Huronia, but returned to Quebec until 1623, when he and two other Récollets, Gabriel Sagard and Nicholas Viel, once more took up the mission, again with little noticeable effect. In 1626 the first two Jesuits, Jean de Brébeuf and Anne de Noue, came to Huronia. Their efforts ended when they and other Jesuits were forced to leave after Quebec was captured by the English in 1629.

When the Jesuits returned to Huronia in 1634, they came determined to make a concerted effort to convert the Hurons. The key to their plan was the establishment of colonies of French families among the Huron to present the example of "good and virtuous Christians". The principle behind this plan was the belief that to Christianize the Indians it was first necessary to "civilize" them – Le Caron even believed that Indians could not understand the Christian mysteries until they were "regulated by French laws and modes of living".[31] The plan, however, never came to fruition; the closest it came to realization was the continuous presence of French traders and missionaries in Huronia from 1634 on.

Coincident with the return of the French was the beginning of a series of disasters which weakened and ultimately hastened the fall of the Huron empire. When the French returned to Huronia in 1635 from the annual expedition to Quebec, they brought with them an epidemic (either smallpox or measles). So virulent and so deadly were these new maladies, especially among the children and old people, that in six years the Huron population was reduced from 30,000 to less than 12,000.[32] Along with the epidemics, the Hurons suffered two famines due to inclement weather in 1636 and 1643. Lalemant, writing in March 1644, reported that the famine was "universal among all these tribes for over a hundred leagues around. Indian corn, which is the sole staff of life here, was so scarce that those who had the most had hardly enough for sowing their fields. Many lived on a kind of acorn, on pumpkin and on paltry roots".[33] Thus when Iroquoian ambitions, sharpened by the scarcity of beaver in their own trading area, turned northward, the Hurons were in no condition to defend themselves or their French allies. Famine and disease were not, however, the only cause of Huron weakness in the impending struggle for ascendancy in the fur trade. The Jesuit missionary efforts, at last bearing fruit, were also a divisive factor among the Hurons.

The Jesuits were by no means unanimously welcomed by the Hurons when they returned in 1634. However, because the French had made it clear that they considered the presence of the missionaries of great importance, the Hurons tolerated them out of consideration for the fur trade. With the rapid spread of disease (and even the Jesuits observed that children tended to die soon after baptism) the rumour spread that the Jesuits were practicing a deadly form of witchcraft.[34] By 1639 many Hurons were proclaiming that since the Jesuits had arrived the whole country had gone to ruin, and the Hurons "no longer dream, their charms and Ascwandics [familiar spirits] have no more power, they are unlucky in everything".[35] Although a majority of the people wanted to kill the missionaries (according to Huron customs the killing of a witch carried no penalty), their leaders repeatedly stressed that they could not afford to rupture their trade alliance with the French by such an act. Here lay the heart of the Huron's economic dilemma. Because they had tied themselves almost entirely to trading relationships with the French, they had lost much of their ability to live without that trade. But the trade brought two disastrous side effects: war with the Iroquois and internal divisions created by the Jesuits.

It is clear that the Jesuits were well aware of the importance of the French-Huron trade alliance as a guarantee of their safety. In 1645 when the Hurons were considering giving up the fur trade out of a desire to end the war with the Iroquois, Lalemant pointed out the likely fate of the missionaries if the fur trade was ended. The missionaries would be exposed to an angry people who would no longer hesitate to kill them through fear of losing the fur trade with the French.[36]

Although the missionaries' position remained dangerous until the end, they became increasingly successful in winning converts to Christianity. Prior to 1640 most converts had been Hurons on the point of death who hoped that baptism would, somehow, save their lives.[37] After 1640, however, an increasing number of Hurons, including several prominent men, became Christians. Many factors seem to have worked to bring about conversion: admiration for Jesuit bravery, the desire to follow a Christian friend to heaven, the belief that the new God would help overcome their problems, and, by no means least, the Christian's economic advantages in the fur trade[38] – in 1648, when only fifteen per cent of the Hurons were Christian, half of the men in the Huron fleet were either converts or were preparing for baptism.[39]

Although a minority, the new Christian converts, like the missionaries, would not be content with treating their religion as a strictly private affair. Instead they attacked the traditional Huron customs and kept up a constant agitation for reform. By 1648, just before the destruction of Huronia, the Christians in La Conception were strong enough to prevent those ancient Huron practices which they considered "sinful". These agitations produced a strong reaction among the unconverted Hurons, who from 1645 on attempted to persuade their fellow villagers to expel the missionaries and break off the fur trade in a last desperate attempt to preserve the ancient beliefs and to save the country from a disastrous war with the Iroquois. The hope of the anti-Christian majority in 1645 seemed to lie in arranging a trade treaty with the Iroquois. When this proved impossible the rate of conversions accelerated, especially after the Seneca Iroquois had attacked and burned the large Huron town of St. Joseph in 1648.[40] No doubt the arrival of a small contingent of French troops aided in increasing the rate of conversions during that year. Thus, decimated by disease and famine and racked by internal dissension, the Hurons faced their final trial.

The precise cause of the Iroquoian attack on Huronia has caused much scholarly dispute. One thing, however, is clear. The Hurons had furs and held access to the northern and western hunting territories. At the same time the Iroquois sources of furs had been trapped out, and they were anxious to divert the rich northern trade south through their hands. Thus the intermittent Iroquois raids on the Huron trade routes were aimed not merely at capturing the furs, but also at forcing the Hurons and Algonquins to trade with them instead of the French. The success of these tactics was demonstrated in 1642 when Iroquois raiders spread fear and terror through all of Huronia, and in 1644 when the Iroquois temporarily cut off contact between Quebec and Huronia – a situation that had caused traditional Hurons to question the value of the Huron-French alliance and to demand a treaty with the Iroquois instead.

When all attempts to force the Hurons into an Iroquoian-Huron alliance had failed up to 1648, the Iroquois, growing desperate for furs, determined on one last all-or-nothing gamble – they would attempt to destroy Huronia and seize the avenues to the riches of the north. During the summer of 1648, St. Joseph was destroyed by the Seneca and in the spring of 1649 the Iroquois unleashed an attack that resulted in the famous deaths of Fathers Lalemant and Brébeuf. Although only two small towns, St. Ignace and St. Louis, were captured by the Iroquois in 1649, the long years of famine, disease and religious dissension seemingly had destroyed the Hurons' will to resist. Convinced that they could never prevail against their bad luck, they fled their villages. By May 1, fifteen villages had been abandoned and burned by the Hurons themselves, as six to eight thousand men, women and children crowded onto barren Christian Island. Even before winter, people began dying of starvation, and by the next spring the hand of death was everywhere. Of the once proud and powerful Huron nation only a few thousand remained. Most of these sought protection from the friendly Indian nations to the south, west and north, where they were quickly absorbed. The remainder, about 500, set out for Quebec in June 1650, where they settled on a reservation at Loretto. They live there to this day. Thus weakened by economic dependence, external attacks and internal dissension, the Huron nation was dispersed.

From the spring of 1650 when the remnants of the Hurons had abandoned their last refuge on Christian Island, the Iroquois expanded their attacks, driving out the Neutrals and Tobacco Nation, until the whole of southern Ontario was in their hands. Their victory, however, was illusory. In 1653, intent upon carrying the war against the Erie Nations, the Iroquois concluded a treaty with the French, assuming that they were now the middlemen in the fur trade. They were wrong. In June of 1654 a great canoe fleet which was first thought to be an Iroquois army on the attack, was sighted from Montreal, but soon the Montrealers recognized it as a Huron-guided Odawa (Ottawa) trading fleet. The Odawas, an Algonkian tribe, were seizing the initiative and stepping into the void left by the collapse of the Huron nation.[41] The Iroquois were now faced with the difficult task of protecting their west flank against a series of enemies roused by their expansionist tactics, while at the same time trying to prevent the Odawan trading expeditions. The latter proved impossible, although constant harrassment of the trading fleets and of outlying French settlements kept trade in a chaotic condition. While they could not halt the

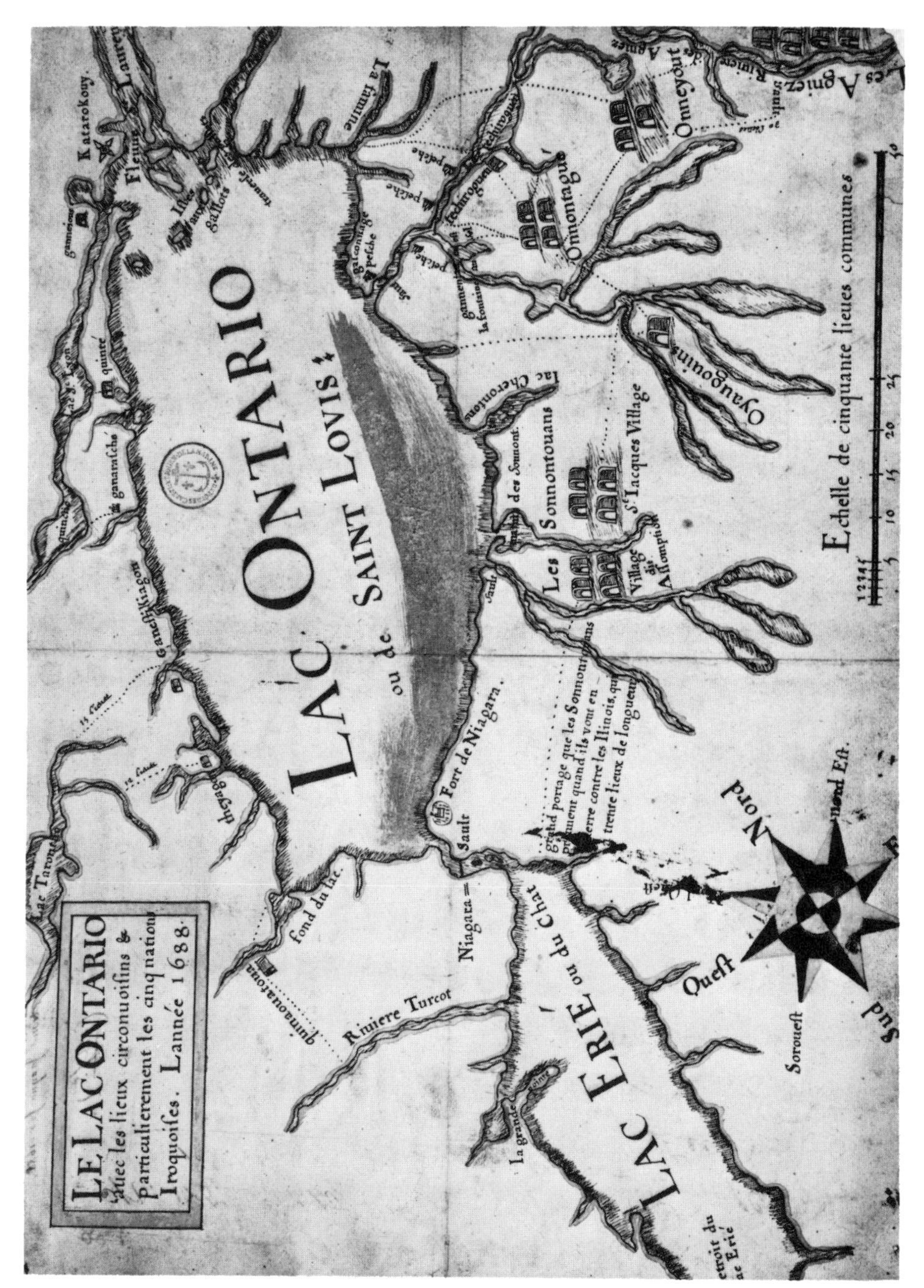

MAP I *Franquelin's Map of the Iroquois Nations, 1688*

Public Archives of Canada: Serv. hist. de la Marine, Recueil 67 (ancien 4044 B), par Franquelin, 1688.

fur trade, the Iroquois could and did prevent any other Indian tribe from moving into Southern Ontario.

During the 1660s small bands of Iroquois gradually began migrating to the north shore of Lake Ontario and establishing themselves in villages at the point where trails to the north entered Lake Ontario. Thus Ganneious (Oneida Nation) was established on the present site of Napanee; Kente on the Bay of Quinte, Kentsio on Rice Lake, and Ganaraske at Port Hope (these three Cayuga); Ganatsekwyagon in Pickering Township near the mouth of the Rouge and Teiaiagon at the mouth of the Humber (both Seneca).[42] Ganatsekwyagon was founded close to the mouth of the Rouge because it afforded access to one of the most used portages between Lake Ontario and the upper lakes region – the famous *Passage de Taronto* which paralleled the Rouge and Holland Rivers through Ontario and York counties.

The route followed by the Rouge-Holland trail, as indicated by Joliet's and Raffeix's maps, did not follow the rivers themselves, but followed the path just east of Vandorf (where archeologists have discovered the remains of a fortified village), passed east of Newmarket, and terminated at Holland Landing. Another trail followed the valley of the Rouge itself, and yet another ran just east of Bond Lake parallel to Yonge Street.[43] The Ganatsekwyagon trail was well known to the French explorers: for instance, Joliet and Péré used the trail on their way north to search for copper near Lake Superior in 1669.

The Senecas of Ganatsekwyagon, far from their allies south of the lake, desired peace with the French and thus in 1669 decided to request a missionary from the French as a goodwill gesture. In response, Abbé Fénelon came up to Ganatsekwyagon from the mission at Kente on the Bay of Quinte. As part of his duties he established a school at Ganatsekwyagon where he attempted to teach the Indian children their letters and the gospel. Fénelon's labours were quickly terminated, however, when a food shortage forced the villagers to take to the woods in an attempt to live on game, and Fénelon was forced to follow them. So scarce was food that at times they were reduced to gnawing on fungi which grew at the base of the pine trees. By spring Fénelon's health was broken and he returned to Kente sick and discouraged. Although he is said to have reported to Bishop Laval that it would be best if everyone forgot his work at Ganatsekwyagon,[44] the name of "Frenchman's Bay" still commemorates him; near its shores his school, the first in Pickering Township and Ontario County, was erected.

Although the Senecas of Ganatsekwyagon desired peace with the French, they continued to trade with the English of Boston and the Dutch from Manhattan and Orange. The Intendant of Quebec, Jean Talon, in 1670 wrote to Colbert, the French Minister of Marine, explaining his intent to cut off the fur trade from the Dutch and English traders using the two *Passages de Taronto* (the Humber-Holland and the Rouge-Holland routes). It was Talon's intention to build two posts, one on the north and the other on the south side of Lake Ontario, and to build a small vessel which could be either sailed or rowed to wherever there was trading on the lake, and thus direct the greater part of the trade naturally and without violence into the hands of his Majesty's subjects.[45] In 1673, Frontenac, anxious to cut off the Dutch trade (and equally anxious to get it into his own hands) revived Talon's plan and built Fort Frontenac at Cataraqui, near Kingston. Although both the French government and the Montreal traders objected to the erection of forts in the interior, Frontenac stood his ground, and the fort remained as a trading rival of the Iroquois towns.

Although the presence of Fort Frontenac no doubt reduced the profitability of the fur trade for Ganatsekwyagon, by penetrating farther and farther into the interior to attack the Ottawa fur brigades and to conduct trading expeditions of their own, the Iroquois, English and Dutch managed to maintain a profitable trade. Finally, in an attempt to keep the fur trade for the French, Denonville, the Governor of Quebec between 1685 and 1687, had a chain of forts built from Lake Champlain to Michilimackinac and the Illinois country. Included in Denonville's plans were forts to block off the *Passage de Taronto* and Detroit. In a letter explaining his plans Denonville wrote:

> The letters I have written to Sieurs du Lhu and de La Durantaye, of which I send you copies, will inform you of my orders to them to fortify the two passes leading to Michilimaquina. Sieur du Lhu is at that of the Detroit of Lake Erie, and sieur de La Durantaye at that of the portage of Taronto. These two posts will block the passage against the English should they attempt to go again to Michilimaquina, and serve as retreats for our Indian allies either while hunting, or making war against the Iroquois.[46]

Denonville's plans to monopolize the fur trade drew the natural response from the English and Iroquois. In 1686 a band of Dutch and English soldiers and traders, aided by the Iroquois, crossed the *Passage de Taronto* and attacked the new French post at Michilimackinac. Although the attack failed, Denonville decided to invade the Seneca territory to punish them for their audacity. On his way back from the Seneca territory in what is now New York State, Denonville built a fort at Niagara.

The Iroquois exacted a terrible revenge for Denonville's ill-considered raid. Through 1687 and 1688 they totally disrupted both the fur trade and farming in Quebec by a series of raids which culminated in the destruction of the French settlement at Lachine in 1689. Fort Niagara and Fort Frontenac were abandoned by the French and Lake Ontario again passed into Iroquois control for a time. The Iroquois triumph was short-lived. With Count Frontenac's re-appointment as Governor and with more vigorous aid from France, the French gradually won the upper hand. With the rebuilding of Fort Frontenac in 1695 the French re-established control of the fur trade in the Lake Ontario region.[47] Nor were the French content merely to take up a defensive position. During the 1690s the French formed an alliance with the Indians of the

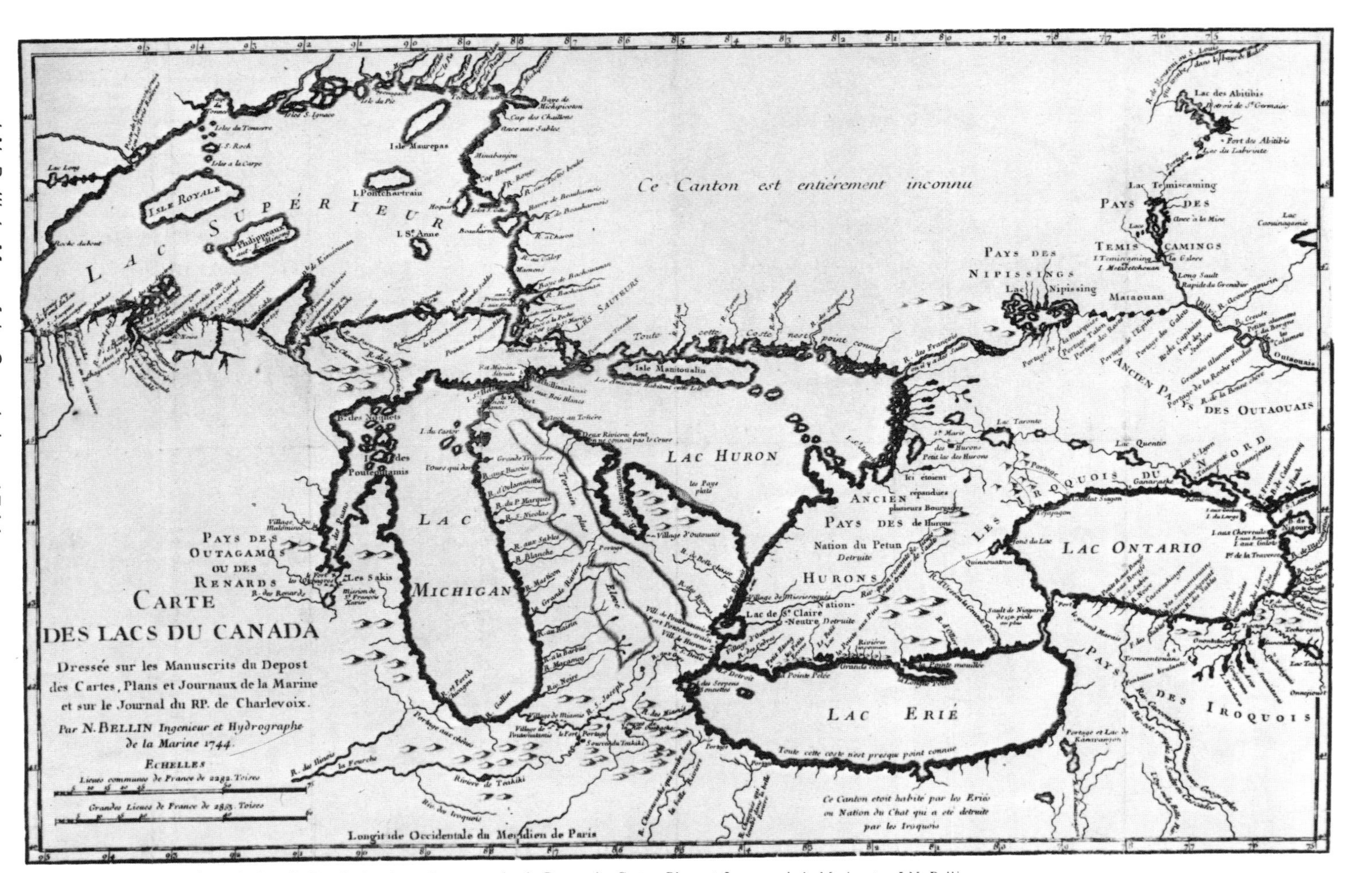

Public Archives of Canada: Carte des lacs du Canada dressée sur les manuscrits du Depost des Cartes, Plans et Journaux de la Marine, par J.N. Bellin.

MAP II *J.N. Bellin's Map of the Great Lakes, 1744*

"Council of the Three Fires" to drive the Iroquois from the north shore of Lake Ontario.

The Indian nations who made up the "Council of Three Fires" (the Ojibway, Odawa and Potawatomi nations) had long been enemies of the Iroquois. Prior to 1650 they had inhabited the lands bordering Lake Huron, but with the fall of their allies, the Hurons, they moved west to escape the reach of the Iroquois. For the next forty years a state of intermittent warfare existed between the Council of the Three Fires and the Iroquois Confederacy for control of the fur trade, but nothing was resolved. With the alliance between the Council and the French, however, the northern Iroquois villages faced an irresistible two-pronged pressure.[48]

The position of the inhabitants of the Iroquois villages along the north shore of Lake Ontario was not an enviable one. Under Frontenac the French rejected all the conventions of war and broke peace treaties at will. In particular the treacherous kidnapping and enslavement of the inhabitants of Ganneious and Kente at the customary Feast of Peace at Fort Frontenac in 1687 must have convinced the Senecas of Ganatsekwyagon that their position was intolerable. The re-establishment of Fort Frontenac in 1695 which gave the French complete control of the fur trade on Lake Ontario was the final blow.[49] Convinced at last that they had no alternative, the Seneca abandoned Ganatsekwyagon and returned to their ancestral home south of Lake Ontario. Thus, just as the Hurons had fallen victim to the struggle for trade dominance between the French and Iroquois, so too had the Iroquois north of Lake Ontario suffered from the trade rivalry between the French and English. With the departure of the Senecas of Ganatsekwyagon, Ontario County was left unoccupied for a second time in a half-century.

Into the vacuum left by the retreating Senecas moved a very different poeple – the semi-nomadic Ojibways, one of the partners in the triumphant Council of the Three Fires. The Ojibway were of Algonkian stock and were divided into two closely related groups; one known as the Mississaugas and the other called simply Ojibway or Chippewa. There was no clear-cut division between the lands claimed by the two groups, but in general the Mississaugas occupied the area east and south of Georgian Bay, while the Ojibway remained in the vicinity of Georgian Bay itself.

Just when the Mississaugas first entered the region of Ontario County is hard to determine. In 1700 envoys from the Five Nations (Iroquois) presented a series of "Propositions for Ye Commissioners of Trade" at Albany. Among the "Propositions" was the statement that

> Some of the Dawaganhaes [Odawas] having had a conference with our Indians at their hunting last winter, conclude to desert their inhabitants and to come and settle upon ye Lake of Cadarackque [Lake Ontario], near the Sinnekes' country at a place called Kanatiochtiage

> [Ganatsekwyagon], and accordingly they are come and settled there and have sent five of their people to Onondaga to treat being sent from three Nations who are very strong, having sixteen castles.[50]

Other references to the Mississaugas make it clear that they were never very populous. An "Enumeration of Indian tribes" of 1736 showed Mississaugas in a number of places in southern Ontario and stated, "The principle tribe of that of the Crane. Warriors 150".[51]

The economy of the Chippewa and Mississauga newcomers to southern Ontario was very different from that of their predecessors, the Hurons and Iroquois. Whereas the latter were agricultural people who lived in villages, the new arrivals' economy was based on a minimum of agriculture combined with extensive hunting and gathering activities. Thus while the Chippewas and Mississaugas might grow patches of corn, pumpkins and beans during their summer residence, in other seasons they found it necessary to move long distances to areas that provided the staples of their economy. In spring they collected sap from the maple trees for syrup, in summer they grew small gardens and dried large quantities of fruits and berries which were stored for the lean months of winter, and in fall they collected the wild rice which grew in the shallow water around the edges of the lakes. In addition to their farming and gathering activities the Chippewas and Mississaugas were keen hunters and trappers. In winter the families scattered to their favoured locations in the woods to hunt moose; in spring and summer they trapped beaver and hunted small game, and fished for suckers, pickerel and pike; and in autumn they speared trout, whitefish and sturgeon, which spawn close to the shore in that season.[52]

For semi-nomadic societies such as the Chippewas and Mississaugas, the need to be constantly on the move affects every aspect of their social organization. Because of the great labour involved in transporting goods from one area to another, they were unable to accumulate many material possessions, or to develop social organizations around that accumulation. Status within the Chippewa and Mississauga tribes was therefore related to an individual's leadership in hunting or war, not to his ability to accumulate large amounts of wealth.

Each tribe was subdivided into numerous bands, each of which had its own hunting territories and traditional camping grounds. Because of the scarcity of game there was a functional limitation of band size to about three or four hundred individuals. Each band had its own leader who generally handed his position down to his son; but the power and status attached to this position varied with the individual. The chief of a band was generally, but not always, its war leader.[53] With the Chippewas and Mississaugas, as with the Hurons, the chief had no power to force anyone to follow him. If he decided to carry out a raid on an enemy, he first had to consult his own followers and obtain their agreement and then attempt to persuade the warriors of other bands to take part in the endeavour. Strong leaders such as Sahgimah, the Ottawa war chief who led a great victory over the Iroquois in about 1696, had little difficulty in obtaining followers.[54]

The replacement of the Iroquois by the Chippewas and Mississaugas was of great importance when white settlers began to take interest in the fertile lands of Upper Canada. Whereas the Hurons and Iroquois had erected elaborate palisaded villages, cleared extensive fields and maintained a land title system which placed great value on personal and tribal ownership of land, the Chippewas and Mississaugas erected only temporary habitations, did only a little crop growing and attached very little value to a particular piece of land. To them, land was something which was permanent and autonomous – to be used, but not possessed in the European manner. Because they had little sense of ownership, when settlers began to arrive in large numbers after 1783, the Mississaugas freely sold their rights to their lands with little conception that they were being permanently dispossessed. In contrast the Five (after 1720, Six) Nations of the Iroquois south of Lake Ontario clung tenaciously to their lands in New York State and were dispossessed only with great difficulty.

Meanwhile events elsewhere were shaping the future of Ontario County. In 1720 the French intensified their control of Lake Ontario by building *Magasins Royals* (government stores) at the mouth of the Niagara and Humber Rivers. While these were closed in 1729, Fort Rouille was built, again at the Humber, in 1749. Finally, with the fall of Quebec in 1759 and of Montreal in 1760, the whole country passed into British hands. With the burning of Fort Rouille by its occupants in 1759 (to prevent its falling into British hands) the last vestiges of French control in the Ontario County area ended. The forests quickly reclaimed the blackened embers of forgotten campfires, and the remnants of French trade goods, previously exchanged for the precious beaver pelts, were soon discarded or buried with their owners. When the first white settlers arrived in Pickering and Whitby, Uxbridge and Reach, nothing of two hundred years of Huron, Iroquois and French occupation remained. Only the Mississaugas stood in the way.

PREPARING FOR SETTLEMENT: TREATIES AND SURVEYS

Just as the fate of Ontario County's first peoples had been the result of struggles whose origins were far removed from its borders, so too was the coming of the first white settlers the result of distant events. With the fall of Quebec in 1759 and the Treaty of Paris in 1763, all of New France, an area which included present-day southern Ontario, passed permanently into British hands. To the British the acquisition of a thousand miles of forest inhabited only by a few nomadic Indians and fewer white traders was of less immediate importance than the pacification and incorporation into the British Empire of the 60,000 French inhabitants of the eastern half of the new Colony. Thus the Quebec Act of 1774, which returned to the French their civil laws, land tenure laws and religious rights, did little to change conditions in the western part of the Colony, and attempted only to prevent Indian wars by licencing fur traders and controlling the limits of settlement.

With the growing likelihood of revolution in the Thirteen Colonies, the British Government sought to retain the Crown's alliance with the Indian nations by the enforcement of a "good neighbour" policy – particularly as it applied to the acquisition of Indian lands. In 1775, in order that no mistake be made regarding British intentions, Governor Carleton was instructed:

> No purchase of Lands belonging to the Indians, whether in the Name and for the Use of the Crown, or in the Name and for the Use of proprietaries of Colonies be made but at some general Meeting, at

> which the principal chiefs of each Tribe, claiming a property in such Lands, are present; and all Tracts, so purchased, shall be regularly surveyed by a Sworn Surveyor in the presence and with the Assistance of a person deputed by the Indians to attend such Survey; and the said Surveyor shall make an accurate Map of such Tract, describing the Limits, which Map shall be entered upon Record, with the Deed of Conveyance from the Indians.[1]

It is clear, however, that in the case of the Ontario County area, these instructions were generally neglected.

The first notice paid by the British authorities to the Ontario County region was necessitated by the dangerous military situation during and shortly after the American Revolution. In May 1780, Governor Haldimand caused orders to be given to "open a Communication with Michilimackinac from Niagara by way of Toronto", and "to explore that useful route making observations upon the Naviagation of the Rivers or Lakes, and the length and nature of the ground and woods by which they are intercepted . . . "[2] These orders were carried out by an officer leading a party of regular soldiers and Indian scouts and bearers. The little party travelled by way of the old Humber Trail, reaching Hackett Lake and the Holland River on June 25, 1780. The journey overland had been difficult and the Indians were tired. According to the officer's journal, the party camped on the banks of the Holland, and the next morning continued the journey.

> Monday—26th
>
> Set off in the Morning, and from here the Creek [the Holland River] is about 50 yards wide and runs very crooked. Went down about 23 miles, then we entered a small lake [Cook Bay, Lake Simcoe] in the breadth about 6 miles, the Creek runs East: where the Creek enters, in the Meadows are 4 Miles in breadth—
>
> This lake runs from appearance from the Mouth of the Creek N by W.—On the East Side of this Lake are a great many Indians, we go down the West Side—Went about 12 miles and encamped, the Shore rocky & thick bush, and opposite is an Island [Snake Island] about 2 miles long.
>
> Tuesday—27th:
>
> We leave this in the Morning, go about one mile, where are two more Islands, here the Lake widens greatly, can't perceive what breadth believe it to be about 10 miles; went about 15 miles further and came to a Bay [Kempenfelt Bay] runs west that is about 8 miles deep & ½ mile broad; Here the Lake appears to be 20 miles broad: Here we stayed about 3 Hours the wind being too high to cross the Bay, in the evening crossed & went about 4 miles where we encamped; Still a rocky

Shore & very low thick woods; opposite where we slept is another Island [Thorah Island] about 8 miles from the North Shore about 2½ miles long.—

Wednesday—28th:

Set off in the morning crossed several Bays & passed two Islands about 8 miles from the N. shore & 10 miles distant from one another—went about 10 miles and came to the mouth of the River [the Narrows at Orillia], where went past several Islands where Indians had corn-fields on. Our course from here is North. the River [Lake Couchiching] here is about 1¼ mile wide several Islands in it: One small Island in the middle of the River, were about 10 Hutts of Indians, who saluted us as we came nigh the Shore, & we returned them the Compliment—remained here about an Hour, the Chief wanted us to remain there as it was likely to Rain, but excused ourselves and went on about two miles, and began to blow very hard, was obliged to encamp on a large Island [Chief's Island] about two o'clock, remained there all night—

Thursday—29th:

The Wind still blowing very fresh, & rain. Was obliged to remain here all night—

Friday—30th:

Set off about 7 o'Clock went about 5 miles, our course then N.E. went about 3 miles further, came to a very broad Island [Rama Island], went down the West side about 1½ miles, where the Water runs rapid, and at each end of the Island there is a small Fall—here we carried over our Canoes & Baggage the Carrying place is about 50 yards broad: Here the River is about fifty yards broad . . . Rocks on each side; about ½ a mile from the carrying place, runs in a Creek [Black River] comes seemingly from S.E. is about 20 yards wide.—We go now N.N.W.—went about 3 miles came to another Carrying place [the second Fall of the Severn] about 30 yards wide where we carried our Baggage & Canoes over; from this our Course is West—Several small Islands—went about 10 miles & came to a small Lake [Sparrow Lake] about one mile wide and 3 long, here we encamped; very low Land until we came to this Lake—[3]

The party continued on down the Severn, reaching Georgian Bay on Sunday, July 1, returning along the same route to reach Niagara on July 11.

Although no immediate action was taken, on August 9, 1785 an agreement was signed with local chiefs which stated that

the King shall have a right to make roads through the Niagara country,

> That the Navigation of the Rivers and Lakes, shall be open and free for his Vessels and of his Subjects, that the King's Subjects shall carry on a free trade unmolested, in and through the Country, That the King shall erect Forts, Ridouts, Batteries, and Storehouse, & ca. in all such places as shall be judged proper for that purpose—respecting Payment for the above right, the Chiefs observed they were poor and Naked, they wanted Clothing and left it to their good Father to be judge of the quantity.[4]

No record remains as to whether the Indians' trust was justified. Included in this surrender, as later remembered by J.B. Rousseau, the translator, was the land for one mile on each side of Lake Couchiching and the Severn River from the Narrows to Matchedash Bay.[5] This one-mile strip, through Mara and Rama, therefore, was the first land in Ontario County obtained by the Government.

With the final defeat of the British by the American revolutionary forces in 1783, thousands of colonists who had remained loyal to their King were forced to flee persecution and to seek their fortunes elsewhere. In 1783 and 1784 more than 5,000 Loyalists treked north to begin life again in Britain's newest colony, in the uncharted wilderness of Upper Canada. The first and most immediate demand of the Loyalists was land to replace that lost in the Thirteen Colonies. Again, just as in 1775, the military situation dictated that Britain had to retain the loyalty of the Indians while acquiring their lands. Because of his long experience and his history of good relations with the Six Nations Indians in New York State, Sir John Johnson was made responsible for Indian affairs.

On October 9, 1783, a meeting was held with several Mississauga chiefs on Carleton Island at the east end of Lake Ontario. According to Captain Crawford's report to Johnson, he had

> purchased from the Mississaugas all the land from Toniato or Onagara to the River in the Bay Quinte within eight leagues of the bottom of the said Bay, including all of the Islands, extending from the lake back as far as a man can travel in a day.[6]

According to at least one witness the circumstances of the meeting were peculiar, to say the least. Instead of following the instructions given to Carleton in 1775, Crawford had apparently persuaded the Indians to sign a blank deed for the whole area from Etobicoke Creek west of Toronto to the Trent River. Nathaniel Lines, the interpreter at the meeting, remembered the circumstances of the signing as follows:

> Mr. Nathaniel Lines Indian Interpreter at Kingston says he was present at the Bay of Quinte when he witnessed the Blank Deed supposed by him at the time to be a proper Deed of Conveyance of Lands from the Mississaugas resorting the Bay of Quinte, the Rice Lake and Lake La

> Clie [Lake Simcoe] – Commencing at the Head of Carrying Place of the Bay of Quinte to a Creek called Tobeka from seven to fourteen miles above Toronto. . . . The lands sold and intended to be purchased at that time are connected all the way in front of Lake Ontario running in depth 10 or 12 miles nearly as far as Rice Lake and above the Rice Lake a Common day's Journey back as far as Toronto.
>
> Mr. Lines further says that Sir John Johnson, Mr. Collins the Surveyor and several others were present, and that immediately after delivery of the goods which were the Consideration for the Lands, he, Mr. Lines, was called to Witness the Blank Deed . . . [7]

This treaty (commonly called the "Gun Shot Treaty") had immediate repercussions. Because it was improperly drawn and signed, no survey was ordered of the area and no legal description was filed. Moreover, Sir John Johnson received crisp instructions that henceforth

> No person belonging to or employed in the Indian Department is to be permitted to trade directly or indirectly, or to have any share, profit or concern therein.[8]

Such an order suggested that even Line's testimony did not cover all improprieties that had occurred in 1783.

The Government now called a second meeting which took place on September 23, 1787. At this meeting, held at the Carrying Place of the Bay of Quinte, the Government purchased about one-third of York County (an area stretching from the Don River to Etobicoke Creek, and reaching inland twenty-four miles) for £1,700 in cash and trade goods.[9] This treaty (called the "Toronto Purchase Treaty") was later confirmed in 1805 at yet another meeting where certain minor problems were negotiated.[10] Map III shows the general areas covered by this and subsequent treaties in the region. In 1788 the area covered by the "Toronto Purchase" was surveyed by Alexander Aitkins, who found that the Indians were still somewhat unhappy with the treaty, but were persuaded by the interpreter, Nathaniel Lines, that all was in order.[11]

While the Toronto Purchase Treaty was settled satisfactorily in 1787 and 1805, the remainder of the land supposedly covered under the Gun Shot Treaty was not. When Lieutenant-Governor John Graves Simcoe reviewed the case in 1795, he made it clear that he did not consider the Gun Shot Treaty to be valid and binding. On the other hand, since the Mississaugas did not contest it, Simcoe's decision was to let it stand as long as the Indians continued to recognize it.[12]

Even more peculiar was the lack of a treaty covering the areas lying in Home District just east of the Toronto Purchase. Not only was no good treaty signed for the townships of Uxbridge, Reach, Scott, Brock, Thorah, and Georgina, but also, if Nathaniel Line's testimony was correct, most of Markham

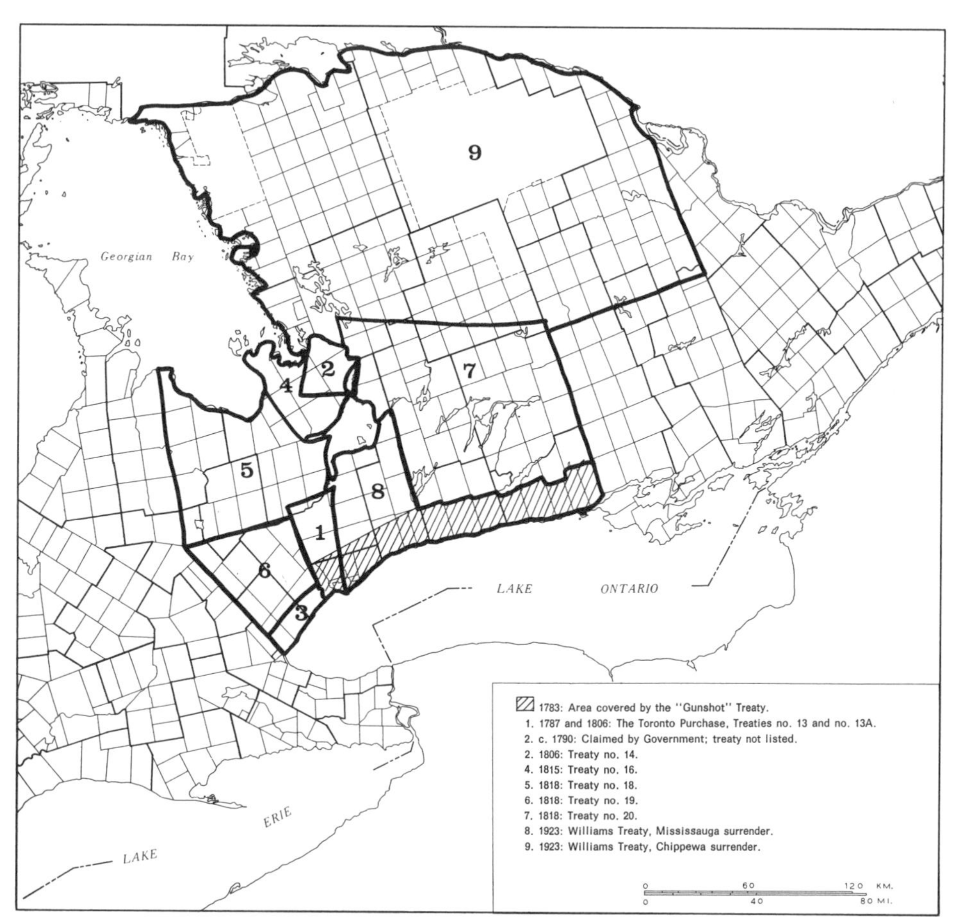

MAP III *Indian Treaties*

Compiled from *Indian Treaties and Surrenders*, 3 vols. (Queen's and King's Printer, Ottawa, 1891 and 1912), Williams Treaty, File 2.

and Whitchurch were not covered by the Gun Shot Treaty. It would appear, since the surveying of the area was begun in 1796, that government policy was to take everything that the Indians did not actively claim.

While some authors excuse the subsequent events as having resulted from the confused state of land administration,[13] it is clear from an official map of Indian surrenders printed in 1847[14] that the Indian Department and the Government were fully aware that the Indians had never surrendered the area. Moreover as later testimony would show, the Mississaugas were aware of the true state of affairs as well. Again and again, decade after decade, the little bands at Alnwick, Rice Lake, Mud Lake and Scugog protested the injustice of having been dispossessed of their lands without proper treaties or payment. Always their pleas went unheard.[15]

The public position taken by the Government throughout the nineteenth and early twentieth century was that the Gun Shot Treaty was valid and binding, and that no claim existed. This position was made clear in the 1850s. When the Gun Shot Treaty had been concluded, the Mississaugas had apparently kept for themselves a large block of land which became the Alnwick Indian Reserve at the east end of Rice Lake. During the 1850s certain ambitious entrepreneurs, discovering the lack of a valid treaty, challenged the Indians' right to the area and demanded that the Government seize the reserve and sell it to "progressive" white settlers.

In the succeeding investigation held in 1858, Captain Anderson, the civil servant responsible for Indian affairs, quashed these claims. As Anderson's evidence made clear, if the Indians had no valid treaty title to Alnwick, then the Government's right to a hundred miles of the richest farm land in the province was also invalid.[16] Needless to say, the Government immediately dropped the issue, and continued to maintain their right to the area covered by the Gun Shot Treaty as well as backing the Mississauga's right to Alnwick. Except for the repeated requests by the Mississaugas for a review of their case, the matter passed from the public eye. It would not reappear until the twentieth century when the British Columbia Indian land claims forced a review of all aboriginal land rights in Canada.

While the Mississaugas of southern Ontario were struggling to get their land rights case heard, a second dispute between the Chippewa Indians and the Government was brewing. In 1818, the area covering Mara and Rama as well as all of Northumberland, Durham and Peterborough counties north of the first tier of townships (area 7 on Map III) was negotiated and signed without incident. On November 5, 1818 the Mississauga chiefs Buckquaquet, Pishikinse, Pahtosh, Cahagaghishinse, Cohagagwin and Pininse signed away the area containing more than 1,590,000 acres of land lying east of Lake Simcoe and south of Haliburton in exchange for an annuity of £740 in trade goods "at the Montreal Price".[17] This treaty did not, however, cover the area of Muskoka and Haliburton which the Mississaugas continued to share with the Chippewas as a hunting ground.

In 1850 the Government signed a treaty with the Ojibways of Georgian Bay (the Huron-Robinson Treaty), which gave to the Government all the "unconceded lands within the limits of Canada West to which they have any just claim".[18] According to the terms of the treaty this area included not only the areas north of Georgian Bay, but a thousand square miles of territory lying east of Georgian Bay as well. The latter term was immediately disputed by the Chippewa bands of Christian and Georgina Islands and Rama Reserve, who argued that the area east of Georgian Bay, ceded in the Huron-Robinson Treaty, was part of their own hunting lands for which no treaty had as yet been made. This claim was repeated regularly for more than seventy years by the Chippewas, but to no avail.[19]

Later, just as with the townships lying south of Lake Simcoe, the Government not only opened the contested area for settlement, but began to survey and place settlers in the huge area of Muskoka and Haliburton, and north to Lake Nipissing and east to the Ottawa river for which no treaty – even a disputed one – had ever been signed. After Confederation the area was mapped, the timber cut, roads built and settlement begun without consideration of the lack of a treaty.

The refusal to acknowledge or settle the Chippewa and Mississauga claims to their northern hunting grounds lay, at least in part, in a longstanding constitutional dispute between the Federal Government and the Province of Ontario. As one federal civil servant put it, when reviewing the situation with his superior:

> The delay in settling this claim seems from the fyles largely to have resulted from a controversy between the Dominion and the Province of Ontario on this point: the Dominion contending that inasmuch as the lands when free from the Indian title will belong to Ontario absolutely while at present under the 109th Section of the British North America Act they belong to that Province "subject to any interest other than that of the Province in the same" the duty to assume the monetary obligation independent to the quieting of the Title should fall, while the Province has taken the position that inasmuch as the right to legislation to "Indians and Lands reserved for Indians" comes within the exclusive jurisdiction of the Dominion it is the duty of the Dominion to assume this obligation and hand over the lands to the Province free therefrom.[20]

Because the province had already seized the lands under question, and the only injured parties were the Indians who had neither vote nor economic power, there was little pressure to rectify the injustice done. The situation might have continued indefinitely had it not been for the public controversy raised by the Indians of British Columbia concerning lands which had been seized there without a treaty.[21] While federal spokesmen later stated that there was no direct relationship between the two claims,[22] it is clear that the public anger over the unjust situation in British Columbia provided an impetus towards settling other outstanding claims.[23]

In 1916, E.L. Newcombe, the Federal Deputy Minister of Justice, instructed R.V. Sinclair, a lawyer frequently employed by the Department of Justice, to investigate the claims of the Chippewas and Mississaugas to the disputed areas north of Lake Simcoe and the area ceded in 1818. After a careful investigation Sinclair concluded that though there was no proof that the Ojibways had ever hunted in the area (or indeed that the Ojibways had ever *claimed* to have hunted in the area) there was ample testimony that the disputed thousand square miles included in the Huron-Robinson Treaty were the property of the Chippewas and Mississaugas, and that the title to ten thousand square miles of territory lying between the forty-fifth parallel, the Nipissing and Ottawa Rivers and Georgian Bay "was never extinguished".[24] There the matter rested until 1921.

After the election of the Drury Farm-Labour Government in Ontario in 1919, the Federal Government, smarting from criticism of their behaviour towards the Indians in British Columbia, decided to make one more attempt to resolve the Chippewa and Mississauga hunting rights claims. Duncan Campbell Scott, the poet and Deputy Superintendent General of Indian Affairs, explained the situation in a letter to the Honourable W.E. Raney, Attorney General for Ontario:

> The Chippewa Indians of Lakes Huron and Simcoe and the Mississaugas of Mud, Rice and Scugog Lakes have been for a number of years preferring a claim against the Government for compensation for a tract of land approximately as shown on a map enclosed herewith [the map shows the hunting area north of the 45th parallel], which tract has been taken up for settlement but which, it is alleged, has never been surrendered. Before going further into the merits of these claims it is thought that the matter should be taken up with the Province for the purpose of ascertaining whether the Provincial Government would be disposed to join the Dominion Government in ascertaining the extent and validity of these claims, and whether the Provincial Government would undertake to make provision for their settlement if such claims should be established, in view of the fact that these lands when free from the Indian title belong to the Province.[25]

The Province's reply was prompt, if cautious. On December 20, 1921 the Deputy Minister of Lands and Forests replied:

> Inasmuch as this territory comprises a very large and important area over the Province of Ontario, part of which is in the old settled and part in the more recently occupied areas, the Department deems it advisable for the Province to join with the Dominion in ascertaining the extent and validity of these Indian claims, on the understanding that the questions of provision for the settlement of the claims should be left in abeyance until a claim has been established.[26]

The next eighteen months were spent in a lengthy exchange of correspondence between the two Governments laying out the terms and conditions under which an investigation of the Indian claims would be made. This agreement was signed in April, 1923. By its terms the Federal Government was to appoint the head of the three-man commission while Ontario was to appoint the other two members. The Federal Government was to be responsible for all expenses.[27] This agreement was confirmed by Orders-In-Council of the Federal and Provincial Governments on June 23 and 29 respectively.

It is clear, from the preamble of the agreement that, as yet, neither level of government realized the true extent of the treaty situation. The agreement begins:

> Whereas certain Indians of the Chippewa and Mississauga tribes claim that the said tribes were and are entitled to a certain interest in lands

> in the Province of Ontario to which the Indian title has never been extinguished by surrender or otherwise, the said lands being described parts of the counties of Renfrew, Hastings, Haliburton, Muskoka, Parry Sound and Nipissing. . . . The area in question including about 10,719 square miles.
>
> And whereas a department enquiry made by the Department of Indian Affairs that the said claim has such probable validity as to justify and require further investigation, and if found valid to be satisfied on such just and fair terms as may be settled by a surrender.[28]

Nowhere was there any suggestion that the Government realized that most of the north shore of Lake Ontario was held under similar questionable conditions.

As soon as the agreement between the Federal and Ontario Governments was approved, the Federal Government appointed A.S. Williams, a Toronto lawyer as the chairman of the commission, and the Province appointed R.V. Sinclair (who had made the original report in 1916), and Uriah McFadden, a Sault Ste. Marie lawyer, as its representatives. After more than a month of debate and innumerable letters between the commissioners and the Governments about salary (they finally were given $100.00 per day rather than the usual $25.00 per day of the period[29]), the Commission began its work.

In analysing the role of the Commission and Governments in the subsequent events it is necessary to understand the position of Indians at that time. Under the British North America Act and subsequent "Indian Acts" those Indians who were on the band rolls were legally the wards of the Crown. In other words, for legal purposes their position was similar to minors, while the Government through the Indian Affairs Department held the position of guardian with full control over their lands, property, money and rights. No Indian could make a will, sell property or engage in any of the normal legal adult activities without the approval of the Indian Affairs Department or its representatives. For example, a common practice on the Rama Reserve was for the local Indian agent to intercept the annuity money of Indians who were in debt to local merchants and to pay their bills for them.[30]

Moreover, in their dealings with the Government regarding land, mineral rights, water and treaty rights, the Indians were not represented by a lawyer to defend their interests. An exchange in the House of Commons between the Honourable Charles Stewart, Minister of the Interior, Minister of Mines and Superintendent of Indian Affairs, and Mr. Garland, the member from Bow River, Alberta, made clear the attitude of the Government:

> *Mr. Stewart* (Argenteuil): . . . The federal government through the superintendent general has complete control of the funds . . . of the Indians so long as an Indian remains in existence.

> *Mr. Garland* (Bow River): Are the Indians represented by counsel when agreements of this kind are arranged?
>
> *Mr. Stewart* (Argenteuil): No.
>
> *Mr. Garland* (Bow River): The department undetakes all that for the Indians without any separate counsel for them.
>
> *Mr. Stewart* (Argenteuil): Yes. . . . The responsibility of the government of Canada is to take care of the Indians, who are known as wards, and certain lands are allocated for the use of the Indians. To all intents and purposes the Department of Indian Affairs stands to protect the Indians in every way it can, to work in the interest of the Indians. The Indians I am free to say, do not always think so. They are human, like the rest of us, and sometimes the feel that, perhaps, what we consider is in their best interest, is really not the thing that should be done for them.[31]

The Department of Indian Affairs, then, in arranging the treaties with the Mississaugas and Chippewas, was placed in a position of direct conflict of interest. On the one hand it controlled the lands it was selling on behalf of the Indians, and on the other hand, it represented the Government as purchaser. In the case of private guardians the courts tend to exercise extreme care in guarding the interests of the ward. In the case of the Indians no such protection existed - other than that provided by the commissioners and the Opposition Parties in parliament. These protections, as it turned out, failed.

When the Williams Commission began its investigations in September, 1923,[32] it encountered open suspicion on the part of the Indians. As the commissioners reported:

> The Indians [had] unfortunately become imbued with the idea that the object of the Commission was to minimize the claims and to require such strict legal proof of them as would be required by a Court of Justice in a contest between litigants.
>
> The Commission being aware that it was not the desire of either of the Governments to have the Commission approach the consideration of the claims in any such attitude, sought to impress the Indians with a view that any evidence whether it might be direct or indirect . . . would be received and considered, and the Commission is glad to be able to state that the attitude of doubt referred to was entirely dissipated and beyond any question when the commission left each of the reserves it had secured the entire confidence of the Indians.[33]

Later this confidence would be put to good use.

The results of the investigation of the Commission were a bombshell to the Provincial and Federal Governments. First of all, as R.V. Sinclair had forecast in 1916, the claims of the Chippewas and Mississaugas to the hunting grounds north of the forty-fifth parallel were fully supported. In the Commission's words:

> It is the opinion of the Commission that the claimants have submitted ample and satisfactory proof of the occupation by them referred to as the ancient hunting grounds of the ancestors of the claimants. These hunting grounds cover an area of over 10,000 square miles of territory, the value of which is almost incalculable.[34]

In addition, the Chippewa claim to more than a thousand square miles of territory which had been acquired from the Ojibways under the Huron-Robinson Treaty of 1850 was completely vindicated. Thus the claims which had been rejected by the Federal Government for more than seventy years were upheld in every detail. Given the previous correspondence, however, it is clear that both levels of government had expected this result.

The Commission, however, had not contented itself merely with investigating claims to the hunting lands. In the September interviews the Mississaugas had re-opened their old claims to most of Ontario and York counties, and the Commission had looked into these as well. The results were shocking indeed to the publicity-conscious government. Of the Mississauga claims the commissioners said:

> It was claimed by the Mississauga nation that seven townships lying immediately south of Lake Simcoe, belonging to them, had never been surrendered. A moderate estimate of the value of these townships alone would be $30,000,000.00. The area comprised in these townships alone is somewhat over 355,000 acres. The Commission has not been able to find that a surrender of the townships in question has ever been made.[35]

Even more disturbing was the discovery that the 1783 Gun Shot Treaty which covered the lakeshore townships from the Don River to the Trent was also invalid – a fact of which even the Mississaugas were not aware. The recommendation of the Commission was that all the latter areas, as well as the hunting territory, be covered in a single treaty.

In considering a recommendation for compensation the commissioners chose not to raise the question of the value of the lands as of 1923. Rather they offered two calculations based upon treaties which had been signed previously for areas in remote regions of the Province. In arriving at their recommendations the Commission argued that:

> The claim made by these Indians has been continuously pressed for the last seventy years; that for over fifty years the claimants have practically been deprived of the use of the lands as hunting grounds because of the encroachment of the whites, both settlers and trappers, so that

> the view which is to be found in the files of the Indian Department, that these claimants should be now compensated for the deprivation of use which they have suffered for fifty years, is one which must be considered in arriving at a sum.
>
> If one were to approach the question of compensation from the foregoing point of view, and were to settle with these claimants on the basis of the settlement which is provided for under the Robinson-Huron treaty, the capitalization of the amount which would be required to be paid at the present day would be $840,000.00, in addition to which the claimants would be entitled to 156,000 acres of land as reserves. If, however, the claimants should be dealt with on the basis which prevailed with respect to Treaty Nine, the capitalization of the amount required would be $1,372,800.00, in addition to which the quantity of land required to be set aside for reserves would be 320,000 acres.[36]

Considering the basis laid out by the commissioners in their report, and the fact that the lands in question were much more valuable than those acquired in either the Huron-Robinson Treaty (the rocky north shore of Georgian Bay) or Treaty Nine (the even rockier north shore of Lake Superior), one might have expected an award larger than either treaty. Instead, and completely without other explanation, the commissioners reported that they had

> come to the conclusion that the sum of $700,000.00 will be a fair and equitable compensation for the rights which the Indians will be called upon to release.[37]

The Commission requested that they, therefore, be given the right to pay up to $700,000.00 to the Indians for their rights, and from this

> such cash payment as may be necessary to procure the signing of the surrenders. The latter payment, however, it is believed, will not exceed $30,000.00.[38]

In other words, the Indians were to be offered a cash bribe for signing – which of course would be deducted from the over-all settlement which would be paid into the capital funds of the bands involved.

The haste with which the two Governments responded to the Commission report reveals the consternation they felt at its revelations. Now, in the midst of the public outcry over the occupation of Indian lands in British Columbia (a controversy which had drawn world-wide attention and created the most bitter feelings) the Government was in danger of being revealed as having systematically and knowingly usurped Indian rights in Ontario as well. Not only could such a revelation bring Indian rights advocates into the picture in Ontario with the result that a high price, indeed, would have been demanded for the Indians' lands, but the British Columbia controversy might have been made more acute. The situation called for drastic action.

The one barrier which appeared likely to complicate the settlement of the Indians' claims was the Ontario Government's refusal to pay even the Commission's very modest recommendation of $700,000.00. The Honourable James Lyons, Minister of Lands and Forests of Ontario, informed the Federal Government that the Province was unprepared to pay one penny more than $500,000.00.[39] The question facing the federal government was a difficult one: should it attempt to negotiate for terms more in line with the actual value of the land rights involved and face the danger of public revelation of the true situation in Ontario, or should it abandon its responsibilities as guardian of the Indians' interests in the hope that the Indians might be persuaded to accept quickly the sum offered by the Province. It was decided to pursue the latter course as being the least dangerous.

From the Federal Government's point of view, several circumstances stood in its favour: the Indians had not seen the report and knew neither the strength of their case nor the valuation of their rights made by the Commission; the Indians involved were extremely poor and could be expected to be amenable to the promise of a cash payment; and finally, the Indians, while still distrustful of the Indian Affairs Department, had been convinced of the honesty and objectivity of the commissioners. The last two situations would prove decisive in the subsequent negotiations.

In order to make maximum use of the good will with which the commissioners were regarded by the Indians, Williams, Sinclair and McFadden were instructed to carry out all negotiations with the Indians. They, in turn, strengthened their hand by requesting that a cheque for $400,000.00 be drawn immediately in favour of the Indians in order that they could approach the Indians as beneficiaries.[40] The province agreed with the strategy, and on October 31 an Order-in-Council approved the issuance of the cheque.[41] Thus equipped the commissioners were ready to undertake negotiations.

The itinerary which the commissioners followed and the speed with which they covered it illustrate the urgency felt by the Government. They visited seven reserves, made their explanations and had the treaty signed by all bands within twenty-two days. The treaty was signed by the various bands on the following dates:

Date	*Reserve*	*Tribe*
October 31	Georgina Island	Chippewa
November 3	Christian Island	Chippewa
November 7	Rama	Chippewa
November 15	Alderville	Mississauga
November 16	Rice Lake	Mississauga
November 19	Mud Lake	Mississauga
November 21	Scugog Lake	Mississauga

In the signing of the treaty, only one minor concession had been made: whereas the Commission report had suggested that a cash payment of approximately $15.00 per head might be necessary to induce the Indians to sign the treaty, it had been necessary to give them $25.00 each instead.

The terms of the treaties (separate treaties with identical wording were signed with the two groups of Indians) were simplicity itself: the Indians were to give up all "right, title, interest, claim, demand or privileges" to the areas under question. In return they were to receive $500,000.00 ($250,000.00 each to the Chippewas and Missassaugas) with a cash advance of $25.00 per person and the balance to go into the band funds under the administration of the Federal Government. Each band received the following amount in its trust fund:[43]

Chippewas	*1923*
Beausoleil (Christian)	$75,432.28
Rama	74,931.68
Snake (Georgina)	33,036.04
Mississaugas	
Alnwick	$74,092.98
Rice Lake	28,772.55
Mud Lake	73,339.67
Scugog Lake	7,469.80

There can be little doubt that the Federal and Provincial Governments were relieved when the last signature was affixed to the treaty on Scugog Island. For a mere $375.00 each, the 1328 Indians involved (663 Mississaugas and 665 Chippewas) had been persuaded to give up their claims to much of the Province of Ontario including almost half of the City of Toronto, to say nothing of Whitby, Oshawa, Port Hope, Cobourg and Trenton. If the federal ministers, civil servants or the commissioners felt any qualms in abandoning the interests of their wards in this conflict of interest, none showed any remorse - then or later.

With the signing of the treaties, just one hurdle remained - the parliamentary Opposition. Each year every governmental department is required to give a report when it makes its budgetary request for the following year. Here was a situation which might prove exceedingly embarrassing should some alert member raise the question of just how it was that the department had neglected to negotiate treaties to cover such valuable territory, in the case of most of Ontario and York counties and the lake shore townships for a period of 140 years, and in the case of the northern hunting rights for 73 years.

The solution, as it occurred to Mackenzie King's ministry, was simple. The Opposition was not told. Rather than reveal the true extent of the treaties, the annual report of the Department of Indian Affairs contained only the first

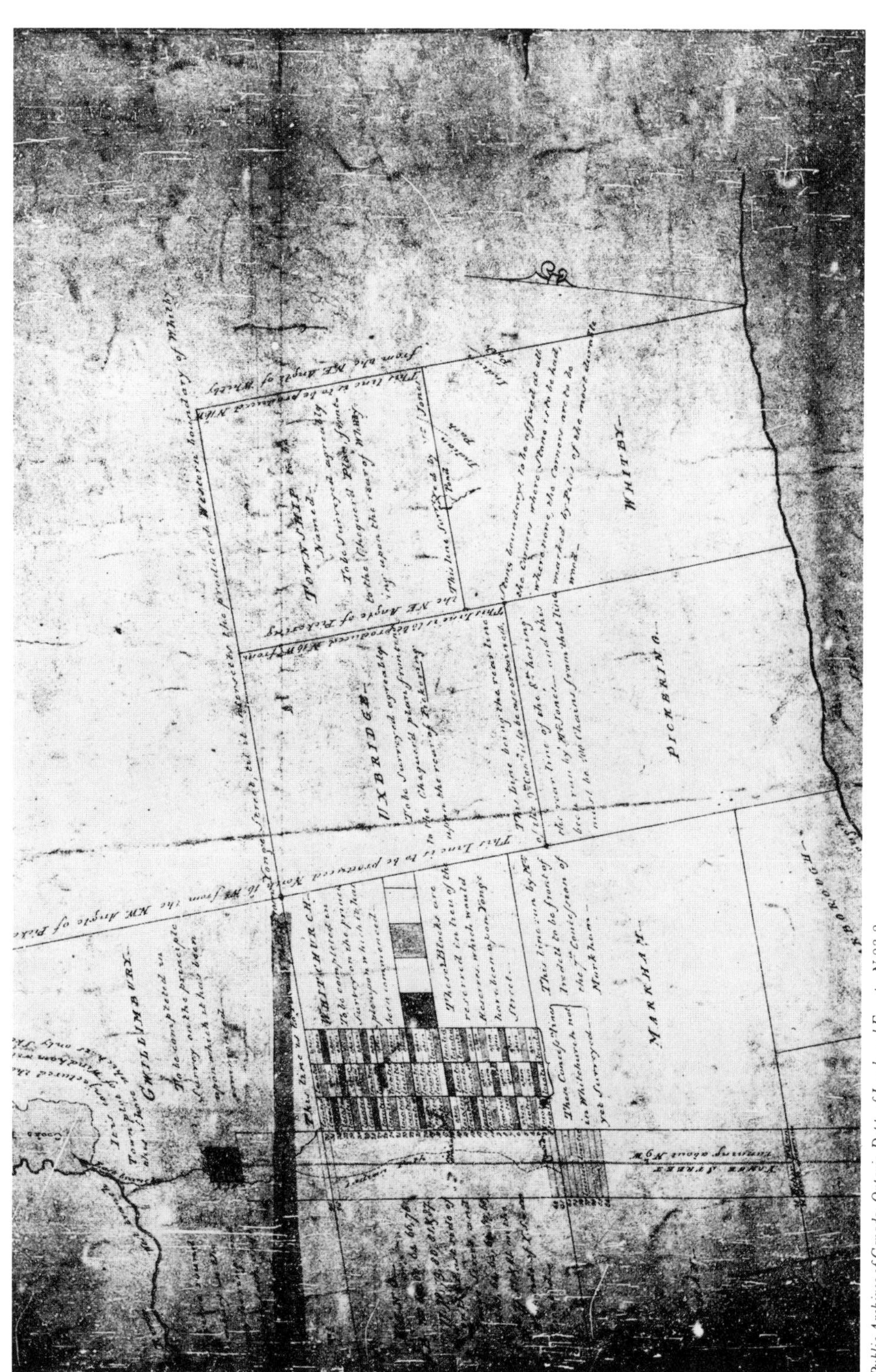

Public Archives of Canada: Ontario Dept. of Lands and Forests, N 23-2.

MAP IV *Early Plan of the Township of Pickering, Uxbridge and Whitby.*

section of the treaties – that covering the northern hunting grounds. No mention was made of the second section which covered the southern area. As a result, the Opposition was left with the impression that the Indians had received $500,000.00 as compensation for hunting rights in the area north of the forty-fifth parallel.[44] Thus the matter stands to this day.

After the Government had acquired the Indian lands, the second step in preparing the area for settlement was the laying out of townships and the survey of the lots and concessions. The procedure for surveying lands along the shoreline was to run a "base line" sufficiently far inland to miss any bays or coastal identations, and on this line lay out townships approximately nine-by-twelve miles in size. In each township the concessions were run parallel to the base line, 1¼ miles apart. The land between the base line and the lake shore was divided into "broken fronts", and where the broken front was deeper than 1¼ miles, further concessions (in Pickering Township called "ranges") were laid out.[45] Using this method, in 1791 a base line was run from Murray township on the east to York on the west, and eleven townships were established on it. In this row of townships, Whitby was eighth and Pickering was ninth. All these townships were given names which were later changed. Thus Darlington, Whitby, Pickering, Scarborough and York were called, respectively, Bristol, Norwich, Edinburgh, Glasgow and Dublin.[46]

While Uxbridge and Scott have the same basic survey pattern – the "single front", 1¼ mile concessions, and so forth – as Pickering and Whitby, they were laid out as squares, nine miles to a side. The reason they deviated from the normal nine-by-twelve mile size was that Governor Simcoe, in planning his military and settlement roads, had decided to make Yonge Street a base line similar to that along the lake shore.[47] Thus Markham and Whitchurch and the Gwillimburys were laid out with fronts nine miles along Yonge Street and running twelve miles back from the base line. When the division lines between Pickering and Whitby, and Whitchurch and East Gwillimbury were extended, a nine mile square resulted, the township of Uxbridge. Similarly Scott was formed by extending the boundaries between Pickering and Whitby, and East and North Gwillimbury. Since settlement was progressing more rapidly along Yonge Street than it was along the lake shore, it was natural to treat Uxbridge and Scott as extensions of the Yonge Street townships. Thus the concession lines in Uxbridge and Scott run north and south, parallel to Yonge Street rather than east-west, parallel to the shore base line. While there were good reasons for making Uxbridge and Scott only nine miles deep, one difficulty did result. Seven concessions were too few to fill each township, while eight were too many. The result was a bad compromise – an eighth, narrow concession no more than a quarter-mile deep on the eastern edge of each of the two townships.

In surveying the land, strict orders were given to set aside one-seventh of the land as reserves for the support of a "Protestant" clergy, and a similar one-seventh for the revenue of the Government.[48] These reserves, which were to be the basis of much bitter debate in later years, were ordered to be distributed regularly through the townships in such a way "as nearly as the circumstances and the nature of the case will admit" to equal the quality and value of the surrounding lands.[49] It was hoped that as settlement came and land values rose, these reserves could be leased, thereby requiring little or no general taxation.

While the survey patterns in themselves do not appear of great importance, still the presence of boundaries did restrict the kinds of decisions that were available to settlers. Where the concession lines did not follow good land, roads were difficult to maintain and proved an economic hardship to the neighbouring settlers. Similarly, where farms were cut by streams or swamps it was difficult to farm profitably. Finally, the presence of reserves which were rented late or not at all created hardship in a period when the farmers were required to build and maintain the roads in front of their farms, for in some areas, two out of seven farms (that is, the reserves) were unoccupied and long stretches of road were neglected and generally impassable. On the other hand, the "Lines on the Land", the work of the surveyors, gave a form and order to life on the frontier, which would have otherwise been absent.

LAND GRANTS AND EARLY SETTLEMENT, 1790-1820

The first lands granted in Ontario County went to two very different kinds of petitioners: the "official" grantees who received their lands because of statutory rights, and the "unofficial" grantees who had to justify their grants by the payment of fees and the performance of settlement duties.

The "official" grants were made in recognition of the hardships and losses suffered by the Loyalists in the Revolutionary War. In 1784 Governor Haldimand had set up a scale of grants for the Loyalists which allowed the head of a family 100 acres, with an additional 50 acres for each member of the family. A single, non-military man was to get 50 acres; privates, 100 acres; non-commissioned officers, 200 acres; and officers, up to 1,000 acres depending on rank.[1] All these "official" grants, however, were soon increased. In 1787 Lord Dorchester ordered that an additional 200 acres be given to heads of families who had already improved their lands. The local Land Boards took this to mean that all who had borne arms would be entitled to 300 acres or more, according to their rank, and other Loyalists would receive an initial grant of 200 acres. Moreover, the Executive Council ordered that a registry of the names of Loyalists be kept so that their descendants might be distinguished from future settlers, and that the Land Boards grant 200 acres to the sons of Loyalists, when they came of age, and also to their daughters at that time or at their marriage. Finally in 1788, the grants to officers were raised to a maximum of 5,000 acres depending on rank. While it is clear that the recipients of these grants were expected to occupy and improve these lands, and that Loyalist sons and daughters would receive their lands only if there were "no Default in the due Cultivation and Improvement of the Lands already assigned to the Head of the Family of which they were members",[2] these conditions were soon forgotten or ignored. All too often the result of this official generosity was that large acreages, sometimes whole townships, were granted and then were left vacant to impede the orderly spread of settlement. These vacant lands, like the Clergy and Crown Reserves, would become a constant source of grievance in Upper Canada. To a military claimant, Major John Smith of the Fifth Regiment of Foot, goes the distinction of being the first person to patent lands in Ontario County. On November 6, 1795, Major Smith, who had been commanding officer at Detroit, 1790-92, and at Niagara, 1792-95, received 5,000 acres - 200 in York and 4,800 in Pickering Township.[3]

In Ontario County a second factor worked to cause delay and confusion in settlement. In his anxiety to persuade settlers to come to Upper Canada, Governor Simcoe followed a practice of his predecessors in Quebec, namely that of granting large tracts of lands, frequently whole townships, to middlemen who were expected to bring in settlers. The choice of middlemen was not haphazard, however. As Simcoe explained to the Colonial Secretary, Henry Dundas, he had taken special care that grants of townships were assigned only "to those persons who seemed likely to bring an acquisition of settlers into the country".[4] Simcoe's judgment, however, was not infallible.

On December 31, 1792, William Willcocks, a citizen of Cork, Ireland, petitioned the Executive Council of Upper Canada for 1,000 acres of land for himself and his associates, in addition to the 200 acres already granted him personally at Toronto.[5] The lands desired were in the township of Norwich (now Whitby). Willcocks claimed in his petition that he had come to Upper Canada earlier in the year, and "spent many months exploring that fine country." According to his story, he was grieved to see it uninhabited at a time when thousands of his countrymen, ignorant of its resources, were emigrating to the United States. So he had decided to undertake a settlement scheme. Confronted by these admirable sentiments, the Executive Council granted his petition and awarded an additional 200 acres for each settler he and his associates could bring out. Willcocks then returned to Ireland to gather settlers.

Immediately after he returned to Ireland, Willcocks had advertisements distributed praising the merits of the new land, and setting forth the terms to emigrants. "Free" grants would be given to persons who could prove they were able to cultivate and improve the land, at two guineas for a 200-acre lot, 400 acres for six guineas, 600 acres for eighteen guineas, and so on up to 1,200 acres for sixty guineas. Also there would be a small rent of a penny per acre the first year, and threepence in succeeding years. A ship would be provided, on which cabin-passengers would pay twenty guineas and provide their own wine, while common passengers would pay six guineas if Britain were at peace and seven if at war. All passengers must provide their own bed and bedding.

Tradesmen who could not pay their passage might be granted special terms. The country was painted in glowing and somewhat exaggerated terms. According to Willcocks the land was covered with timber and abounded in valuable fur-bearing animals, delicious fish, and so on, and every form of produce found "ready sale at Montreal and other towns on the river".[6] This advertisement clearly contravened the terms by which Willcocks had been granted the lands, since the lots were to be given free to *bona fide* settlers, who were to pay only the customary fees.

Circumstances as diverse as his election as Mayor of Cork and the war between Britain and France prevented Willcock's return to Upper Canada until 1795, but in that year he brought out thirty-three settlers. Unfortunately he came by way of New York, necessitating a long trip overland to Upper Canada, during which his settlers were gradually enticed away by American land agents who offered more attractive opportunities for settlement.

Since Willcocks had brought part of his family to Canada, he decided to remain here and leave the recruiting in Ireland to his son. In the meantime he turned his attention southward in hope of attracting settlers from the United States.[7] On August 25, 1795 the following advertisement appeared in the Schenectady *Mohawk Mercury*:

> Upwards of 30,000 Acres of most excellent Land on the north side of Lake Ontario, in the Township of Whitby, about 18 miles East of the new Town of York, now building for the seat of Government, 20 miles west of the Bay of Canty, and 30 north of Niagara, divided into 200 acre Lots; – Will be disposed of on moderate terms by Wm. Willcocks Esq'r who will give good Encouragement to the first ten industrious Settlers, that close with him before the first day of November next; Apply to him at Niagara or York, or at the printers of the Mohawk Mercury in Schenectady.
>
> N.B. This Township is nine miles front on Lake Ontario, and twelve miles deep: it has three Good Harbours and several Capital Millseats.[8]

This further contravention of the regulations brought an immediate reprisal from the Upper Canadian officials. On January 6, 1796 E.B. Littlehales (Governor Simcoe's military secretary) wrote to Acting Surveyor General D.W. Smith:

> You are desired by his Excellency the Lieutenant Governor to transmit to Mr. Willcocks a copy of the letter which I wrote to Messrs. Watson and Prior on the subject of their offering for sale Lands in the township granted to them under the conditions of the Proclamation issued at Quebec; by which Mr. Willcocks will see that having advertised the lands in Whitby for sale, He has forfeited all claim and Pretension to the same –
>
> You will also be so good to inform him that the lands for which He

> has obtained an Order in Council (if the proceedings at York have been confirmed, which is doubtful) are expressly on his being a Resident in York or cultivating the same, on and for that purpose.[9]

Following this order, on May 25, 1796 Governor Simcoe ordered that Whitby (and eleven other townships seized for similar reasons) be declared open for granting to settlers.[10]

The Executive Council, in rescinding Willcocks' grant, did not wish to impose undue hardship on him. On June 28, 1797 the Council ordered that

> in consideration of the great expense Mr. Willcocks has been exposed to in his efforts to fulfil his engagements to Government, & in crossing the Attlantic [sic] twice in consequence of that Township having been appropriated for the purpose of being filled by him with Irish settlers, it is further ordered, that 1,200 acres each shall be immediately located & appropriated to W. Willcock's wife Phoebe, his Daughters Maria, Phoebe Junior, & Eugenia, his Son Charles and his Son's wife Ann Willcocks to be confirmed by the King's Deed to each as they shall respectively come into this Province to reside but not before.[11]

In all, the Willcocks family would receive some 7,000 acres in Whitby Township under the terms of this concession, one of the largest holdings in Ontario County.[12]

Despite the failure of the Whitby experiment at mass settlement, one more such attempt would be made in Ontario County. During the French Revolution large numbers of Royalists had fled to England where they quickly became a serious burden on the charitable organizations and tax revenues of the country. As early as 1792 various plans had been put forward to settle the Royalist Emigrés in Canda, but these plans had been dropped when events in France had temporarily taken a turn for the better. In 1796, however, the dashing Comte de Puisaye, ex-commander of the Royalist forces in Brittany, revived these plans. Finding himself betrayed by a jealous subordinate and out of favour with the heir to the throne (the future Louis XVIII), de Puisaye persuaded the British Prime Minister, Sir William Pitt, that the British Government should establish the Emigrés in Canada and support them for three years.[13] Although the Upper Canadian officials were at first reluctant to see large numbers of French-speaking immigrants settle in Upper Canada, in the end they bowed to British wishes and made provision for the expected influx. The centre of Emigré settlement was to be at Windham Settlement (present day Oak Ridges) on Yonge Street, where four square miles embracing the corners of Vaughan, King, Whitchurch and Markham townships were set aside as a townsite. In addition, on November 22, 1798 the townships of Uxbridge and Gwillimbury, another (unnamed) township north of Whitby (probably Reach) and the ungranted portion of Whitchurch were all granted to de Puisaye for his followers. De Puisaye himself was to receive 5,000 acres in whatever part of this area he chose.[14]

Again, as with William Willcocks, strict terms were laid down. Every Emigré settler had to remain seven years on his land or have it forfeited and no one was to be granted lands in these areas except through de Puisaye or by special order of the Executive Council. The whole project, however, was a complete failure. Only a few Emigrés ever arrived and those that did were quickly disillusioned by the labour required to clear the land from the stubborn forest. By 1802 only thirteen Emigrés remained in Upper Canada.[15] A pitiful letter, written by Le Chevalier de Marzeul (an Emigré nobleman who had settled on Yonge Street, concession I, lots 57 and N½ 56, Markham Township) to de Puisaye in 1799, shows the difficulties that inexperience and ignorance imposed on the Emigré settlers;

> I determined to write to you, to let you know what obstacles oppose themselves to my establishment. A felon [a kind of abscess] which has made me lose the joint of a finger has long prevented me from working. Add to this the time I had laboured on another lot. When seed-time the fences being poor the oxen ate everything. Those which you had the goodness to send me strayed two months ago and notwithstanding my search I am not able to get news of them. I am afraid I shall lose them. After having worked to repair some of the imperfection of my house, the fall of the great oak crushed the front part of the roof and damaged the floor and other parts. The house is repaired now, but I sleep on the ground.[16]

It is not surprising that they quickly became discouraged and returned to England to take their chances on fate returning them to power in France. In despair at the Emigrés' failure, in 1803 the government resumed control of all lands not actually occupied by them. Thus Uxbridge and the other townships reserved for them were opened again for regular settlement. Just as they had done when seizing Whitby from William Willcocks, the Executive Council granted the Emigrés extensive lands in Uxbridge, Scott and Whitby in compensation for this seizure.[17] Thus the romantic dream of noble families dwelling in a rural Arcadia faded before the harsh reality of life in the uncleared forest.

Neither the Loyalists' migration nor attempts at settlement through middlemen brought the first permanent pioneers to Ontario County. Instead it was the frontier "squatter" who cleared the first fields and planted the first crops. According to tradition, Benjamin Wilson, a native of Putney, Vermont, his wife and two sons, and two young men named L. Lockwood and E. Ransome were the first to arrive as permanent settlers.[18] Some time between 1788 and 1794 (the tradition varies), the little party travelled from Niagara to their new home on lot 4, broken front, Whitby Township. The trip was not easy: the boys drove a yoke of oxen and four cows along the shore while the family kept pace in a boat loaded with household effects.[19]

Although military and Loyalist claimants received their land patents automatically, "unofficial" settlers, such as Benjamin Wilson, were required to fulfill strict terms in order to gain ownership. On February 7, 1792 Governor Simcoe had issued a proclamation, which was smuggled into the western frontier of the United States, and which offered free land to all who would cultivate it and would sign an oath of loyalty to the King. The only charge entailed would be the various clerks' fees which were kept at low level by a published fee list. Farms were to be granted in 200-acre lots, but could be increased to 1,200 acres at the discretion of the Executive Council.[20]

While Simcoe's proclamation immediately attracted thousands of American-born settlers northward, it was not an open invitation, nor were settlers allowed to "squat" where they pleased. The key to Simcoe's administration was order and a careful attention to duties. Thus because Benjamin Wilson had not followed directions to settle in an "open" township, he was not able to apply for a location ticket until July 4, 1796, some six weeks after Whitby had been seized from William Willcocks.[21]

In order to receive ownership of a farm it was necessary to perform certain settlement duties. One such list of duties required that:

> They must within the term of two years clear fit for cultivation and fence, ten acres of the lot obtained; build a house 16 by 20 feet of logs or frame, with a shingle roof; also cut down all timber in front of and the whole width of the lot . . . 33 feet of which must be cleared smooth and left for half the public road.[22]

Moreover, the payment of fees to all the clerks and officials tended to discourage settlers from getting final title (the patent) to their lands. In Wilson's case the patent was not received until February 17, 1819.[23]

For Pickering and Whitby, therefore, in the early years far more land was held by Loyalists, the military and self-seeking officials than was received by settlers intending to make their home in Ontario County. After Major Smith's military grant of 4,800 acres in 1795, there followed a whole series of large grants to officials and their relatives. A list of the grants made in Ontario County in 1796 shows the extent of this practice:

Grantee	*Area (acres)*	*Township*	*Date*
Captain George Hill	1,200	Pickering	May 6, 1796
William Holmes	1,200	Pickering	May 28, 1796
Hon. John McGill	1,000	Whitby	Nov. 11, 1796
Catherine (Mrs. John) McGill	1,200	Pickering	Nov. 11, 1796
Elizabeth Russell	800	Whitby	Dec. 15, 1796
Rev. Thomas Radenhurst	600	Whitby	Dec. 31, 1796
Anthony Neverville	1,200	Whitby	Dec. 31, 1796
Meredith Melvil	1,200	Whitby	Dec. 31, 1796
Alexander Burns	700	Whitby	Dec. 31, 1796

Other large grants patented in Ontario County before 1800 include:

Grantee	Area (acres)	Township	Date
Lieut. James Givens	1,000	Whitby	March 14, 1798
William Willcocks, Sr.	1,000	Whitby	March 14, 1798
Hon. John Elmsley	4,600	Pickering	April 16, 1798
Mrs. Mary Elmsley	1,200	Pickering	April 16, 1798
Benjamin Hallowell, Esq.	1,200	Pickering	April 16, 1798
Capt. George Law, M.C.	3,000	Pickering	May 4, 1798
John Shaw	1,200	Whitby	May 4, 1798
Isabella Shaw	1,200	Whitby	May 22, 1798
William Holmes, Esq.	2,000	Pickering	May 22, 1798
Elizabeth Tuck Macauley	1,000	Whitby	Aug. 8, 1799

In all, between January 1, 1795 and December 31, 1799, over 28,400 acres were patented in Pickering and 15,200 in Whitby Townships.[24]

Between January 1, 1800 and December 31, 1805, another 8,300 acres were granted in Pickering, and 25,780 acres in Whitby.[25] Large grants between 1800 and 1805 include:[26]

Grantee	Area (acres)	Township	Date
William Ross	1,200	Pickering	Sept. 4, 1800
Eugenia Willcocks	1,200	Whitby	Sept. 4, 1800
Hugh Earl	1,200	Whitby	Sept. 4, 1800
Maria Willcocks	1,200	Whitby	Sept. 11, 1800
William Harffy	1,400	Pickering	June 30, 1801
Bernard Fry	2,300	Whitby	Aug. 10, 1801
Isabella Hill	1,200	Pickering	May 17, 1802
John Scadding	1,000	Whitby	May 17, 1802
Charles Willcocks	1,200	Whitby	May 17, 1802
Phoebe Willcocks	1,200	Whitby	Nov. 25, 1802
Arthur McCormack	1,200	Whitby	June 4, 1803
Phoebe Willcocks Baldwin	1,200	Whitby	March 15, 1804

By 1805 some sixty-nine per cent of the land available in Pickering, and ninety-four per cent of the land available in Whitby (exclusive of Reserves) had been granted. Moreover, of the lands granted, more than sixty-four per cent in Pickering and more than fifty per cent in Whitby had consisted of grants of 1,000 acres or more.

With the repossession of Uxbridge Township from the French Emigrés, it was now possible to grant lands in it to other types of applicants. With the available lands having largely been taken up in Pickering and Whitby, and with other townships in the area, such as Markham and Whitchurch, already heavily settled, people with "official" land rights turned to Uxbridge as being the closest open township to the rapidly growing Town of York. As soon as Uxbridge was surveyed in 1804, large numbers of applicants began patenting lands. Unlike those taking lands in Pickering and Whitby, almost all patentees in Uxbridge received only 200 acres. In 1804 alone, fifteen of these 200-acre patents were made.

Despite the rapid spread of land ownership in Pickering, Whitby and Uxbridge, settlement progressed very slowly in the area. Few of those receiving lands were interested in farming them or settling in the area, with the result that large tracts of vacant lands discouraged those who might have settled near them. Nonetheless a few hardy pioneers did begin to purchase lands from the patentees to whom it had been given and to build a small community in the southeast corner of Whitby Township. Early records show that by 1801 settlers including Elizar Lockwood, Adam and David Stephens, John McGahn (or Magahan), David Lloyd and Abraham Townsend, had joined Benjamin Wilson, L. Lockwood and Ebenezer Ransome in the Oshawa-Harmony area.[27] In the next few years these were joined by Levi Annis, Thomas McGahee, Joseph Wiley, Matthew Terwillegar (or de Willigar), Acheus Moody and William Farewell, Jabez Lynde (the first settler west of the Town of Whitby) and William Pickle.

The first settler in Pickering Township was William Peak who settled near the mouth of Duffin's Creek about 1800. Peak was joined immediately in Pickering by other settlers near Duffin's Creek as well as by a few settlers who moved across the northwest boundary from Markham Township. Such names as Judson Gibson, John Majors, David Crawford, Peter Crawford and Anthony Rummerfeld appear on early lists of municipal officers, and by 1805 these were joined by Samuel Munger, David Spicer and David Thatcher.[28]

Though settlement was progressing, the spread was slow chiefly because most potential settlers preferred to go to areas where land was free rather than puchase that already patented. By 1805, nearly fifteen years after Benjamin Wilson's arrival, Whitby's population was only 104 (28 men, 23 women and 53 children). At the same time Pickering's population had grown only to 96 – 27 men, 18 women and 51 children. By contrast, in 1805, Markham's population was 889, York Township's 494, and that of Whitchurch, 348.[29]

The assessment summaries for 1805 show how slowly agriculture had developed in Ontario County. In 1805 only 263 acres were under cultivation in Whitby and 104 in Pickering. In Whitby there were 11 horses, 26 oxen, 50 milk cows, 47 young cattle and 20 swine. In Pickering there were 7 horses, 29 oxen, 40 milk cows, 39 young cattle and 5 swine. Pickering had the only sawmill, possibly that of Timothy Rogers on Duffin's Creek which is reported in 1810.[30]

Between 1805 and 1810 the process of land alienation (patents being taken out by absentee "official" grantees) which had begun in Uxbridge in 1804 was completed in that township, and continued on in much of Scott.[31] By December 31, 1809 a total of 36,812 acres in Uxbridge (the entire area not

Reuben Crandell's House, built in 1821, Reach Township *Public Archives of Ontario*

set aside for Crown or Clergy Reserves) had been granted. In 1807 Scott Township had been opened and by December 31, 1809, 23,240 acres, some sixty-six per cent of the land available for granting had been patented. In addition to these grants, another 5,100 acres in Whitby and 2,600 acres in Pickering were patented.[32]

In 1811 Reach, the last township in Ontario County in which large scale "official" grants were allowed, was opened. In the two years, 1811 and 1812, 43,820 acres of land, nearly all in 200-acre plots, was granted to absentee "official" landowners. This was almost ninety-eight per cent of land available in the township. In Scott during 1810, 1811 and 1812, an additional 10,450 acres was patented, bringing the total patented in that township to ninety-six per cent of the lands available outside the reserves. By the end of 1812 almost a hundred per cent of Whitby, Pickering, Uxbridge and Scott had been patented, as well as almost ninety per cent of Reach Township.[33]

The major exception among the pioneers who were forced to purchase their lands were a few Quaker settlers who arrived in Uxbridge during the great land rush of 1804-1807. The first of this group was William Gold (later changed to Gould) who patented lot 31, concession V on April 13, 1804. Following him in 1805 Dr. Christopher Beswick, Elijah Collins, James Hughs, George Webb, Robert Wilson and Joseph Collins all patented lots around the Uxbridge-Quaker Hill area on the fifth and sixth concessions. So quickly were

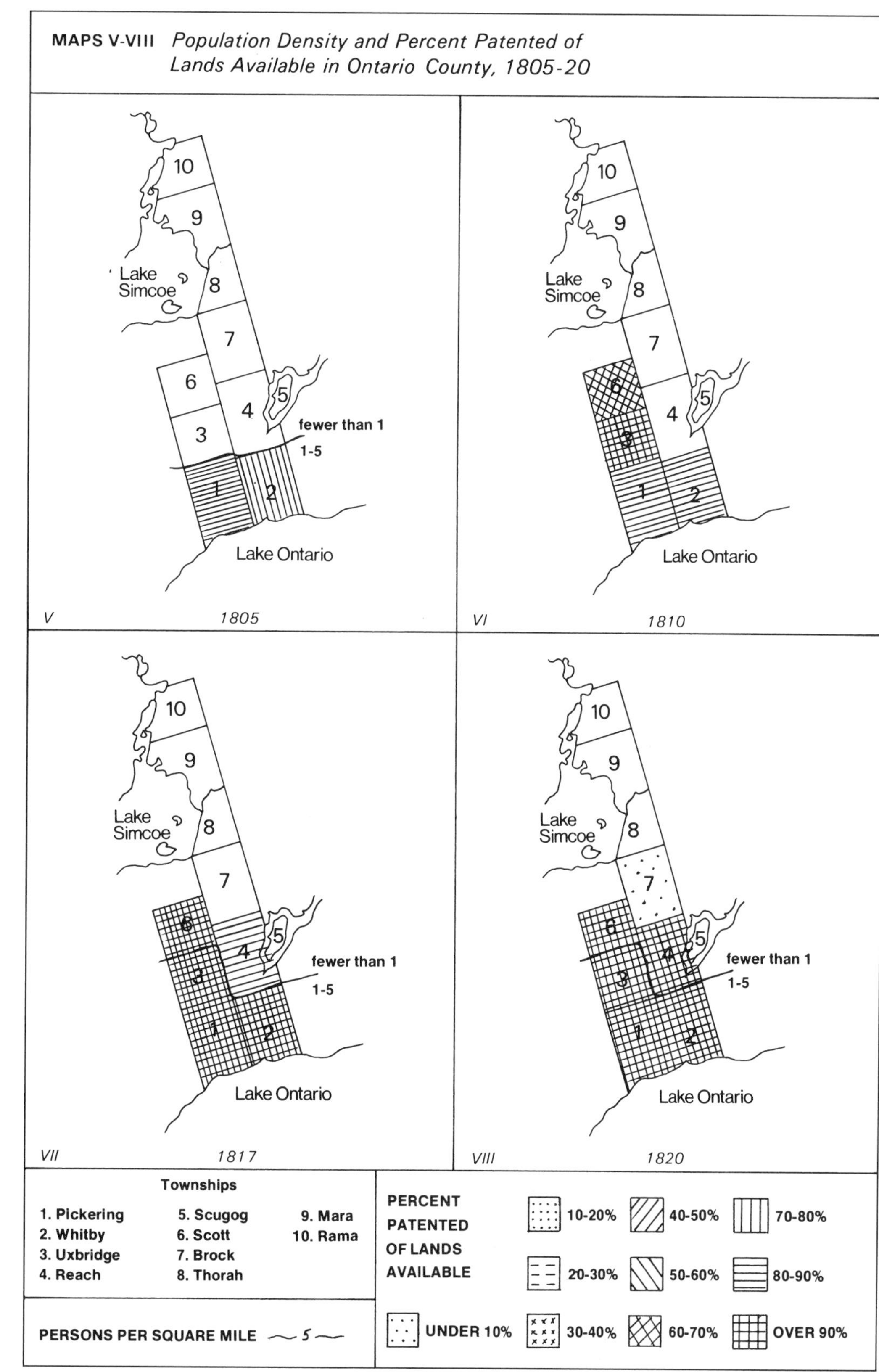

MAPS V-VIII Population Density and Percent Patented of Lands Available in Ontario County, 1805-20
10
9
Lake Simcoe
8
7
6
5
4
3
fewer than 1
1-5
1
2
Lake Ontario
V
1805
10
9
Lake Simcoe
8
7
6
5
4
3
1
2
Lake Ontario
VI
1810
10
9
Lake Simcoe
8
7
6
5
4
fewer than 1
1-5
3
1
2
Lake Ontario
VII
1817
10
9
Lake Simcoe
8
7
6
5
4
fewer than 1
1-5
3
1
2
Lake Ontario
VIII
1820
Townships
1. Pickering
2. Whitby
3. Uxbridge
4. Reach
5. Scugog
6. Scott
7. Brock
8. Thorah
9. Mara
10. Rama
PERSONS PER SQUARE MILE
5
PERCENT PATENTED OF LANDS AVAILABLE
10-20%
40-50%
70-80%
20-30%
50-60%
80-90%
UNDER 10%
30-40%
60-70%
OVER 90%

the vacant lands taken up by "official" patentees, however, that other Quaker settlers, such as Ezekial Roberts, Amos, Stephen and Thomas Hilborne, Jonathan Gold, Abraham Bagshaw, William Fergusson, John Johnston, George Hutchinson and Peter Thompson were forced to purchase their lands from the non-resident patentees. Similarly, of the pioneers in the Glasgow-Goodwood area in the southwest corner of Uxbridge, only Jacob Wideman (lot 13, concession V, patented April 25, 1804) was able to get free land. Other early settlers who arrived in the area from 1806 on, such as the Mordens, Kesters, Browns, Forsyths, McWains, Townsends and Frenches, were forced to purchase their lands from the original patentees.[34] For these settlers, land-locked amid an untouched, absentee-owned forest, life would be rendered almost impossible by the lack of roads and the distance from other settlements.[35]

With the outbreak of the War of 1812, both land patenting and settlement came to a halt, but for much of Ontario County a strong set of characteristics had already been established. While settlers were, as yet, few in number, they were grouped together in small, cohesive settlements which were able to maintain their national identities and traditions even when later and larger immigrations swamped them numerically. Thus the southern part of Whitby took on a distinctly "Yankee" tradition from its early settlers from Vermont and New York, while Pickering, with its strong New England Quaker contingent, was less given to commerical ambitions. In Uxbridge, the Pennsylvania Germans who moved across the township line from Markham to the Glasgow area, and the Pennsylvania Quakers of the Uxbridge Village region both left vital cultural traditions in their regions. The postwar immigration period would, however, introduce quite a different set of elements into the area.

From 1812 to 1820 there was a relatively small amount of new land patented, although some important new areas were opened for settlement. In 1817 Brock Township was surveyed, and in 1820 J.E. White surveyed parts of Thorah. There was not the customary rush of absentee patentees into the area, as had been true of the earlier townships. The reason for the change was the Government's determination that the errors made before 1812 would not be repeated. To prevent absenteeism and speculation, Lieutenant-Governor Peregrine Maitland ordered that all those receiving lands, whether Loyalists or not, would be required to erect habitable houses and to clear and fence five acres in every hundred before receiving the title.[36] As a result of this order, in 1820 Brock Township was less than ten percent patented three years after it was opened.

While the settlers before the War of 1812 had been almost entirely Americans, after the war they were almost all British. Thus as settlement spread north in Whitby and Pickering, a band of British settlement was established north of the American. Because it was necessary to purchase these lands from their original owners, only the wealthier (usually English) settlers could afford to settle in these areas. In this way the region around Columbus acquired its title of "English Corners" from its neighbours,[37] while the area around Greenwood developed the same English character.

At the same time settlers looking for free, unpatented land began to enter Brock Township from the north, having followed the long road from York through Newmarket and Georgina. The first of these, James Reekie, arrived in 1817, but he was soon followed by Colonel James and George Vrooman. Almost immediately these settlers were followed into Brock by the British military grantees whose presence would give that township a unique "loyal" character.

While the War of 1812 was still in progress, various British regiments serving in the Canadas were promised that any soldiers discharged in Upper Canada and recommended as settlers would receive one hundred acres of land free of fees, provisions for themselves and their families for one year, and all necessary farm implements. This privilege was subsequently extended to soldiers discharged elsewhere as well.[38] While most of these military claimants were settled in Lanark County, a few were directed to Home District (previous to 1849, Home District comprised, roughly, York, Ontario, Peel and Simcoe Counties) where they settled in Brock and Toronto Townships.[39] During 1817 and 1818, about two hundred English and Irish families who had emigrated by way of New York City were forwarded by James Buchanan, the British Consul in New York. He had been authorized to spend up to $10.00 per person in forwarding them to Canada so that these loyal citizens might be saved for the Empire.[40] Among those sent on from New York were William Smith, Mark MacManus, Samuel Stephenson, Thomas Morgan, Samuel and Richard Marshall, John Gutherie, William Bagshaw, Alex Cathcart, and Philip St. John, the colourful "King of Brock".[41]

St. John was probably typical of those settlers who entered Upper Canada via New York City at that time. He had left Rathkaly, Limerick County, Ireland in 1816 with his wife and two children to settle in the United States.[42] Dissatisfied with the "rampant democracy" of his new home, he eagerly turned north in 1817 when the opportunity was offered to assert once again his loyalty to the British Crown. Philip St. John and the other "Loyalist" Anglican Irish who settled in Brock made that township a bastion of conservatism and unquestioning loyalty to the government that remained unshaken for generations.

By 1820 both the faults and successes of Simcoe's policies had left a profound mark upon the development of Ontario County. The sparse settlement and vast empty distances would allow the development of separate, homogeneous groups with their own values and attitudes. When, in later periods, new problems and issues arose, they were debated and contended over, not just in terms of the issues themselves, but also in terms of older divisions and rivalries which often hindered their solution and all but rendered them insoluble.

PIONEER SOCIETY, 1790-1820

In spite of the difficulties imposed by the high degree of absentee ownership, Whitby and Pickering's favourable position close to the lake and their fertile soil attracted settlers at a rate slightly higher than did the Home District as a whole.

Table I
Population of Whitby and Pickering Township, 1805–20[1]

	1805	*1817*	*1820*
Whitby	104	296	505
Pickering	96	330	575
Total Home District	3,784	7,229	10,833
Percent Whitby	2.7	4.1	4.8
Percent Pickering	2.5	4.6	5.7

Thus between 1805 and 1820 Whitby's population grew from 2.7 to 4.8% of the Home District total and Pickering grew from 2.5 to 5.7%. In contrast Uxbridge grew much more slowly. In 1826 when the first separate figures are given, Uxbridge had only 228 inhabitants compared with 891 in Pickering and 1,098 in Whitby.[2]

According to assessment records this growth fell into three periods. First, a period of slow but steady growth from 1790 to 1812; second, a slowdown during the war years; then third, a rapid growth from 1815 to 1820. For example, in 1812, 47 households were assessed in Whitby and 53 in Pickering. By 1815 the number had dropped to 38 in Whitby and 48 in Pickering. By 1820 these numbers had more than doubled to 90 in Whitby and 100 in Pickering. As Table I confirms, within just three years from 1817 to 1820 the number of new British settlers almost equalled in numbers all those who had come in the previous twenty-five years.[3]

Table II
Economic Development of Whitby Township, 1805–20[4]

	1805	*1812*	*1815*	*1817*	*1820*
Number Assessed	—	47	38	48	90
Acres Uncultivated	4,844	7,862	6,565	7,282	11,671
Acres Cultivated	263	660	838	1,012	1,491
Horses	11	33	41	43	74
Oxen	26	40	21	34	68
Milch Cows	50	115	114	128	194
Young Cattle	7	84	49	53	111
Assessed Value (£ Sterling)	798.5s	3,579.8	3,229.0	4,202.8	6,785.4
Value per Person Assessed (£ Sterling)	—	76.3s	84.19	84.1	75.8
Value per Capita (£ Sterling)	7.14s	—	—	14.4	13.9
Acres per Person Assessed	—	181.3	194.8	172.8	130.0
Acres Cultivated per Person Assessed	—	14.0	22.1	21.1	16.6
Acres Cultivated per Capita	2.5	—	—	3.4	2.2

As Tables II and III show, the years 1805 to 1820 display a pattern of economic development closely related to the overall growth in population. Several aspects, however, should be emphasized, because they bear on the future development of the area. First, the rapid changes in the average size of farm suggests that the War of 1812 and its aftermath significantly affected the lives of the local inhabitants. Before the war, farms averaged 181.3 acres in Whitby and 195.5 acres in Pickering. During the war, with fourteen of the original families selling out and leaving the area, farm sizes increased to 194.8 and 221.7 acres respectively. With new settlers pouring in after the war, the tendency was to divide the already settled farms rather than to open new areas. This trend is particularly noticeable in Pickering where farm acreage increased very slowly from 12,335 acres in 1817 to 12,709 acres in 1820, while the number of persons assessed jumped from 69 to 100. Through such subdivisions the average farm size dropped sharply to 130.0 acres in Whitby in 1820 and to 127.1 in Pickering. This process of subdivision would continue until

Table III
Economic Development of Pickering Township, 1805–20[5]

	1805	*1812*	*1815*	*1817*	*1820*
Number Assessed	—	53	48	69	100
Acres Uncultivated	4,936	9,540	9,546	11,156	11,134
Acres Cultivated	104	819	1,098	1,179	1,575
Horses	29	48	53	74	82
Oxen	40	46	30	43	66
Milch Cows	39	129	116	168	205
Young Cattle	5	35	75	61	109
Assessed Value (£ Sterling)	778.16s	4,426.0	4,154.4	5,264.4	6,534.16
Value per Person Assessed (£ Sterling)	—	83.10s	86.11	76.6	65.7
Value per Capita (£ Sterling)	8.4s	—	—	15.19	11.8
Acres per Person Assessed	—	195.5	221.7	178.8	127.1
Acres Cultivated per Person Assessed	—	15.3	22.9	17.1	15.8
Acres Cultivated per Capita	1.1	—	—	3.6	2.8

1851 when the average farm size in Whitby and Pickering was 74.0 acres and 78.2 acres respectively.[6]

During the period 1815 to 1820 the first division of society into different economic classes began to appear in the local population. Before that time almost every adult male in Ontario County owned land. However, with the completion of land patenting by absentees and with Sir Peregrine Maitland's new rules which greatly raised patenting fees, working-class immigrants found that they must first labour for years to accumulate capital in order to buy patented land or to pay the high fees on upatented land.[7] Thus while in 1817 only 18 of 66 males (16 years and over) in Whitby, and 8 of 77 males (16 and over) in Pickering were without land, in 1820 some 65 of 178 men in Whitby and 48 of 161 men in Pickering were landless. Included among the landless in 1820 were 49 men and 11 women described as servants.[8]

Finally it should be noted that the percentage of cleared acreage per inhabitant remained very low throughout the period, as did the cleared acreage per person assessed. In circumstances where so little land was available, it was necessary to cultivate it very intensively. Thus the labour of children and women was used extensively in the care of livestock and of large gardens. In busy seasons, they laboured in the fields as well. The scarcity of land also made it difficult to raise enough hay for livestock. Thus the number of cattle did not rise above three per farmer at any time during the period. Similarly, the number of horses and oxen remained at less than one per farmer until 1820.

For the first white settlers in Ontario County life on the frontier was a difficult and demanding task which left little time for non-productive activities. Although most had come with the intention of becoming farmers, many were forced by circumstances to become backwoodsmen as well. The struggle to clear the forest left profound marks on the social, political and economic organization of the pioneer community. Gradually these attitudes and institutions, isolated from other centres by distance and poor communications, developed into a community on which the local inhabitants based an intense pride and identity which prevailed for generations. Just as these pioneers shaped the environment, so did the environment shape them.

For the first few years, distance from grain and produce markets and the difficulties faced in clearing the forest meant that many of the early settlers were forced to depend on non-agricultural pursuits for much of their income. Thus pioneers such as William Peak, the first settler on Duffin's Creek in Pickering, and the brothers Moody and William Farewell in Whitby Township, became traders in areas north of the little settlements.[9] Other settlers "hired out" on a part-time basis as surveyors, labourers and teamsters on government projects such as the Danforth military road between York and Kingston. Still others set up small shops or taverns in rooms in their houses as a means of adding to their incomes.[10]

When the settler first arrived on his lot, he faced the necessity of getting a quick harvest in order to survive the following winter. To get this without undertaking the slow and difficult task of clearing the land, he usually "girdled" a few acres of trees by chopping a ring in the bark of the larger trees; then having cleared away the underbrush, he broadcast his grain between the trees. Since girdling killed the trees quickly by preventing the development of leaves, the settler could get a crop the first year. While this method saved time, it had severe drawbacks. First, the dead trees left standing quickly became iron-hard and difficult to cut down. Their falling limbs were dangerous to men and animals alike. Moreover, as time went on and wind toppled them, they created a "slash", impossible to cultivate and an enduring fire hazard for the whole settlement. Thus girdling was resorted to only in the first year or so of settlement.[11]

The most usual method of clearing land was that described by David Gibson of York Township in 1827. According to Gibson, clearing was undertaken after the harvest, but before the snow fell. At that time the farmers cleared out all the underbrush and piled it into heaps, and cut up the fallen dead trees that would later be covered by snow. Later in the winter, they cut the trees so that the tops fell near the brush piles. Then they cut the trunk of the tree into large pieces; these were left to lie until the succeeding summer, when the brush piles were burned along with the deep leaf mould on the ground which the pioneers considered to be harmful to the crops. After the brush was burned off, the most difficult task still remained: the logs had to be rolled into piles so that they would dry out and could be burned as well. This work required the combined efforts of three men, a yoke of oxen and a driver. As Gibson noted:

> Logging is very hard work having so many heavy lifts, and the men are as black as chimney sweeps when at this work, the logs get burned on the outside when the brush is burning.[12]

After these logs had dried, they were burned and the ashes collected for sale in York.[13] Since the clearing and burning of new land was a difficult time-consuming job, wealthier settlers hired new immigrants as "choppers" who cleared and fenced the land at a price of $12.00 to $20.00 per acre.[14]

While the forest presented an immediate barrier to progress, the sale of ashes from burning the cleared timber often provided the only cash income a pioneer family might receive. Thus the Kendrick brothers established a potashery in York as early as 1799 where ashes could be exchanged for trade goods, and in 1800 William Allan, the future banker and member of the Executive Council, advertised that

> he conceives it his duty to inform those who may have ashes to dispose of, that it will not be in his power to pay cash, but merchandise at cash price.[15]

It was calculated that ashes from ten acres of forest would make about five barrels (2,500 lbs.) of potash, for which a price from nine shillings to twenty-five shillings or more per hundredweight could be obtained – the price depending upon the condition of the market and the grade of the product.[16]

Despite the vast amount of labour expended in chopping and burning the trees, the land remained covered with stumps for many years after the clearing was complete. Most pioneers, rather than expend the huge effort necessary to root out the stumps, sowed among them until they rotted out. For most hardwood varieties this occurred after eight or ten years, but pine or hemlock stumps, preserved by the pitch, often remained sound for a lifetime. Thus land having a larger percentage of evergreens was less attractive to the settler and brought a lower price than areas covered by hardwood.

By all accounts, the original pioneers were poor farmers. While few critics went so far in their condemnation as did the British traveller, John Howison, who stated that "the Canadians in addition to their indolence, ignorance, and want of ambition, are very bad farmers",[17] his criticism was shared by many knowledgeable observers. As Howison pointed out, the pioneer farmer's object was

> to have a great deal of land under improvement; and consequently, they go on cutting down the woods on their lots and regularly transferring the crop to the soil last cleared, until they think they have sufficiently expanded the bounds of their farms; then they sow different parts randomly.[18]

A later observer, W.H. Smith, remarked that "the universal Canadian practice has been followed in clearing the land, that of sweeping away everything capable of bearing a green leaf, although it requires a generation to repair the devastation of a few hours".[19] Viewing the devastation of the forest and the wasteful cultural practices of the times, Patrick Sherriff was no doubt correct in his remark that the province was overrun rather than settled in the early years.[20]

The first crops planted were generally either wheat or potatoes, although Indian corn was frequently sown in more southern areas. For the first few years after clearing, the rich forest soil produced excellent crops – wheat, for instance yielded thirty to forty bushels per acre from a single bushel planted. After eight to ten years, however, the stored up fertility of the soil was exhausted and yields dropped drastically.[21] Since the pioneer farmers neither manured their fields nor practiced the rotation of crops, many early pioneers would farm until the cleared land was exhausted, then sell to a newcomer and move to a new location on the edge of settlement. In Ontario County the continuous movement inland of many of the earliest settlers would seem to follow this pattern.

Agricultural practices were simple and tools and implements were rudimentary at best. Wheat was generally sown broadcast and covered by dragging over it a heavy branch or a crude harrow made of a log with long wooden teeth set in holes. Plows were made of wood bound with a piece of iron strapping to give it strength, while grain was cut with the sickle or scythe and cradle. Threshing was done with a simple flail made from two pieces of wood joined by a leather strap.

One of the most significant factors in shaping the developing society of Ontario County was the necessity of economic self-reliance, created by the bad roads and distance from markets. Not only did these latter create great hardships for the early settlers, but the struggle to overcome them, and the social and economic limitations imposed by them combined to create a society markedly different from that of England or the urban centres such as York or Kingston.

The hardships created by distance and bad roads is illustrated by the reminiscences of William Paxton, Sr. who settled on the third concession, Whitby, in 1820:

> The County north of that [was] one unbroken wilderness. . . . With no grist mill in the Township, the nearest being situated at Duffin's Creek, which was of the rudest character, and hence often out of repair, the family was obliged for weeks at a time, to go without bread. Meat of any kind was only a rarity which few could afford. The nearest store was at Little York [now Toronto], where the journey, for years, had to be made on foot.[22]

As Paxton observed, "Comparing his time to the present, he lived as the poorest of the poor".[23]

Similarly, those who settled farther north in Uxbridge Township faced great hardships in reaching markets. While a small gristmill had been operated in Uxbridge by Dr. Beswick and Joseph Collins in 1806 and 1809, as Joseph Gould remembered it:

> The renting of the premises, the constant removal of tenants, and the need of proper repairs and due attention led to the total delapidation of the sawmill, so that in time it rotted altogether. The gristmill was but a poor thing at best, and it was allowed to get so much out of repair that it did not run half the time, and it sometimes remained altogether idle for more than a year at a stretch. For nearly twenty years the people of the settlement were obliged to go to Newmarket to mill to get their gristings done.[24]

Nor were the settler's troubles over when he arrived at the mill with his grain. Philip St. John of Brock township recollected that he

> was the first settler that ever sold a load of wheat out of Brock. He took it to Newmarket, and when he got it there he had to take the whole price in store pay [i.e., merchandise]. He wanted to get $2 cash to pay his hotel bill and other small payments, but he could not get even $2 in cash. There were no blacksmith shops nearer than Newmarket or Toronto, and the settlers in Brock had to go to one of these places were it only to get a plow point sharpened or horse shod.[25]

Because of the difficulties of transportation and scarcity of money, most necessities of life were made by hand within the family or the local community. Thus hides were tanned into leather which was then made into boots, outer clothing and harnesses. Wool and flax were grown, carded, spun and woven into cloth from which the rough durable "lindsey-woolsey" clothing was made. Furniture and utensils were carved from wood; shingles were split from cedar blocks; and fences were built of rails made from split cedar logs. Dried hardwood pegs served as nails; fruit and meat were dried; soap was made from rendered animal fat and lye leached from ashes; rakes, flails and even shovels were carved from wood. In the early years almost everything the family used, wore or ate was produced by the members themselves. Only a few necessities and luxuries could be traded for: axes, tinware and bar iron which was forged locally into shoes for oxen and horses; luxuries such as tea, or a piece of fine cloth for a christening or wedding dress or a shroud; paper, books (often a bible); such were the few amenities to which the pioneer family might aspire, and for which they traded their potash, grain and maple sugar.[26]

Through these innovations and techniques a family could survive and, in time, expect to live reasonably well on a pioneer farm, but to do so required unremitting toil for adults and children alike. Moreover, the development of so many different skills within a family or small community meant that none could be carried above minimal levels of utility. Technology was crude and farming practices bad, not merely from ignorance, as John Howison asserted, but from the practical necessity of doing most things for oneself without either capital or sufficient division of labour to allow specialization and higher levels of craftsmanship. Once established and found successful, pioneer techniques changed very slowly.

The isolation of the settlements, the small population and the general scarcity of money and materials meant that a large amount of cooperation was necessary for survival. Thus, for large projects the trading of labour through the form of "bees" became a general practice which was continued by the British newcomers in later years. The bee, of course, became much more than merely an example of economic cooperation. Since opportunities for visiting and socializing were limited both by distance and scarcity of free time, the bee offered an opportunity to visit with old friends, meet the new neighbours, and exchange the latest news and gossip.

William Thompson, a British traveller described a bee which he attended in 1840:

> A new settler has not much difficulty in getting the neighbours to turn out and assist him to build a house; but idle drunken fellows are always most forward on such occasions; and many of them will go to these routes rather than work at home. . . . I was on the ground early, and found the settler and his wife busy cooking at a large fire, surrounded by fallen trees and brushwood. The neighbours came by twos and threes, from different quarters, with axes over their shoulders; as they came up each got a drink of whiskey out of a tin can. . . . Some had straw hats, some Scotch bonnets, some had wincy coats, some had none; all had strong boots, and most of them had torn "inexpressibles". . . .
>
> Four blocks of wood, about a foot and a half above the ground, marked out the corners of the dwelling that was to be erected before night. On these blocks were laid the first tier of logs, dove-tailed in a very rough way. Four of the most experienced hands took their station, one at each corner, whose duty it was to make the joints and carry up the angles perpendicular.
>
> At first they set to work moderately and with quietness, but after the whiskey had been handed about several times they got very uproarous—swearing, shouting, tumbling down, and sometimes like to fight. . . .
>
> In all there were about twenty-four men . . . , on the whole about the roughest specemine of humanity I have ever seen. . . . The walls of a house, 15 by 26, and 12 feet high, were up before night; and some of the nearest neighbours were to return the next day and cut out the doors and windows. When all was done they sat down, all about eating bread and drinking whiskey.[27]

As the array of pioneer techniques developed, and social behaviour was modified by the necessities and limitations of the primitive economy, the gulf broadened between the local inhabitants and the wealthier government elite in York and the well-to-do businessmen and farmers who were not forced to share the hardships of pioneer life. All of these latter groups saw the settlers as being quite different from themselves, and spoke of the rough clothing, and crude, practical ideas and manners of the pioneers with ill-concealed contempt. Thomas Hamilton, for example, stated:

> Of the lower orders in the Upper Province it is impossible to speak favourably. They have all the disagreeable qualities of the Americans, with none of the energy and spirit of enterprise which often convert a bad man into a useful citizen. They are sluggish, obstinate, ignorant, offensive in manner, and depraved in morals, without loyalty and without religion.[28]

Upper class immigrants in the eighteen-twenties and thirties were shocked that lower class settlers assumed an air of familiarity toward the high-born and wealthy. As Mary Gapper O'Brien of Yonge Street noted with astonishment:

> We were amused by the parties at the Inn [in York], some with the appearance of gentlemen, others that of greasy farmers strangely mingled together, as it seems by politics, which they were discussing freely before us but in terms too enigmatical for us to understand:—it seemed that they were all somehow connected with the *house* [Legislative Assembly], either as members or informants, I could not make out which, probably both. . . . Mr. Thorne [a well-to-do British merchant and miller of Yonge Street] says he never has seen so ill-qualified an assembly before.[29]

Of course, not all British immigrants were either so superior in attitude or wealthy enough to live as gentlemen merchants or farmers. Most were as poor as the first settlers had been and shared the same hardships and struggles, with the result that most quickly adopted both the way of life and outlook of the original settlers.

For the first sixty years of settlement in the Ontario County area, local government was carried on, not by the township, town, county and city as we know them today, but by an older form of administration, the district, which was administered by Justices of the Peace meeting in the Quarter Session. In 1788 when Sir Guy Carleton, under pressure from the Loyalists, found it necessary to establish British forms of freehold land tenure, rather than the seigneurial system which existed in Quebec, he divided the area making up present-day southern Ontario into four districts. These he called (from east to west), Luneburg (later Lunenburg), Mecklenburg, Nassau and Hesse, which were soon renamed Eastern, Midland, Home and Western. The eastern boundary of

Ontario County was the eastern boundary of Home District. In 1789 these four districts were subdivided into eight, and further subdivisions continued to be made so that by 1842 there were twenty districts in all.[30] Through all the changes in boundaries, however, Ontario County remained part of Home District and for local purposes was administered from York.

Throughout this period the administration of local affairs and justice lay in the hands of the Justices of the Peace who met in Quarter Session – so called because their meetings were held regularly four times a year. The office of the Justice of the Peace had been established by Edward III and as the Justices' powers were increased over the years, they became the key to local administration both in England and in many of the colonies. Singly the Justices could try minor infractions of the laws and settle local disputes. When two or more Justices met at the Quarter Sessions, however, they wielded very extensive administrative and magisterial powers, and were responsible for all municipal legislation as well. Since no salary was attached to the office, the system was inexpensive to operate. Furthermore it had the advantage of being easy to establish since it required little more than the swearing in of two or more Justices resident in an area to bring British law and administration to it.

There was, however, a serious drawback to the system which soon became evident in Upper Canada. Because the Justices (or magistrates, as they were commonly termed) were appointed by the Governor for life, the local inhabitants had no direct control over either local legislation or administration. Moreover the system carried the danger that when such wide powers were placed in the hands of a few men who did not have to face an electorate at regular intervals, the powers could be used irresponsibly to reward friends and to punish enemies.

The appointments of Justices of the Peace were made by the Lieutenant-Governor on the advice of his Legislative Council. Because the British and Upper Canadian Governments feared the "republican" and "democratic" elements among the original settlers, the tendency developed that those appointed as Justices were from the Tory elite, such as retiring army officers, wealthy landowners, and the Governor's favourites from among the provincial office-holders. Unfortunately few of these sympathized with or even understood the kind of problems which faced the pioneers. In particular the granting of money to make repairs or to build new roads and bridges brought charges of partiality and arrogance.[31]

In addition to their powers over roads and bridges, the magistrates controlled such diverse affairs as: erecting and managing court houses, jails and asylums; assessing and taxing property for the costs of highways, paying the wages of the members of the Assembly; appointing district and township constables, street and highway surveyors, and inspectors of weights and measures; fixing the fees of jailers, town clerks and pound-keepers; and licensing both those who sold liquor and the "dissenting" clergymen to perform marriages.[32] It is little wonder that the capacity to exercise so many powers in an arbitrary manner soon caused antagonism between the justices and many of the settlers.

Though counties existed in the early period, they had no administrative or legislative function. Simcoe had intended to base both local government and administration on the English county system, but when he introduced the necessary legislation in 1792 he found that entrenched interests so strongly opposed the idea that he was forced to leave the district government system intact. As a result the only function of the county was that it was the basis of parliamentary representation and the local militia commanded by the County Lieutenant.[33] The county as it exists today would not come into being until 1849.

The township originally was intended to be a geographic unit existing only for the convenience of the surveyors and the land-granting department. It was not the intention of the government that either law-making powers or an administrative function should be attached to it. Indeed, according to Governor Haldimand's original instructions in 1783, they were to be numbered, not named.[34] It was not long, however, before it became clear that some administration at the local level was necessary to the proper functioning of government. Under the circumstances the township appeared to offer the only convenient basis. The attempt to establish township government, however, set off a debate which revealed the fundamental political cleavage which existed in the province.

In 1792 two local government bills were presented to the newly-created Legislative Assembly. Their titles made clear the contending principles involved. The first, presented by the "democratic" elements, was entitled "An Act to Authorize Town Meetings for the Purpose of Appointing Divers Parish Officers" and proposed that township officials such as pound-keepers, fence viewers, assessors and collectors would be elected annually by the property owners.[35] The second bill, entitled "An Act to Authorize Justices of the Peace to Appoint Annually Divers Public Officials",[36] was introduced by the Tories who wanted to keep all power and all appointments within the hands of the "loyal" elite; this faction not only distrusted the loyalty of the settlers, but also believed that the mere introduction of "republican" institutions such as local elections was the first step toward revolution.

Since neither bill was passed, in 1793 Simcoe proposed a compromise: local officials would be elected, but they would be entirely under the control of the Justices of the Peace.[37] Nowhere in the new act was there any suggestion that the townspeople were to be allowed any independent powers to regulate their own affairs: they were merely to appoint officers to carry out the orders of the Quarter Sessions. By the act, any two of his Majesty's Justices of the Peace were enabled to authorize by their warrants the constable of any "parish, township, reputed township or place" to assemble the inhabitants on the first Monday in March (later changed to the first Monday in January) of each year to choose for the following year: a parish, town or township clerk, two assessors, a collector, a number of overseers of highways, a pound-keeper, and two town wardens who were in charge of the property of the township. In addition to these appointments only two very minor pieces of legislation were allowed the town meetings: the height of a lawful fence, and the determination of what animals should be allowed to run at large, and for what periods.[38]

According to contemporary witnesses, the annual township meeting and election of officers was a lively affair. Until 1841 township meetings were held outdoors by custom, and elections were by "acclamation"; that is, the supporters of a particular candidate were expected to shout at the top of their voices when their man's name was put forward by the township clerk. The candidate whose supporters seemed most numerous from the volume of noise was declared elected by the chairman of the meeting. Thus supporters with unusually loud voices were a real asset to a candidate, as were muscular gentlemen who roamed through the crowd casting baleful glances at non-supporters. The general melee of dogs barking, boys skylarking, and men shouting amid the mounting tension as candidates names were announced made elections an exciting break in the montonous round of daily life.

The first recorded town meeting in Ontario County was held on June 4, 1801 at Samuel Munger's farm in Pickering Township. At this meeting of the combined ratepayers of Pickering and Whitby, the following officers were elected: Ebenezer Ransom, town clerk; John Majors, Pickering, and Elizar Lockwood, Whitby, assessors; Anthony Rummerfeld and Adam Stephens, town wardens; David Stephens, collector; Samuel Munger, Mathew De Williger (Terwilliger) and John McGahn, pathmasters; William Peak, David Lloyd, David Crawford and Abraham Townsend, fence viewers; and Silas Marvin, pound-keeper. In conformance with the act which allowed the meeting to decide upon fences and animals-at-large, the meeting voted upon and passed the following resolutions:

> That no hogg shall be free comener [commoner] except that they will wey more than forty weight,

and

> That no fence shall be lawful except it measure 4½ ft. high and 2 feet at the bottom, the rails not to be more than 4 inches apart.[39]

In addition to those officers chosen at town meetings, the Quarter Session appointed town constables who were charged with keeping the peace and apprehending law-breakers. For the first five years after the townships were organized the constables were:

1801: Whitby, Elizar Lockwood and David Stephens
Pickering, Peter Tuttle
1802: Whitby, Levy Annis (replaced by Thos. McGahee because Annis could not read or write)
Pickering, Samuel Munger

1803: Whitby, David Lloyd
Pickering, Jacob Crawford
1804: Whitby, Joseph Wiley
Pickering, Daniel Spicer
1805: Whitby, John Magahan
Pickering, David Thatcher.[40]

In spite of the formidable array of local officials, there was in reality little actual government involved. For one thing, taxes were low (seldom above the statutory minimum of one penny per pound of assessment) which meant that there was little money for district projects. In 1802 the total taxes for Pickering and Whitby amounted to 5 pounds, 19 shillings "Halifax Currency",[41] and in 1805 to 7 pounds, 13¼ pence.[42] Even in 1820 taxes amounted to only £28.14s.9½d. in Pickering and £29.16s.10d. in Whitby. For the whole of Home District the taxes were £712.15s.11¾d.[43]

For all the careful restriction of local initiative by Lieutenant-Governor Simcoe and his successors, one important aspect of local affairs, the education of their children, was for a time left almost entirely in the hands of the inhabitants. Although an act[44] passed in 1807 had provided salaries of 100 pounds per year for the schoolmaster of each of the eight district grammar schools (that for Home district was, of course, established in York), nothing was done to aid the local "common" schools until 1816. Unfortunately, the high tuition of the grammar schools and the great distances involved for children from the remote areas such as Ontario County meant that the York grammar school was patronized almost exclusively by the children of the wealthy and socially prominent in the capital.

The first schools established in Ontario County were conducted by individuals on a profit basis without government subsidization of any kind. Parents desiring to give their children the rudiments of reading, writing and "cyphering" were expected to pay a stipend to the teacher for each child taught, take turns boarding him, and to supply such necessities as fuel, furniture and rude equipment to the school. In these circumstances, teaching was never a very lucrative profession, but one which was often the refuge of those who had failed at all else. The first school recorded in Ontario County was one conducted in Whitby in 1811 by a Miss Cross.

The introduction of the Common School Act of 1816[45] was a landmark for several reasons. Not only was it the first concerted effort to improve the quality of education for those unable to afford the Grammar Schools,[46] but it was also the first measure to grant some larger degree of control to a local government. The Act provided that when a "competent number of the inhabitants" of any "Town, Township, Village or Place" had built or provided a schoolhouse, had engaged to provide twenty or more pupils, and had provided in part for a salary for a teacher, they could then call a meeting to select three trustees who were empowered to appoint a British subject as a teacher. The Government maintained a general control of these local school boards through an appointed district board of education (for Home District they were all residents of York[47]) which was empowered to specify what books might or might not be used, to rescind or alter local rules and to remove the teacher if he should prove unsatisfactory for any reason. After 1824 this board acquired the power to examine and licence teachers as well. In addition, the Act of 1816 set aside 6,000 pounds annually for common school support and for the payment of a portion of teachers' salaries.

While this Act certainly appears to have greatly encouraged the building of schools, it by no means solved all the difficulties facing those who hoped to secure even a modest education for their children. For example, while the Common School Act of 1816 appears to have been at least partially responsible for the decision to build the first school in Uxbridge, the poor quality of both school and schoolmaster was remembered by Joseph Gould:

> Until I was about ten years old, there was no school in the township; nor was there any nigher than the Quaker schoolhouse on Yonge Street, almost twenty miles west of our place. In 1817 or '18, a log schoolhouse was built on the north-west corner of lot 31, in the 6th concession. A little Irishman was employed to teach the school. But the teacher was like the house, a poor one. I had been taught the alphabet by my mother, before I went to school, and was able to spell and read a little. . . . The people were all poor, and poor as was the school, they could only keep it open for three or four months during the winter season. I got a smattering of the three R's there, and such was the extent of my schooling.[48]

Without proper schools and teachers, the literacy of the inhabitants declined steadily until 1820. Whereas the early minutes of township meetings are generally neatly written with a fair attention given to correct spelling, in later years there was a sharp deterioration in both writing and spelling. For example, the Pickering minutes for 1815 note that "our townd meting war omited in the year A.D., 1814 and our Town officors war Put in the same manner."[49] In addition, land records show that sons of literate fathers often signed their names with a cross.[50]

While in the early years most events by-passed the settlers of Ontario County, the War of 1812 did make its presence felt. Many of the first settlers were Quakers who found themselves in a doubly difficult position: not only were most of them recent arrivals from the United States with both family and friends still in the land of their birth, but also being pacifists, they were charged with disloyalty by their neighbours for their refusal to fight. As we have seen, there was a drop in population in both Pickering and Whitby, but in Uxbridge the problem was particularly acute. Many of the original settlers were from Pennsylvania and most had not been in Upper Canada long enough to become naturalized. As a result many returned to the United States and settled near Buffalo. The township did not recover from this loss for almost twenty years.[51] Other Quakers volunteered for service in the transportation or medical corps.[52]

Although Danforth Road was a main military communication between York and Kingston, and several early settlers such as the Farewell brothers, Jabez Lynde and Hawkins Woodruff served as dispatch riders, only one minor skirmish was fought in the area. During 1812 a flotilla of boats carrying stores was attacked by an American gunboat opposite the Hall farm in Whitby. The boats were drawn up on shore to prepare for an attack, and the soldiers guarding them were joined by the settlers. During the night the gunboat bombarded the defenders, and several attempts were made by American Marines to land and seize the supplies. In spite of heavy fire, the British soldiers and the settlers managed to hold off the attackers, who sailed away in the morning. The boats and supplies reached York safely.[53]

The society which was being shaped in Ontario County during the first three decades of white settlement had begun to take on definite outlines by 1820. It was a society based upon and limited by the total, unremitting labour of the whole family. While such toil exacted severe penalties in cultural areas such as education and craftsmanship, it was capable of producing, in time, a good deal of wealth when conditions eased. Moreover, while isolation created a harsh economic situation, it encouraged both self-reliance and a sense of identity and social cohesion in the settlers which persisted for generations.

With the development of toiler farming methods, Simcoe's visions of an aristocratic society based on vast estates owned by a landed gentry became an impossibility. As long as an immigrant could get land of his own, he saw little reason to toil for others. It was not long before the elite who had received huge grants in Pickering and Whitby were forced to acknowledge that, because of scarcity of labour, they might as well sell off their grants. Thus the Buchanans, McGills, Holmes and the French emigré noblemen who had been intended as Ontario County's gentry failed in their own and Simcoe's purpose.

The failure of Simcoe's plans did not, however, remove the basic social division between the aristocratic-minded government elite and the York officialdom who had been placed in control of local government and the new class of independent land-holding farmers. Rather the isolation of pioneer life and the grinding toil which it required delayed the inevitable conflict for another generation. The eighteen-twenties and thirties would see these divisions and conflicts come to a head.

IMMIGRATION AND SETTLEMENT, 1820-40

During the eighteen-twenties government land-granting policies underwent rapid changes as the British and Upper Canadian Governments attempted to solve many of the accumulated problems of the province through changes in the land laws. In 1824 the Government put the first real teeth into land taxation laws. Henceforth if an owner of wild land defaulted on his taxes for eight years his lands could be seized and sold for back taxes. Although this freeing of lands for sale did not bring about an immediate upsurge in settlement, it did spur the sale of patented wild land in areas close to York, such as Pickering Township.[1] After 1824, settlement and land patenting in new areas show a much closer inter-relationship than they did previously. No doubt the fear of seizure of their lands made the "official" patentees more cautious.

A second policy – the termination of free grants in 1827 – had even more far-reaching consequences. Henceforth working-class immigrants would find it much more difficult to acquire land and thus rise to the status of landowner. In the British Colonial Office's consideration of Upper Canadian problems, three major difficulties stood out. First: because the Governor was dependent upon the Legislature for funds in the growing struggle between the Lower and Upper Houses, the Lower House was bound, in the long run, to win unless a source of funds other than taxes could be found.[2] Second: there was a severe shortage of capital in the colony. This shortage, it was argued, was caused by the scarcity of labour and the high cost of wages. This argument contended further that, so long as men could get free land, they would prefer to farm rather than work for wages. As William Allan, banker, member of the Family Compact, and Legislative Councillor put the case in 1845:

> The greatest drawback to the employment of Capital in this country . . . consists in the *high price of wages*, and the *extreme difficulty of procuring the labor* requisite for its profitable employment in *any* pursuit; and more especially in the *agricultural* ones. Everything therefore, that tends to lessen the *quantity of labor in the Market*, will tend also to *exclude capital from it*. But the main cause of the scarcity of hired labor in a new Country is the *Cheapness of Land*, and it seems to follow, as an irresistable conclusion, that the *Free gift of Lands*, must increase that scarcity an hundredfold.[3]

The logical conclusion to be drawn from Allan's position was that if land were made expensive, poor immigrants would be forced to remain workers; there would be a surplus of labourers; wages would drop; consequently, those with capital could make profits by hiring cheap labour. Thus if the Government could force the wages of working people down, then entrepreneurs with money to invest would flock to Upper Canada.

From the viewpoint of those who supported Simcoe's dream of creating an aristocratic society of land-owning gentry, the new egalitarian society of small, self-sufficient landowners which was emerging in Upper Canada, presented the third problem. "How", these aristocrats wondered, "could there be an educated, wealthy elite if no one was forced to be a servant?" In particular, Lord Goderich, the Colonial Secretary, strongly opposed any continuance of free land grants to the poor immigrants. The basis for Goderich's objections was made clear in a letter to Lord Aylmer, the Governor of the Canadas, in 1831:

> It has been said that by a strict adherance to [a land sales] system, by refusing Land to the poor man whose labour is his only wealth, a most useful class of Settlers will be discouraged. I see no ground for such an apprehension; whatever promotes the prosperity of the Colony will naturally attract Settlers, both of the labouring and of all other classes. . . . Has it, on the other hand, been sufficiently considered by those who made this objection, whether it would conduce to the real prosperity of the Province to encourage every man who can labour to do so only on his own account, to obtain and cultivate his allotment of land without giving or receiving assistance from others? Without some division of labour, without a class of persons willing to work for wages, how can society be prevented from falling into a state of almost primitive rudeness, and how are the comforts and refinements of civilized life to be procured.[4]

Goderich's objects in pursuing a policy of high-priced land and the prevention

MAPS IX-XII *Population Density and Percent Patented of Lands Available in Ontario County, 1825-50*

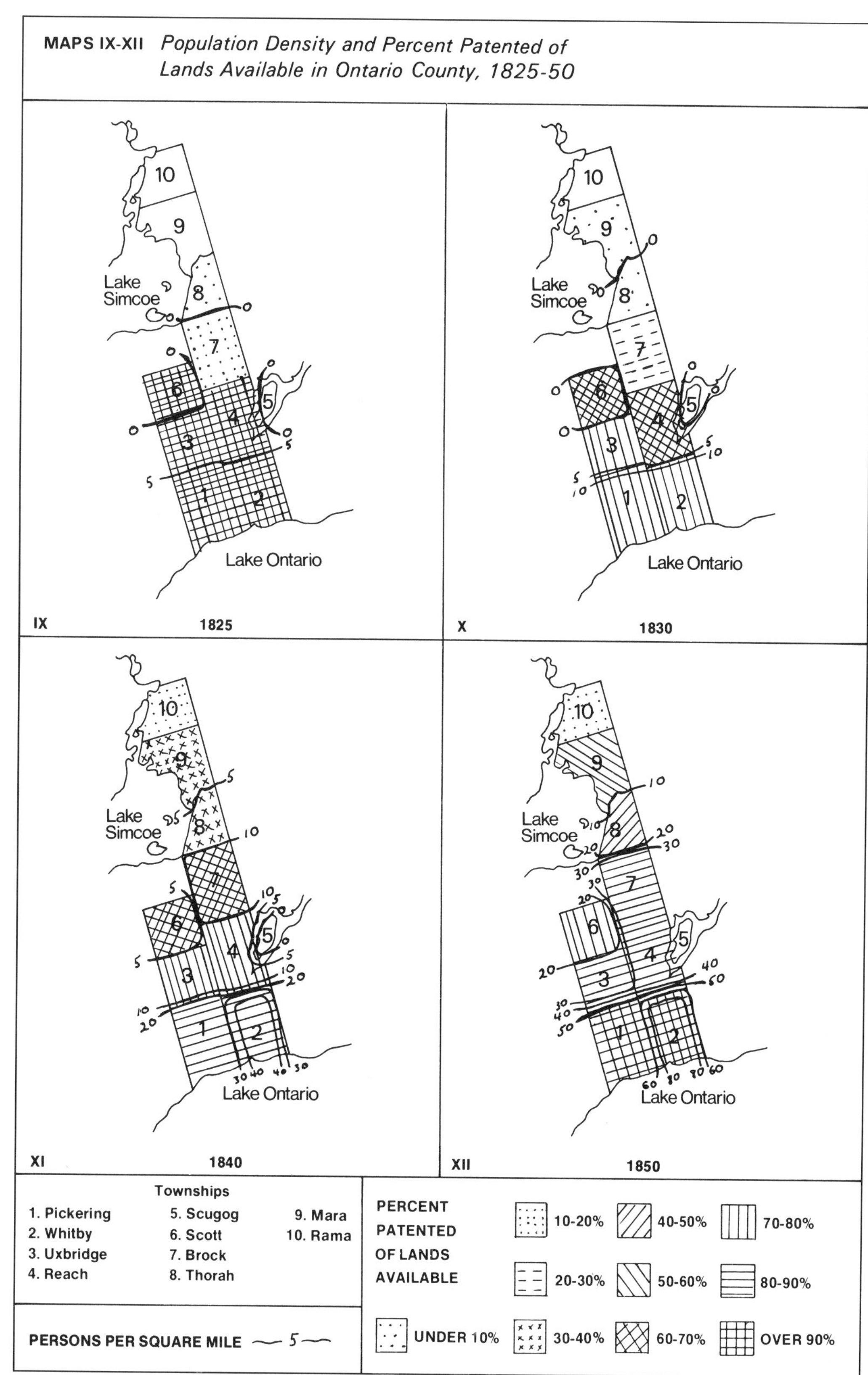

of its acquisition by the working class was made even more clear in an official dispatch sent in 1833:

> I know not how to propound in plainer terms that I have already done . . . , the necessity that there should be in every society a class of Laborers as well as a class of Capitalists or Landowners. The high rate of wages and the scarcity of labour, is the complaint of every growing Society. To force that condition artificially, by tempting into the class of Landowners those who would naturally remain laborers, appears to me a course opposed to the dearest interests of the Colony . . . because, as I have stated, to the good of every Society a supply of labour and a division of employment must be indispensable.[5]

The sale of Crown land rather than the free land policy of previous years seemed to offer a solution to all of these major problems at the stroke of a pen. The income from land sales was not subject to control by the Legislative Assembly; this freed the Governor from Parliamentary control. It also kept the poor immigrant off the land and in the working class and attracted capital to the colony and preserved a hierarchical class society. Thus, it was the poor immigrant who had hoped that through hard work he might some day join the ranks of the land-owning who paid the price for these changes.

The possibility of selling all Crown lands rather than granting them was attractive to others outside the Government as well. With immigration to Upper Canada increasing from the post-war low, John Galt, a well-known Scottish novelist, conceived a brilliant idea to make himself and his backers rich men in the land-settlement business. After a number of false starts,[6] an agreement was struck between Galt's Canada Company and the Imperial Government by which the Company agreed to purchase 1,000,000 acres of land in the Huron tract as well as some 1,384,013 acres of Crown Reserves which had been laid out in those townships surveyed before 1824.[7] The latter term affected all townships in Ontario County other than Rama. In all, more than 60,000 acres of Crown Reserves in the county were made available to the Canada Company.[8] The sale price of 3s. 6d. per acre was a bargain indeed when land in the area commonly sold for 10s. to 15s. per acre.[9] Those Crown Reserves which had been leased previously to farmers were used to endow King's College. These lands totalled, in all, some 8,941 acres made up primarily of 4,524 acres in Pickering, 3,050 acres in Whitby and 800 acres in Uxbridge. There were, as well, minor acreages in Reach, Brock and Thorah.[10]

The impact of all the new rules was felt strongest in the three "new" townships, Brock, Thorah and Mara. In previous times when a new area was opened, there was an immediate land-rush, as those having Loyalist or military rights vied to acquire the most desirable locations. In spite of the fact that some 312,800 acres worth of warrants and fiats (that is, rights to acquire "official" lands) had been issued to U.E.L., Militia and Military claimants, no post-war land-rush developed. During the period 1820-28 patented lands totalled only 9,200 acres in Brock, 1,184 acres in Thorah and 1,600 acres in Mara. In addition, in the "old" townships of Pickering, Whitby, Uxbridge, Reach and Scott, a total of only 1,500 acres was patented – all in Pickering and Whitby.[11]

While the decision to sell the Crown Reserves opened up one-seventh of all lands in the county for sale, there was in fact little immediate impact. Primarily this was because the Canada Company possessed a monopoly on the Crown Reserves and demanded such a high price that, in most cases, the potential settler preferred to purchase vacant lands from among those held by absentee owners. Had it not been for the decision of the Government to allow the Clergy Corporation to sell one-fourth of the Clergy Reserves, there would have been no land available for patenting by actual settlers.

Because the Canada Company's main purpose was to make a profit, it concerned itself mainly in exploiting its monopoly of Crown Reserves in the well-established areas of Ontario County. Its practice was to patent and pay for only those lots for which it had immediate sale. As Table IV shows, almost two-thirds of Canada Company patents were taken out in the "old" townships. On the other hand, the ordinary settler was forced either to buy already patented land or to move to the "new" townships. Thus, between 1820 and 1840 only 10,201 acres were patented by private individuals in the five old townships, while 71,296 acres were patented by private individuals in the four new townships.

Table IV
Land Patented in Ontario County, 1821–40[12]

	1821–1825		*1826–1830*		*1831–1835*		*1836–1840*	
	Private	*Canada Co.*	*Private*	*Canada Co.*	*Private*	*Canada Co.*	*Private*	*Canada Co.*
The "Old" Townships*	900	—	1,600	2,454	3,750	13,067	3,951	2,742
The "New" Townships†	6,950	—	14,106	1,236	23,070	8,892	27,170	953

* These townships include Whitby, Pickering, Reach, Uxbridge and Scott.
† These townships include Brock, Thorah, Mara and Rama.

Not all of the patents taken out by private individuals in the new townships were those of settlers. In 1835 under extreme pressure by those holding Loyalist land rights, the Government completely removed the strict regulations regarding settlement duties and fees upon Loyalist lands.[13] This resulted in the kind of land rush which had not been seen since before the War of 1812. Thus in the years 1835-36, 11,400 acres were patented in Mara, largely by absentee owners. Because of the high degree of absenteeism this land-rush created, Mara would suffer the same problems of scattered land-locked settlement and retarded growth which had plagued Uxbridge township in previous years.

Government land policy, particularly its favouritism, exclusion of poor from the land, and the whole Canada Company affair, created a deep-seated bitterness among those whom it injured. There can be little doubt that some of the policy changes in the 1820s had beneficial effects, for example, as Maps IX to XII show, after 1820 there was a much closer relationship between land patenting and population growth than there had been before that date. However, most of the changes made were in fact for the benefit of the few at the expense of the many.

In 1824, after a journey through Peel County, William Lyon Mackenzie strongly attacked the high fees which the settler was required to pay in order to acquire his land. The effect of these imposts was that the working-class settler was at a distinct disadvantage. As Mackenzie said:

> Not one-tenth of the settlers have got deeds. It is really bad policy to deprive those industrious settlers, who have left their homes in Britain, to seek an asylum in the woods of North America, of their birthright, because they cannot pay £5, £10, or £20 of fees; yet such is the case. Not one of these people who have done settlement duty, and built houses on their farms, can obtain deeds.[14]

Moreover, the monopoly of lands given the Canada Company formed the basis for one of Mackenzie's strongest attacks on the Government. It was to the working-class immigrant deprived of the possibility of owning land to whom Mackenzie appealed in this broadside issued in November, 1837:

> CANADIANS! It is the design of the Friends of Liberty to give several hundred acres to every Volunteer—to root up the unlawful Canada Company, and Give *free deeds* to all settlers who live on their lands . . . so that the yeomanry may feel independant, and be able to improve the country, instead of sending the fruit of their labour to foreign lands.[15]

In spite of the constant agitation and political controversy surrounding the disposal of the Clergy Reserves, it actually had little real effect on settlement in Ontario County. These reserves, no doubt, created considerable hardship because they broke up settlements, and road duties were not performed where they were vacant, but the same was true of Crown Reserves against which there was much less agitation.

The Clergy Reserves had originally been created to provide an income to support the "Protestant" clergy of Upper Canada.[16] For the first three decades they were directly in the control of the Executive Council, but in 1819 the Clergy Corporation was established for the specific purpose of managing the clergy lands. Because the Clergy Corporation had been established at the request of Bishop Mountain of Quebec and was controlled entirely by the hierarchy of the Anglican clergy, other "Protestants" immediately set up a demand for a share in the control and management of the corporation and of the funds which resulted from the leasing of the lands. This quarrel would, until the 1850s, remain one of the most bitter disputes in Upper Canadian society.[17]

The intention of renting Clergy Reserve lands was frustrated by the abundance of free lands available for the mere payment of fees in the early period. Thus only in especially desirable townships, such as York, Vaughan or Markham, were leases taken up before 1830. In Ontario County only two leases were given in Pickering and five in Whitby before the end of 1828. In 1829 three additional leases were granted – one each in Pickering, Whitby and Thorah. The first Clergy Reserve lot leased in Pickering was lot 6, concession II, received by Moses Winter, November 10, 1820. In Whitby the first lot leased was lot 31, concession I, leased by Jabez Lynde in 1818 and renewed by him on February 24, 1825.[18]

After 1829 the rate of leasing stepped up rapidly, as the scarcity of vacant lands and the high cost of purchase from either the Government or the Canada Company began to force the price of land upwards. Within four years (1830-34) an additional 4,800 acres in Pickering and 5,800 acres in Whitby had been leased. Moreover, even the less desirable northern townships shared in the upsurge. For example, 3,200 acres in Reach, 2,500 acres in Brock, 1,200 acres in Thorah, 1,000 acres each in Uxbridge and Mara, and 400 acres in Scott were leased. Only in Rama were no leases taken. In all, in just four years the Clergy Corporation was able to lease 20,900 acres in Ontario County.[19]

Over the years, from 1826 on, the Clergy Corporation was authorized to sell large sections of its lands, which it proceeded to do as soon as the leases were terminated. In most cases, this was accomplished by the lessee either saving or borrowing the money and acquiring outright title to lands he had previously leased. By 1854 when the clergy lands were finally secularized, most of the leased farms in Ontario County had been acquired by the original lessees. Thus although the reserves posed a barrier to compact settlement and good roads before 1830, after that date their leasing and sale removed them as local problems. The political problem concerning the division of the moneys gotten for them, however, persisted for another generation.

The period 1820-40 was a time of enormous growth and expansion of settlement in Ontario County. Whereas in 1820 most settlement was concentrated in Pickering and Whitby, with no more than 200 settlers in Uxbridge and a dozen in Brock and Reach, by 1840 the population had increased by 1,000 per cent and covered the entire area with the exception of Scugog Island and the back areas of Rama. Table V shows how rapidly settlement spread. In general, the population showed its greatest proportional growth in the periods 1820-25 and 1830-35 when in each case the population doubled.

The immigrants who arrived after 1820 were almost all from the British Isles, but they were far from being an homogenous group. Distinctive in religion, racial origin and social organization, each group on arriving strove to create the society of its choice in its new home. For this reason newcomers tended to settle near their national and religious compatriots when possible. As a result distinct communities were formed, such as the Pickering Quakers, the Catholic Irish and Scots in Mara and Rama and the Anglican Irish in Brock.

Table V
Population Growth in Ontario County, 1820–40[20]

	1820	*1825*	*1830*	*1835*	*1840*
Whitby	508	1,136	1,659	3,808	5,013
Pickering	575	830	1,356	2,642	3,450
Reach	①	57④	93	444	771
Brock	①	282④	453	1,077	1,330
Uxbridge	②	228④	253	431	708⑥
Scott	—	—	—	55⑤	
Thorah	—	③	184	337	514
Mara	—	—	—	153⑤	214
Rama	—	—	—	—	14

① No Return.
② Combined with Whitchurch: Estimated population, 200.
③ Combined with Georgina: Estimated population, 50.
④ Totals are for 1826.
⑤ Totals are for 1836.
⑥ In 1839 the population for Uxbridge was 537, and Scott, 76.

There was, in addition, a geographical barrier which divided the county into "old" and "new" areas. Scott township was settled very late for two reasons: first, it had been among the earliest areas patented by absentees, and second, the soil was so light and sandy and the terrain so rolling and difficult for road-building that it formed a barrier to further settlement and to the transportation of people and goods into the back areas. To complete the barrier between north and south, the extensive swampy areas lying along the Nonquon and Beaver Rivers made road building extremely difficult, with the result that even in the 1840s there was still no good north-south road. Thus settlers who acquired the fertile lands of Thorah and Brock were forced to travel by way of Yonge Street and Lake Simcoe to reach them, and when they wanted to sell produce or to buy supplies they were forced to go to Holland Landing or Newmarket.

Because of the lack of north-south roads, the old and new areas of Ontario County followed very different paths of development between 1820 and 1840. While Pickering and Whitby were well settled by 1840 (see Map XI) with a more diversified economy beginning to appear, the northern areas in 1840 still possessed most of the characteristics of a pioneer settlement, and the inhabitants were still engaged in clearing the fields and undergoing the struggle for survival that pre-war settlers in the south had experienced. By contrast the southern areas of Reach, which were settled at the same time as Brock but which were easily accessible by roads from Whitby, developed in the Whitby-Pickering pattern.

In spite of the difficulties imposed by distance and bad roads, Brock township, which had been "opened" by the Anglo-Irish military settlers in the 1817-1820 period, grew rapidly after 1820 with such familiar names as Smith, Ruddy, O'Leary, Keenan, Doble, Shipman, King, Campbell, Amey, Carmichael, Brethour, Brabazon, Valentyne, Thompson, Bolster, Cowan, Hart, McPhaden, McLean, McDonald, Baird, Malone, Taylor and Acton joining the assessment rolls. The vigour and ambition of these settlers were so pronounced that Brock, despite its many drawbacks, grew much more rapidly in population and wealth than did other similar townships such as the Gwillimburys or townships in the southern part of Simcoe County which shared similar geographic characteristics.[21]

Like Brock, Thorah township was settled by ex-military men, but their history was quite different from that of their Anglo-Irish neighbours. Thorah had been surveyed in 1820 by John Edward White, who received some 1,978 acres as payment for his services. He settled on the shore of Lake Simcoe just north of Beaverton (N. 1/2 of lot 14, concession VI) in 1822.[22] In the same year

Colonel Kenneth Cameron Residence, Thorah Township *Public Archives of Ontario*

Ensign William Turner settled in the southwest corner (lots 21 and 22, concession I) of the township.

It was not until 1824, however, that large-scale settlement was actually begun. In that year Donald Cameron, a Scottish half-pay army officer from Lancaster, Glengarry County, brought a group of settlers from Glengarry to Thorah as part of a large settlement scheme. Cameron had for some years been bringing out settlers from Scotland on a private basis, but in 1823 he petitioned Lord Bathurst, the Colonial Secretary, for aid and for a tract of land upon which to settle them. In his letter he pointed out the desperate need of the Scottish poor for land of their own, the precarious financial condition of his own endeavours, and his own personal investment of £1,200 that had been used to transport and establish 140 families that he had brought out.[23] When he was refused aid by Lord Bathurst, a further petition to Lord John Wilmot-Horton, the Undersecretary of State for the Colonies brought better results.

In southern Ireland the clearing of estates, unemployment and famine had created serious political disturbances with the result that the British Government decided to solve their political difficulties by assisting the displaced Irish to emigrate to Canada. In 1823 the Government aided a total of 568 persons with free passage, land, rations and farming tools to settle in Ramsey and

Ensign Turner House, Thorah Township *Public Archives of Ontario*

adjacent areas in eastern Ontario.[24] Wilmot-Horton decided to offer Cameron's settlers the same terms that had been offered the Irish immigrants, and in 1824 Cameron decided upon Thorah and Eldon townships as his field of operation. In Thorah, each adult male between the ages of 18 and 45 would receive a location ticket for 70 acres, and a further 30 acres would be purchasable for £10 within ten years. Each lot would be subject to a quitrent of 2d. per acre per annum after six years which would be redeemable on the payment of twenty years' rent as a purchase price. No other aid would be given. Patents would be issued on completion of settlement duties and payment of fees.[25]

When Cameron approached the Upper Canada Executive Council he found them in an unexpectedly generous mood. Rather than the 70 acres proposed by Wilmot-Horton, the Council offered Cameron's followers 200 acres to heads of families who had five children or more, and 100 acres to heads of small families and single male settlers. Cameron himself was given 1,200 acres "on account of his great exertions . . . by way of remuneration".[26]

As a nucleus for his settlement, Cameron encouraged a number of ex-soldiers who had served with him in the Napoleonic Wars to leave their homes in Glengarry and move to Thorah. This group included Donald McRea, Alexander Stewart, Christopher McRea and John McRea. In addition, a second group of military claimants were brought out from Scotland. These included John McDonald, Alexander McKenzie, William Stewart, Donald McPherson, Kenneth Campbell, Donald Grant, Robert Bailey, John Cain, Ronald McPhail, Donald Chisholm, Allan Grant and a large number of their relatives.[27] In 1827 Donald Calder and a number of Scots who were natives of the Isle of Islay (these included families named McMillan and McFadgens) immigrated from North Carolina where they had settled for a time and joined the Cameron settlement.[28]

In spite of this auspicious beginning the plan to settle poor immigrants was a failure. Cameron was unable to recruit and settle them and was forced to ask for several extensions of time in order to prevent the termination of his project. In 1830, its patience exhausted, the Executive Council ordered an investigation of Cameron's affairs and appointed Arad Smalley to conduct it.

Smalley's report was a dismal one indeed. After four years of effort by Cameron, there were only 16 lots in Thorah and 13 in Eldon actually occupied by his settlers, while 110 lots in Thorah and 270 in Eldon which Cameron had reported occupied, were, in fact, vacant. Of the 41 settlers in Eldon previously reported by Cameron to have completed their settlement duties, 37 had done nothing. Similar conditions were noted in Thorah. The report concluded that Cameron was guilty of making false returns and perjury. Cameron immediately rejected these claims, arguing that Smalley was a "tool of the Robinsons" and demanded a new hearing. The events then degenerated into a political football with the Reformers taking Cameron's side and the Tories asserting the accuracy of Smalley's report. No clear resolution of the degree of Cameron's falsification was ever arrived at,[29] and Cameron lived to a dignified old age on his lakeside farm.[30] The settlers who had actually arrived were given one year to do their settlement duties, after which all vacant, unlocated or neglected lots were to be declared open to settlement by others. In spite of the failure of Cameron's plans, the strong Scottish and Irish-Catholic character of the half-pay officers and the poor settlers remained the main characteristic of the township.

Mara township was surveyed in 1821 by James G. Chewitt who received 2,484 acres for his efforts. The Mara settlement was an extension of that in Thorah, although the first settler, an Irishman by the name of Patrick Corrigan, was the only pioneer in 1823. Actual settlement began in 1827 when Patrick Kelly took up residence. He was followed by the Cameron, McDonagh, McDermott, Doyle, O'Boyle, Flinn, Haraby and Duffy families who, with later immigrants, gave the area an Irish- and Scottish-Catholic character.[31]

In contrast to Thorah and Mara, the first white settlement in Rama did not occur until 1835. The township was surveyed in 1834 by William Keating and in 1835 a number of British officers took up lands along the lake. The first to arrive was Captain John McPherson, and in 1836 he was followed by Captains Garnett, Coppinger, Yarnold, Rouke and Pass. The settlement was a failure economically, however, and the Bank of Upper Canada seized a number of the estates for debt.[32] These were later sold to the Indian department as a reservation for the Chippewa Indians who had been pursuaded to leave the Orillia townsite. As a result of these setback, by 1840 only 14 white settlers lived in Rama Township.

In contrast to the strong ethnic and religious concentrations of northern Ontario County, the southern area retained its homogenous population. Thus the enormous tide of immigration as well as natural growth which increased Whitby's population ten-fold (from 508 in 1820 to 5,013 in 1840) created a society in which no religious or ethnic group enjoyed a paramount position. While Pickering had grown less rapidly (from 575 in 1820 to 3,450 in 1840) a similar mixing of nationalities occurred, although the closeknit Quaker community, which had been augmented by a large contingent of Irish Quakers (the Richardson, Collins, Wright and Valentine families and the numerous American Quakers of the Brown family in 1825[33]), resisted the tendency towards absorbtion more strongly than did most groups. Of course, the passage of time, the death of many of the first settlers and the necessity of close co-operation which led to intermarriage, all contributed to a gradual blurring of group distinctions. Table VI, which gives the ethnic composition of Ontario County in 1842, shows the degree to which time and immigration had reduced the dominance of the original immigrant groups in southern area. Only in Whitby did the "Americans" retain a prominent position although even in that township they were outnumbered three to one by the native-born British Canadians. Unfortunately the increase in diversity of population did not bring with it an immediate reduction in inter-group hostility. In particular the whole "Alien Question" of the 1820s reveals the depth of the divisions.

Table VI
Origins of the Inhabitants of Ontario County, 1841–42[34]

	British Canadians	*French Canadians*	*English*	*Irish*	*Scottish*	*Americans*
Pickering	58.9%	0.2	12.5	12.2	6.8	7.9
Whitby	61.8	3.8	5.1	0.8	7.7	19.5
Uxbridge	59.0	4.1	16.1	2.9	8.6	5.9
Reach	59.7	0.6	15.7	7.4	8.0	8.2
Brock	57.0	1.4	1.7	21.7	15.7	1.9
Scott	59.0	4.1	16.1	2.9	8.6	5.9
Thorah	40.7	2.1	3.7	3.0	50.2	0.9
Mara & Rama	39.7	5.1	2.2	15.6	35.5	2.9

The few persons characterized as "other" in the census are omitted.

An examination of religious affiliations points out even more strongly the greater diversity of the older southern area. Whereas in the new northern sections most inhabitants tended to be members of the Church of Scotland and Roman Catholic Church, in the south a whole spectrum of religious pursuasions was represented, with none holding a commanding position. The most remarkable group in the south was the 73.1 per cent of the inhabitants

Table VII
Religious Affiliation in Ontario County, 1842[35]

	Church of England	*Church of Scotland*	*Presbyterians: not C. of S.*	*Church of Rome*	*Methodists: all varieties*	*Baptists and Anabaptists*	*Quakers*	*Other religions*	*No affiliation*
Pickering	17.4%	13.6	5.6	4.7	17.2	4.1	7.1	30.0	0.8
Whitby	4.5	3.6	1.7	3.6	8.2	0.9	0.7	3.7	73.1
Uxbridge	30.0	12.7	4.7	4.1	17.6	7.0	14.6	9.3	—
Reach	40.0	10.3	0.8	2.3	25.0	7.7	1.3	4.9	7.7
Brock	35.7	23.5	0.5	14.9	19.1	4.3	—	1.4	—
Scott	30.0	12.7	4.7	4.1	17.6	7.0	14.6	9.3	—
Thorah	9.4	78.6	—	10.3	2.0	—	—	—	—
Mara and Rama	4.2	50.6	—	43.7	1.5	—	—	—	—

of Whitby who declared that they had "no religion". Nor was this a mere passing aberration or fancy. In 1839 the annual census reported to the Provincial Secretary that some 1615 residents of Whitby had reported "no religion."[36] As time went on, however, most of these either died or became affiliated with one of the denominations. By 1861 only 233 "free thinkers" remained.[37]

The growth of agriculture in Ontario County between 1820 and 1840 showed both the similarity of growth and the diversity of pattern that marked the increase in settlement.

Table VIII points out the great contrast in degree of development between the old and new townships. Whereas in Pickering and Whitby between 20 and 25 per cent of all land was under cultivation in 1840, in the northern area only Brock showed signs of developing into a comparable agricultural area. These ratios, of course, are almost exactly parallel to the varying degrees of population growth in the areas. The growth in livestock (Table IX gives the figures for milk cows) follows a very similar pattern. Both Tables VIII and IX make it clear that Reach and Uxbridge were lagging far behind Brock, thus strengthening the geographical division between the north and south areas.

Table VIII
Acreage Cultivated by Township, 1820–40[38]

	1820	*1825*	*1830*	*1835*	*1840*
Pickering	1,575	2,527	4,469	10,171	15,501
Whitby	1,491	2,989	5,900	14,523	23,371
Uxbridge	①	1,031③	1,220	1,660	2,456
Reach	②	127③	188	1,006	2,618
Brock	②	630③	1,287	3,187	5,777
Scott	—	—	—	②	239
Thorah	—	②	231	813	1,814
Mara and Rama	—	—	②	②	573

① Uxbridge was combined with Whitchurch township until 1826.
② No figures given.
③ Figures are for 1826.

The rapid growth of cultivated acreage and the increase in livestock brought signs of a developing prosperity among the better-established farmers. With this came the desire to abandon the pioneer shanty for roomier and more fashionable houses. In order to encourage settlement, the pioneer log shanty was not taxed, but houses of better quality were. Thus log houses built of squared timber were assessed at £20 (with each additional fireplace above one assessed at £4) while frame, brick or stone houses of two stories were assessed at £60 (with additional fireplaces at £10). Other types of houses were assessed at commensurate rates. The great difference in the numbers of taxable houses in Whitby and Pickering in comparison to those of the northern areas in 1835, 1840 and 1842 is a particularly dramatic example of the difference in prosperity and development between the older and newer settlements. The rapid rise in numbers of taxable houses in Whitby after 1830 was the result of the beginnings of the two villages of Windsor (later Whitby) and Oshawa. In spite of these signs of prospertiy, however, it should not be forgotten that most inhabi-

Table IX
Milch Cows by Township, 1820–40[39]

	1820	*1825*	*1830*	*1835*	*1840*
Pickering	205	316	578	889	1,238
Whitby	194	372	572	1,163	1,853
Uxbridge	—	107①	111	149	210
Reach	—	91①	29	125	268
Brock	—	18①	157	312	463
Scott	—	—	—	—	33
Thorah	—	—	54	101	212
Mara and Rama	—	—	—	—	72

① Figures are for 1826.

tants were still living in the cramped log homes of the pioneer. Of the 2,466 houses in Ontario County in 1842, 1725 (almost 70 per cent) were still the original pioneer shanties.

In Ontario County, the disparity between wealth and poverty among the settlers was almost entirely related to the ability to acquire land and to the length of time it had been settled. In one sense, the economic theorists of the

Table X
Taxable Houses by Township, 1820–40 and
Total Houses and Taxable Houses, 1842[40]

	1820	*1825*	*1830*	*1835*	*1840*	*1842*	
	Taxable Houses					*Total Houses*	*Taxable Houses*
Pickering	12	24	33	92	134	622	168
Whitby	16	43	75	179	388	1,080	465
Uxbridge	—	4①	12	17	40	149②	47
Reach	—	0①	0	1	8	168	6
Brock	—	1①	5	9	15	281	20
Scott	—	—	—	—	0	②	1
Thorah	—	—	5	5	10	116	29
Mara and Rama	—	—	—	—	6	50	5

① Figures are for 1826.
② Uxbridge and Scott were united for census purposes in 1842.

time such as Robert Gourley, Edward Gibbon Wakefield, and William Allan were correct: the standard of living of the pioneer settler was related directly to the amount of capital he had accumulated.[41] Such capital could be accumulated directly by working for themselves in clearing fields, or indirectly by selling their produce in order to purchase capital goods such as livestock or tools and machinery. The difficulty facing the poor settler was that because he was poor, he could not easily acquire the capital goods necessary to increase productivity. Thus the settler who came to Upper Canada with considerable monetary capital could pay to have his land cleared quickly and purchase the tools, machinery and livestock to make it profitable, while the poor settler was required to struggle for decades to reach the same affluence.

One traveller who passed through Whitby Township in 1837 testified to the enormous importance of having a large capital when one began farming in the area. On visiting a Mr. Dow (probably Peter Dow concession II, lot 23[42]) this anonymous traveller said of Dow that

> I drove out to his house and found him to be one of the most intelligent men in the country. He settled here in 1833 and is making a fortune. He told me that he sold £300 pounds worth of wheat this winter and about £60 worth of pork. He has 300 acres of land which cost him about £1,300. He is raising a fine stock of cattle and a Teeswater Bull which belongs to an agricultural society which formed here . . . Land can not be got here now without paying a great sum for it and for 5 or 6 miles back it cannot be had under 3 pounds per acre, and on the front road throughout this Township there can be none got under £5 an acre.[43]

The effect of these problems is shown in Table XI. During the period when a small proportion of settlers had become sufficiently wealthy to afford better homes and a few luxury items such as carriages and pleasure wagons,[44] the average wealth of the area showed little increase, and in some areas, such as Uxbridge and Scott, actually declined.

Table XI
Per Capita Assessment by Township, 1820–40[45]

	1820		*1825*		*1830*		*1835*		*1840*	
	£	*s*	*£*	*s*	*£*	*s*	*£*	*s*	*£*	*s*
Pickering	11	7	11	14	11	0	12	5	12	16
Whitby	13	9	11	0	12	19	11	16	13	13
Uxbridge	—	—	14	7①	16	10	13	4	12	11
Reach	—	—	10	1①	11	2	9	0	10	5
Brock	—	—	12	15①	12	9	10	6	12	3
Scott	—	—	—	—	—	—	—	—	②	—
Thorah	—	—	—	—	17	8	10	19	12	0
Mara and Rama	—	—	—	—	—	—	—	—	10	19

① Figures are for 1826.
② United with Uxbridge in 1840.

In a society where the disparity between rich and poor was becoming wider all the time, the existence of a power structure based upon birth, favouritism and political and religious alliances could only deepen the cleavages. It offered no comfort to the landless or landed poor that a social organization which aided the upper class at the expense of the lower was deemed as necessary and right by the Governor, the Bishop and the leading merchants and landowners. In this situation reformers such as John Rolph, the Bidwells, the Baldwins and William Lyon Mackenzie found an eager audience among those who were hindered in their rise by the social system of the time.

The growth and development of Ontario County between 1820 and 1840 produced a situation of cleavages and divisions, wealth and poverty. However, it also produced a population large enough and compact enough to allow the area to begin to move away from primitive forms of production. Before 1820 in the southern area each family or locality had to be virtually self-sufficient. After 1820 with a growing population, greater specialization and higher levels of technology and craftsmanship became possible. Thus after 1820 an economic takeoff would occur that would greatly change the life of the area. Instead of a pioneer community, a full-fledged agricultural community would appear. The north, on the other hand, would be forced to wait another generation for that development.

THE DEVELOPING AGRARIAN SOCIETY, 1820-40

Although the increased population, growth in capital and greater productivity all contributed to Ontario County's development from a primitive pioneer community to a more mature agricultural economy, several additional aspects, particularly the development of an adequate transportation network, made possible and determined the geographical location of these economic changes. Because specialization in higher levels of technology and craftsmanship was dependent upon having relatively easy access to a large market area, the development of good roads was necessary before higher forms of commodity production and exchange were possible.

When Benjamin Wilson and his family came to the Oshawa area in the early 1790s there were no roads of any sort in Ontario County. Travellers through the area either followed the Indian paths or canoed along the lake shore and up the many small streams.[1]

In building roads three methods were used to finance construction: first, every settler was responsible for clearing one half of the road allowance in front of his property, as well as for a certain number of days of road work (on a sliding scale according to the assessed value of his property[2]) to be performed at the direction of the township road overseer; second, the Provincial Government and district Quarter Sessions used tax money for major projects; and third, privately-owned road companies were given monopolies on certain roads where they charged tolls both to cover the expenses of building and maintenance and to earn a profit. In Ontario County all three methods were used.

It was originally intended that the road duties of the settlers would be used to build all the main highways, but with settlement growing so slowly, the threat of war with the United States made it necessary for the Government to construct military roads between the main centres of population and military installations. For this reason, in 1799, it was decided that a contract should be let to a private contractor, Asa Danforth, for the clearing of a highway between York and Kingston. As the Provincial Administrator, Peter Russell, reported to Lord Portland, the British Home Secretary:

> After having for more than two years experienced the very great inconveniences resulting to the public Service from the Want of a free land Communication with the Seat of the Government & long lamented that I could not in Consequence comply with the Wishes of the People by assembling the Provincial Parliament in Winter and considering that the Thinness of the Population in these new Settlements precluded all Hopes of the Inhabitants being soon in a Condition of themselves to open sufficient Roads for that purpose; I judged it proper to submit to the Executive Council the propriety of immediately adopting some Measures for removing the difficulties we labored under.[3]

The contract given to Danforth called for a payment of $22.50 per acre or $90.00 per mile, with the stipulation that he would be paid one-half the price as each ten-mile section was cleared, and would receive the balance upon completion of the entire route to the Bay of Quinte. By July 26, 1799 work had been completed thirty miles east of York, and on December 23 the road was reported passable from York to the Trent River.[4]

The Danforth Road, however, would for a long time remain little better than a trail through the bush. In spite of enormous amounts of statute labour expended upon it, it was hardly more than a bog in spring and fall, passable only for foot traffic or a rider on horseback.

In order to get the statute labour applied to a particular road, it was necessary for the settlers to get up a petition, have it signed by their neighbours and then present it to the Quarter Session or the Justices or Commissioners for action. At each session it was the duty of the District Road Commissioners to decide which petition they would act on. Thus the minutes of the Home District Quarter Session for April 18, 1803 reported that:

> David Crawford, overseer of the Highway in the Township of Pickering, applied for leave to open a road from Dundas Street to the Settlements in the rear of the Concessions of that Township.[3]

While the minutes of Oct. 11, 1809 recorded that:

> The inhabitants of the Township of Whitby then presented a Petition concerning the alterations necessary to be made on Dundas Street in

> the said Township of Whitby. Ordered that a Warrant be issued to the Sheriff of the Home District to Summon Twelve Jurors to report upon the same.[6]

The administration of the local roads by the Justices of the Peace brought about the typical problems created by an absentee and authoritarian government in conflict with a local populace. In Ontario County the local inhabitants often protested against what they considered to be bad and wasteful management.

A constant complaint arose upon the issue of where the labour and road money were to be spent.[7] One such dispute in Pickering township in 1808 was taken all the way to the Executive Council. When the road commissioners ordered that the line of road be altered, the local inhabitants complained that one of the commissioners, Mr. Graham, was a total stranger to the area, and that much of the statute labour which had been applied to the road would be wasted. The Executive replied in its haughtiest tone that:

> His Excellency, having confided to gentlemen of the first respectability, does not feel inclined to interfere with the detail of it and trusts that the best possible effects will result to the public from the Zeal & Cooperation of the Commission.[8]

Needless to say, replies such as these did little to inspire the settlers with confidence in the concern of the Government for their special problems.

Because of the poor condition of the roads and the scant population, there was no stage service along the Danforth Road until 1817 when the Montreal-Kingston service (established in 1816) was extended to York.[9] During the winter of 1823, the Kingston-York service was carried on by J. Powers of Darlington, who advertised that the service would be continued as long as sleighing was good. He did not, however, state how often the stage would run.[10]

The first regular bi-weekly summer stages were operated by Jonathan Ogden in 1827. They left the head of the Bay of Quinte on Tuesdays and Fridays and returned on Thursdays and Mondays. The trip took about twenty-four hours and cost £1.10s. In 1829 this service was taken over by William Weller, and a competing line was operated by Norton and Company.[11] Thus by the mid-1820s Danforth Road had reached a degree of improvement that offered the possibility of year-round commercial traffic.

In the development of roads connecting the more northern areas of the county to Danforth Road, the seemingly limitless possibilities for trade and profit offered by the Scugog-Trent-Lake Simcoe waterways caused the Government to be unusually generous in its expenditures on roads into Reach township. To the Government and leading commercial men, the Scugog-Trent-Lake Simcoe route seemed destined to join Lakes Huron and Ontario and to draw the trade and prosperity of half a continent through the villages along its route. For example, in 1826 William Lyon Mackenzie speculated on the possibility of such a public work:

> There are various routes in the home district through which the navigation from Simcoe could be continued into Ontario, the most eligible of which seems to be a connection of the Black River, which enters Lake Simcoe in the township of Thora with a creek that flows into Ontario near Long Reach in Whitby—the expense of this latter cut would be trifling when compared with the immense advantage offered by a navigation through the very heart of the colony. The lands in Whitby, Reach, Brock, Thora and the surrounding townships are considered one of the best tracts in the province.[12]

In 1827 John Smith, the Deputy Provincial Surveyor, examined the Lake Scugog system and pointed out the importance of building a road into the area. The area north of Scugog, he said, had been surveyed and thrown open to settlement in 1825, but because of a lack of roads and mills, it was feared that few would be able to complete their settlement duties.[13]

As a result of proposals such as these, the Government authorized the opening of two major roads running north from the Danforth Road in 1828. The first, Simcoe Street, ran from Oshawa north through English Corners (now Columbus), O'Boyle's (now Raglan), Dayton's Corners (Prince Albert), Crandell's Corners (Borelia), and then north to the Nonquon River. The second road ran north from Windsor Habour (Whitby) through Winchester (Brooklin), Well's Corners (Myrtle) and Fitchett's Corners (Manchester) then turned eastward through Borelia to Lake Scugog.[14] These roads were later planked throughout their length and provided the first easy access into Reach Township and to Lake Scugog. A third road running in a direct line north from Whitby was built in 1831. Called Brock Road, it ran from Whitby through Butler's Corners (now Asburn), McKercher's Corners (Utica), Jockey Hill (Epsom) and ended near Reach township.[15] None of these roads, however, were continued into Brock for several years to come.

The more northern areas of Ontario County were not so fortunate. In this area the settlers were thrown largely on their own resources and no provincial help was given. In the back areas of Pickering township in 1831, roads were so primitive that wheeled traffic was generally impossible, and the trip to Oshawa with a sleigh and oxen in winter, or in summer a "jumper", required a two-day round trip.[16] Joseph Gould remembered that in 1828 it required a hard four-day's journey to make the return trip from Uxbridge to York.[17] In 1832 the Reverend Mr. Carruthers, a Presbyterian missionary, spoke of a twelve-mile journey on foot from Plank's tavern in Uxbridge village to Whitchurch through dense forest without seeing a house or settler.[18] As for Brock, Thorah and Mara, the roads remained so bad that local settlers preferred the boat trip from Beaverton to Holland Landing to a struggle over the bad roads between Brock and Newmarket. Once they reached Holland Landing, the relatively well-cared-for Yonge Street made the trip to York almost a pleasure.[19]

Between 1831 and 1840 no new major north-south road-building projects were undertaken, although the local inhabitants continued to improve and to extend those already in existence. By 1842 these had been sufficiently improved that in winter sleigh-loads of grain could be hauled from Brock and Thorah to Whitby and Oshawa, although in other seasons the roads were barely passable for the traveller on foot or horseback.[20]

The major road-building undertaken in the 1830s was the improvement of Danforth Road. To carry out this project the Government created a road corporation responsible for building and managing the road and collecting the tolls. It had been the original intention to macadamize the road, but the high cost and scarcity of materials induced the trustees to experiment with planking. In 1837 they built a mile of plank road for £525, and found that the cost of upkeep was little more than one fourth that of a stone road. As a result of this experiment they abandoned the idea of macadamizing and, in spite of the disruption of the rebellion, had fourteen miles built by the end of 1839.[21]

In spite of the improvements to the Danforth Road, the presence of an excellent natural harbour at Whitby and a second, less sheltered, but still usable, harbour at Oshawa, meant that most goods could be transported more cheaply by ship than by road. With those harbours and the excellent north-south transportation provided by the Simcoe, Scugog and Brock roads, the south Ontario County area presented the possibility of the development of an economy not subordinated to that of York. Moreover, when businessmen looked to the future and envisioned an inland waterway uniting Lakes Ontario, Scugog, Simcoe and Huron, they speculated about the day when the Whitby-Oshawa area might surpass York as the chief commercial centre of the province.

Although the "Big Bay" harbour at Whitby had been used for local traffic since the arrival of the first settlers, its lack of a customs house barred its use as a port for the American grain and timber trade. With the growing volume of traffic and increased flow of produce generated by the opening of the main north-south roads, the government decided, in 1831, to declare Windsor Harbour a port of entry and appointed P.K. Tincombe as customs collector on September 6, 1831.[22]

After 1830 the volume of trade increased rapidly and entrepreneurs recognizing the area's potential, soon began establishing enterprises based on the local grain trade. In 1833 James Welsh built a storehouse and tramway for loading wheat and flour aboard ships at Whitby,[23] and in 1837 the first attempt to create a local transportation monopoly was undertaken. In that year the "Windsor Harbour Railway or Macadamized Road Company" was incorporated with an authorized capital of £5,000. By its charter the company was authorized to construct a railway or a macadamized road or both from the harbour to Dundas Street. With the economic depression of 1837 and the disruption caused by the rebellion, the promoters were unable to raise the required capital, and the project was abandoned.[24] In spite of this reversal, by 1840 the general outline of trade patterns in Ontario County had been established. For the next thirty years most of the trade from the area would flow through Whitby and Oshawa rather than York, and the ambition of local entrepreneurs to extend this pattern to the north would dominate the economic thinking of the leading businessmen of Whitby and Oshawa for years to come.

In contrast to development of an excellent transportation system through long settlement, government aid and private enterprise in the south, northern areas still lagged far behind at the pioneer stage of primitive bush roads and difficult, expensive travel.[25] Thus the economic changes which fundamentally altered the nature of production and distribution in the southern area between 1820 and 1840 had little effect on the north.

In the development from the period of self-sufficiency of family or neighbourhood to one in which a wide range of products were manufactured and exchanged locally, three prior changes of condition were necessary: a great increase in accessible population to allow for division of labour and specialization of production; the introduction of craftsmen who had high level skills; and a good transportation network which both facilitated internal trade and made possible the sale of local produce outside the area. Such external sales were necessary to purchase both the capital equipment required to increase local productivity and the raw materials necessary for local manufacture. In the early years, the key men initiating these changes were the local merchants.

Although William Peak of Pickering and the Farewell brothers of Whitby Township had traded with the Indians in the early days of the settlement, a major hardship of the first settlers was the lack of merchants from whom goods could easily be bought and to whom local produce could be sold. In the years before 1820, several attempts were made to establish stores, but all failed because of the scant and scattered population and the lack of sufficient cash crops which the farmers could trade for manufactured goods. The first such attempt was made in Pickering in 1817 and 1818 when a Mr. Smith kept a store beside Timothy Roger's mill in Duffin's Creek.[26] At about the same time two storekeepers named Losie and Storey attempted to set up business in Whitby,[27] but so shortlived were their efforts that they were never entered on the census rolls.

It was not until the sharp increase in settlement in Whitby after 1820 that the first permanent store was opened. In 1823 William Warren kept a store in conjunction with the first post office at Hamar's Corners. He later moved his store to Dundas Street between Oshawa and Whitby. In 1825 Warren's was

Table XII
Merchant Shops by Township, 1820–40[28]

	1820	*1825*	*1830*	*1835*	*1840*
Pickering	0	0	0	9	6
Whitby	0	1	6	14	19
Uxbridge	—	0①	0	0	0
Reach	—	—	0	0	0
Brock	—	0①	0	0	0
Scott	—	—	—	—	—
Thorah	—	—	0	0	1
Mara and Rama	—	—	—	—	0

① Figures are for 1826.

still the only store in Ontario County, but between 1825 and 1830 several others were built in Whitby in order to take advantage of the trade opened up by the new north-south plank roads. Table XII shows the rapid growth in the number of merchants in front townships in contrast to the slow growth in the northern areas. In the immigration boom of 1830-35 small villages containing several stores sprang up at the terminus of the main north-south roads in both Whitby and Pickering. Thus by 1840 there were mercantile establishments at Oshawa, Whitby Harbour and Duffin's Creek. The latter village, however, because of competition from Markham Village and Stouffville, experienced a sharp set-back in the depression of 1837 and the unsettled conditions after the Rebellion. The only other store to survive more than year or so was that of Kenneth Cameron in Thorah[29] at the landing at Milton (now Beaverton) which shared the same favourable location at the terminus of a road network as did the stores in Whitby and Pickering. Stores without this advantage seldom survived for long. Thus a store begun by Richard Shier in Brock[30] had a difficult early career, while several would-be merchants who began business in Uxbridge before 1840 soon failed.[31]

The successful merchant in a pioneer society quickly became a man of affairs. Peter Russell explained the back country merchant's position in 1825:

> Young men often begin business here without any capital at all; they find security or are known in Montreal, consequently obtain a credit from $500 to $2,000 in goods at such a price as the wholesale dealer chooses to charge, say 15 to 25 percent above the money value, on an average. These young men then establish themselves either in the village or in places where they have the fewest competitors or capital; and sell out their stock to the country farmer for ashes, pork, wheat stillgrain and other articles of produce, or on credit, for a promise of payment in produce the following winter, the farmer agreeing to deliver the produce at *cash* price, and taking the goods at a dear rate,—

> they get a little cash now and then, but their chief dependance is on produce. They build grist and saw mills, distilleries, and potash works, and pay the workmen chiefly in trade, that is, in goods.[32]

The bane of pioneer life, as William Lyon Mackenzie never tired of pointing out, was the credit system. As Mackenzie said:

> The whole together is a system revolting to the feelings of every independent thinking colonist. Our farmers are indebted to our country merchants, our country merchants are deeply bound down in the same manner, and by the same causes, to the Montreal wholesale dealers. Few of these Montreal commission merchants are men of capital; they are generally merely the factors or agents of British houses, and thus a chain of debt, dependence, and degradation is begun and kept up, the links of which are bound fast round the souls and bodies of our yeomanry.[33]

The basic economic problem at the root of the credit system was that Upper Canada was at the initial stage of capital accumulation. Because almost all commodities other than farm produce were in short supply and few of the needed capital goods were manufactured in the colony, it was necessary to send what little currency and coinage there was out of the colony to buy manufactured goods. As a result, there was always a shortage of cash. Unfortunately the high rate of credit, high transportation costs and the British tariff all combined to make everything that the farmer bought extremely expensive, while that which he sold was in competition with similar goods from all other British colonies as well as farm producers in England itself. The result was that much of the wealth the farmer produced was in the hands of those who had sufficient capital to give credit at the high rates demanded.

Not only did the credit system make prices extremely high, but far too often these debt relationships were manipulated for political advantage. Since voting was open, a farmer who voted against the candidate favoured by the merchant to whom he was indebted could expect to have his credit cut off or his debt called in. Similarly, when the local merchant was indebted to his principal in York or Montreal, and to the government of the day for purchase of pork and flour (to say nothing of the patronage in post offices, magistracies, and other fee-collecting positions) he was also required to deliver both his own vote and those of his creditors to the favoured party. In these circumstances it was a brave and independent man indeed who dared cross party lines.[34]

The key to success for merchants and villages alike was a favourable location on a main thoroughfare that gave them a "natural" monopoly. In the 1820s and 1830s both Whitby Harbour and Oshawa enjoyed such a monopoly position at the terminus of the only passable roads running north. With roads generally poor, the additional cost of by-passing the closest merchant with one's produce in order to deal with his competitor was so great and so time-consuming that it generally was not worth the trouble.

Not only were monopolies a major source of merchantile success, they were recognized as such by the businessmen of the period. When government grants for road-building were in the offing, the merchants of the various localities competed vigorously to have them allocated for their own benefit. Such rivalries would become especially bitter after 1840 when Whitby and Oshawa battled for dominance in Reach. Later both struggled to prevent that township from becoming a rival trading centre. Finally, in the 1860s and 1870s Whitby would fight a desperate battle against Toronto for dominance in the northern townships.

Parallel to the increase in the number of merchants in the southern villages was the rise of manufacturing in the area. Just as those merchant shops which had been founded before 1820 generally failed, early attempts at manufacturing were also failures for lack of a good transportation system and a sufficiently large market. In Ontario County, manufacturing in the early days was tied directly to the products and needs of the local inhabitants, and was, in many cases, merely an extension of the processing of goods made in the home or grown on the farm.

The first attempts at manufacturing and processing were the early grist and sawmills. While both processed locally produced primary products into goods used on the local farms, the sawmills produced lumber exclusively for the neighbourhood, while the gristmill owners very soon began to export grain and flour to larger centres and to the United States. Both, of course, did custom work on a share basis, keeping a portion of the finished flour or lumber for payment.

Table XIII
Grist- and Sawmills by Township, 1820–40[35]

	1820		*1825*		*1830*		*1835*		*1840*	
	Grist-mills	*Saw-mills*	*Grist-mills*	*Saw-mills*	*Grist-mills*	*Saw-mills*	*Grist-mills*	*Saw-mills*	*Grist-mills*	*Saw-mills*
Pickering	1	1	1	3	2	4	2	11	3	12
Whitby	1	3	2	4	3	9	3	14	5	15
Uxbridge	—	—	1①	2①	1	4	1	4	1	3
Reach	—	—	—	—	0	0	0	0	0	0
Brock	—	—	1①	0①	1	1	2	3	3	3
Scott	—	—	—	—	—	—	—	—	0	0
Thorah	—	—	—	—	0	1	1	1	0	0
Mara & Rama	—	—	—	—	—	—	—	—	0	0

① Figures are for 1826.

As Table XIII shows, there was a rapid growth in the number of sawmills in comparison to the number of gristmills. The reason for this phenomenon is that sawmills were relatively simple to construct and were designed to serve a local market. The poor condition of local roads made it impossible for any one operator to tempt distant business except by offering ruinously low prices for services. In other words, the bad roads operated as a form of tariff which protected the small operator from his competition. On the other hand, because the same bad roads made it impossible to haul locally sawn lumber to the ports for shipment to larger centres, it kept the local sawmills small in size and dependent upon the neighbours for business.

In the early years the first gristmills were operated, as Paxton, Gould and St. John have testified,[36] to serve only a local market. A first class flourmill and storehouse was expensive to build. Unlike lumber, however, the sale of flour was profitable even with the cost of shipment. Thus, once a fairly large volume of grain was produced locally, the miller with sufficient capital to buy stocks of grain in the winter (when good sleighing allowed the backwoods settler to bring his grain to market), soon found himself in a highly profitable business.

Gristmills were even more sensitive to monopolies of location than were stores. Mill-sites with a volume of water large enough and steady enough to allow large-scale, year-round operation were scarce. In addition, good road and good port facilities were required to build a business larger than a mere custom operation for neighbouring farmers. For all these reasons, before 1840 gristmills tended to be fewer in number and to be larger scale operations than were sawmills.

As with the local merchant, farmers selling grain to the local miller found themselves the last link in a chain of debt that reached all the way to England. Accordingly, the local farmer received only a small portion of the value of his produce. For example, in 1827 wheat which sold in York for 2s. 6d. per bushel, sold in Montreal for 4s. 8d. The price spread on flour was similar: 17s. 6d. per barrel in York and 30s. 0d. in Montreal. By contrast, the price of wheat in Rochester was 3s. 7d. per bushel (75 per cent higher), while the New York price was identical to that in Montreal.[37] It seems unlikely that the difference in transportation costs would explain the great discrepancy in price. Mackenzie said that often the miller paid for the wheat he bought in goods that he marked up to double their value.[38] The local monopoly created by the debt relationship and location placed the farmer in a position of dependency from which he could extricate himself only with great difficulty.

Around the ports and major mill sites there grew up a series of small industries which were dependent upon the attraction of the primary enterprise for customers. These industries were either complementary to, or the same as, the activities which had been carried on in the pioneer home, but in the factory they were carried on at a higher level of technology and craftsmanship. For example, the fulling mill provided a process complementary to the spinning and weaving which was still carried on the home, while tanning and carding replaced home processes. Similarly, a distillery or ashery provided services of a nature qualitatively different from those which could be provided in the home, while a brewer or chair-maker replaced home occupations. In all cases, however, these services were closely related to the rural pioneer or farming economy and produced only those things of most common use and simplest production.

The list of industries which grew up around Oshawa provides an excellent example of the nature of the industries which developed out of the pioneer community. In the early years, as Table XIV shows, the industries (gristmills, carding and fulling mills, tanneries and asheries) were closely connected to the earliest stages of pioneer agricultural development.

Table XIV
Oshawa Industries, 1820–41[39]

Year	*Name of Owner*	*Type of Industry*
1822	Cleveland	Gristmill
1822	Joseph Gorham	Carding & fulling mill
1829	Thomas Gibbs	Gristmill
1832	T. N. & W. H. Gibbs	Gristmill
1836	Niles Luke	Tannery
1836	Luke & Ash	Tannery
1836	Bartlett Bros.	Tannery
1837	J. B. Warren	Gristmill
1837	J. B. Warren	Distillery
1837	J. B. Warren	Ashery
1837	Thomas Fuller	Chair Factory
1839	Patrick Wall	Cooperage
1840	Gibbs Bros.	Oshawa Cabinet Co.
1841	Henry Pedlar	Blacksmith
1841	Moscrip	Foundry
1841	Spalding	Brewery
1841	Lockhart & Wilson	Distillery

In 1840 a markedly different kind of industry, a cabinet works, requiring high level skills and a disciplined, stable labour force, appeared for the first time. Thus it can be said that the years 1840-41 mark the transition to a much more advanced form of production. Since cabinet-making and foundry work were highly skilled and specialized, their products were costly and required both a large market area and a largely cash economy to survive. Their introduction shows that by 1840 there had been a major development away from pioneer production methods towards a "mature" economy with good transportation, more advanced technology, and high levels of craftsmanship.

The major exception to the gradual evolution from lower forms to more advanced forms of production in southern Ontario County was the shipbuilding industry. Attracted by the fine natural harbour several owners of ships made their homes at Whitby in the 1820s. Because of the need to renew their ships from time to time and a desire to oversee the construction and repair of their vessels, these owner-captains brought skilled shipwrights to the area rather than having their ships constructed or repaired in another port. Thus, as early as 1828 a twenty-ton vessel was constructed at Windsor Harbour, Whitby, and a small five-ton boat was built at the mouth of the Rouge River in Pickering,[40] while in the 1830s David Annis built two vessels, the *Dianah* and the *Lord Durham* in Whitby Townships.[41]

In contrast to the rapid development of industry in southern Ontario County between 1820 and 1840, the northern areas remained, in 1840, a generation behind in development. As Table XIII shows, in 1840 neither Reach, Scott, Mara nor Rama as yet possessed a grist or sawmill, while Brock, the leading township of the north, had three of each, thereby standing approxi-

Toll Gate, Centre Line Road, Whitby Township *Public Archives of Ontario*

mately where Whitby Township had in 1825. Joseph Gould's description of Uxbridge Village in 1832 provides a useful basis of comparison between the north and the more dynamic south. As Gould remembered it:

> In the fall of 1832, the whole of the buildings standing within . . . the limits of the town of Uxbridge were the little old gristmill and barn built by Joseph Collins [1809] a small log house and blacksmith shop, built by John Lyons; a small frame tavern and driving house, occupied by J.P. Plank, a small cooper shop built by Thomas Arnold, the store of Carleton Lynde, and the sawmill, house and barn purchased by Mr. Gould from Mr. Plank, and situated a quarter mile south of the other buildings.[42]

In 1836 Uxbridge's industries were expanded by the addition of a small tannery built by Joseph Bascome who also operated a shoe-making business and kept the post office. It would be another generation before northern Ontario County began to reach the degree of economic maturity which would allow the advanced kinds of industries which were already developing in Whitby and Oshawa.

SOCIAL CRISIS: CONFLICT AND REBELLION, 1820-40

The years 1790 to 1840 during which Ontario County was being settled were troubled years economically, socially and politically, which had shaken the world. In England the Industrial Revolution and the "clearances" of the great estates of Scotland and Ireland had created a mass of homeless, desperate poor who provided the labour for the great mills. The rise of industry would ruin the craft workers who had followed their ancient and honourable trades for centuries. In Europe revolution had swept aside the rulers of a dozen countries only to see them replaced by yet other rulers as the revolution foundered on the reaction of the newly-risen middle classes. Even in England the fear of revolution – fuelled by the revolt of her most valued colonies and the example of bloody Europe – shook the confidence of the ruling class. This class had, however, learned the lesson that France had been taught. Instead of excluding from power the new, aggressive industrialist and merchant classes, they invited them to share it, recognizing that the monopoly of property represented by the new *bourgeoisie* could be a valuable, if sometimes uncomfortable, ally of the monopoly of land and position represented by the aristocracy, against the common threat of "*liberté, fraternité, égalité*" of the unleashed working classes. The Great Reform Bill of 1832 cemented this new alliance.

Meanwhile in Upper Canada all these themes and more troubled the minds of ruler and ruled. Settlers coming from the British Isles and the United States brought with them memories and loyalties hardened by battles won and lost.

In Upper Canada they discovered economic, social and constitutional arrangements which, while generally similar to those of Britain or America, also had some novel aspects which fitted uneasily into preconceived molds. The social and political development of Ontario County displayed all the complexity and disorganization which its multiple inheritances and diverse patterns of development foreshadowed.

While no attempt can be made here to outline all the issues at stake in the pre-1837 period in Upper Canada, those which would find direct expression in Ontario County's political life generally fall into four categories: differences in vision as to what constituted the ideal society, legal and constitutional abuses in the community, economic problems, and religious and social prejudices and oppressions. The events preceding and occurring within the rebellion period itself contained aspects of all these problems.

The essence of the Tory vision of the ideal society was the conception of an ordered, differential and graded society which, centred around an elite in government and an established church, would provide stability, peace and contentment for each and every citizen. It was assumed that men were naturally unequal and as such had a proper place and role in society. To attempt to rise above one's divinely ordained position and responsibilities was to threaten society with chaos. As John Strachan, Archdeacon of York (and later Bishop of Toronto), and his Tory allies agreed, human nature was plagued by an "evil tendency"[1] and vice was "deeply woven in our propensities".[2] As a result, liberty and order could be maintained only by a system of government in which men's natural passions and "insatiable cupidity"[3] were held in check. To the Tory the American Revolution, the French Revolution, and the invasion of Canada in 1812 all represented the inevitable product of the evils of democracy. As the Kingston *Chronicle* ironically pointed out of the Republic,

> In that birth place of genius, political and legislative science is considered easy and obvious, level to the meanest capacity and most unlettered education. Even the commonest beggar thinks himself qualified to give gratuitous advice on the science of legislation, though his qualities, abilities and judgment have been totally inadequate to the task of advising ways and means for keeping himself from rags and starvation.[4]

Thus, to the Tory, the ideal society was one in which each would be contented with his lot, the lower classes were to bear in mind that the aristocrat's life carried with it both advantages and burdens. As the *Chronicle* observed:

> [O]ur obligations increase with our opportunities. Wealth, power and education are gifts of Providence accompanied by proportionate duties which render them a little dangerous to the possession.[5]

This philosophy found expression in the Upper Canadian constitution and political life with life appointments for members of the Family Compact and their friends to the Legislative and Executive Councils, and in its control of appointments to all junior offices of the Crown from the Justices of the Peace to the most junior civil service or postal clerk.

The rise to independence of the "lower orders" of immigrants brought about a crisis in social relations. As that keen observer Susanna Moodie discovered, the economic opportunities afforded by Upper Canada quickly broke down the social controls that had kept the labouring and servant classes subservient in England.

> [O]f all follies, that of taking out servants from the old country is one of the greatest, and is sure to end in the loss of the money expended in their passage, and to become the cause of deep disappointment and mortification to yourself.
>
> They no sooner set foot upon Canadian shores than they become possessed with this ultra-republican spirit. All respect for their employers, all subordination is at an end; the very air of Canada severs the tie of mutual obligation which bound you together. They fancy themselves not only equal to you in rank, but that ignorance and vulgarity give them superior claims to notice. They demand the highest wages and grumble at doing half the work, in return, which they cheerfully performed at home. They demand to eat at your table, and to sit in your company, and if you refuse to listen to their dishonest and extravagant claims, they tell you that "they are free . . . "
>
> Why they treated our claims to their respect with marked insult and rudeness, I never could satisfactorily determine. . . . Then I discovered the secret.
>
> The unnatural restraint which society imposes upon these people at home forces them to treat their more fortunate brethern with a servile deference which is repugnant to their feelings, and is thrust upon them by the dependent circumstances in which they are placed. This homage to rank and education is not sincere. Hatred and envy lie rankling at their heart, although hidden by outward obsequiousness. Necessity compells their obedience; they fawn and cringe, and flatter the wealth on which they depend for bread. But let them once emigrate, the clog which fettered them is suddenly removed; they are free; and the dearest privilege of this freedom is to wreak upon their superiors the long-locked-up hatred of their hearts. They think they can debase you to their level by disallowing all your claims to distinction; while they hope to exalt themselves and their fellows into ladies and gentlemen by sinking you back to the only title you received from Nature – plain "man" and "woman".[6]

The key to this emancipation was land. The struggle to get and keep land would be crucial in Upper Canada.

The Tories believed that the lower classes, because of their mental and moral weakness, were constantly subject to the seduction of self-seeking demagogues who posed as social reformers. As the Kingston *Chronicle* asserted;

> [No instance] can be produced where an individual has embarked his all to bring about the political reformation of a country, without having some sinister object in disguise, without some view of self-interest and aggrandisement.[7]

This view of the subversive role of reform was echoed by the *Upper Canada Gazette*:

> It has always been the case that those who intend to subvert good order in society begin by making extraordinary pretentions of public virtue and crying up a necessity for reform.[8]

Anyone who raised questions concerning the power and authority of the Family Compact was characterized by its leaders as either American subversives intent upon treason, or British revolutionaries bent upon overthrowing the most enlightened of constitutions. As Strachan said of the latter group:

> Many have no religion and are inimical to regular government. Flying from the ranks of radicals at home they came here with increased assurance and think that in a colony they may go to greater lengths than they durst at home.[9]

The terror with which leaders like Strachan viewed the social and political changes of the period was revealed in his speeches and in the letters that he wrote his intimates:

> Never was sedition more barefaced—never was there such a degree of tension and blasphemy abroad in the world—never did opposition to decency and order march with a bolder front than at present—and never was such vigor and skill displayed in the dissemination of licentiousness.[10]
> My Tory Friends as well as myself consider nothing stable either in England or here [.] We believe Revolution to have virtually commenced—it may be quicker or slower in its movements as circumstances fall out but it will never rest till the Glorious Fabric of the Constitution is crumbled in the dust.[11]

Given this hatred and fear of reform and reformers, it is little wonder that the Tories reacted with such extraordinary harshness whenever a challenge to their authority was raised by a Thorpe, Gourlay, Bidwell or Mackenzie. In their struggle against reform their weapons were their control of the Anglican church, the Legislative and Executive Councils, and the provincial officialdom. When under threat these were wielded without restraint.

In contrast to these theoretical pretensions and the garrison mentality which they created, the opposition which arose grew from a basis of practical grievances, and only in latter years reached the proportions of an opposing social theory. The key to the reformer's vision was the concept of the "sturdy yeoman", the independent producer - farmer, craftsman or merchant - who provided the solid basis of Upper Canadian society. In such a society all those who did not produce - whether bankers, lawyers, clergymen, government officials or paupers - were seen as existing either as aids to those who produced or as outright parasites. William Lyon Mackenzie expressed this sentiment clearly in 1828:

> The merchant thrives when the people thrive, and . . . is a fit man for the people to send [elect to the Legislative assembly], for he can only thrive when the country thrives. But the lawyer prospers best in times of misery—like Mother Carey's chickens, he is seen in his glory in a storm of scarcity, with his warrants, summonses, and executions.[12]

Because labour was the source of wealth, there could be no natural antagonisms between those who produced wealth in a free society. In his "Address to the People of the County of York" Mackenzie enunciated the basic premises of this belief:

> Labour is the true source of wealth. The farmer produces Wheat—the Miller converts it into flour—the Labourer breaks Stones and Macadamizes Roads and these roads with the aid of Steamers and Boats convey the flour to the place where the Foreigner will buy it at the highest price. The owner of the flour receives his money, be it one thousand or ten thousand dollars—this is wealth, it was wealth before paper money was in existance—and I hope it will be so considered when a paper currency will be no more.
>
> To produce this wealth, the Farmer, the Miller, the Labourer, the Sailor, the Merchant, each contribute his share, by useful industry in an honest calling.[13]

Other occupations and callings were useful as they lent their "beneficial aid" to the producers of wealth.

While the source of wealth was labour, there were various forms of labour relations, some good and some evil, which could be used in the creation of that wealth. The good forms of labour were those which exalted the dignity and independence of men; the evil were those based upon subservience and exploitation of the weak. Attempts by the Colonial Office and Upper Canadian Government to create a class of landless labourers through the manipulation of land prices, and to attract capitalists to Canada, through the creation of high tariffs, to employ these labourers, were rejected because they threatened to bring to Canada the evils of class differences and class warfare which had swept Europe:

> Great establishments of manufacturers require great numbers of very poor persons to do the work for small wages; These poor persons are

> to be found in Europe in large numbers, but they will not be found in North America until the lands are all taken and cultivated, unless unnatural laws should be framed to prevent the cultivator from being supplied from the cheapest market.[14]

Above all, the reformers wanted no pauper class to be created which they believed would threaten both the stability of society and, through its exploitation, bring about the degradation of the independent producers through "unnatural" competition:

> Heaven in its mercy forbid that the legislature of Upper Canada should inevitably conspire with rich, covetous and ambitious capitalists to reduce the Canadian population to the condition of living machinery moving for the benefit of concentrated and in many cases ill acquired wealth.[15]

Yet while the producers, the "creators-of-wealth", might resent the pretensions of the high-born or highly placed to be all-knowing and all-powerful, they were not, on the other hand, entirely social "levellers". For example, when Mackenzie's journeymen printers formed a union and demanded better pay, he condemned their action as unjust. While he was ready to admit that "Labour sometimes needs protection",[16] such was not the case in Toronto, he asserted, and moreover, such demands upon their employers were themselves dangerous to society.

> It would be well for these journeymen if they would employ their evenings in studying the true principles of economy which govern the rule of wages. Had they so done previous to their present ungrateful movement, it never would have been made. They would have seen that combinations among workmen, intended solely to keep up the rate of wages, are of precisely the nature of combinations among masters to keep up the rate. . . .
>
> Combinations like that of the printers are useful when not carried too far. But, when they begin to foment divisions and animosities in society, when they array classes against each other who could otherwise be united by a common interest, when they attempt to deprive the youths of a city (Toronto for instance) of the privilege of choosing the trade they would desire to pursue, when they attempt to establish a monopoly in the rate of labour instead of leaving it to be regulated by supply and demand, they become injurious to society.[17]

The political basis of the reformers, then, was the independent, productive owner and operator. The duty owed to those without property (and thereby without a stake in the community) was no more than an open and unconstrained marketplace where the able and energetic might, through their own honest efforts, rise to the status and social value of owner-producers. The reform leadership, landowners, farmers, professionals and craftsworkers, reflected these ideals and interests.

To the reformers, the constitution, far from being a bulwark against and curb upon the people, was nothing more than a contract among them. In 1828 Mackenzie argued:

> The constitution of a country is not the act of its government, nor of any distant authority, but of the people constituting a government suited to their necessities—a constitution contains the principles on which the government shall be established, the manner in which it shall be organized, the powers it shall have, the mode of elections, the duration of parliaments, assemblies, or congresses; the authority to be given the executive, and the principles on which it shall be bound.[18]

The message of this argument was clear; what the people create, they can destroy, change or retain as it suits them. Thus whether their demands were for Responsible Government (as the moderate reformers led by Robert Baldwin advocated) or republicanism (as Mackenzie ultimately struggled to achieve), the lesson was the same: the people, and only the people, have a right to decide. The "people", of course, might have just as readily been called "the producers" - to most reformers the terms were synonymous.

The continued frustration of the "will of the people" by the Family Compact (which controlled the Legislative and Executive Councils and was therefore in a position to reject reforms passed by the elective Legislative Assembly) and by the Colonial Office and Governor who failed to bring reform through executive action, gradually split the reform movement between those who favoured direct action and those who did not. In the weeks before the rebellion, Mackenzie printed a poem which appealed to those who had opted for direct action. Entitled "The Strength of Tyranny" it enunciated many of the basic philosophical positions of the independent producers:

> The lords of earth are only great,
> While others clothe and feed them
> But what were all their pride and state
> Should labor cease to heed them? . . .
>
> We toil, we spin, we delve the mine,
> Sustaining each his neighbor;
> And who can hold a 'right divine'
> To rob us of our labor?[19]

But in Upper Canada the "lords of the earth" were the Tory Family Compact who fattened on the wealth created by those who laboured. The rulers had failed to discharge their duty of "beneficial aid" to those who produced the wealth of the country, and it was now time for the independent yeomanry to assert their right to change the constitution. To fail to do so was to lose the right to be considered free men and to sink to the level of slaves. The poem continued:

The swain [swine] is higher than a King:
   Before the laws of nature,
The monarch was a useless thing
   The swain a useful creature.

The tyrant's chains are only strong,
   While slaves submit to wear them;
And who could bind them on the throng
   Determined not to bear them?

Perish all tyrants far and near
   Beneath the chains that bind us: -
And perish, too, that *servile fear*
   Which make the slaves they find us.

One grand, one universal claim -
   One peal of mortal thunder -
One glorious burst in freedom's name,
   And rend our bonds asunder!

Thus, confronted by an obdurate and entrenched elite which, feeling its power slipping away, opted for a greater and greater authoritarianism, the reform movement split between those who were willing to wait for better days and better ways, and a few who refused to accept further repression. The abortive revolt of 1837 was the result.

In Ontario County the first issue which stirred widespread interest and local political action was the Alien Question. The issue, while not a new one, became critical with the expulsion from the Legislature of Barnabas Bidwell, an American immigrant, who had been elected as a reformer in 1821. When the electors of Lennox and Addington returned Bidwell's son, Marshall Spring Bidwell, in his place, his Tory enemies attempted to bar his election on the grounds that, although he had been born a British subject in pre-revolutionary Massachussets, he had failed to migrate to a British territory with the Loyalists in 1783 and could therefore no longer claim British citizenship. He was, on these grounds, ineligible to sit in the Legislature.

Whatever the legalities of that debate, the question raised an even more serious problem. According to British law at the time, aliens could not legally own land: if all those immigrants from the United States who had depended upon their British birth and subsequent oaths of loyalty were not legally citizens, then virtually every inhabitant of Ontario County who had arrived before 1812 was threatened by the loss of his property.[20]

Between 1821 and 1828 decision after decision in the courts and the provincial legislature went against the "aliens". As the issue dragged on and anxiety mounted, a province-wide campaign was begun to petition the British Government to pass legislation guaranteeing the "alien" immigrants their hard-earned property. In February, 1827 John Warren, a Whitby Justice of the Peace and postmaster (brother of William Warren, the Oshawa tanner and ashery keeper), and a number of his prominent Whitby neighbours decided to call a meeting to add their voices to the mounting chorus of those demanding reform. The date set for the local gathering was March 6, 1827.

On the appointed day, the excited citizens gathered at the township meeting hall in Whitby to discuss the issues. All afternoon the debate raged as to the proper mode of presentation and language of the petition. Finally, written in the secretary's best hand, the petition was ready for presentation. It read:

> *Resolved*—That this meeting consider that the naturalization bill, as passed in the last session of our provincial parliament is derogatory to the affectionate and loyal feelings of the people composing this meeting, and the province at large, and subversive of their peace and prosperity. [This bill allowed all American born immigrants who had been domiciled in Upper Canada for seven years to swear an oath of allegiance. It rejected their claims to have been loyal citizens before this, but confirmed their property rights.]
> *Resolved*—That it is therefore expedient to petition the imperial parliament praying that the said bill may not pass into law.
> *Resolved*—That Messrs. Ezra Annis, Jabez Hall, and Reuben Hudson, be a committee to solicit subscriptions in aid of funds now raising in the province, to defray the expense of one or more agents to proceed to England with the said petition, and have the same presented to the imperial parliament.
> *Resolved*—That John Warren, Esq. be treasurer, to receive all monies so collected by the committee, and transmit the same to Mr. Jessie Ketchum of York, the standing treasurer for the Petitioners.
> *Resolved*—That the meeting hear with regret rumours of personal violence having been offered to any members of our provincial parliament, on account of supporting said bill—that they disapprove of such conduct, and will use their influence to discountenance and prevent anything of that nature.[21]
>
> Jabez Hall, Chairman of the Meeting
> William Moore, Secretary

The Family Compact retaliated almost immediately. John Warren who had helped call the meeting and had been nominated treasurer was struck from the Commission of the Peace for his participation.[22] Since the office of Justice of the Peace was one which offered a comfortable living through fees, it was a severe punishment indeed. The lesson of the occasion was not lost upon William Lyon Mackenzie:

> We are credibly informed that Mr. Warren the postmaster of Whitby has been struck off the commission of the peace for having, in consequence of the request of some of his neighbours, attended a meeting upon the alien question in the township, consented to remit their subscriptions to York, although he neither spoke nor voted on the occasion—It is useless to talk of an independent unpaid magistracy in a country where such examples are placed before those in the commission of the peace. One turnout will serve for a district in silencing the bench from speaking what they think.[23]

Happily, John Warren's sacrifice was not in vain. In 1828 the British Government was under pressure both from the colony and from reformers in England. When Robert Randell, a Virginia-born member of the Upper Canadian Legislature carried the petitions to England, the British authorities made an almost complete about-face. The provincial Legislature was invited to pass a bill which immediately naturalized all persons who had previously received lands from the government, held any public office, taken the oath of allegiance, or who had come in before 1820. Persons who had immigrated after 1820 could be naturalized after seven years' residence.[24] While the battle had been won, the lesson of many years' struggle was not forgotten. Henceforth the reformers of the area took an active and partisan interest in the issues of the day.

The election of 1828 was the first in which the new political activism found expression.[25] The election was fought around three main issues: the alien question, the attempt by the Anglican church to obtain all the Clergy Reserves (and the discovery and exposure of an "Ecclesiastical Chart" drawn up by Strachan which included innumerable fraudulant claims aimed at bolstering the Anglican Church's case), and the arbitrary dismissal of Judge John Walpole Willis who had quarrelled with Governor Maitland and members of the Family Compact concerning the legality of the Colony's court system. The last issue created the greatest response because it threatened the independence of the whole legal system.

When Willis was dismissed a wave of protest swept the province. Local meetings were called to discuss the issue, and, just as with the alien question, it was decided to petition the British Government for redress. The meeting held in Brock was typical of those in Ontario County.

On July 9, 1828, the inhabitants gathered to discuss the issue and to decide upon a course of action. After naming Oliver Taylor chairman of the meeting and Randal Wixon secretary, a series of motions was made and debated which resulted in the following resolutions:

> *1st Resolved*—that from every information which we have been able to obtain respecting the conduct of the Hon. John Walpole Willis, he has acted a fair, legal, unbiased, and Just part, as a puisne judge of his majesty's court of Kings bench, in Upper Canada.
> *2nd Resolved*—that the Hon. Mr. Justice Willis's conduct merits the highest approbation and applause of all who are true friends of the British Constitution, and who wish to see the purity and independence of our high courts established upon the true principles of British freedom.[26]

Other resolutions thanked the king for having appointed a man of Willis's "honest and upright principles", and asked for his reappointment.

The election struggle in 1828 was a vigorous (and sometimes vicious) one, but the reformers across the Colony were generally victorious. The contest for York County (which then included the Ontario County area) was particularly bitter. York County had been a stronghold of Tory sentiment for a generation. Indeed, as Robert Gourlay had reported in 1817, Home District was so much under the influence of Archdeacon Strachan that not a single township in the area had replied to Gourlay's questionnaire.[27] Thus from the War of 1812 on, a succession of supporters of the Family Compact had been elected with the single exception of William Warren Baldwin, a moderate who had been elected in 1820 as one representative of the two-member riding. However, with the succession of public issues which affected that area, the Tory hold was broken and the two reform candidates, William Lyon Mackenzie and Jesse Ketchum, were elected. The overwhelming vote in favor of Mackenzie and Ketchum showed the depth of discontent which the continued arbitrary acts of the Family Compact had generated. The vote was Ketchum, 869; William Lyon Mackenzie, 759; and W. W. Baldwin, 277. William Thompson, the only Tory incumbent trying for the seat, fared so badly that he withdrew after the second day of voting.[28]

With a reform majority in the Assembly the political situation degenerated rapidly. The Upper House was entirely in the hands of the Family Compact and a situation of deadlock existed. What the Assembly passed, the Upper House defeated. With sufficient funds under the control of the Governor to carry on most necessary functions and to pay the salaries of government favourites, the reformers were unable to bring about any of the needed changes. In 1830 on the death of George IV, the Assembly was dissolved and new elections were held. While Mackenzie and Ketchum were returned with handsome majorities, the reformers were generally defeated when the new Governor, Sir John Colborne, appealed directly to the electorate's loyalty and promised to redress many of the old grievances.[29] These promises, however, were not fulfilled.

The period 1830-34 was a tumultuous one in Upper Canada. Of particular interest to Tories and reformers alike was the halting progress that Great

Britain was making toward reform. During the session of 1830-31, the reformers, drawing hope from the efforts of British reformers, leveled attack after attack on their entrenched opposition. But in spite of the Tory's disorganization, numbers told and all attempts to bring about reform were rejected. Facing a road block in the Assembly, the reformers turned again to the strategy which had proven successful in the alien question – the township meeting and petition to the British Government. This time, however, the local meetings were to play a far greater role than they had previously. They were to become a permanent institution for education and agitation. As Mackenzie said of these "Societies for the Preservation of the Constitutional Rights of British Subjects":

> These, and constitutional tract associations, with one or two auxiliary branches in every township, will probably be the immediate result of the attempt now making by the government utterly to annihilate and destroy the salutary influence of the Assembly. . . . If the people will be but true to themselves, the evil intended them will pass away, and the discomfiture of their enemies be assured. The periodical press of London and the provincial cities will aid in awakening the British nation to a due sense of the wrongs done the colonists.[30]

The petitions of 1831, moreover, did not propose merely a simple solution to a single grievance. Instead they incorporated both a detailed analysis of many constitutional and economic problems and the means proposed to solve them. They were designed not merely to inform the British Government but, more importantly, to educate the Upper Canadians to their rights and duties as British citizens.

The method of the organization of the meeting illustrated the growing political sophistication of the reformers. In May of 1831 Mackenzie informed his supporters that a broad campaign of political action and education was necessary if a solid political base and lasting reform were ever to be achieved. In the *Colonial Advocate* during May and June, he discussed his fears concerning the economic future of the colony and the necessity of constructive action on the part of the public. In the meantime at the grass-roots level, reformers began circulating petitions directed to the clerks of the townships requesting that a meeting be held of the "Freeholders, Householders, and other Inhabitants" to discuss the "Condition of Canada". Reiterated again and again was the theme that the act of petitioning the King was not an act of disloyalty, but the inalienable right of every British subject. The petition presented to the Pickering Township clerk was typical of those circulated:

> To Mr. William Sleigh, Town Clerk of the Township of Pickering.
> Sir: The undersigned hereby request that you would call a general meeting of the Freeholders, Householders, and other Inhabitants of the said town—to be holden on an early day in a place convenient to the inhabitants, for the purpose of considering of the propriety of uniting

> in dutiful and affectionate address to His Majesty King William 4th, assuring His Majesty of the unalterable sincere attachment which the people of Pickering entertain for his royal person and family, and of their confidence in the zeal, patriotism, and wisdom of his confidential advisors: and also to address His Majesty and the two houses of the provincial legislature on the state of affairs in this Province.[31]

Attached to the petition were the signatures of forty voters resident in Pickering Township. Similar petitions from Whitby (twenty-six signatures), Uxbridge, Brock and the other townships of Home District were presented.[32]

The careful organization which went into the whole affair was revealed in the scheduling of the meetings. Beginning on Saturday, July 16, 1831, a series of eighteen meetings was set up, with only Sundays omitted. These were laid out in such a way that Mackenzie could attend them all. The meetings in Ontario County were held in Pickering, July 20; Whitby, July 21; Uxbridge, July 22; and Brock, July 28. The Reach meeting was held with the one in Uxbridge.[33]

Mackenzie's appeal to the citizens of the townships, printed on July 14, was moderate and reasoned in language:

> Mr. Mackenzie respectfully acquaints his constituents that he considers these public meetings highly expedient at the present time, and it is his intention to meet the people . . . to consult with them for their interest upon subjects connected with the general welfare; to learn their opinion, desires and intentions respecting future road appropriations, the late British Act authorizing American produce to be brought free into Canada, the duty on salt, the condition of the courts of law, the collecting and applying assessed taxes in the district, the expediency of further augmenting the provincial burthens by loans to the Welland Canal Company and for War Losses, and the best means of promoting education and obtaining the control of the whole revenue of the country, as well as of putting a stop to the sale of public lands in a secret manner. . . . Mr. M. considers the present time highly favourable for a general application to his Majesty's government for the practical recognition of those inalienable rights and privileges.[34]

At each of the meetings a prepared "Petition and Address" was presented to the meeting, discussed and voted upon. The twelve main points enunciated in the petition struck at the heart of the Family Compact's base of power. It requested equal representation (i.e., representation according to population) in the Assembly; the abolition of the Crown and Clergy Reserves and of all religious preferences; that the granting of land be regulated by law; that the Assembly be given control of all the Government's money; that the town or township meeting be given control of all statute labour, assessment, local taxation and town officers; that judges and clergymen be barred from election or appointment to the Assembly, Legislative Council or Executive Council; and that the right of impeachment of all government officials be granted to the Legislature.

The series of daily public meetings in the townships amounted almost to a triumphal procession for Mackenzie. Not only were all of Mackenzie's proposals overwhelmingly accepted at all the meetings, but, beginning with the meeting in Whitby (July 21), additional proposals were added to the petition by local inhabitants. The Whitby proposals regarding elections and a fairer method of selecting jurors were strongly approved by later meetings. As Mackenzie joyfully reported:

> Travel through these counties, as we have done, gentle reader, and you will perchance find various opinions with regard to public men; but with reference to the great questions involved in the address to His Majesty adopted in this town on the 16th July last, one opinion prevails, and that opinion is decisive in its favor. In Etobicoke, in Scarboro, in Pickering, in Whitby, in Uxbridge, in Markham, in Whitchurch, in East Gwillimbury, in Brock . . . in nineteen public meetings . . . one voice was heard . . .
>
> Lawyers and doctors, priests and placemen, merchants and mechanics, have had their societies and associations . . . but now the people will have their associations also; they will go regularly and steadily to work, and we will see whether complete success will fail to attend their honest and united efforts. THE FEW may continue to cry out, that wisdom remains with them, but THE MANY will cease to regard the voice of the charmer.[35]

Although the petitions gathered so carefully in the townships failed to bring any redress of the grievances enunciated, the meetings and local associations established to gather signatures did have one important effect. A leadership began to appear in the reformer's ranks which would have profound effects on local political life for the next two generations. Thus Joshua Wixon, and David and Peter Mathews in Pickering; Doctor James Hunter in Whitby; John B. Plank in Uxbridge; and Randal Wixon and James Reekie in Brock began to take a prominent place in politics through their roles in the local reform associations.

Nor were the reformers satisfied merely to meet to discuss the constitutional and economic questions of the day. Through the media of tracts, speakers and the reform press, their vision of the "good society" of producers and the overthrow of illegitimate rule by "parasitical aristocracy" was disseminated. Of course Mackenzie's *Colonial Advocate* was one of the main sources of their arguments and social analysis. For example, with his characteristic flair for language, Mackenzie demanded to know, "What is Aristocracy!" and answered:

> "What is Aristocracy!" In reply to the question of an ultra, what is aristocracy? General Foy, a distinguished orator in the French

> Chambers, gave the following definition:—"I can tell what it is, said he:—aristocracy in the nineteenth century, is the league, the coalition of those who would consume without producing, live without working, know everything without learning, carry away all the honours without having deserved them, and occupy all the places of government, without being capable of filling one.[36]

The Family Compact lost little time in striking back at Mackenzie. Earlier in the year the Tory members had attempted to expel him from the Assembly because of his endless demands for investigations and constant motions attacking the Government, but the move was so blatantly improper that the more moderate government supporters refused to risk the public outcry that would have resulted. Now, however, Mackenzie gave his enemies better grounds. In November in the *Colonial Advocate* he referred to the Assembly as "a sycophantic office for registering the decrees of as mean and mercenary an Executive as ever was given as punishment for the sins of any part of North America in the nineteenth century".[37] On the basis of this statement Mackenzie was accused of libel and expelled from the Assembly on December 13, 1831.

Never one to suffer injury in silence, Mackenzie filled the pages of his paper with attacks on the Tories. Public indignation was so widespread that on election day, January 2, 1832, forty sleighs filled with his supporters escorted him to the polls where speeches were made in his favour, and a presentation was made to him of a gold medal worth two hundred and fifty dollars which was inscribed with the words, "Presented to William Lyon Mackenzie, Esq., by his constituents of the county of York, in token of their approbation of his political career".[38] Mackenzie's opponent, Mr. Street, received only one vote of the first 120 cast, and withdrew from the contest.[39]

In spite of the overwhelming support for Mackenzie displayed by his constituents, the Tories promptly returned to the attack, and for a second time voted to expel Mackenzie, this time with the additional motion that he was ineligible for re-election. In spite of the latter motion, Mackenzie again declared his candidacy and began a whirlwind campaign for re-election. In the Ontario County area the excitement was intense. This time the Tories were determined to make a strong showing, and nominated Colonel Washburn to contest the seat. In addition James E. Small, a moderate, argued that he should be elected, since Mackenzie was now ineligible; Small was subsequently nominated. On election day (January 30, 1832), the voters of Ontario County turned out in strength to support their hero. By sleigh, on horseback and afoot they came from Pickering, Whitby, Uxbridge and Brock. In spite of the long distance to be travelled to the polling place (the Red Lion Inn on Yonge Street), when voting ended Mackenzie had scored a smashing victory, receiving 628 votes. His opposition, Small and Washburn, received 96 and 23 votes respectively. Those electors who had travelled from Ontario County polled their votes in an even more decisive manner: Mackenzie, 59; Small, 6; Washburn, 1.[40]

With his successful re-election Mackenzie and the reformers once again went to the attack, holding meetings, circulating tracts, and gathering signatures on innumerable "petitions of grievance". The rage felt by the Tories at Mackenzie's success was almost inexpressible. The following example from the *Courier* showed something of their attitude toward their farmer enemies:

> Every wheel of their well organized political machine was set in motion to transmute county farmers into citizens of York. Accordingly, about nine in the morning, groups of tall broad-shouldered, hulking fellows were seen arriving from Whitby, Pickering, and Scarborough, some crowded in wagons, and others on horseback; and Hogg, the miller, headed a herd of the swine of Yonge Street, who made just as good votes at the meeting as the best shopkeepers in York.[41]

The Tories, however, did not stop with just harsh words against the reformers. Faced with the growing success of the reformers, the Tories began, first to threaten violence, then to resort to strong-arm tactics in order to break up the reformers' meetings. For example, when the reformers announced a meeting in York for March 23, 1832, the *Courier* threatened that if the reformers attempted "deception", they most assuredly would not ensure the leading revolutionary tools a whole skin, or a whole bone in their skins.[42] In March, an attempt was made on Mackenzie's life in Hamilton by a gang led by William J. Kerr, a Tory merchant of that city, and other meetings were disrupted by government supporters, often in the presence of government officials who did nothing to halt the attacks.[43]

In spite of the British Government's advice to the Governor, Sir John Colborne, that the Assembly had no power to keep Mackenzie out permanently, he was again expelled. In all, between 1831 and 1834, Mackenzie was expelled five times - and five times his supporters re-elected him, once when he was absent in England. The struggle against the improper explusions of Mackenzie, however, did have one important effect. For the first time men began to question whether justice could ever come about through constitutional means when the constitution was so abused by those in power. Henceforth the language of the motions passed and petitions circulated was couched in more and more radical phrases. Gradually the hint of something more dangerous than mere petitions began to appear in local discussions. A petition circulated in Whitby by the reformers in January, 1834 and signed by 159 residents demonstrated the new mood. After demanding to know why the Governor had not dismissed the officials responsible for Mackenzie's expulsions, particularly when the British Government had declared the expulsions to be illegal, the petition concluded:

> The activity and zeal displayed by these personages, in the different expulsions of the representative of this county, coupled with the oppro-

> brious language they have used towards its inhabitants, cannot be otherwise viewed by petitioners, than as rendering suspicious the sincerity of His Majesty's Government as well as of your Excellency's professed disapprobation of the measure.
>
> Loyal as the inhabitants of this county unquestionably are, your petitioners will not disguise from your Excellency, that they consider longer endurance under their present oppressions neither a virtue nor a duty. For though all mankind admit to the claims of good government to the respect and support of the governed, yet very different considerations are due to that which is regardless of public interests, wars with public inclinations and feelings, and only aids or connives at oppression.[44]

Other townships went even further. King Township, for example, refused either to nominate its township officers or to pay its taxes in 1834.[45]

The growing pessimism of the reformers concerning the intentions of the British Government, the increasing threats and acts of violence by the Tories, and the downward spiral of events in Lower Canada all worked to transform the Upper Canadian reformers from a broad and generally united movement into a number of fragments whose internal differences over strategy did much to injure their effectiveness. In spite of these difficulties, however, unity might have been preserved had not both William Lyon Mackenzie and Egerton Ryerson, the Methodist leader, gone to England in 1832. Although they left Upper Canada as allies, what they saw in England made them permanent enemies. To Ryerson's horror he discovered that the British reformers were, in his words, "infidels in religion, republicans in politics, and insincere and inconsistent in their concern for human welfare".[46] In other words, Joseph Hume and his British reform allies were primarily concerned about the material welfare of the British lower classes, rather than concentrating on their religious welfare which was Ryerson's primary interest. Indeed, when Ryerson considered that many British reformers were outright atheists, he concluded that he and the Tory Anglicans had more in common than did the Methodists and reformers.

In contrast to Ryerson's conclusions, Mackenzie had spent a good deal of time travelling through the industrial areas of Britain viewing the miserable condition of the British working class. When he visited his old home in Dundee tremendous changes had occurred in the quiet country town that he had left in his youth:

> The number of mills for spinning flax into yarn in Dundee is now very numerous. The smoke of their steam-engines darkens the face of the heavens, and many a poor and miserable boy and girl eke out a wretched existence by long and incessant toil in these ever-to-be detested establishments—the graves of morality, and the parents of vice,

> deformity, pauperism, and crime. Long may Canada be free of all such pests! Let our domestic manufacturers be those which our children can easily carry on under the eyes and in the houses and homes of their fathers and mothers.[47]

The depths of horror that Mackenzie felt at the social changes which had occurred in England, and which government policies threatened to bring about in Canada, were revealed in a long letter that he wrote for publication in the *Colonial Advocate* in January, 1833:

> As to those miserable dungeons of factories in England and America, where human nature drags out a tedious and weary existence, they shall never, with my consent, *be protected* in the Canadas. I trust it shall never fall to my lot . . . to present a petition against cruelty in making infants and young children work 14, 15 and 16 hours a day in factories in the Canadian Yorkshire, for a bare pittance, just on the borders of starvation.
>
> How well the poet expresses the feelings of young children in these dens when he puts into the mouth of the *factory girl*[48] such language as the following:—
>
> At night my mother kisses me, when she has
> combed my hair,
> And laid me in my little bed, but—I'm not
> happy there—
> I dream about the factory, the fines that
> on us wait—[49]
> I start, and ask my father if—I have not
> laid too late?
> And once I heard him sob and say "O better
> were a grave,
> Than such a life as this for thee, thou little
> sinless slave?"[50]

Mackenzie returned to Canada haunted by the memories of human degradation which he had witnessed in England. Never again could he rest as long as he saw Canada threatened by the future that had befallen his old home.

There were, however, many reformers in Upper Canada who, while they were opposed to Strachan's aristocratic Toryism, did not reject the development of capitalism as it had appeared in England and Europe. Around the banks, land companies, large merchants and the developing manufacturing establishments began to appear a new class of ambitious men intent upon building fortunes. Of course, these rising capitalists entirely rejected Mackenzie's vision of a society of egalitarian producers. Thus Peter Perry and Mackenzie clashed bitterly over Perry's support for a bill which allowed those who had speculated in Loyalist rights to realize their profits in 1836. Perry had been such a speculator and between 1835 and 1837 had acquired some 5,800 acres.[51]

Similarly, Mackenzie's bitter opposition to the expansion of the powers of the Bank of Upper Canada and the founding of new banks created a great deal of anger among many of his reform allies. For example, in 1834 when the British Government, on Mackenzie's advice, rejected a major bank act which increased the capital stock of the Bank of Upper Canada and created a new Commercial Bank for Kingston, the fury of both Tory- and Reformer-Capitalists was turned upon Mackenzie and the British Government alike. Since Robert Baldwin, William Cawthra and William Proudfoot, all leading reformers, were shareholders of the Bank of Upper Canada, it is easy to see why they objected to Mackenzie's attacks upon the power of banks. Moreover, the bill to create the People's Bank in 1836 showed John Rolph as president; James Lesslie, cashier; and Marshall Spring Bidwell and James Price, solicitors.[52] Thus Mackenzie's growing fears of capitalism, which lent such drive to his demands for reform, were not shared by many of his erstwhile allies. As a result, while James Dryden, A.M. Farewell, Peter Perry, John Warren, Joseph Gould, William Paxton and other rising businessmen-reformers of Ontario County might support Mackenzie in his attacks upon the entrenched power of Tory authority, they were far from agreeing with him when he attacked the large expenditure of public funds and provincial debt which were intended to aid the province's businessmen. R.B. Sullivan, a leading Tory, put the matter nicely:

> Mercantile men, those possessing large landed property which they wish to make productive [,] speculators in land and others interested in money transactions have naturally been most forward in urging what is called public improvement . . . and the most opposed to theoretical and organic changes for the sake of mere political abstract principle.[53]

Thus when Mackenzie, on his return from Britain, once again re-entered the struggle to bring about his society of equal, independent producers, he and his associates found themselves caught between two contradictory forces: on the one hand, there were the Tories who fought to prevent the rise of the lower classes to independence; on the other, there was the new aggressive class of bankers, great merchants, industrialists – in Mackenzie's words, the "capitalists" – who were equally opposed to the Tory aristocracy, but whose every triumph threatened the ultimate degradation of the independent producers into wage slavery. The dilemma facing the reformers who agreed with Mackenzie was, therefore, a difficult one indeed. Unfortunately for Mackenzie and his associates, the attempt to fight on both flanks at the same time so confused the issues that to most viewers the attacks on one side, then the other, began to appear both random and intemperate. This problem would ultimately destroy public confidence in Mackenzie's leadership and doom the revolt of 1837.

With Mackenzie's return from England, and with yet another re-election and expulsion, a new and more militant form of organization was undertaken, the Committees of Vigilance. These committees were established at the township level; they sent delegates to a centralized district committee, which in turn elected members to a provincial council. The fourth resolution, passed at a meeting of reformers in Whitby, January 6, 1834, spelled out their goals:

> That in order to attain this all important object [of a "judicious and careful exercise of the Elective Franchise"] alike connected with the peace and prosperity of the province, and the permanency of its institutions, we deem it essential that standing committees should be appointed in every township in the province, to watch over its interests, direct and concentrate public opinion, appoint delegates to county conventions, to aid and assist in nominating fit and proper persons as representatives, and to take all constitutional steps for securing an able, efficient, and faithful representation.[54]

To accomplish these goals a committee was established in Whitby consisting of some thirty-seven residents, including many who would have a long-time influence on local life. Among the committeemen were A.M. Farewell, Jabez Hall, James Hunter, M.D., John Ritson, William Paxton, James Dryden and Thomas Henry.[55] Similar meetings were held in other townships; for example, the Pickering delegates nominated to the county convention were Peter Mathews, Joshua Wixon, Andrew Hubbard, Joseph Wixon and John Tool,[56] while the East Gwillimbury-Whitchurch-Brock meeting nominated John Marr, James Reekie, Archibald McFadden, Webster Stevens, and Randal Wixon to represent Brock.[57]

The election of 1834 demonstrated the effectiveness of the Committees of Vigilance. Under an election act passed in 1833, Home District had been divided into four ridings, of which the third riding consisted of Scarborough, Markham, Pickering and Whitby townships, while the fourth was made up of Whitchurch, East and North Gwillimbury, Georgina, Scott, Uxbridge, Reach, Brock, Thorah and Rama.[58] All four ridings returned Reformers, York Third being represented by Dr. Thomas David Morrison of Toronto, one of the leaders of the reform party; and York Fourth, by John Mackintosh, a resident of Toronto, president of the Metropolitan District Reform Convention (as the Home District central Committee of Vigilance had called itself) and a relative by marriage of Mackenzie.[59]

The tragic history of the political deadlock, and growing frustration and bitterness of the Upper Canadian Assembly from 1834 to 1837 need not be recounted here, although the deepening anger of the reformers in the Ontario County area must be understood against that background. In spite of the reformers' domination of the Assembly from 1834 to 1836, little could be accomplished as long as the Tories and Governor used their control of the Legislative and Executive Councils to frustrate change. Moreover, the extreme partisanship of Sir Francis B. Head, the new Lieutenant-Governor sent out in 1836, convinced men like Mackenzie that no hope could be expected from the Colonial Office. With the defeat of the Reformers in the 1836 election in which Mackenzie was personally defeated (although both Morrison and Mackintosh were returned in York Third and Fourth Ridings), many who had continued to hope for peaceful constitutional change began to look to other means.

In opposition to the reformers, the Tories also began to adopt new organizational tactics as well. In particular, the introduction into Upper Canada of the Orange Order provided the more extreme elements of the Tories with both the ideological explanations and the organizational framework to justify and carry out their violent attacks on reform meetings. Thus, in spite of what the more responsible elements among the Order's leadership might do to prevent violence, after 1830 more and more of the violent political attacks which occurred were done in the name of Orangism and loyalty to Protestantism and the British Crown. As S.D. Clark concluded:

> Orange votes may have been important in influencing the results [of the 1836 election], but even more important was Orange intimidation of voters who were wavering in their sympathies or who had shown partiality for the reform cause. Something approaching gangsterism was introduced into the politics of Upper Canada, and mob violence came increasingly to be relied upon in the two years before the rebellion as a means of suppressing efforts to secure by free and open discussion a solution of public questions.[60]

While British authorities were unanimous in viewing the Order as being dangerous to public peace,[61] local officialdom was inclined to shut its eyes to their activities. As John Elliot reported to Lord Durham,

> The members of this dangerous Confederacy have always been found first and foremost (encouraged and led on by the Magistracy) in creating violent disturbances.[62]

and, as Sir George Arthur reported of one reform meeting, "The Irish Orangemen attacked them furiously and put an end to the affair without any loss of Life, but with many broken heads."[63]

In response to the growing violence of the Tory and Orange Order attacks, Mackenzie proposed that the reformers arm themselves in order to protect their lives and political liberties. While there can be little doubt that Mackenzie envisioned that the arms might be used for more than defence, it is equally clear that many reformers who armed themselves genuinely feared for their lives. For example, at a joint meeting of political unions No. I of Uxbridge and No. II of the northeast and southwest corners of Pickering and Markham, held on November 11, 1837, the members proposed that they should meet once a month to "discuss and take into consideration the state of our country, which now stands like a girded tree in the beautiful continent of North America", then, to protect their meetings, they decided on the following arrangement:

> Resolved. That every man in this township who has not got a good rifle, do forthwith prepare himself with one, as we do intend to maintain our political rights inviolate, let the consequences be what they will. We know our cause is a great and honest one, and we will have one who is stronger than man to go with us; therefore brother reformers, be encouraged, be true to each other, and be united, as union is strength.[64]

Thus, as S.D. Clark observed, the violence and aggressiveness of the Orangemen did much to bring about the conditions for the rebellion which they claimed they intended to prevent.[65] On the other hand, the constant discussion of guns, and the violent clashes, caused many supporters of reform to abandon the reform movement in the hope that in spite of a decade of disappointment, the British Government might yet intervene with reforms to prevent the coming bloodshed.[66]

The revolt of 1837, in many ways was an anti-climax considering the almost classic escalation of repression and resistance, violence and counter-violence which had been developing. Premature in every way, badly conceived, and poorly led, it has taken on almost comic opera proportions in Canadian history. For those involved, however, there was nothing comic about either the grievances and injuries they had suffered under the rule of the Family Compact or the price they would pay for their attempts to bring about change, first through peaceful, constitutional methods, then through revolt.

The year 1837 was one in which disaster followed disaster. First, Lord John Russell, the Colonial Secretary, announced on March 2, 1837 that no more concessions would be made to the Lower Canadian Reformers, and he allowed the Governor to take funds from the provincial treasury without a vote by the Assembly. For Upper Canadian reformers locked in a similar struggle against the Government the lesson was clear – no hope for reform from England could be expected. Canada was not merely a more distant part of Mother England, but a colony in the worst sense of the word. As Mackenzie said in denouncing Russell's rejection of reform, the situation was one "more suitable for the Meridian of Russia in its dealing with Poland".[67]

Equally important in the developing situation was the collapse of the economy in the fall of 1836 and spring of 1837. Farmers who had undertaken large mortgages in the boom years of 1833-34 were now caught in a desperate squeeze as prices fell and loans dried up. Banks suspended specie payments both in the United States and Lower Canada, and only the calling of a special session of the Upper Canadian Assembly prevented the Upper Canadian banks from following suit.[68] Here was proof, indeed, to many that Mackenzie's attacks on currency speculation and heavy provincial debts were justified. The Bank of Upper Canada bore the full venom of Mackenzie's attack: this bank, he said, had

> controlled our elections, corrupted our representatives, depreciated our currency, obliged even Governors and Colonial Ministers to bow to its mandates, insulted the legislature, expelled representatives, fattened a host of greedy and needy lawyers, tempted the farmer to leave his money with it instead of lending it to his worthy neighbour, shoved government through its hands, sent many thousands of hard cash to foreign lands as bank dividends, taxed the farmers and traders at £18,000 a year for the use of its paper, and supported every judicial villainy and oppression with which our country has been afflicted.[69]

It is not surprising, therefore, that farmers, who were feeling the threats of foreclosure, resented the support that the Government was giving to the bank while ignoring their economic difficulties.

The Mackenzie plan to create a new republic in North America began to unfold in July, 1837, when he offered for approval of his fellow Toronto reformers his "Declaration of the Reformers of the City of Toronto to their Fellow-Reformers of Upper Canada". The Declaration was a frankly republican document which called upon all reformers to demand their rights, and to seek common cause with Louis Joseph Papineau and the Lower Canadian French in their common struggle against British tyranny.[70]

The huge campaign of meetings which he launched to discuss the Declaration was marked, first, by attacks by Tories and Orangemen, and then by an increasing militancy on the part of the reformers. As Mackenzie extended his tour first through the West Ridings, then through Brock, Pickering, Whitby, Uxbridge, Markham and the other East Riding Townships, the increased tendency of reformers to appear bearing rifles drew his enthusiastic approval:

> A meeting in Vaughan lately numbered 150 fine fellows. The taste for manly exercises increases greatly and military manoeuvres are all the rage. In a meeting last Saturday in York Township, we counted 183 rifles, and perhaps the best marksmen in Canada.[71]

At the meetings Mackenzie adapted his program according to the degree of sympathy displayed by his audiences. Where he found favourable conditions, he would go so far as to advocate peaceful separation from Great Britain, often suggesting that a money payment might be considered to cover Britain's loss.[72] The meetings, however, provided a cover for more serious business – the recruitment of those who promised to bear arms under Mackenzie's leadership. By the beginning of November, 1837, some 1,500 men were enrolled across the province who were ready to take up arms on one hour's notice, if arms could be found for them.[73]

Mackenzie's secret military organization did not, however, coincide with the public "Committees of Vigilance". While many men belonged to both organizations, care was taken to maintain both a public legal "front" organization, and the illegal military body. As Mackenzie explained the situation:

> Some of the members of our brand societies were kept in ignorance of the intended revolt–Others were fully aware of it. Some whose names were attached to no association were leaders in the revolution–other very active republicans took no part.[74]

The actual call to rebellion was decided upon in late November. Mackenzie explained the plan as follows:

> About the third week in November it was determined that on Thursday the 7th of December, our forces should secretly assemble at Montgomery's Hotel . . . and proceed from thence to the city, join our friends, there, seize 4,000 stand of arms, take [Sir Francis Bond Head] into custody with his chief advisors, place the garrison in the hands of the liberals, declare the province free, call a constitution, and meantime appoint our friend Dr. Rolph, provisional administrator of the province.[75]

When Dr. John Rolph sent out the call to rebellion (changing the planned date from the seventh to the fourth) the reformers of the Ontario County area responded in a variety of ways. Although it had always been expected that the Yonge Street reformers of King, Whitchurch, and East and West Gwillimbury would make up the majority of Mackenzie's forces, strong contingents from Pickering, Brock and Uxbridge also took part. In particular, the reformers of Pickering led by Peter Matthews, Landon Wurtz and George Barclay played an active part.

The Pickering cotingent had been among the first to arrive at Montgomery's Tavern on Yonge Street when the call went out, and it shared in the general confusion and uncertainty of the first two days. On December seventh, it was decided that a diversionary feint should be made in hopes that the impending government attack on Montgomery's Tavern would be delayed until reinforcements for the rebels would arrive. To accomplish this end about sixty men, under the leadership of Peter Matthews, were sent eastward to burn the Don bridge and to intercept the Monteal mail.

The march to the bridge was accomplished without incident, and, according to plan, Matthews and his forces crossed the bridge shortly after noon and advanced some distance along King Street into the city. Soon, however, a detachment of militia under George P. Ridout was sent out from city hall, and the Pickering contingent retreated. When the rebels attempted to burn the bridge, however, it refused to catch fire, although a nearby tavern and stables were destroyed. Meanwhile shots were fired on both sides without much effect, although the hostler of the tavern was killed, apparently by the militia bullets. Early in the afternoon, the disastrous events of Montgomery's Tavern were learned by Matthews and his men, who then abandoned the fight at the Don bridge and scattered in various directions to avoid arrest. Matthews and several of his neighbours hid in the Rosedale ravines until Saturday night, then walked north into East York township where they intended to spend the night at the house of John Duncan, a sympathiser.[76] There they were captured.

When the call to the rebellion reached Randal Wixon in Brock on December 4, he, Joel Wixon and John Marr quickly rounded up their fellow conspirators and slipped away through Uxbridge on their way to the rally at Montgomery's.[77] In Uxbridge they gathered with Bartholemew Plank, Robert Taylor and Philip Wideman to persuade Joseph Gould to join them in their fight for liberty. As Gould remembered the events:

> On the same day that the attack was to be made [December 4th] I found myself surrounded by about fifty of my friends from Brock, Scott and Uxbridge, who insisted upon my going with them. They refused to give heed to my remonstrances. They claimed that I should be manifesting a great deal of cowardice if I did not go with them after all I had said about the abuses we had complained of and from which the country was suffering. I therefore went with them. They were determined to go, and there was nothing else left for me, but to take my place amongst them.[78]

When the men from Brock, Scott and Uxbridge reached Montgomery's, they found not the disciplined, confident force which they had expected to join, but a chaotic situation where nothing had been planned and all was in confusion as to what to do next. Joseph Gould was particularly angry at what he found:

> We arrived that evening at Montgomery's hotel, which was Mackenzie's headquarters, two miles north of the city. . . . I found that there was no order or discipline; that there had been no picket-guards put out, and that the whole party was liable to be surprised at any moment, and that probably before morning they would be surrounded and cut off. Tired as I was, after our long march, I determined to set pickets at once. This I did, and had the guard relieved until morning.[79]

In spite of Gould's preparations, little could be done to save an impossible situation. The element of surprise had been lost by Rolph's premature call to arms, and the militia and Orange units quickly rallied to the defence of the capital. When the government forces attacked the rebel headquarters at Montgomery's Tavern, resistance quickly collapsed. Joseph Gould remembered his experiences as follows:

> Next morning [December 7] they sent Captain Matthews with a few men (my brother Joel was one), to make a feint attack on Toronto, by

> way of the Don Bridge, on the east side, while the main body was to make the attack on the north. But we had not got fairly organized when a messenger was sent to us from Toronto to say that the troops were marching up Yonge Street to attack us at Montgomery's. We soon got under arms and started down Yonge Street to meet them. The troops, however, turned to the west, and made as though they wanted to get round the west side to our rear. We hastened through the woods, climbing over dead hemlock trees and through the underbrush, and rushed to head them off. We had no arms but our rifles, and some had only rude pikes and pitchforks. The troops, beside their muskets and plenty of ammunition, had two small field pieces—one controlled by a friend of ours, and the other by an enemy. The friend fired grape shot, and fired over us into the tops of trees, cutting off the dead and dry limbs of the hemlocks, which falling thickly amongst us scared the boys as much as if cannon balls had been rattling around us. The other gun was fired low and so *careless* that I did not like it. One of the balls struck a sandbank by my feet and filled my eyes with sand, nearly blinding me. Another struck one of those dry hemlocks, scattering the bark and splinters about, and into my face. Captain Wideman was killed on my left side, and F. Shell was shot through the shoulder, to the left of the fallen captain. But we got to the west of the troops. They then turned and crossed to Yonge Street behind us. It was soon known that Montgomery's hotel was on fire and that the day was lost.[80]

Gould and several of his fellow rebels were now trapped to the west of Yonge Street and decided to get to the United States if possible. They penetrated deep into the woods and stopped for the night, but were surrounded and captured there.

Meanwhile, in the Ontario County area, the air was filled with rumours and alarms. According to those bearing the news, the Government had decided to unleash both the Orangemen and Indians to pillage the towns. Cooksville was reported burned, and Indians were said to have swept down from Lake Simcoe and attacked either Mariposa or Brock.[81]

Led by Doctor Hunter (who had broken off political relations with Mackenzie about three months earlier[82]) about 150 residents of Whitby met and formed defence units in order to protect their families against the expected attacks. Similar preparations were made in Reach, where at an open meeting the residents unanimously passed a resolution proclaiming their neutrality in the conflict.[83]

In Brock, the "defence" of the township was led by Joseph Thompson. His diary clearly illustrates the state of mind and uncertainty which the population experienced as they waited for news of the situation in Toronto:

> [December] 7. This morning while at breakfast M. Cowan came in breathless to tell us that Lieut. Gibbs had just arrived with orders for

> all persons to proceed to Newmarket to join with a party going to Toronto—that the Governor was taken prisoner together with the garrison. . . .
>
> Arranged with Gibbs that a public Meeting of the Inhabitants sh'd be held the next morning for adopting measures to protect property & preserve peace. . . .
>
> 8. This morning there was a meeting of about 40 persons at our house, who after some discussions, concurred in the propriety of forming a Society to protect property & preserve the peace & signed a Document agreeing thereto. . . .
>
> One report is that 5,000 Americans from the U.S. have come over & assisted in the capture of Toronto.
>
> One affirms that only 7 lives have been lost—another that there are heaps of slain. . . .
>
> In the night two persons brought word to Cowan's that Toronto was not taken, with some other information. They fired a gun on reaching the House, and were nearly fired at in return by Cowan Sen'r.[84]

In spite of the preparations and the news that the rising had been put down, there continued to be rumours of Indian attacks and massacres for the next week.

The most serious problem that faced the Brock society, however, was the activities of the local Orangemen. As Thompson reported the events:

> 13. While winnowing here this morning K. McCaskill & I. McKay came & informed me that they brought unpleasant news—that a mob of orangemen were going about threatening to burn down the houses of such persons as they chose to visit—carrying away fire arms etc.
>
> Mr. McKay stated that they had been to his house & ransacked every thing and refused to shew any authority for what they did.
>
> From these representations we concluded that they must be acting illegally and that the Society for protecting property etc. ought to be summoned.[85]

After investigation, it was discovered that warrants had been issued to search certain houses, but that the Orangemen had decided not to show them in order to heighten the local tension and to terrorize their political enemies. After almost two weeks of constant excitement, things quieted somewhat and local life returned to close to normal.

For the rebels, however, life would not return to normal for a long time – and in some cases, would result in their jailing, exile or execution. As soon as the rebels had been routed at Montgomery's Tavern, a number were arrested and sent to Toronto where they were confined in the jail, court house and even the parliament buildings. Included in the group first arrested were Joseph Gould and Philip Widemen of Uxbridge. Many escaped, however, and when later on the same day, the Lieutenant-Governor issued a proclamation offering a free pardon to all those not guilty of murder or arson, most returned to their homes. In spite of Governor Head's promise, many officers and local "Loyalist" groups continued to arrest individuals whom they suspected of involvement in the rising. On the tenth a somewhat tougher stance was taken by the Government, and the order went out that no one was to be released that had been arrested on suspicion. This order was again changed on the fourteenth, however, when accommodations for prisoners became too crowded. Henceforth, it was ordered, arrests should be made only by militia officers upon warrants issued by the civil magistrates.[86]

The vast majority of those arrested in Ontario County were taken during the period of chaos before the December 14 proclamation was passed, although arrests continued on a more orderly basis for another month. Because of the great number of arrests and few magistrates, a special commission was set up on December 11 to examine all those arrested in order to determine who from among those arrested should be held for trial. In spite of the examinations of the special commissioners, many of those arrested as the result of personal enmity (for example Doctor James Hunter had been arrested because a personal enemy, James Fewster, had attempted to get even for an unpaid debt[87]) lingered in jail for months waiting for trial. As the Upper Canadian Solicitor-General reported, "I regret to say that many prisoners have been confined on charges as indifferently supported by evidence as to make it appear a hardship that they have not been much sooner released".[88]

In spite of the failure of their expedition, and the punishment which was sure to follow, most of the leaders who had been arrested continued to assert the rightness of their cause. For example, when Joseph Gould was examined by the commissioners, Robert S. Jameson, Jonas Jones, George Gurnett, Robert B. Sullivan and William B. Robinson, he replied to Jameson's questioning as follows:

> Jamieson [sic] asked me where I lived. I told him I lived at Uxbridge. "What do you do for a living?" he asked. I told him I had a sawmill. "A sawmill!" he exclaimed, as if that was a strong reason why I should not be there. "Yes, and a small farm, too," I added. "What! a farm and a sawmill! What more do you want?"—was his next remark. "What more do you want that you should rebel?" he continued. "I want my political rights," I answered. "Why," said he, "you have got them now—quite enough for so young a man as you are." I then had all our political grievances at the tip of my tongue, and began a rehearsal of the most prominent of them, when he stopped me.
>
> After a pause he asked, "Do you believe all these complaints?"
>
> I answered that the evidence was plain enough, and that the way the government of the country was administered was quite enough to show that, and that the people were denied their rights.
>
> He then turned on his heel, and told me—"You are a dangerous

> fellow and you ought to be hung for believing and for spreading your treason."
>
> I could only reply—"I am in your power, you can act your pleasure. I am neither afraid nor ashamed to express my sentiments."[89]

With the arrest of so many prisoners charged with high treason,[90] a crime which carried a mandatory death sentence if proven, the British authorities were faced with a difficult problem. With their enemies at last delivered into their hands, the Tories were determined to exact the last drop of their revenge. The *Patriot*, the leading Tory paper, for example, called for the most violent measures against all insurgents.[91] With so many involved, however, and the widespread public sympathy for their goals, if not their means, the Government soon concluded that too drastic an action would lead inevitably to a disastrous reaction. Thus a policy was evolved which was designed to strike terror into the hearts of anyone who dared to assume a leadership role, while at the same time dividing the general populace from them through a general amnesty. In Lieutenant-Governor Sir George Arthur's words:

> It was my opinion . . . from the time of my arrival in this Province that it was not necessary to make many examples either in the way of capital punishment or otherwise in proceeding against criminals where large numbers are in the nature of the offence concerned. The ends of justice I think are best advanced by the punishment of a few, with comparative severity, sufficient to mark the sense entertained by the government of the heinousness of the offence, and by mercy and complete indemnity towards all others.[92]

To provide an example for other would-be leaders of political opposition, the Government chose Samuel Lount, a blacksmith from Holland Landing, and Peter Matthews, a farmer from Pickering,[93] to stand trial for treason.

Because there was no doubt that from a legal and technical sense both Lount and Matthews were guilty as charged, their lawyer, Robert Baldwin, advised them to plead guilty and to ask for clemency on the grounds that they had been encouraged to act as they had by the oppressive political circumstances of the time.

As candidates for mercy, both Lount and Matthews had much to recommend them. Samuel Lount was a prosperous businessman and farmer, the father of a large family of young children and the elected representative of Simcoe County from 1834 to 1836. Peter Matthews was

> A jolly, hale, cheerful, cherry-cheeked farmer of Pickering, who lived on his own land, cultivated his own estate, and was the father of fifteen children . . . Capt. M. had fought bravely for the King of England in the war of 1813, was a man of unstained reputation, well beloved by his neighbors, unassuming, modest in his deportment, a baptist, unfriendly to high church ascendancy.[94]

In all likelihood, it was the high regard held by the rebels for Lount and Matthews which had determined their choice. Matthews, in particular, had borne up well under the harsh conditions of his imprisonment and remained firm in his belief in the rightness of his cause until his death. As Charles Durand said of him:

> Matthews always bore up in spirits well. He was, until death, firm in his opinion of the justice of the cause he had espoused. He never recanted. He was ironed and kept in the darkest cell in the prison like a murderer. He slept sometimes in blankets that were wet and frozen. He had nothing to cheer him but the approbation of his companions and his conscience.[95]

On March 29 the sentence was passed. The Chief Justice, J.B. Robinson, delivered a long and impressive speech, in which he dwelt upon the heinous nature of the crime of rebellion. The sentence was delivered: death to both men. The date of execution was set for April 12.

Throughout the province a wave of shock and horror followed the sentence. Petitions bearing thousands of names were circulated, signed and presented to the Governor – but to no avail. Examples were needed to impress the disaffected of the gravity of rebellion, so examples were to be made. When the newly-arrived Governor, Sir George Arthur, requested the opinion of his Executive Council, their answer was clear and to the point:

> The Council are of opinion that the cases in question are of great urgency; that severe public example is actually required in some instances; and that the crimes which these prisoners are shown to have incited, abetted and countenanced the committal of, in addition to the crime of high treason, point them out as particularly fit to be selected for capital punishment.[96]

At eight o'clock on April 12, the stage for the public execution was readied, and a huge crowd gathered to witness the spectacle. The two condemned men, each accompanied by a minister, mounted the scaffold firmly, betraying neither fear nor regret. General Edward Theller, one of the rebel leaders left this account of the scene:

> Lount . . . appeared firm and perfectly prepared for his doom. . . . We saw him and Matthews walk out with the white cap on their heads and their arms pinioned, preceded by the sheriff and his deputy dressed in the official robes and with drawn swords, followed by two clergymen and a few of our prison guard. . . . Lount looked up and bowed to us; then kneeling upon the trap underneath one of the nooses, the cord was placed about their necks by the executioner, and the cap pulled over their faces. One of the clergymen, Mr. Richardson, made a prayer, the signal was given by the sheriff, and in an instant these two heroic souls, the first martyrs to Canadian liberty, were ushered into eternity.[97]

The trials did not, of course, end with the deaths of Lount and Matthews. The remaining Home District rebels who, in the opinion of the special commissioners, were deserving of punishment were divided into three classes based upon such points as actual participation in the criminal acts which had accompanied the rising, their moral character, and the extent of their hostility to British Government. The first group, numbering twenty-two, were to be transported to Van Dieman's Land (Australia) for life; a second group of thirty-two were to be transported for shorter periods or to be merely banished from the province; and a third group of ten were to be sentenced to penitentiary. All were to lose their property. A last group of fifty-five it was thought fit to pardon on condition of giving security of good behaviour. Although later a number of changes made in the actual numbers of prisoners to be placed in each class, this pattern was retained.[98]

The most severe sentences handed out to residents of the Ontario County area were received by John Marr and Randall Wixon of Brock who were sentenced to transportation to the penal colony in Van Dieman's Land. Marr, however, escaped from the Kingston jail and fled to the United States. Joel Wixon of Brock was banished from the province, while George Barclay of Pickering was sentenced to three years in penitentiary and then banishment. Finally, a large group which included Michael Corrigan, Andrew Hill, Arthur Kelly, Joseph McGrath and Solomon Sly of Brock; Joseph Gould, Bartholomew Plank, Robert Taylor and Philip Wideman of Uxbridge; and Russell Baker, Joseph Matthews and Townsend Wixon of Pickering, were found guilty of treason, but pardoned and freed upon giving security to keep the peace and to be of good behaviour for three years. By the end of May, 1838 most of the prisoners released upon giving security had returned home.[99]

The persecution of those who had rebelled or who had stayed neutral in the crisis did not end with the sentences. For a considerable time tavern licences were refused to suspected sympathisers and neutrals, postmasters were dismissed, and many citizens were refused jury duty because of government suspicions.[100] The result of this continued harassment was that many old settlers decided to sell their farms and move to the United States. This move was encouraged by American papers such as the Cincinnati *News* which editorialized:

> Emigrate ye Canadians. If England will not treat you with decency, shake the dust from your feet, cross the border and build up a home where tyranny does not dare show its head.[101]

So anxious were some to sell that William Gordon, a Scottish immigrant, was able to buy one of the finest farms in Whitby (the site of the Ontario Hospital) for £400, a sum less than half its true value.[102]

More serious, from the Government's point of view, was the continued anger among the populace. Even in areas such as Whitby where no one had taken part in the rebellion, the harshness of government repression, the execution of Matthews, and the severity of the reprisals taken against the reformers had led to an open hostility on the part of many previously loyal citizens. Indeed, a kind of underground warfare of individual reprisals was begun which caused the Government to fear that a second rising might occur. The climate of opinion in Whitby was revealed in a letter to Sir George Arthur:

> The people of known Loyalty are annoyed in various petty ways, by injury to their property, such as pulling down small Huts, Offices, Gates, Fences, etc. . . .
>
> The Magistrates are averse (tho' instigated by me to do so) to take any Active Measure to repress this Conduct, fearful that they themselves may be sufferers.[103]

That Governor Colborne's opinion of the depth of disaffection was shared by many of the citizens of Ontario County was made clear in a letter to Arthur:

> With reference to your suggestion of stationing a detachment of militia, at Whitby, I have no doubt from the character of a portion of the Settlers of Whitby, Reach and Pickering, that those Townships should be closely watched; . . . If the Americans disembark at any point between Port Hope and the Highlands [Scarborough Bluffs] the invasion would be made, in expectations of being joined by a large proportion of the Townships.[104]

This reputation for unrest would long remain part of the Ontario County tradition. Indeed, for decades to come none but reformers could expect election in the area, while charges of republicanism against the local inhabitants and their leaders were constantly made. The rebellion experience and its aftermath left a deep impression on all who lived through it.

The tragic irony of the whole affair was that within a decade, as England's interest in retaining an iron grasp on her colonies diminished, all those things which had been refused to the Reformers through all those years of bitter struggle were now granted, not because of a new generosity on the part of the British Government, but from its indifference. With the granting of Responsible Government, the Tories were swept aside and a new political order established. But the twin rebellions of Upper and Lower Canada had not been entirely in vain. Lord Durham's Report opened the way for many local reforms, such as elected municipal government, whose benefits would be realized long before Responsible Government would be granted.

Although the Upper Canadian rebellion had been crushed and its leadership scattered, the ideals which had spurred the farmers and small holders of Home District to take up arms remained. The vision of an egalitarian society composed of independent producers of wealth and those who rendered them "beneficial aid" lived on. It would reappear again and again for more than a century. But as Mackenzie had feared, while it ultimately would see the defeat of its oldest enemy, the aristocratic Toryism of Bishop Strachan, it would fall prey to that new, rising class of entrepreneurs whose version of "progress" was the accumulation of capital and the employment of men.

MERCANTILE DEVELOPMENT: VILLAGES AND ROADS, 1840-51

In spite of the severe depression of the late eighteen-thirties and its attendant political and social disruption, Ontario County continued to develop at a rapid rate. Indeed, so rapid was the growth of the area between 1840 and 1850 that by the mid-century, for most areas, the pioneer period had been left behind. Even in the more remote regions settlement had taken place and the development of a good system of transportation and commercial agriculture had begun. With the rapid expansion of agriculture and the improvement of roads, old villages expanded and new villages sprang up. By 1850, Ontario County had begun to take on its modern face.

In the eleven years from 1840 to 1851 Ontario County's population grew from 12,015 to 29,571. In the northern areas the increase was particularly dramatic: Reach's population grew by over 400% from 771 to 3,897, while Scott, Uxbridge and the other northern townships grew at similar rates. As Table XV shows, 1851 was the peak of population growth. While population continued to grow after that date, it did so at much slower rates. Indeed, after 1861 population growth slowed almost to a standstill. Between 1861 and 1871 a decline in the rural population of the southern townships had begun. Only in the northern areas and the towns of Whitby and Oshawa did growth continue, but at a very slow rate.

Table XV
Ontario County: Population by Municipality, 1840–51[1]

	1840	*1851*
Whitby Township	5,013	7,996
Oshawa	—	1,142
Total Whitby	5,013	9,138
Pickering	3,450	6,737
Reach	771	3,897
Brock	1,330	3,518
Uxbridge	708 (Uxbridge and Scott)	2,289
Scott		1,028
Thorah	514	1,146
Mara	215	1,403 (Mara and Rama)
Rama	14	
Scugog	—	415
	12,015	29,571

The growth in population in the 1840-51 period fundamentally altered the composition of the area's society. Because many of the original American settlers died during this decade, and because the great majority of new settlers were natives of the British Isles (particularly England and Ireland), the British-born portion of the population rose from 25.4% in 1842 to 39.2% in 1851. During the same period the proportion of American-born residents declined from 12.1 to 4.1%.[2] With the influx of immigrants, land soon became scarce in the more settled areas, and the newcomers were forced to take land in neglected areas such as Scott and Rama Townships. One result of the growing scarcity of land was that Scugog Island, hitherto bypassed because of the difficulty of access, began to attract settlers.

In the early days there was no large lake surrounding the ridge which today is Scugog Island. Rather, there was a shallow meandering stream which drained a large swampy area; the south end was covered by a fine tamarack forest.[3] For a very long time, so little was known of the area that it was supposed that the Scugog area was part of the western limits of Rice Lake. In the wave of land granting which had swept Reach township in 1811 and 1812, the present-day lake bed was all patented by Loyalist and military claimants. The major portions of the island, which lay in Cartwright Township, was surveyed in 1816 by Major Wilmot. Because of the slow rate of settlement immediately after the War of 1812 and the difficulty of access, much of the Cartwright land was left unpatented for a long time.

The lake itself was created as the result of the building of a dam across the Scugog River at Lindsay. In 1837 William Purdy petitioned the Lieutenant-

Governor, Sir Francis Head, for the right to build a dam at Lindsay which would flood much of the land above the site. In his petition Purdy stated:

> Your petitioner is apprehensive that unless some order of your Excellency is made, some of the lands necessarily overflowed by your petitioner's mill-dam may be granted unconditionally [to settlers] . . . which would . . . prevent your petitioner from using his mill.[4]

Unfortunately, most of these lands had already been granted to absentee owners many years before. In spite of this fact, Purdy and his brother Hassard went ahead and built their dam, raising the water of the lake by four feet and flooding thousands of acres of privately owned land.

Not unexpectedly the owners of the flooded land objected to the dam, and over the years exhausted every legal means of getting it removed. But the grant to the Purdy brothers was perfectly legal and their opposition failed. Allied with the Purdys in this dispute were the leading merchants and millers of Port Perry and the lumbermen of Victory County who benefited by the improved navigation: the higher water levels allowed steamboat navigation and the floating of rafts on the inland waterway. In spite of innumerable petitions, the contest was an unequal one when farmers opposed businessmen and the government refused to intervene. The dam remained and Scugog Lake became a permanent feature of the landscape.[5]

In the early days of settlement in Ontario County, Scugog Island had been a favourite winter camping ground and meeting place of the Mississauga Indians. Before the War of 1812 the Farewell brothers of Oshawa traded in the area, and the first Methodist missionary efforts to the Mississaugas in Ontario County were made there. With the gradual depletion of game, however, the local Indians settled farther north in the 1830s and did not return until their present reservation was purchased for them in 1843.[6]

The actual date and name of the first settler on Scugog Island is in dispute. It would appear, however, that the first permanent white resident was Joseph Graxton, who arrived in 1834.[7] Large-scale settlement did not occur until after 1840. Among new settlers were Charles Nesbitt, Joseph Reader (and his six sons), Grosvener Pickle, Stephen Scoville, Joseph and John Thompson, the Rodmens, Robert Walker, E. and J.W. Gamble, Will Mossworth, Henry Cole and William and Sarah Ann Burr.[8] The spread of settlement on the Island did not, however, solve the main problem which faced the first settlers – the lack of easy access to markets and the necessity of a municipal government which would be aware of their problems and concerned about their needs. More than a decade would pass before solutions to these problems were undertaken.

While those settlers who were attempting to farm Scugog Island would continue to face grave problems in reaching markets and clearing their lands, farmers in other areas of Ontario County rapidly improved their position between 1840 and 1851. As Table XVI shows, not only did the total acreage occupied by farmers greatly increase, but more important, the proportion of that acreage which was under cultivation greatly increased as well. Again, just as with population, agricultural development was greatest in the northern areas, although even Pickering's area under actual occupation by farmers doubled from 32,447 acres to 64,160 acres by 1851.

Table XVI
Acreage Occupied and Under Cultivation in Ontario County, 1840–51[9]

	Acres Occupied		*Acres Cultivated*		*Percent Cutivated*	
	1840	*1851*	*1840*	*1851*	*1840*	*1851*
Whitby	33,623	61,154	23,371	40,312	69.5	65.9
Pickering	32,447	64,160	15,501	38,772	47.8	60.4
Uxbridge	7,913	25,983	2,456	8,980	31.0	34.6
Reach	12,759	42,812	2,618	18,231	20.5	42.6
Brock	25,802	49,416	5,777	17,604	22.4	35.6
Thorah	12,164	16,436	1,814	4,846	14.9	29.5
Mara	4,660	18,434 (Mara and Rama)	488	3,645 (Mara and Rama)	10.5	19.8 (Mara and Rama)
Rama	2,007		85		4.2	
Scugog	—	5,369	—	1,195	—	22.3
Scott	2,606	17,964	239	4,768	9.2	26.5
Oshawa	—	1,533	—	1,060	—	69.1

With the rapid increase in settlement in Ontario County came both a period of growth and prosperity for the old market and manufacturing centres and the appearance of new villages around the main crossroads in the northern areas. Throughout Reach, Brock, Uxbridge and the other northern townships, taverns, merchant shops, blacksmithing establishments and the first small service industries began to appear. Soon churches, meeting houses and schools

Table XVII
Exports from Whitby (Windsor) Harbour, 1843–50[10]

Article	*Measure*	*1843*	*1844*	*1850*
Lumber	feet	353,500	646,000	1,745,000
Flour	barrels	28,562	21,597	35,337
Wheat	bushels	29,674	14,563	107,101
Pork	barrels	1,656	1,435	63
Oatmeal	barrels	860	285	83
Ashes	barrels	1,064	610	549
Oats	bushels	6,684	1,682	5,466
Peas	bushels	1,000	290	84
Potatoes	bushels	140	1,240	50

were built as the previously backward areas began to take on the appearance of prosperous farming communities.

The increased population of the northern areas greatly benefited the two well-established towns of Whitby and Oshawa which had a monopoly of the trade in the area. Because of its good harbour and customs office, Whitby became the centre of the export trade to the American market. Table XVII shows the rapid growth in exports from Whitby harbour of lumber, wheat and flour between 1843 and 1850. By 1850, moreover, the exports were no longer restricted to the basic staples of lumber and farm produce. In 1850 the exports included 1,200 cords of cordwood, 17,700 pipe staves, 457,210 West India staves, 210,000 cases of shingles, and 52 cases of panel doors.[11] Indeed, in 1851 Whitby ranked third among lake ports in exports to the United States. Only Kingston, which exported goods valued at £421,016, and Toronto with £327,368, exceeded the Whitby total of £201,164. Behind Whitby came Port Credit with £181,268; Belleville, £147,368; Oakville, £122,880; and Port Hope, £100,408.[12] In contrast, the import trade was funneled through the commercial houses centred in Toronto and Kingston. Whereas Whitby ranked eighth with £26,456, Toronto imported goods valued at £1,525,620 and Kingston imported £743,232 worth.[13]

The contrasting descriptions given of Whitby by W.H. Smith illustrate the rapid growth of the village. In 1844, "Windsor" was described as:

> A Village in the township of Whitby, situated on the eastern road, two miles from Windsor Bay, and about thirty-one from Toronto. The plank road from the bay to Skugog Lake passes through the village. There is a Congregational Church in the village.
>
> Population about 500.
>
> Post office, post every day.
>
> *Professions and Trades.*—Two physicians and surgeons, two lawyers, eight stores, two druggists, one bookseller and stationer, three taverns, one watchmaker, one ashery, one brewery, three saddlers, two cabinet makers, one chair maker, one fanning mill maker, two waggon makers, one tinsmith, one baker, three blacksmiths, four shoemakers, four tailors.[14]

Similarly, Smith described "Windsor Harbour" as:

> A Village and shipping place in the township of Whitby. . . . An excellent harbour has been formed here, by constructing a breakwater and building two piers; within the breakwater is enclosed a basin of about 120 acres in extent. . . .
>
> The Steamboat "America" (a British boat) calls here daily, on her passage to and from Rochester and Toronto. Seven schooners, whose collective tonnage amounts to about 400 tons, are owned here. . . . There are two churches in the village, Episcopal (built of stone), and Methodist.

The Brick Mill, Brooklin

Whitby Historical Society

Gibbs Brothers' Mill, South Oshawa

Public Archives of Ontario

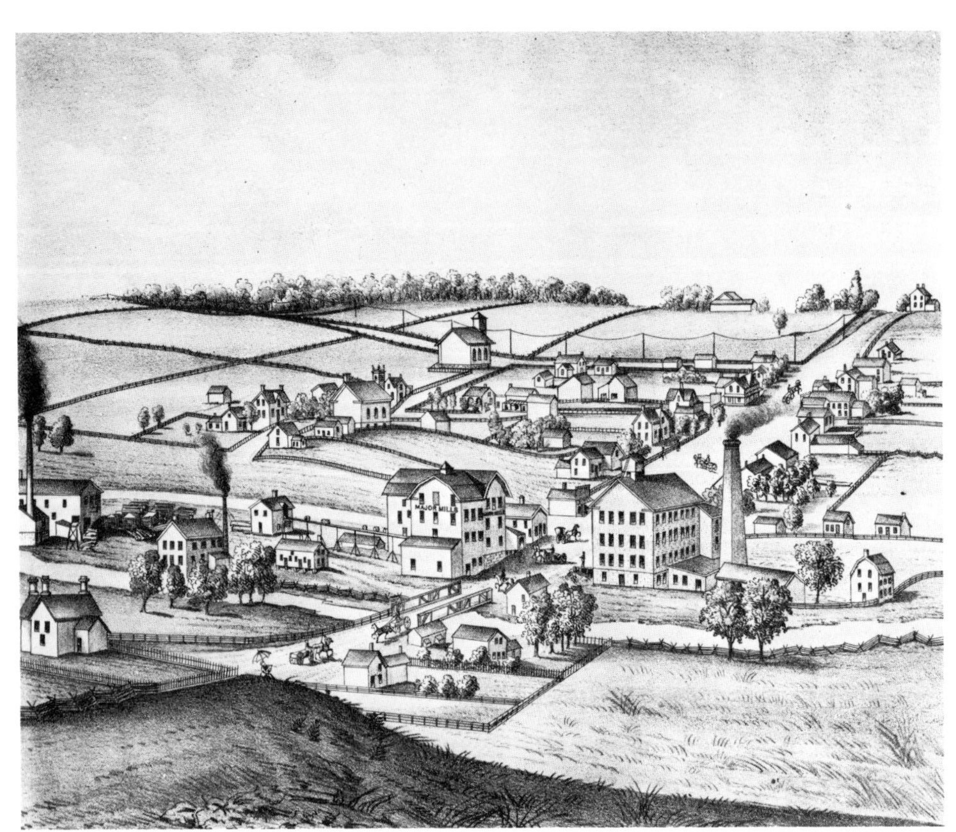

Whitevale, Pickering Township, c. 1860 *Public Archives of Ontario*

> Population about 250.
> *Professions and Trades.*—One brewery, three stores, four taverns, one saddler, two blacksmiths, two shoemakers, two tailors, one wheelwright, one baker, one ship carpenter.[15]

Between 1844 and 1850, not only had Whitby grown, but it had changed its name as well. Smith described the village in 1850 as follows:

> This village was formerly called Windsor, and the settlement on the shore of Big Bay was known as Windsor Bay and Windsor Harbour. In consequence of the frequency of mistakes from the name, and in order to distinguish it from Windsor in the Western District, an Act of Parliament was obtained, changing the name to Whitby; the village at the bay was included in the limits assigned to it, and it is now known as Port Whitby. Whitby or Windsor, however, has been long known as "Perry's Corners," so called after an old and enterprising settler, Mr. Peter Perry; and this name it continues to hold with a large majority of the old settlers in the neighbourhood. . . .
>
> Whitby is a place of considerable business, notwithstanding it is destitute of . . . a water privilege. The formation, some years since, of the plank road to Scugog by the Government, as an adjunct to the harbour, has had the effect of considerably increasing the prosperity of the village, by giving the farmer facilities for reaching the market. . . .
>
> Whitby contains a brewery, tannery, Congregational church, and a grammar school; and a newspaper, called the "Whitby Reporter," is published here. A small settlement, about half a mile to the east of the village, called East Windsor, is now included in the limits of Whitby. . . . The harbour is capacious. . . . A number of houses have been erected here; but the principal business transacted is in storing and forwarding goods and produce, for which purpose there are large warehouses, and others are in the course of erection. There is also a brewery, and an Episcopal church built of stone. . . . The population, including East Windsor and the Port, is said to be about eleven hundred.[16]

In contrast to the mercantile and shipping basis of Whitby's growth, Oshawa, which grew more slowly than its sister town, owed much of its prosperity to the industrial basis laid by men such as Messrs. Cleveland and Gorham, the Gibbs brothers, and John B. Warren. W.H. Smith's description of Oshawa in 1844 shows its diversified economy:

> Oshawa is a place of considerable business, having a good farming country behind it; it contains about 1,000 inhabitants. Churches and chapels three, viz., Catholic, Methodist and Christian.
> Post Office, post every day.

> *Professions and Trades.*—Three physicians and surgeons, two lawyers, two grist-mills (one containing five run of stones), one foundry, one brewery, one carding machine and fulling mill, two distilleries, one ashery, eleven stores, one machine shop, one trip hammer driven by water, one bookseller, one chemist and druggist, one auctioneer, three hatters, seven blacksmiths, four taverns, two watchmakers, five tailors, five shoemakers, one grocery and bakery, one chair factory, four cabinet makers, three waggon makers, one bank agency, "Commercial".[17]

In addition, Smith listed two small suburbs, Gibbs' Mills and Oshawa Harbour, which had been established just south of Oshawa:

> *Gibbs' Mills.* A Settlement . . . about one mile south from Oshawa. It contains about 150 inhabitants, grist mill, oatmeal do., pot barley do., distillery, tannery, and cloth factory (the machinery of which is worked by water), where excellent coarse cloths and blankets are made.[18]
> *Oshawa Harbour.* A small shipping-place on Lake Ontario, three miles from the village of Oshawa. There are store-houses for storing produce, one tavern, and houses for the warfinger and deputy customs-house officer.[19]

While Oshawa did not have as good a natural harbour as Whitby, it was ambitious to supplant Whitby as the centre of the area's mercantile trade. Without major shipping facilities, farmers would be required to go to Whitby to sell their grain, and would naturally buy their goods from the Whitby merchants and craftsmen. In an attempt to improve their competitive position with Whitby, a group of Oshawa merchants and businessmen formed the Sydenham Harbour Company in 1840, with Elder T. Henry as president. This company undertook the first harbour improvements, and built a pier and breakwater to create a sheltered harbour. In 1850, the harbour company was reincorporated as the Port Oshawa Harbour Company, and the works expanded.[20]

Table XVIII
Exports from Oshawa Harbour, 1844–50[21]

Article	*Measure*	*1844*	*1850*
Lumber	feet	145,000	726,000
Flour	barrels	18,690	29,516
Wheat	bushels	11,314	24,330
Pork	barrels	599	281
Oatmeal	barrels	819	17
Whiskey	barrels	377	690
Ashes	barrels	544	684
Oats	bushels	2,715	2,544
Potatoes	bushels	521	1,065

While the harbour company did increase the volume of trade flowing through Oshawa (see Table XVIII) it was never as good a harbour for shipping grain as that of Whitby. In spite of this, Oshawa grew steadily from 1844 to 1850. In 1850, Smith gave this description of the village:

> Oshawa . . . has the advantage of a small but good mill stream, on which are erected two grist mills, one with five run of stones, the other having two; two distilleries, carding and fulling mill, manufactory for machinery etc. There is also in the village a brewery, foundry, axe factory, etc. There are three churches, Episcopal, Wesleyan Methodist, and Roman Catholic. A newspaper, the Oshawa Reformer, is published here. . . . About half a mile from the village is a small settlement called South Oshawa, or "Gibbs Mills", where is a grist mill containing three run of stones, oatmeal mill, and tannery. . . .
>
> The population of Oshawa, including South Oshawa, numbers between eleven and twelve hundred.[22]

So impressive was Oshawa's industrial development that when the Municipal Act of 1849 was passed,[23] Oshawa was named a town - an honour not shared by Whitby until a special act was passed in 1853. These acts came into force on January 1, 1850 and January 1, 1855 respectively.

The rapid increase in population in the northern and rural areas of Ontario County brought a rapid economic expansion as well. This was reflected in the increase in cleared acreage, numbers of livestock and mills and in the appearance of a number of small villages at the main crossroads in the area. Table XIX shows the increase in agricultural development in Ontario County. In

Table XIX
Acres Cultivated, Number of Grist- and Sawmills, Number of Milch Cows, and Assessed Value by Municipality, 1840–50[24]

	Acres Cultivd		*Gristmills*		*Sawmills*		*Milch Cows*		*Assessed Value (£)*	
	1840	*1850*	*1840*	*1850*	*1840*	*1850*	*1840*	*1850*	*1840*	*1850*
Pickering	15,501	27,043	3	6	12	23	1,238	6,475	44,111	87,317
Whitby	23,371	32,810	5	11	15*	15*	1,853	6,713	68,322	114,721†
Uxbridge	2,456	2,898	1	2	3	7	210	1,269	7,738	20,211
Reach	2,618	5,271	0	1	0	8	268	2,665	7,096	36,796
Brock	5,777	12,638	3	2	3	7	463	3,016	16,150	36,786
Scott	239	1,959	0	0	0	1	33	690	1,140	7,553
Thorah	1,814	3,694	0	2	0	2	212	1,136	6,179	13,671
Mara	488	1,832	0	0	0	1	65	879	1,975	8,529 (Mara and Rama)
Rama	85	112	0	0	0	0	4	18	523	

* Includes Oshawa.
† Excludes Oshawa. Taxable property in Oshawa was assessed at £15,460.

particular, with the growth of milling centres in Reach, Scott, Thorah and Mara, life became much easier for northern settlers.

The rise of villages in the northern area provided the basis for a significant change in the rural economy there. Not only did it make available to the farmers a variety of goods which had hitherto been generally unavailable, but an influx of tradesmen reduced the necessity of complete self-sufficiency of the farm family and made way for better craftsmanship and higher levels of technology. Thus by 1850, the northern areas reached the level of economic development attained by the front townships in the mid-1820s.

The rise of the inland villages was significant in two ways. First, they tended to create a cohesive economic unit out of their area or township by providing services and markets which hitherto had been located at a distance; and second, their rise provided a challenge to the monopoly previously enjoyed by the main villages on the lake shore. The following sketches of the rise of the largest of these villages and their condition, as observed by W.H. Smith in 1850, illustrates many of the changes that were occurring:

In Pickering three villages of importance had appeared by 1850. Duffin's Creek or "Canton", as it styled itself, had grown up around the first mill established in Ontario County. In spite of its early beginning, its lack of either a good road north or a trade monopoly over a large area (because of the vigorous growth of Markham and good roads from there to Toronto) prevented it from reaching the stature of its lake shore rivals, Whitby and Oshawa. In 1844 Smith described Duffin's Creek as follows:

> Contains about 130 inhabitants. Churches and chapels, 4; viz., Presbyterian, Catholic, British Wesleyan, and Quaker. . . .
> Post Office, post every day.
> *Professions and Trades.*—One grist mill, one brewery, one tannery, three stores, two taverns, three shoemakers, two tailors, one blacksmith, one waggon maker.[25]

By 1850 Duffin's Creek had grown steadily although it was still a relatively small village. Smith described it as "a thriving village containing between three and four hundred inhabitants, a grist mill with four run of stones, a brewery, tannery, and four churches, Presbyterian, Methodists, Quaker and Roman Catholic".[26]

The two other villages, Majorville (later Whitevale) and Dunbarton, had their beginnings in the prosperous 1840s and 1850s. The site of Majorville contains one of the best mill seats in the township on the headwaters of Duffin's Creek. When the British decided in 1843 to allow American grain into England duty-free, provided that it was ground in Canada, good water-power sites close to harbours became very valuable. In 1845 Truman White, then only twenty years of age, acquired the Majorville water rights and built a large gristmill and sawmill which immediately prospered. Later he added a large woolen mill to his works. A little village composed of his workmen grew up around the mill.[27] To serve the booming grain and flour trade created by White's mill, William Dunbar and a number of associates formed a harbour company which built a dock and warehouses on Frenchman's Bay and laid out a town plot which was named Dunbarton after its founder.[28]

In Whitby Township two new villages, Brooklin and Columbus, developed around mills between 1835 and 1850. Of the two Columbus, which was founded in the mid-1830s, grew more slowly. By 1844 it contained about 400 residents, and there were two churches (Methodist and Episcopal) in the area. In the village there was one ashery, four stores, two taverns, two wagon makers, two tailors, two blacksmiths and four shoemakers.[29] In his description of Columbus in 1850, W.H. Smith put his finger on the reason that it had not grown in the previous six years:

> Columbus . . . contains about three hundred inhabitants; it is a tolerably thriving settlement, although it is too near Oshawa to do a large business, indeed it appears to have remained nearly stationary for the last three or four years. It contains a grist mill, with two run of stones, a saw mill, tannery, ashery, and soap and candle factory, Post Office and three churches; United Presbyterian, Wesleyan Methodist, and Bible Christian; and there is an Episcopal Church about one mile west from the village.[30]

By contrast to Columbus which had only a small stream available for milling purposes, Lynde's Creek which crossed the main north-south road at Brooklin provided a good location for mills when American grain was made available for use in Canadian flour exports to England. In 1840 two brothers, John and Robert Campbell, built a large flour mill on the stream at Brooklin (then called Winchester) which was later replaced by a large impressive brick structure after a fire. Shortly after the first mill was built, a second grist- and sawmill was erected just north of the first mill.[31] The rapid growth and prosperity of Brooklin are shown by the fact that while it was too small to be noticed by Smith in 1844, by 1850 it had reached a respectable status indeed:

> Winchester . . . now named Brooklin, . . . contains a population of about five hundred and fifty, two grist mills with three run of stones each, one of which is built of brick, and another containing two run of stones. There are also a tannery, a woollen factory, foundry, ashery and brewery; two saleratus factories, and a soap and candle factory. The village also contains a circulating library.[32]

In contrast to the villages in the two old "front" townships which were growing rapidly, Uxbridge village made very slow progress. In the 1840s it was handicapped by its lack of a large captive market to the north and its distance from the lake which excluded it from the flour trade.

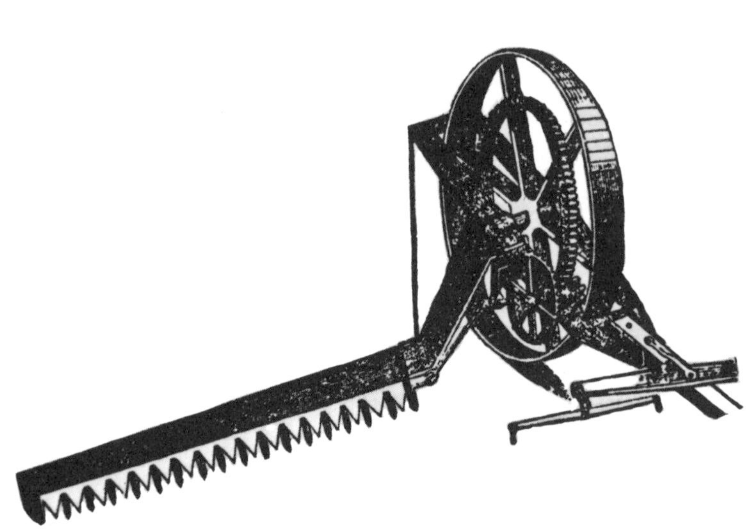

Early Mowing Machine, 1848 *Public Archives of Ontario*

Horse Powered Threshing Machine, 1850 *Public Archives of Ontario*

The most important development of those years was the rise to prosperity of the area's most important businessman, Joseph Gould. In spite of the severe setback his fortunes received in the Rebellion, he gradually built up a good business at his mill, and in 1843 added a small woollen factory to his operations. In 1844 and 1845 he renovated and expanded his gristmills and sawmills into large and imposing structures.[33]

Around the enlarged mills, a number of merchants set up stores, and cooperages, tailor shops and other small service trades. In 1847 and 1848 Uxbridge village received an economic boost when Joseph Thomas and Robert Johnson established warehouses and undertook a grain-buying business for the Toronto market.[34] As yet there was no good road for farmers from Uxbridge to Whitby and Oshawa. Later, when a road was opened between Uxbridge and Manchester, the grain trade would shift to the latter village because of its proximity to the excellent harbour at Whitby.[35] By 1850, Uxbridge's slow growth meant that several other, much newer, villages had passed it in size. W.H. Smith described it as follows:

> Uxbridge village . . . is pleasantly situated, but at present has rather a *backwoods* appearance. It contains about three hundred and fifty inhabitants, two grist mills, two saw mills, carding and fulling mill, distillery, tannery, ashery and Post Office. That portion of the village situated to the south, is distinguished from the rest by the name of Gouldville.[36]

Of all the areas which underwent rapid development, none grew more quickly than the four villages of Reach township, Prince Albert, Port Perry, Manchester and Borelia. Each came into being as the result of a specific geographical or economic condition, and all prospered. The oldest, Prince Albert, owed its prosperity to its location on Simcoe Street, the main line of communication between Lake Ontario, Lake Scugog and the townships lying to the north. In 1845 Abner Hurd, a local merchant, explained its advantages:

> [Because] Scugog Lake . . . and the ridges and various other obstructions prevent any direct line of communication between Ops and Fenelon and the front being practicable, their market is principally at Whitby [township] and this street is their only Road, and a very great proportion of the Inhabitants of Reach, Brock, Thoro, and Mara depend exclusively on this Road as their [*sic*] is no line of road west of this equal in grad[e]ness. Swamp and Ridges are insuperable barriers, [thus] travel from Windsor, Oshawa and Bowmanville to all those Northern townships concentrate on the Village of Prince Albert & termination of the plank road.[37]

In 1844 Smith reported that Prince Albert contained two hundred inhabitants, a Methodist Church, five stores, two taverns, two asheries, one blacksmith, one wagon maker, two shoemakers, and two tailors.[38] Six years later he reported that

> Prince Albert, which contains about three hundred inhabitants, appears to be a busy little place, being at a sufficient distance from Oshawa and Whitby to enable it to command a tolerable trade of its own. It is pleasantly situated, and will probably become a thriving little town; it has been settled about eight years, and contains two tanneries and three asheries, and a Post Office.[39]

Thus in just eight years Prince Albert had achieved almost the same growth as had Uxbridge which was thirty years older. With the development of the area a mail stage which carried passengers began to operate on Simcoe Street in 1848.[40]

By 1850 Prince Albert had become a thriving grain-buying centre, and in later years would rival Brampton as the largest grain market in Canada. Among the grain merchants who would set up business there were James and Andrew Laing of Oshawa, J.B. Warren, T.N. Gibbs, A. Farewell, P.A. Hurd, George Curry and T.C. Foreman.[41]

As the demand by the United States for Canadian lumber increased, a number of far-sighted businessmen led by Peter Perry began to look for a way to enter the timber trade. Perry, who had moved to Whitby in 1836 after his election defeat in his home riding of Lennox and Addington in that year, had built up a prosperous merchant business at the "four corners". As a result, that rising village had for a time called itself "Perry's Corners". In 1844 he became interested in the present site of Port Perry as an excellent prospect for land speculation (an activity for which Mackenzie had denounced him in 1837).[42]

The chief attraction of the site was the possibility that the beginning timber trade of Victoria County might be directed down the Scugog River and Lake and over the plank roads to Whitby and Oshawa, rather than to Port Hope or Trenton. Perry purchased the site and began business by building a store which was managed by Chester Draper. Soon Perry added a wharf and warehouses, and then erected temporary houses for his workmen.[43] Perry's endeavours paid off almost immediately. In 1846 the partnership of Thomas Sexton, George Paxton and Daniel S. Way erected a large steam-powered sawmill in the village, and in 1847 a second sawmill was built by Samuel Hill, a resident of Whitby. In 1852 a third mill, owned by Stephen Doty, was established. With these large-scale undertakings the future of the village was assured.[44] Logs were rafted down the lake to these mills and the lumber was exported to Rochester and Oswego, New York, via Oshawa and Whitby harbours. To serve the lumber trade in the northern areas, a steamer (the *Woodman*) was built on Lake Scugog by Hugh Chisholm for the partnership of Rowe and Cotton of Whitby in 1850, and in 1851 the boat began making regular trips to Lindsay.[45]

When W.H. Smith passed through Port Perry in 1850, it was just beginning to take on the outlines of its future importance. Its population numbered about one hundred fifty, and it had two steam sawmills in operation.[46]

The other two villages, Borelia and Manchester, were just beginning to take shape in 1850. Borelia was at the crossing of two important roads: the Whitby-Port Perry plank road, and the Nonquon road from Prince Albert to the northern townships. Originally called "Crandall's Corners" after the first settler, Reuben Crandall, Borelia assumed its new name in 1850. Its population then was about one hundred.[47] Manchester, too, was at an important crossroad, and had the added advantage of the township hall which was built there in 1850. Manchester had originally been called "Fitchett's Corners" after a local tavern owner. It had only a few inhabitants in 1850.[48]

North of Reach township, villages were still little more than crossroads settlements. Whereas Beaverton had been founded more than two decades before, in 1850 it was still a struggling hamlet. As W.H. Smith noted, it contained a gristmill and sawmill, two distilleries, two asheries, and a tannery. It also had a Presbyterian church.[49] The only other northern village of consequence was Cannington which had been laid out by Messers. Davidson and Munro in 1849.[50] In 1850 it contained a gristmill and sawmill, a woollen factory and a distillery.[51]

Up to 1850, all the towns and villages in Ontario County were still in the early stage of industrial development. Although Whitby and Oshawa had a greater diversity of manufacturing and trades, as yet all were activities directly related to the basic needs of the pioneer rural communities. In spite of the employment of crafts techniques in their industrial production, the system of economic organization throughout the area had clearly advanced from the earlier stage when only the most primitive forms of manufacturing techniques of family production had been used. Specialization had become possible, and farmers throughout the area now had access to these specializations through the appearance of merchant shops in even the more remote northern areas. Moreover, with the expansion of the export trade in grain, flour, lumber and similar products, the local economy began to change from one of subordinate debt relations to one of freedom of exchange which a cash economy allowed.

Of greater importance, perhaps, was the rapid accumulation of capital in the area, as the growing export trade allowed the purchase of more and better tools, machinery and livestock, which in turn accelerated the growth of local productivity. Suddenly, almost without warning, there was money available, surplus to the immediate material needs of the community. At last it was possible to build churches, schools, libraries and similar social institutions. This sudden expansion of capital accumulation and productivity was a province-wide phenomena, which meant that at long last many projects of provincial importance could be undertaken from taxes which could now be raised on imports. Although the end of British preference in 1849 shook the confidence (and loyalty) of some of the more enterprising new merchants and entrepreneurs, the reciprocity arrangement in 1854 and the high grain prices caused by the Crimean war renewed the rapid expansion of the economy which had begun in the 1840s. Thus for Ontario County by 1850 the hardships, poverty, and economic restrictions of pioneer life were gradually being left behind.

Although both Whitby and Oshawa had grown and prospered in the 1840-1850 period, the leading merchants and businessmen of each recognized that future prosperity depended upon their towns having a monopoly of trade over the expanding northern area. In order to retain and enhance their position, the leaders of each centre fought hard to improve the roads north from their village, or when that failed, to prevent the improvement of their neighbours' roads. This bitter rivalry existed not only between Whitby and Oshawa, but as the new northern centres became prominent, was extended to Prince Albert, Port Perry, Uxbridge, Cannington and Beaverton as well. Whenever a government road or harbour grant became available, or whenever the possibility of some improvement (such as large investment) seemed imminent, open rivalries and vicious infighting was bound to occur. The bitterness created by these struggles affected almost every facet of municipal life from 1840 on.

The first major controversy which arose (and one which would persist in one form or another for the next thirty years) was centred on the spending of public funds to improve internal transportation. The chief struggle that developed was between the supporters of the Oshawa-Prince Albert-Nonquon route (Simcoe Street), and the supporters of the Whitby-Brooklin-Manchester-Sunderland route (Centre Line). Since Prince Albert and Oshawa depended on Simcoe Street for much of their prosperity, the improvement of Centre Line presented a real threat to their control of the back townships' grain trade. Whitby's superior harbour intensified the threat. With the founding of Port Perry the situation became even more dangerous.

Between 1840 and 1845 both Simcoe Street and the Centre Line road were under Home District jurisdiction. Thus the Provincial Assembly had an excellent excuse for refusing all petitions for improvements. In 1845, however, under constant pressure from local residents, both roads were brought under provincial jurisdiction.[52] Particularly instrumental in persuading the Government to take over the roads was Peter Perry who had once again been elected to the Assembly.[53] Perry's interest in seeing the Whitby-Port Perry road built was twofold: as the leading Whitby merchant he was interested in seeing northern produce flow through that town rather than Oshawa, but, more important, as a land speculator at Port Perry, Perry was anxious to see a good road built from Lake Scugog to Whitby Harbour in order that timber from Victoria County might be shipped by way of his new town.

No sooner had the Centre Line road been completed in 1845, than a second serious dispute broke out between the merchants of Prince Albert and Oshawa and those of Whitby and Port Perry. Throughout 1845 and 1846 the residents of Brock, Thorah and Mara had sent letters and petitions asking that a better road be built north from Reach township through to Lake Simcoe.[54] The importance of such an undertaking was shown in a letter from J.R. Thompson of Brock to Robert Baldwin written in 1845:

> Low prices and bad sleighing were severely felt by the settlers in Brock last winter. It is some satisfaction, however, to know that there is at length a prospect of a road being made by which we shall be able to get to the front in summer as well as in winter.[55]

In response to these requests, a sum of £2,000 was voted for improvements to a road running north to Lake Simcoe.

While no one objected to the expenditure of government funds to build such a road, the merchants of Prince Albert and Oshawa were anxious to see the money expended on improvements to the Simcoe Street-Nonquon route so that they could regain the competitive advantage which had been lost with the improvement of the Centre Line road to Port Perry. Of course, the Whitby merchants were just as anxious to see the money spent on an extension of the Centre Line.

The controversy raged for months as innumerable petitions, letters and resolutions from local meetings piled up on the desks of government members.[56] The arguments presented by the disputants were typical of the differing ambitions of the towns involved. The Whitby merchants and businessmen led by Peter Perry put forward the argument that the Centre Line must some day become the key to a great inland transportation system connecting Lakes Huron and Ontario. They argued that should such a great project be successful, Whitby would, because of its excellent harbour and superior position, rise to pre-eminence among the cities on Lake Ontario's north shore. By contrast, Oshawa and Prince Albert businessmen stressed the cheapness and practicability of their less ambitious project. Whereas the Centre Line road would have to cross wide stretches of swamp and uncleared forest, the eastern or Nonquon route was already open and required only a little work to serve the pioneer areas of Brock, Mariposa, Ops and Emily, all of which as yet had no easy access to a port on Lake Ontario. The sum of £2,000 already voted was sufficient, they argued, to make the Nonquon an excellent road, well-suited for pioneer needs. The Centre Line road was denounced as visionary, unnecessary, and, above all, too expensive for a pioneer society.[57]

Not only did such disputes set one town or township against another, but they created dissention within townships as well. The inhabitants of Brock Township split into "East" and "West" factions depending on whether they would be best served by the Centre Line or Nonquon route. This bitterness, of course, would be reflected in township politics as each faction attempted to gain control of the situation.[58]

Peter Perry, aided by the influence he could wield as a member of the Assembly, and his Whitby backers carried the day. Abner Hurd, the Prince

Albert merchant, commented bitterly on Perry's tactics in a letter to Robert Baldwin:

> Altho' the estimates contain [an] item for an additional outlay for [the Nonquon] road, the opening and improving of which would be of great advantage to the . . . back country . . . this I fear will not be done as the voluminous Petitions with P.P. [Peter Perry] and 2621 others, or even without the others, will doubtless have more influence in some quarters than all the country besides, while I venture to predict that not one out of 100 of those petitioners even had that long and abused document. . . . We in the first place Petitioned for the improvement of Simcoe Street . . . where as Uxbridge, Scott and Georgina [where Perry used a paid agent to collect signatures] have but little interest in the said road whether made on one line or another.[59]

As the merchants of Prince Albert and Oshawa had predicted, the expenditure of £2,000 to improve the Centre Line road was insufficient to make it usable in all seasons. The road remained in such poor condition that in spite of annual expenditures, the road was often impassable. In all, up to December 31, 1849, the Government spent a total of £9,510 on the "Windsor and Scugog" section, and an additional £1,340 on the Scugog-Lake Simcoe Narrows section. In addition, a total of £28,498 was expended to improve Whitby harbour.[60] In York currency, the total expenditure totalled no less than $196,740. In spite of this enormous outlay, little benefit was received by the inhabitants of the northern townships because the northern section of the Centre Line road remained impassable for much of each year. With northern farmers forced to use the Nonquon, both Prince Albert and Oshawa continued to prosper.[61]

Although the battle over road financing continued to rage, a new element was introduced in 1849. When the "Businessmen-Reformers", Hincks and Baldwin, took over leadership of the Provincial Government, "economy" immediately became the watchword of the Assembly, and local improvements such as roads were once again the responsibility of the various local governments. To enable local governments to shoulder the burden of heavy capital expenditures, the Municipal Corporations Act of 1849 removed the ceiling on local taxation rates and allowed municipalities to go into debt for the first time.[62]

The Provincial Government then decided to sell all toll roads to the local municipalities. But when Home District refused to pay the £60,000 demanded by the Province for the district toll roads, an act was passed which permitted their sale to private toll road companies.[63] Thus, in 1850 the Centre Line road and Whitby harbour were sold to Peter Perry, who incorporated them as the Port Whitby, Lakes Scugog, Simcoe and Huron Road Company. The transaction was a most controversial one, since the sale price was $80,400 – less than half the original cost of the works. Rumours of favouritism, collusion and dishonesty among government and district officials were circulated. In addition a mysterious New York financier, Major Hoople, was supposed to have financed the takeover. Needless to say all charges were denied, and no proof was obtained.[64] After Perry's death, the road passed into the hands of "Captain" James Rowe and John Watson who incorporated themselves as the Port Whitby and Lake Huron Railway Company in 1853.[65]

Not content to let Whitby business interests triumph in the battle for the inland trade, a group of Oshawa businessmen and merchants decided to form their own toll road company to improve Simcoe Street between Oshawa and Prince Albert. The Nonquon Road Company, promoted by Dr. McGill, Abraham Farewell, T.N. Gibbs, Colonel G.H. Grierson and Colonel Fairbanks (all of Oshawa), laid out a new road to the east of the old line of Simcoe Street in an attempt to find easier grades and a more sheltered location for winter sleighing. In all £5,700 ($28,000) was spent on the venture.[66]

The purchase of the roads by private businessmen, however, created a fundamental conflict of interest. Though the businessmen proposed to improve the roads so that the northern grain trade would flow through their town, they also intended to show a profit on their investments. They needed low tolls to get the farmers' custom; on the other hand, high tolls were required to make a profit. It was not long before it became clear that the anticipated monopoly of trade was an illusion and the roads were a losing business proposition. The primary reason for their failure was the fact that although the farmers desperately needed improved roads in spring and fall, in winter when the bulk of their produce was hauled to market, they required little more than brushed out "winter roads" for good sleighing. Thus, while in theory good quality toll roads should create a monopoly situation where high tolls could be charged, in winter when an attempt was made to charge high tolls, the farmers simply used the parallel concession roads.

Faced with these problems, the road company owners turned to the muncipalities for aid. In 1853 the owners of the various private road companies approached the County Council of the United Counties of York, Peel and Ontario with the proposal that the Council borrow £100,000 to invest in the road companies, with the promise that the proceeds would go for large-scale improvements. The basis of their proposal was that the road companies bestowed such benefits on the area that they should be aided by public financing. This rationale was stated as follows: resolved,

> 1. That the improvements of the leading roads in these counties is an object much to be desired, as well as for the pecuniary advantage of the inhabitants as for their comfort and convenience, and the want of such improvement is a serious and continued drawback to the industry of the country.
>
> 2. That the several roads in these counties which have been constructed by joint-stock companies (though they have not an-

> swered the expectations of their promoters in direct profitable returns for the outlay,) have been of great benefit to the inhabitants in their vicinity; but the bad success which has attended them, as means of investment, will probably deter capitalists from assisting in such works for the future.[67]

This line of argument raised a number of questions which the rural members of Council wanted answered. Why, they asked, should private road companies be treated differently from any other business? After all, if the roads were profitable the owners would not be before Council offering to share the profits. Moreover, why should public money be invested in order to fill the pockets of private investors? If the counties had money to spend on roads, why not spend it on the development of the roads owned by the public, where all the benefits would go to the taxpayers? After a bitter debate the motion was defeated 18 to 16, with voting split along rural-urban lines. Only T.N. Gibbs, president of the Nonquon Road Company, was awarded help: by the narrowest of margins (a 17 to 17 tie, with the chairman casting the deciding vote) the council voted a grant of £50 for the improvement of Simcoe Street.[68] This was not the last attmpt to use public money to make privately-owned undertakings profitable. Indeed, in the next generation many such road and railway projects - privately owned but publicly financed - would be put forward as businessmen from the rival centres struggled for supremacy.

In spite of the constant quarrels and resulting bitterness, it was a period in which major strides were made in road improvement. In particular, the Mara and Thorah road, which ran from the Talbot River to the Narrows at Atherley, was a boon to the northern part of the county. Begun in 1846, the project dragged on for several years while the usual barrage of petitions and quarrels over route went on.[69] Because of the continued shortage of funds, work was frequently interrupted when unpaid contractors and labourers quit in protest. In spite of all these problems, by 1848 the road was in serviceable condition. In all, the River Talbot-Narrows road cost the Province $8,000 to build.[70]

Yet in spite of the expenditure of large sums of money on the main roads; and the use of statute labour on the concession lines, roads in the more remote and newly settled areas still presented great difficulties for the farmer and traveller. In 1849 the Methodist missionary to Brock township (a mission which covered northern Ontario County as well as most of Victoria) wrote of the condition of the roads over which he travelled:

> The roads on this Mission are of the worst description; I never saw any thing before to equal them. There are cedar swamps in every direction. In travelling 10 or 12 miles, you will have perhaps 6 or 7 of them to go through, and some of them from a quarter to nearly a mile in length. The roads through them are made of round logs without any covering [the famous "corduroy" roads]. Some of them are quite worn out so

> that in crossing them you are in danger of getting your horse's legs broken.[71]

Thus by 1850 major problems still existed in the development of the inland transportation system. Much was done, but much still remained to do. While no one disputed the necessity of improved roads, it would be many years before agreement would be reached on methods or priorities.

CONFLICTING VISIONS: EDUCATION AND RELIGION, 1840-51

Not only was the period 1840 to 1851 one of great economic and demographic change for Ontario County, it was a time of great social change as well. The move from the primitive rudeness of pioneer "toiler farming" to more modern forms of commercial agriculture not only allowed for greater specialization and accumulation of capital in economic matters, but also made it possible for social changes to occur as well. Thus education, religion and other organized forms of social life underwent great transformations during the period.

It was not at the level of formal social organizations, however, that the most significant changes occurred. With the growing scarcity of land and its rapid increase in price, more and more of the working-class immigrants and younger sons of landowners found it impossible to acquire land for themselves. For these people the choice was either to work for others or to migrate to the American frontier. By 1851, the "classless" society of William Lyon Mackenzie's dreams was already becoming the society of high and low, landed and landless, which the Colonial Office and British and Canadian capitalists had desired. The local farmers and crafts workers of Ontario County, however, continued their political struggles against these changes.

Under the labour-intensive "toiler farming" of the pre-1850 period, there had developed a strongly marked levelling tendency in landholding. As Table XX shows, by 1851 most farms were between 50 and 100 acres in size, with

Table XX
Number of Occupiers of Land in Ontario County, 1851[1]

	Total Occupiers	*10 Acres and Under*	*10 to 20*	*20 to 50*	*50 to 100*	*100 to 200*	*200 and up*
Whitby	826	198	26	182	275	122	23
Pickering	820	101	22	265	334	86	13
Uxbridge	388	51	4	130	158	36	9
Reach	522	25	24	170	241	62	—
Brock	485	18	6	76	283	98	4
Thorah	152	9	3	12	97	27	4
Mara / Rama	218	25	22	34	113	22	2
Scugog	64	1	3	21	35	4	—
Scott	173	1	—	29	120	22	1
Oshawa	94	79	—	5	5	3	2
Totals	3,742	508	109	924	1,661	482	58

very few holdings exceeding 200 acres. It appears to matter little whether the original grant was larger than 200 acres as many were in Pickering and Whitby, or the minimum grant of 200 (and later 100) acres, as most were in Scott and Mara and Rama; by 1851 the pattern of landholding had become the same.[2] It is likely that, given the situation where most farm tasks were performed by hand, most farmers preferred to sell surplus acreage rather than hold it and be forced to pay taxes on useless land. As a result, farms in most townships in Ontario County averaged between 85 and 95 acres in 1851, with those in Uxbridge being the smallest (75.6 acres average) and those in Thorah, the largest (114.4 acres).[3] Thus among the agricultural producers there was a great deal of economic homogeneity.

In contrast to those possessing land, the great majority of the population found it more and more difficult to achieve or maintain a position of equality. By 1851, as Table XXI shows, almost two-thirds (61.6 per cent) of labouring-age males (15 years and over) were without land. Even more serious was the fact that at a minimum (that is assuming that no single men owned land) at least twenty-five per cent of families were without land either as owners or renters. It would appear likely that perhaps fifty per cent of all families were completely dependent upon wages for their income. One serious aspect of so many men being without land was that the vote depended on the possession of property. Thus more than half of all men 20 years and over (53.9 per cent) were incapable of voting.

The condition of the labouring class in Canada, moreover, was far from enviable. Although men possessing land or skills which were in demand might

Table XXI
Males with and without Land in Ontario County, 1851[4]

	Males 15 and Over	*Males 20 and Over*	*Number of Families*	*Occupiers of Land*	*Occupiers with 10 acres or more*	*% Males with Land*	*% Males with 10 acres or more*
Whitby	2,377	1,922	1,344	826	628	34.7	26.4
Pickering	2,498	2,116	1,052	820	719	32.8	28.4
Uxbridge	467	350	413	388	337	83.1	72.2
Reach	1,384	1,190	696	522	497	37.7	35.1
Brock	1,193	990	531	485	467	40.7	39.1
Thorah	393	335	193	152	143	38.7	36.4
Mara, Rama	507	424	228	218	193	43.0	38.1
Scugog	163	142	62	64	63	39.3	38.7
Scott	340	297	173	173	172	50.9	50.6
Oshawa	415	348	204	94	15	22.8	3.6

expect, through long and hard labour, to achieve a reasonable standard of living, the conditions of labourers had deteriorated steadily since the 1820s.[5] The price of land had risen steadily as it became scarcer and wages had dropped. In 1843, the report from Whitby to the Chief Secretary of the Emigration Service at Kingston stated that wages for male farm servants averaged £2 to £2 10s. per month, and those of female farm servants were fifteen shillings per month. Male labourers averaged two shillings, sixpence per day, but were warned that "labourers can only expect work during the continuance of the Public Works or during harvest".[6] The report went on to say that "there are no farms at present known to be for sale, but cleared farms generally sell here for Five pounds currency per acre". Thus only the wealthiest of immigrants could expect to acquire land.

The poverty of most farmers, however, meant that there was little likelihood that a permanent working class such as had developed in England would be created. Robert Baldwin and Robert Baldwin Sullivan reported that there was little basis for the creation of such a class of agricultural labourers:

> In Canada, a man with a young family cannot maintain his wife and children in comfort upon the wages of agricultural labour, unless he is in possession of a residence of his own; nor however much the assistance of the labourer may be required at certain seasons, can the farmer afford to give such constant employment, as would enable the labourer to maintain a numerous family throughout the year; – the poorer classes will not, if they can avoid it, resume the condition of cotters, or small tenants.[7]

As a result of this situation, rural labourers tended either to drift into the towns or lumber camps, or to emigrate into the American West where free land was still available.

Unlike menial labourers, skilled workers who could find jobs were relatively well-paid. The 1843 Emigration Report from Whitby stated that carpenters, wheelwrights, shoemakers and masons could expect five shillings per day (on a six-day week), while tailors could expect four shillings, sixpence. Blacksmiths could expect £4 per month. Board and lodging cost ten shillings per week.[8] There was, however, a strict limit on how many skilled workers (or mechanics, as they were called) could be absorbed into the economy. The report from Pickering stated that "few or any of this class [the mechanics] could find employment here".[9]

A serious problem from the point of view of the farmers, small businessmen and skilled workers, was the fact that the rising class of urban merchants and manufacturers soon discovered ways to use the poor workers to undermine the position of skilled workers, and to create monopolies in merchandising, manufacturing and transportation which would seriously erode the independence of the farmers and small-town businessmen. It would take a generation, however, for all this to become apparent. In the meantime, the immediate problems of the farmers and small businessmen would be reflected in the great legislative changes brought about under the leadership of Robert Baldwin and Louis H. Lafontaine.

In order to explain the timing and impetus of the development of educational and religious institutions in Ontario County, three aspects must be considered: first, the poverty and the social perceptions of the first settlers; second, the rising tide of vice and lawlessness which accompanied the creation of the poor labouring class; and finally, the needs of the rapidly developing mercantile and industrial economy, particularly after 1850. While none of these was decisive in itself, each contributed to the creation of educational legislation which affected Ontario County.

During the first half-century of settlement in Upper Canada the education system developed very slowly. Although an initial step to support local education had been made through a system of provincial grants in 1816, the poverty of the early settlers, and the system of "toiler" agriculture which developed because of the lack of capital, made school attendance almost impossible for rural children. The whole problem of poverty and necessity as the cause of the lack of education among the pioneers was put clearly by E. A. Talbot in 1824:

> Many circumstances concur to make it impracticable for the Canadians, even if they were capable, to educate their own children. In consequence of the difficulty of procuring labour, . . . the farmer is not only compelled to devote himself entirely to the cultivation of his ground, but also to call in the aid of his sons, as soon as they are able to assist

> him. Boys of seven or eight years old are put to work in Canada, and are kept at it during the remainder of their lives.[10]

The result was a growing indifference to education:

> The inestimable advantages resulting from a well-educated and enlightened population, cannot be experienced in Canada for many years to come. The great mass of people are at present completely ignorant even of the rudiments of the most common learning. Very few can either read or write; and parents, who are ignorant themselves, possess so slight a relish for literature, and are so little acquainted with its advantages, that they feel scarcely any anxiety to have the minds of their children cultivated.[11]

Nor did this condition change greatly during the next twenty years. In 1844 a second writer repeated the observation made by Talbot:

> Education, nothwithstanding legislative efforts which have existed from an early period in the settlement of Western Canada to the present time, continues still in a very unsatisfactory state. This is no doubt much owing to the great stretch of country, thinly populated, and without sufficient means to plant and support the large number of schools required in a country so situated during its early stages of existence. Among a great proportion of the population, too, comprising chiefly a class of older settlers, and the humbler class of emigrants from Britain, the benefits of education are but indifferently appreciated; and where there is found, as is the case in the country parts, joined with this apathy, some foundation for indulging it, on account of long and bad roads for the children, and also the early value of their services in the work of the farm, it is not much matter of surprise to see the road-side school-house thinly attended.[12]

Considering the poverty of the farmers in Ontario County in the early years, it is not surprising that few children of the early settlers received more than a rudimentary education. The obvious indifference of most parents to the education of their children should not, however, be condemned as being merely the result of slothfulness, ignorance or vice on their part. Although this charge was commonly leveled by representatives of the urban upper class (and certainly appears to have a basis of truth for the most demoralized elements of the urban working class), it fell far short of the truth for the rural settlers. For the latter group, considering the lack of capital and the general inability to apply successfully the results of a superior education under the primitive conditions of pioneer life, it should not be surprising that they came to regard education for farm children as being impractical and frivolous.

In Ontario County, the passing of the Common School Act of 1816 had relatively little effect on school attendance. In 1821 when Whitby had 314 children under 16 years and Pickering had 334 in the same age group, only one common school, that taught by William Moore in Whitby, qualified for the £10 annual government grant. In 1822 two additional schools, one taught by James McEnery in Uxbridge and a second taught by William Sleigh in Pickering, were added to the list of those receiving grants.[13]

While many of the reformers' rural followers may have been indifferent to education, it is clear that those leaders who hoped to create an ideal society of independent producers were not. To men such as William Lyon Mackenzie and Doctor Charles Duncombe, education was regarded as being indispensable for the proper management of both the individual's private interests, and of the common interests reflected in good representative government. For example, in 1837 William Lyon Mackenzie spoke of the necessity of education for the farmer:

> The Husbandman—There is one prevailing error among this class of society, which ought to be eradicated and destroyed—it is more fatal to the business of agriculture than the growth of Canadian thistles, or the destruction of May frosts—we mean the neglected education of the farmers' children. It is frequently remarked that education is of little use to the farmer; a very little science will do for him. Great knowledge is only beneficial in the professional man. Expressions of this sort are founded upon a false estimate of the more useful and elevated profession of life.[14]

Doctor Charles Duncombe, a leading radical reformer (and later leader of the Rebellion of 1837 in the Western District) expressed these sentiments in a more elaborate form in 1836. As chairman of the Commission of Inquiry into Education of that year, Duncombe concluded:

> By [the inductive system of education] and the Education of Teachers the youthful mind is disciplined, the Arts and Sciences are improved, the world is enlightened, and above all, by this an army of faithful, intelligent, enterprising, benevolent men are trained up and sent forth to be leaders in the great enterprises of the day. I speak not now of one profession merely. Ministers and Merchants, Lawyers and Physicians, Teachers, and Statesmen, Farmers and Mechanics, Authors and Artists, all are wanted in this work.[15]

In spite of these attempts to persuade their followers of the benefits of education, most farmers could do little to improve their condition and tended to remain indifferent.

In contrast to the view held by Mackenzie and Duncombe that education could be one of the tools in the creation of a new society, Bishop Strachan and the Tories saw education as a primary means of maintaining the old. Education, to Strachan, was not valuable merely as a means of teaching literate skills and the laws of nature. Even more important was the use of schools to inculcate correct moral and religious principles. As Strachan said:

> Anyone acquainted with the human heart and the certain current of human habits and feelings will know that the certain consequences of bringing up youth without religious principles and impressions is to multiply reprobates.[16]

Christian schools, to Strachan, were crucial in overcoming human weaknesses:

> In these institutions the youth are taught those principles of pure religion which guard them against the allurement of vice and prepare them for the practice of virtue—a thirst for knowledge is at the same time excited—industrious habits formed and a behavior orderly, obedient and peaceful almost infallibly produced.[17]

It was not enough, however, that the schools should be merely "Christian"; they should be Anglican-controlled if possible. As Strachan pointed out in 1821:

> The true foundation of the prosperity of our Establishment must be laid in the Education of Youth, the command and direction of which must as far as possible be concentrated in our Clergy. This has hitherto been the silent policy of all the measures taken for the Education of Youth adopted in this Province.[18]

To achieve this control, Strachan proposed to create a monolithic, government-controlled system which would bring all education under the supervision of the Anglican clergy.

Nor was Strachan above a certain amount of deviousness in furthering his plans to gain control of education. For example, in 1816 he wrote the Bishop of Quebec that:

> It was my intention had the bill I proposed last winter passed . . . to point out the propriety of a general Inspector of Education to whom all returns should be made. Such a person the Governor might have appointed without salary at first. This office I should have undertaken and might have carried it into precedent that the Clergyman of York should be always Inspector of Education. By this means . . . the Established Religion would have had a paramount influence over the education of the people.[19]

This control, of course, was strongly opposed by all other religious groups.

Because Strachan and the Tories believed that the lower classes were incapable of making correct moral and intellectual judgments, and because they feared anything that encouraged democratic behaviour or local control, they were strongly opposed to the autonomous control of schools by local trustees. Strachan managed to have himself appointed President of the Board for the General Superintendence of Education in 1823, thereby acquiring control of the government grant to the common schools, but his powers were still very limited. Where local trustees decided to do without the grant (which averaged about £10 per year in the 1820s) they could operate the school to suit themselves.

The bitterness with which the Tories opposed local control of the schools was demonstrated in a report made by the Reverend Robert Murray, later the first provincial Superintendent of Education:

> I consider the present provision to be deficient *in toto*; but more particularly,— First: the manner of selecting Teachers for Common Schools, appears to me to be an insult to common sense. Three individuals, as Trustees, or Superintendents, are appointed by the people in the neighborhood of the School House, without any regard to their education; these three men, thus appointed, have the sole power to judge of the qualifications of candidates for the school, and to appoint and eject the Teacher, while they themselves may not have received even the first rudiments of a plain English education. Such men are, consequently, altogether unfit to judge, either of the qualifications of a School Master, or of the progress of the pupils.
>
> 2. The power of ejecting School Masters vested in three Trustees, or Superintendents, subjects the Teacher to the whim and caprice of every child attending the School; the Teacher is thus left at the mercy of the public, who, proverbially, have no conscience, and his situation is rendered more precarious and more degraded than that of a shoe-black.[20]

The differences between the rural reformers and the Tories created innumerable conflicts over control of local education. As a result, the whole system was neglected for decades.[21]

Because of the general lack of interest in education by the local farmers, and the religious and legislative conflict in the Assembly, education developed slowly before 1840. Thus, no school for white children was built in Reach before 1829 (a missionary school for Indians had been built the previous year),[22] and no school was erected in Beaverton until 1839.[23] The Education Acts of 1841 and 1843 would provide the impetus to create a broader system of education in Ontario County.

The growth of urban centres and the appearance of large mercantile and manufacturing enterprises brought the problems of the educational system to the fore. Not only did the rise of large-scale business require employees with a good education, but also the upsurge of lawlessness and public disorder which accompanied the creation of a populous class of poor, landless workers demanded major changes in the school system.

The increase of vagrancy and lawlessness among the urban poor aroused widespread concern in the 1840s and 1850s, and improved education among the lower classes was commonly advocated as its cure. Doctor Charles Duncombe in his report to the Assembly in 1836 decried the prevalence of juvenile delinquency in Toronto:

> Every person that frequents the streets of this city must be forcibly struck with the ragged and uncleanly appearance, the vile language, and the idle and miserable habits of numbers of children, most of whom are of an age suitable for schools, or for some useful employment. The parents of these children are, in all probability too poor, or too degenerate to provide them with clothing fit for them to be seen in school; and know not where to place them in order that they may find employment, or be better cared for.[24]

The picture that Duncombe painted of the worst of these children was black indeed:

> Accustomed, in many instances to witness at home nothing in the way of example, but what is degrading; early taught to observe intemperance, and to hear obscene and profane language without disgust; obliged to beg, and even encouraged to acts of dishonesty to satisfy the wants induced by the indolence of their parents—what can be expected, but that such children will in due time, become responsible to the laws for crimes, which have thus, in a manner, been forced upon them?[25]

To solve this growing problem Duncombe advocated an elaborate system of care and education of the destitute and neglected young.

Nor were the reformers alone in their alarm at the growing problems created by urban poverty. In 1843, Robert Murray, the Superintendent of Education argued:

> Unless the provision for the support of education is made certain and permanent, this great country must rapidly sink deeper and deeper in ignorance and vice. No man possessed of property in this Province, who attends for a little to the state of ignorance which pervades the great mass of the many thousands who are annually settled among us, and the ignorance in which our native youth are growing up around us could hesitate for a moment to pay any reasonable tax for the support of education as he would thereby be increasing the value of his estate, and securing himself and his posterity in the possession of it.[26]

Egerton Ryerson, the second Superintendent of Education, echoed Murray's thoughts in 1846:

> A system of general education amongst the people is the most effectual preventative of pauperism and its natural companions. misery and crime.
>
> To a young and growing country, and the retreat of so many poor from other countries, this consideration is of the greatest importance . . . that pauperism and crime prevail in proportion to the absence of education amongst the labouring classes.[27]

Ryerson, however, was not content to argue the case for improved education merely on the benefits to be derived from lower rates of pauperism and crime. Ryerson argued that not only did education draw the young from immorality, but it made them into more productive workers as well – an argument aimed directly at the rising class of wealthy merchants and manufacturers. In his *Report* of 1846, Ryerson included the following statement:

> The result of the investigation [in Massachusetts, 1841] is most astonishing superiority in productive power on the part of the educated over the uneducated worker . . . Processes are performed not only more rapidly, but better.[28]

Quoting another report with approval, Ryerson allayed the fears of those who were concerned that education of the working classes might lead them to discontent and disorder:

> In the present state of manufacturers, where so much is done by machinery and tools, and so little done by mere manual labour (and that little diminishing), mental superiority, system, order, punctuality and good conduct,—qualities all developed and promoted by education,—are becoming of the highest consequence. There are now, I consider, few enlightened manufacturers who will dissent from the opinion that the workshops, peopled with the greatest number of well-informed workmen, will turn out the greatest quantity of the best work in the best manner.[29]

On the basis of these ideas and observations, Ryerson undertook a long campaign to bring the educational system under stronger and stronger central control, and through compulsory and tax supported schools, to make its effects universal. It is hardly surprising that such an urban-inspired, industrial-oriented system found strong opposition from the rural areas.

The first major changes made in local education, the Education Acts of 1841 and 1843, had important immediate effects in Ontario County. By their terms, the amount of money to be granted the common schools was raised to £50,000 annually (to be divided among the schools on the basis of the population), and the District Councils were to raise an equivalent amount through local taxation. Local administration of schools was placed in the hands of township Commissioners (five or seven in number depending on the population of the township), who were elected at the annual township meeting. It was the duty of the local Commissioners to divide the township into school districts, purchase school sites, make estimates of the cost of necessary building and repairs of schools, appoint and remove teachers, regulate the local course of study, establish the school rules and determine what books were to be used, and to be responsible for a host of other duties connected to the local schools.

The District Council was made into the District Board of Education. Its main duties were to distribute the provincial grant and to raise local taxes necessary to operate the schools. In 1843 local Superintendents of Schools were named to assist the provincial Superintendent in the preparation of reports and the distribution of money. Thus, while control of curriculum and teachers remained in the hands of the township Commissioners, a hierarchy of superintendencies from the township to the districts to the province had been established to report on the condition of schools and to distribute government grants.[30] In spite of increased provincial aid and local taxation, parents of children attending the common schools were still expected to pay a significant proportion of the cost of their education via a "rate bill" or special school charge.

Although the Acts of 1841 and 1843 contained many weaknesses, they had an immediate beneficial effect on local school building and attendance. For example, in Reach Township only two schools had been built before 1840. But with the additional money made available by the new Education Acts, school construction increased rapidly as population grew. In 1841, one was built; in 1843, three; 1844, one; 1845, three; 1847,one, and 1848, two. Thus in the space of just seven years, eleven new schools were built.[31] As Table XXII shows, by 1847 there were seventy-seven common schools in Ontario County. By 1849 the number of schools had increased to eighty-two including one school in Rama not in the table.

Table XXII
Schools and Provincial Grants in Ontario County, 1847 and 1849[32]

	Number of Schools		*Provincial School Grant*			*Total Teachers Salaries*		
	1847	*1849*	*1847*			*1847*		
			£	s	d	£	s	d
Brock	10	13	82	13	0	215	10	0
Pickering	18	18	185	16	3	849	10	0
Reach	12	13	63	9	1	277	17	0
Scott	1	2	8	5	8	15	0	0
Thorah	4	5	26	15	6	80	0	0
Uxbridge	5	5	33	19	0	90	0	0
Whitby	23	22	243	18	3	1,050	0	0
Mara & Rama	4	3*	23	18	11	20	0	0

* Rama not included.

In all, the provincial grant to the area totalled £668 15s.6d. or 25.8 percent of the total cost of teachers' salaries. Assuming that the County exactly matched the provincial grant, then parents were required to pay directly almost fifty percent of the cost of education via the special rate bills.

Unfortunately, the use of these special charges upon the parents of students created two severe problems which tended to make the system ineffective. First, because of the great differences between areas in ability to raise taxes and assess school rate bills, the quality and payment of teachers varied widely from one township to another. Thus, while schools in Whitby averaged over £40 per school in salaries, schools in Brock averaged £21, and those in Mara and Rama £5. Such salaries even in 1847 were extremely low. Assuming that the schools in Mara and Rama were open the minimum nine months, the teachers earned exactly the same rate as common day-labourers. Little wonder that complaints about the quality of teaching were so prevalent.

The second problem concerning the assessment of school rates on the parents of students was explained by Ryerson in 1852:

> When it is apprehended that the Rate Bill will be high, many will not send their children to the School at all . . . or Parents will begin to take their children from School, in order to escape the Rate Bill. The consequence is, that the School is either broken up, or the whole burthen of paying the Teacher falls upon the Trustees.[33]

Because of these problems, and the attitude of parents to education, many children in Ontario County received little or no schooling in spite of the expansion of local schools. In Ryerson's *Report* for 1853, he noted that some 2,184 school-aged children in Ontario County (26 percent) were not attending school. Moreover, the report showed that the problems of urban growth and poverty were beginning to make themselves felt in Oshawa where 108 school-aged children (30 percent) did not attend school.[34] Ryerson's answer to these problems was an even greater centralization of education and the creation of "free" schools.

It was indeed ironic that just when the local inhabitants were gaining control of municipal government, Ryerson was working to take control of education from the local citizens and to vest it in the provincial government. Ryerson's method essentially was to proceed only as fast as public opinion would allow: first, to pass permissive legislation, and then, after a number of areas had made the changes, to make these changes binding on all. In 1852, in a paper entitled "The Spirit in which the Present Educational Movement Should be Directed", Ryerson laid out his principles of persuasion:

> In the advocacy of any measure, however excellent, or equitable, it may be, and it is expedient and proper, that we should attentively listen to the objection of opponents, and not imperiously attempt to repress the expression of sentiments which, although perhaps erroneous, are, equally with our own, independent and sincere. There is a latent pride and spirit of resistance in the bosom of almost every man, which, if imprudently or incautiously aroused, will result in a settled opposition to the favorite theories of others, however invested with practical utility those plans may be.[35]

Thus Ryerson's methods were frustrating to the utmost degree to his opponents. Couching his purpose in the highest and most general principles, while gradually introducing successive changes towards educational centralization and control, Ryerson gradually removed local control of curriculum from the hands of the trustees, while leaving them with the responsibility for paying much of the cost of the system. As one of Ryerson's biographers has noted:

> Ryerson's claim to distinction rests upon the fact that he organized a system that *worked*. He not only co-ordinated the several parts of the system, but put life into it. This was no easy task. The people were very jealous of their power of local control, and yet unless this local control could be subjected to some central control, improvement was hopeless. It was here that Ryerson did what no other man had done. He lessened local, and strengthened central, control, and did it so gradually, so wisely, and so tactfully, that local prejudices were soothed and in many cases the people scarcely recognized what was being done until the thing was accomplished.[36]

Thus, beginning with the educational system, the century-long process of the destruction of local control of social life was begun – a process which would, in the 1970s, culminate with the amalgamation of the municipalities themselves.

Under Ryerson's direction, the Education Act of 1846 made several significant changes towards centralization. These were both direct and indirect. Terms of local trustees were extended to three years, and they were now required to select all books from a list provided by the Department of Education. The powers of the District Superintendents were greatly expanded, but in ways which appeared to offer the least threat to local control. Their powers were expanded to include the duty to examine candidates for teachers' certificates, and to grant licenses (either temporary or permanent) to successful candidates, to revoke licenses held by incompetent or unsuitable teachers (and, incidentally, to decide what constituted a "competent" or "suitable" teacher), to prevent the use of unauthorized texts, and to make an annual report of all the schools in their district.[37] The local trustees were left the power to hire and fire teachers, but this mattered little to Ryerson so long as he determined what was taught and who could teach it.

The mechanism that Ryerson used to gradually expand his power over the educational system was the government grant. Putnam writes:

> The Legislature placed the grant at the disposal of the Superintendent [Ryerson] for him to apportion among the Districts. Here was a lever of wonderful power, and Ryerson was quick to perceive its possibilities. If Districts wished a grant they must conform to certain requirements. If school sections wished a grant from the District Superintendents, they, too, must satisfy certain requirements as to textbooks, qualified teachers, buildings and equipment.[38]

Needless to say, the rural reformers were bitterly opposed to the centralizing of the educational system, as were Robert Baldwin and George Brown, editor of the Toronto *Globe*. Brown was particularly vehement in his denunciation of centralization:

> We have had hints of the Prussian system being applicable to Canada and we feel convinced that he, who sold himself to the late Administration, would have readily brought all the youth of Canada to the same market and placed them under the domination of an arbitrary and coercive power.[39]

In spite of these objections, however, the 1846 Act was not only passed, but its basic provisions were strengthened in 1850. Control of the educational system was passing from the hands of the local community. Henceforth their children would be taught those ideas and subjects deemed necessary and desirable by the "modernists" and "improvers" who were committed to the idea of progress. The aspirations and views of the independent commodity producers who did so much to build the province would gradually be pushed aside as "old fashioned" and "reactionary". Mackenzie's old vision of a society of equal producers of wealth had begun to crumble before the rise of the "new men" – wealthy merchants, industrialists and financiers whose goals would dominate the future.

The final significant step in the urbanization of education in Ontario County was the building of the grammar school in Whitby in 1846.[4] The grammar schools, which had been established in 1807,[41] were intended to be classical schools, fashioned upon the model of the great English public schools as the training ground of the elite. The grammar schools were much more heavily subsidized by the Government than were the common schools, and generally charged much higher fees.[42] The course of study, which emphasized the study of Latin and Greek, served primarily to prepare the sons of the wealthy for careers in one of the professions. Thus the energy expended by Samuel Cochrane, Peter Perry, John Ham Perry and Ezra Annis to obtain the charter[43] demonstrated the changing interests and social aims of the increasingly prosperous members of the local mercantile community.

Just as the poverty and indifference of the local inhabitants for a long time slowed the construction of schools, so too did these problems present barriers to the building of churches and the development of religious enthusiasm as well. Whatever the religious predisposition of the settlers had been before they arrived in Ontario County, once they settled, they found themselves almost totally neglected by the established churches. Only the Quakers and Mennonites, whose religions were based on lay ministry, therefore, were capable of a full enjoyment of their faiths.

Lack of concern by the established churches was not the only thing that prevented the development of religious institutions and the building of churches. The poverty of most settlers, and the scattered religious communities made it difficult to create congregations capable of erecting buildings and supporting a resident minister. Thus only a compact settlement such as that of the Quakers in Uxbridge could afford a building set aside for worship before

1812. The small meeting house, erected in 1809 on the top of Quaker Hill, would remain for almost a generation the only religious structure in Ontario County.[44]

The problem of serving the religious needs of the settlers was one which the Anglicans never solved satisfactorily. Despite extensive aid given to the Anglicans by the Government, the upper-class backgrounds and social attitudes of the Anglican clergy made them unsuitable for pioneer life, and few remained long in backwoods parishes. Indeed, the contempt in which these ministers held their prospective parishioners was almost proverbial. For example, Strachan once described the settlers to whom he was expected to minister as follows:

> Every parish in this country is to be made; the people have little or no religion, and their minds are so prone to low cunning, that it will be difficult to make anything of them.[45]

As one observer commented in 1850:

> It seems to me that the Episcopal clergy are taken from too high a class for colonial service. They are usually so dissimilar from their flocks in tastes, habits, and prejudices, that they might come from another planet. Their early nurture has been too nice, and their education too academic, to admit of that familiarity . . . which gives such well-earned influence . . . to the Wesleyan in Great Britain,—an influence which pervades both civil and spiritual life.[46]

The Anglican Church, as time went on, concentrated its efforts in the larger centres where upper-class communicants tended to live.

In contrast to the Anglicans, the Methodists quickly adapted to the situations of pioneer life. Rather than expect the people to come to the major centres for their religious needs, the Methodists sent out circuit riding ministers to carry the gospel to the people. As early as 1802, Nathan Bangs, an American-born preacher, attended the Yonge Street circuit (which included Uxbridge, Pickering and Whitby), preaching in houses wherever a few neighbours would gather, and holding open air camp meetings. In 1805, the combined Yonge Street-Smith's Creek circuit reported 80 members.[47] In 1806, the Smith's Creek circuit (which included the Ontario County area) was separated, and over the next fifteen years showed steady growth. In 1806 this station reported 76 members; in 1810, 125;[48] and in 1820, 203.[49] In 1821, the Ontario County townships were added to the Yonge Street circuit where they continued to prosper.[50]

Perhaps no other aspect of the Methodist ministry had as great an impact as the open-air camp meetings. Because it was open to all comers, it took on an important social aspect as well as its religious function. It broke the lonely routine of pioneer life, brought people together to make new friends, and provided one of the few opportunities for the younger generation to find husbands and wives. William Case, one of the first Methodist circuit riders in Upper Canada, described the first camp meeting held in Canada as follows:

> At five o'clock Saturday morning a prayer-meeting was held, and at ten o'clock a sermon was preached on the text, 'My people are destroyed for lack of knowledge'. At this time the congregation had increased to perhaps twenty-five hundred, and the people of God were seated together on logs near the stand, while a crowd were standing in a semi-circle around them. During the sermon I felt an unusual sense of the Divine presence, and I thought I could see a cloud of Divine glory rest upon the congregation. The circle of spectators unconsciously fell back step by step, until quite a space was opened between them and those who were seated. At length I sprang from my seat to my feet. The preacher stopped, and said, 'Take it up and go on!' 'No,' I replied, 'I rise not to preach.' I immediately descended from the stand among the hearers; the rest of the preachers all spontaneously followed me, and we went among the people, exhorting the impenitent and comforting the distressed; for while Christians were filled with 'joy unspeakable and full of glory,' many a sinner was praying and weeping in the surrounding crowd . . . O what a scene of tears and prayers was this! It was truly affecting to see parents weeping over their children, neighbours exhorting their unconverted neighbours to repent, while all, old and young, were awe-struck. The wicked looked on with silent amazement, while they beheld some of their companions struck down by the mighty power of God.[51]

To upper-class eyes, the revivalist fervour of the Methodist camp meeting was simply additional proof of the dangerous mental and spiritual weakness of the lower classes. Innumerable English travellers and Canadian observers found the scene of the camp meetings one which allowed them to exercise their wit,[52] while Strachan levelled some of his harshest attacks upon the practice:

> The Methodists are making great progress among us and filling the country with the most deplorable fanaticism. You can have almost no conception of their excesses. They will bawl twenty of them at once, tumble on the ground, laugh, sing, jump, and stamp, and this they call the working of the spirit. All this arises from the fewness of the regular clergy, there being only six of us in the upper province.[53]

So long as the established churches were either unwilling or unable to supply the backwoods areas with clergy, the Methodists continued to have success in winning converts. Indeed, as late as 1823 Strachan reported to British authorities that even then Anglican services were held in Whitby only occasionally, while the closest Presbyterian minister to the area, the Reverend Mr. Jenkins, lived in Markham on Yonge Street.[54]

Although the evangelistic sects were successful in filling the void left by the neglect of the established churches, there was a general increase in the number of inhabitants who abandoned religion entirely. This decline in religious interest was described in various ways. For example, in 1817 one observer argued:

> New countries are generally settled by adventurers, with whom religion is not a primary consideration. Pious persons are seldom found willing to break off their former connexions, and foresake the land where both their fathers have worshipped God. Persons coming from a country where religious institutions are observed, into one where they are neglected, unless they have known something of the power of godliness, will feel themselves set free from restraints which were far from being pleasant. They will find the profanation of the Sabbath, and the neglect of religion, quite congenial to their unrenewed minds: and, if this is the case when they first settle in the woods, what can we expect when they have lived a number of years without religious instruction? May we not expect that depraved passions will be indulged, that vices will be practiced with avidity, and that the future world will be neglected amidst the clamorous demands of the present?[55]

A second observer argued that the main problem lay in the poor quality of clergy which were sent to Canada:

> One great evil which is observable in all the churches of Canada, and mostly, I feel in truth constrained to observe, in the Church of Scotland as it existed—has been that men of indifferent abilities have usually fallen to the lot of the colonists. This is, without question, the effect of the natural principle (from the influence of which not even ministers of the Gospel are exempted), that the lower the rate of worldly encouragement the more indifferent the description of ability presents itself in the field which calls for occupation.[56]

Whatever the cause of the decline in interest in religion, its effects were strongly felt in Ontario County. Indeed in 1842, 73.1 percent of the residents in Whitby reported that they had no religious affiliation.[57]

By the end of the 1820s a strong revival in the activities of the established churches began to take place. After 1828 the Presbyterians sent out circuit-riding missionaries of their own, and in 1832 the Reverend J. Carrothers commenced his circuits in the Ontario County area.[58] So successful was he that a permanent minister replaced him the next year in Whitby - the Reverend R. H. Thornton who became the first resident Presbyterian minister in Ontario County. The Presbyterians worshipped in the old log Baptist church in Whitby for several years until the "Old Kirk", a fine brick church, was built.[59] Thornton's influence was not confined to his religious activities in Whitby. In the early years he preached regularly in Reach and the northern townships. He was active in education, gave innumerable lectures and papers on educational subjects, published several books, and served for many years both as a grammar school trustee and as the superintendent of common schools in Whitby Township.[60]

The influx of many well-to-do British immigrants into Ontario County in the 1830s and the greater prosperity of some of the original settlers made possible the erection of the first Anglican church there in 1835. In that year the prosperous English immigrant farmers at Columbus built a log church, and in 1839 the area of Whitby, Darlington and Clarke was organized into a parish under the charge of the Reverend T.. Kennedy.[61] A second Anglican church, St. John's Episcopal, was opened in Port Whitby in 1843.[62] Four years later the first Anglican church in Oshawa, St. George's, was built.

Other denominations show much the same pattern of increased activity in the 1830s and church building in the 1840s. When the Union School house was built in Oshawa in 1835, it became the centre of worship for all denominations. The Wesleyan Methodists, Roman Catholics, Quakers, Baptists and Bible Christians all shared the building until 1841, when the Methodists and Catholics built their own churches. The Bible Christians built their first church in Oshawa in 1842.[63] In Pickering, the 1840s saw the same wave of church building that had occurred in Whitby. In 1850 W.H. Smith reported that there were four churches - Methodist, Presbyterian, Roman Catholic and Quaker - at Duffin's Creek.[64]

Typically, the northern townships lagged somewhat behind the south in religious organization and the building of churches. In 1843 the first northern church, erected by the Presbyterians in Beaverton, was built,[65] and the Presbyterians began holding services in Mara in 1845. They also built churches in Reach on the twelfth concession and at Utica in 1848.[66] Catholic services were held for the Scottish and Irish immigrants in Mara from 1840 on, although a church was not built until 1857.[67]

Although the Methodists in the southern townships had passed well beyond the period of saddle-bag missionaries by 1848 with the building of a church in Reach on the Brock Road and a chapel in Brooklin, in the north the old practices were still necessary. The Brock circuit encompassed the northern part of Ontario County and Victoria County and, as the *Annual Report* of the Episcopal Methodist Missionary Society noted, was "composed of destitute settlers, there being no Indians within the bounds of the mission".[68]

The awakened interest in religion in the 1840s, was reflected not only in the increased building of churches, but in the new formations of parishes and congregations, many of which worshipped in schools, halls and private houses. Although the list of "places of worship" in the census of 1851 is by no means complete, it does give some idea of the upswing in religious activity. In 1851, there was a total of 46 "places of worship" in Ontario County. This included 15 in Whitby Township and Oshawa village, 11 in Brock, 5 in Reach, 3 in Uxbridge, and one each in Thorah, Scugog and Scott. The census shows no places of worship in Mara and Rama.[69]

In addition to being a centre of growth for religious sects who have retained large membership to the present day, Ontario County was also noted for two groups whose influence had largely disappeared by the 1850s: the Mormons and the Millerites. The first Mormon missionary came to Canada in 1830, although active attempts at conversion did not begin until 1832. In that year six ordained elders of the Church of Jesus Christ of Latter-day Saints, as the Mormon church is officially called, began active work at Earnstown, near Kingston.[70] These missionaries enjoyed considerable success, and over the next several years the efforts of the church were expanded westward. In 1836, led by Elder Orson Pratt, the Mormons began preaching in the Pickering and Whitby area with some success. In 1837, the leader of the Mormons, the Prophet Joseph Smith, visited Pickering and Whitby, and informed the local converts that all members of the religion were to travel to the "far west". Two groups left Canada in 1837 and 1838, and most eventually settled in Nauvoo, Illinois.[71]

Several families from Whitby Township, among them the Magahans, Seeleys and Lamoureux followed Smith to Nauvoo and later to Salt Lake City, Utah.[72] Mrs. Christiana Gordon Ross of Pickering remembered that when her grandfather, William Gordon, came to Canada in 1838, he was fortunate enough to buy a fine farm in Pickering very cheaply from a Mormon family who had decided to follow Joseph Smith:

> Grandfather . . . bought a large farm in Pickering . . . two hundred and fifty acres and almost entirely cleared, with the same house as stands there today and which was counted as a very fine one at that date; he bought also horses, two spans, cattle, wagons and everything else just as they stood. This purchase was made from Mr. Lawrence with whom Joe Smith, the famous Mormon leader lived. My mother often told me about it, that grandfather paid cash (£1,000) . . . and that upon receiving the money, Mr. Lawrence just handed it across the table to Joe Smith. This was sometime in the summer of 1838 and immediately after Joe Smith and all the Mormons left for the states.[73]

It would be many years before the Mormon wanderers would again find the peace that they had enjoyed in Ontario County.[74]

In contrast to the quiet-living Mormons, the Millerites were the source of considerable local interest and humour. The Millerites, or Second Adventists, were a sect of Millenialists (those who believe that Christ will appear in person to claim his earthly kingdom after a period of time) who followed William Miller, an American Evangelist. Miller preached that the world would end in 1842 or 1843, and his message had considerable effect in Ontario County. Thomas Conant reported that some farmers gave away their goods and farms, while others waited joyfully (or sorrowfully, as the state of their consciences warranted) for the end of the world. Conant's father attended a meeting of the Millerites in Darlington on February 14, 1843, the date set by Miller for the end of the world, and described the scene as follows:

> They . . . stood and listened to some Millerite in the master's rostrum desk, as he told about the terrible fires to come on in a few hours. His words riveted the attention of all, cramped and uncomfortable as they were in the crowded room.
>
> Tallow dips, fastened in tin reflectors, shed a mild light over all, and the heat from the crowded room became so great as to give a taste, an intense one, too, of the awful heat promised when the fires should appear. The old log school-house had been used before as a rude pioneer dwelling, and a cellar had been scooped out below the centre. Without an instant's warning the old floor-beams broke and the crowd, who all expected to go up, as the Millerite preacher assured them, were let *down* with unexpected precipitancy. The scene, my father said, was too ludicrous for description. Screaming, fainting, pulling, praying, squirming, the dense mass fought to get out. Fortunately the tallow dips were fastened to the walls and continued to light up the place. My father dryly said he made his way out, got his load and went home (at Port Oshawa) and to bed.[75]

Needless to say, when Conant's father awoke the next morning, the flames which the Millerites had expected to appear to consume the world were nowhere in sight, and the blowing snows of a February morning greeted his skeptical gaze.

Unlike Conant's father, many people had believed Miller's predictions. One girl, Sarah Terwilligar of Oshawa, made herself a pair of wings from silk, and attempted to fly up to heaven from her father's porch.[76] It would be many years before all those who had believed in Miller's millenarian vision would live down their shame at having been taken in.

The major religious groups made gains in membership through their increased vigour in the 1840s and had greatly enhanced their position through their influence in the schools and other social institutions. In the 1830s and 1840s the major social critics who were alarmed by the rise of crime, immorality and social disorder in the towns and cities all believed that social stability through education could be gained only if the inculcation of religious principles was made part of that education. For example, Dr. Charles Duncombe, in his *Report on Education* in 1836 argued:

> All agree that the Bible teaches that mankind are in danger of eternal ruin; that all have become sinful, that a way of pardon and salvation has been secured through the atoning sacrifice of the Redeemer; that whenever love to God, and the desire to do His will, is the regulating principle of the mind, men are prepared for Heaven; and that without this character no happiness is to be hoped for in the future state; that no man will ever attain this character without supernatural aid from the Spirit of God, and that such influences are to be sought by prayer and the use of the appropriate means of religious influence; that as the

> Bible is the standard of moral rectitude, and employ its solemn sanctions to sustain its precepts . . .
>
> One thing is certain, if religious influences are banished from our provincial system of Education, every denomination will be injured in its most vital interests. For one who would be proselyted by a sectarian Teacher, ten would be ruined by the vice and irreligion consequent on the [lack] of moral and religious influences.[77]

One noted Judge who was also the chairman of a county Board of Education summed up his views of the relationship between the rising tide of urban juvenile crime and the lack of religious instruction in the schools as follows:

> Witness the juvenile offenders in our prisons! Witness the Arabs in the Streets of our Cities! Witness the empty benches of many of our Common Schools! Witness the heathen state of some of our School Sections. . . . I can testify that there are Common Schools never opened without Prayer, or Hymns, where the Scriptures are read, and where children are made to know and feel without God, "nothing is good, nothing is holy". But alas! I can also state that there are places called Schools, in which the voice of Prayer and Praise is never heard! Let the Provincial Council of Education, the Local Superintendents, the Trustees, the Examiners, the Clergy, the Visitors, and, although last, but not least, the Parents, dwell upon this painful contrast.[78]

Egerton Ryerson agreed with these sentiments, and as early as 1846, he had offered a solution to the problem. Not only should Christian instruction be made part of the regular curriculum, but schools should be entirely tax-supported by a tax on property (the principal wealth of the period), and attendance for all school-aged children should be made compulsory.[79] In the 1846 *Report*, Ryerson argued that a non-sectarian form of Christianity should be taught:

> To teach a child the dogmas and spirit of a Sect, before he is taught the essential principles of Religion and Morality, is to invert the pyramid, to reverse the order of nature,—to feed with the bones of controversy instead of with the nourishing milk of Truth and Charity.[80]

Although Ryerson always took great care to argue that the "truths" to be taught would not, and should not, give offense to any other religion, the Catholics and Anglicans took rather different views on the matter. In 1847, the Honourable John Elmsley, a convert and leading Catholic layman, set forth the basic argument for the creation of separate schools:

> It was impossible for the Roman Catholics to send their children to schools where the teachers were Protestants. . . . Many things were taught in these schools which reflected on Roman Catholics—such as the history of Henry VIII, which was given so differently in Protestant

> from Roman Catholic Authors. Above all things there was the Bible, which Protestants made a school book of, but which Roman Catholics, not from disrepsect, but from greater reverence did not give to their children to read, without being accompanied by explanations provided by the priests. . . . If children read the Bible without that safeguard they would become *not* Protestants but infidels . . . . There were many Roman Catholic children running about the streets idle, who would be at school if it were not for the Protestant teachers to whom they must be sent; but this the parents would never do; they would rather they were not educated at all.[81]

With Ryerson's drive to force all school-aged children to attend school, the necessity of the creation of separate schools became more and more crucial to Catholics. There is no need here to go into the long struggle by Catholics to establish separate schools in Ontario, but it should be noted that the first school of this type in Ontario County was St. Gregory's on Prince Street in Oshawa, built in 1859.[82]

The expansion and centralization of schools in Ontario County and their transformation from secular to Christian principles was accepted with general public approval, yet it was a process which won little support from any local residents. For a long time attendance would remain relatively low. But over time the new "Christian" schools and the greater prevalence of religious institutions had their effect. By 1871 very few persons remained who stated their religious preference as "none". Thus, under Ryerson's direction the whole social texture of local society gradually changed.

THE CREATION OF ONTARIO COUNTY

Just as the building of roads became the centre of bitter controversy between rival groups of businessmen, and the point of conflict between localities, so too did the development of local government and the separation of Ontario County from York County produce controversy and bitterness as the various factions struggled to enhance their positions.

When Lord Durham drew up his report on the conditions in the Canadas after the Rebellion, he had been particularly concerned about the lack of local elective government at the municipal level. It was his opinion that local government was necessary to encourage responsibility among the citizens and to check the centralizing and autocratic tendencies of the ruling class which, he believed, had been the primary cause of the revolt. It was Durham's opinion that

> The establishment of a good system of municipal institutions throughout the provinces is a matter of vital importance. A general legislature, which manages the private business of every parish, in addition to the common business of the country, wields a power which no single body, however popular in its constitution, ought to have—a power which must be destructive to any constitutional balance .... Instead of confiding the whole collection and distribution of all the revenues raised in any county for all general and local purposes to a single repre-

> sentative body, the power of local assessment, and the application of the funds arising from it, should be entrusted to local management.[1]

The new district councils which were established in 1841 under the urging of the first Governor of the united provinces, Lord Sydenham, were made up of elected councillors and appointed officials.[2] The councillors were elected according to a voters list of adult male freeholders and householders, which was prepared from the assessment rolls. A township with fewer than 300 votes elected one councillor, while a township with 300 or more electors sent two. The councillors were required to be residents of the township they represented and to possess land within that or an adjacent district valued at £300 above all encumbrances. With this restriction, only the very wealthiest men were eligible to be elected to the district council. Thus the first Home District Council was made up of prominent local landowners and businessmen such as Peter Perry and Colonel Cameron. Councillors were elected for a three-year term, with one-third retiring each year.[3]

Although Lord Sydenham was prepared to establish elected district councils, he was determined to retain close control over their actions. Thus the warden, district clerk and treasurer were to be appointed by the governor, and to hold their positions at his pleasure. The clerk was to be chosen from among three men nominated by the council. The council was not given any power over the actions of these officials who were responsible only to the governor. Moreover, careful checks were established to prevent any "runaway" legislation. District councils were expressly restricted to certain areas of legislation: council meetings were limited by law to four meetings per year with a maximum of six days each; extraordinary meetings could be held only with the express permission of the governor; councils were forbidden to tax government property, to levy fines exceeding £5, or to impose prison terms; and no public work could be begun until it had been reported on by the district surveyor (appointed by the warden), and if the cost of the work exceeded £300, by the provincial board of public works.[4] Most important were two additional restrictions: all council bylaws were to be reported to the governor by the district clerk, and might be disallowed within thirty days; and finally, any district council might be dissolved by the governor with the advice and consent of the Executive Council. The last restriction, of course, was designed to prevent a deadlock between the elected council and the Government or its appointed officials. Should such a confrontation arise, the council would simply be dissolved, and the district would return to the arbitrary rule of the justices of the peace.

In spite of all these restrictions, the councils were given considerable powers in several areas of jurisdiction. Most of the administrative powers of the Quarter Sessions (as well as their assets and liabilities) were transferred to the elected councils, and they were given legislative jurisdiction over roads and bridges, the purchase and sale of district real estate, administration of schools, the fixing of district and township officers' salaries and fees, as well as the responsibility of defraying the cost of the administration of justice. To meet these substantial expenses, the councils were empowered to levy tolls and to tax real estate, personal property, or both. The maximum taxation level, however, was fixed at two pennies per pound of assessed value, or one and one-half penny per acre of land.[5]

It was significant that the statutes and powers of the annual township meeting were generally unchanged under the 1841 Act. The powers and duties of the township meeting still included the appointment of officials who were to serve under the direction and control of the district council, and the determination of what constituted a legal fence and what animals might run at large. The one additional duty given them was the election of representatives to the district council. Thus at the first annual meeting of Scott township in 1843 it was determined that, "Hogs be free cominers [commoners]", "Horses be ditto", "The lawful fence to be six feet high, staked and double ridered".[6]

In spite of the problems of too little money and the quarrels over its allocation, the new system worked well. Of special value was the representation of all the areas on the new council. At last, decisions could be made by men who knew intimately the needs and priorities of all the townships, rather than by men from the urban centres (where most of the justices of the peace had been concentrated). When no great difficulties arose regarding council irresponsibility, an Act[7] was passed in 1846 which provided that the warden henceforth would be a councillor who would be elected to the warden's chair by a majority of his fellow councillors. All other officers were placed under the control of the district council who might hire or fire them as they wished. In spite of this change, the powers of disallowance were retained until 1849 when the whole municipal system was again completely reviewed.

Until 1849 the special powers required by growing urban centres were provided for by the enactment of special legislation as need arose. As C.R.W. Biggar remarked:

> As towns arose, and markets were established therein, the Quarter Sessions of the District were further empowered to make for these towns "such prudential rules and regulations as they might deem expedient" relative to the watching, paving, lighting, keeping in repair, cleaning and improving the streets, regulating the assize of bread, slaughter houses and nuisances, firemen and fire companies; and also for enforcing the laws relative to the inspection of weights and measures, and to horses, swine or cattle running at large in the town.[8]

Because of the difficulties inherent in the administration of such local conditions by the justices of the peace in Quarter Session, the Government gradually began to transfer certain powers to local elected Boards of Police. These Boards of Police, which were elected annually, were given power to appoint and dismiss the town clerk, treasurer and street surveyors, assessors, collectors and bailiffs and to fix their remuneration; to make assessments for purchasing real estate for the use of the town, and for procuring fire engines, aqueducts and a supply of pure water; to make assessments for lighting, paving and repairing the streets; to regulate and license eating houses, public exhibitions, circuses, and so forth; to prevent riding or driving at "an immoderate pace"; and to make such rules and regulations "generally to prevent vice and preserve good order in the town".[9] These powers were not set out in any general act, but rather, special acts were passed for each police village. Thus special Board of Police Acts were passed for Brockville (1832), Hamilton (1833), Cornwall, Port Hope and Prescott (1834), Belleville (1836), and Cobourg and Picton (1837).

Even broader powers were sometimes granted to urban centres which were incorporated as towns or cities. In these centres municipal government was invested in an elected mayor and council, the mayor usually being chosen by the council from among its members. Thus Toronto (1834), Kingston (1838), Hamilton and Cornwall (1846) and Bytown, Dundas, London and Brantford (1847) were all granted these extra powers by separate Acts. It must be made clear, however, that it was not the intention of the Acts to create a "democratic" government. Property restrictions upon both electors and candidates for office were so high that only the wealthiest inhabitants enjoyed any participation in local government.

As time went on, the multiplicity of municipal acts became a problem for the government to administer. Moreover, the undemocratic makeup of the council brought municipal life under the control of precisely the same kind of people who ruled through the Quarter Sessions. In an attempt to solve both the administrative difficulties and to introduce some of the democratic ideals of the reformers, Robert Baldwin introduced the first comprehensive Municipal Act in 1843. Baldwin's Act was designed to provide a method for orderly change in the status and powers of municipalities, and to introduce the democratic principle of elected local government to all municipal bodies. Baldwin's Act passed the Assembly with little difficulty, but the Executive Council objected to the democratic principles which it contained, and the Act died on the Order Paper.[10]

When Robert Baldwin finally came to power at the head of a Reform Government in 1848, he introduced local government legislation which fulfilled most of the ideals for which the independent producers (farmers, craftworkers and merchants) had struggled to implement from 1820 on. In particular, the reintroduction and passing of the Local Government Act (which had been dropped in 1843[11]) confirmed, in Canada, the principle that the autonomous producer was the basis of government and society. As a means of bringing municipal government closer to the people, a second Act was passed which allowed for the sub-division of the districts into counties.[12]

Baldwin's Municipal Act of 1849 established two fundamental principles held dear by the independent producers – subsidiarity and an extended franchise which recognized that the independent producer was the basis of social and political stability and prosperity. Subsidiarity, as a principle, meant that all those things which primarily affect a local community should be directly under their control. Thus the Municipal Act was based on the concept of a hierarchy of governments - imperial, provincial, county, and township - each of which was responsible for taking care of the needs of narrower or wider interests of the population. To each level of government was given both the powers and duties appropriate to the common needs of those under its jurisdiction.

Fundamental too, in the new Muncipal Act, was the extension of the franchise to the forty-shilling freeholder. This was not a new concept (indeed, it was the common basis for the British franchise) but its incorporation into the municipal system was new in Canada where it was to be exercised without the constraint of an Upper House or any manner of governmental review. Henceforth, the only check upon municipal legislation was the judicial test as to whether or not a particular bylaw was within or without its field of jurisdiction. Within the areas of law given to the municipalities, they were to be supreme.

The basic unit of the new municipal government was the town or township council. Each town and township were to elect five-man councils annually. From among its members each local council was required to elect a reeve, who was also the township's representative to the county council. Where there were more than 500 names on the electoral roll, the council also elected a deputy reeve who also became a member of county council. In general, the town and township councils were given powers to regulate all those things - roads, bridges, drains, watercourses, pits, common schools, pounds, fences, animals, weed destruction, taxes, and tolls - which were of immediate interest to the local inhabitants. The county council was given similar duties and powers at a general level, with the additional provision that it had the right to review, upon appeal, the validity of town and township bylaws.

The Act which provided for the creation of counties from the districts was short and to the point. Counties were to remain temporarily united until such time as they had grown sufficiently in wealth and population to be able to afford all the capital and administrative costs which would accrue to a separate administration. Thus both Peel and Ontario Counties were required to remain united with York until they were ready for separation. As soon as they had built a courthouse and jail, the government would appoint a judge, surrogate justice, sheriff, coroner, clerk of the peace and twelve justices of the peace. Thus, in 1849, the way was opened for the establishment of Ontario County as a separate municipal government.

The whole problem of municipal alignment was not new to the area when the Municipal Acts were passed in 1849. In 1837, when Simcoe District had been created from the northern townships of Home District, it had been proposed that Thorah, Mara and Rama should be included in the new

Peter Perry *Public Archives of Ontario*

district. The residents of those townships, however, believed their interests were closer to those of Georgina, Brock or Reach than to those of such distant townships as Mulmur, Essa, Tiny or Tay. Thus they petitioned to remain in the Home District.[13] When the boundaries of Simcoe District were drawn, Thorah, Mara and Rama were included in the Fourth Riding of York.[14]

The political struggle to create a new district out of the ten eastern townships in Home District (originally Georgina Township was included in the plans; Scugog did not yet exist) began in 1848, before the Municipal Acts were passed. Led by Peter Perry, the movement at first consisted almost entirely of Whitby merchants and businessmen who believed that the creation of a new district with Whitby as its capital would strengthen their control over the commerce of the area and make possible the creation of the extensive inland transportation system which would join Lakes Ontario and Huron and capture the trade of an inland empire. Opposing their ambitious undertaking were three kinds of opponents: the farmers who feared that the high costs of separation would raise taxes; residents of townships which already had good roads and access to the district centre at Toronto; and the leaders of rival towns who objected to the enhancement of Whitby's power and prestige to the detriment of their own.

The first round of the battle begun by Perry for separation resulted in almost complete defeat. In the summer and fall of 1848 he toured the townships advocating the creation of a new district, and demanding that it be put to a vote at the annual township meetings in January, 1849. The opposition, lead by rural radicals, such as Joshua Wixon, opposed Perry's plan on the grounds that the benefits to be gained by separation were greatly outweighed by the high capital costs of a new courthouse, jail and administrative offices and the increased annual cost of the duplication of services and officers.[15] In the subsequent township meetings Perry's plan was roundly defeated in all but Pickering where there was a disputed election result. Immediately after the township meetings, petitions against separation (Uxbridge's petition was purported to have been signed by nearly every voter) were sent by local committees to Robert Baldwin for presentation to the Assembly.[16]

Rather than accept defeat, Perry presented his motion to the Home District Council in hopes that pro-separation members from other areas would support his case. Once again he met defeat as the council passed the resolution:

> It is the opinion of the Council, that any dismemberment of the Home District, either at the eastern or western extremity, would be unwise and injudicious, inasmuch as it would impair the credit and contract the means now at the disposal of the Council, for extending the necessary local improvements, instead of which a large portion of the revenue would inevitably divert from those objects so highly beneficial to the whole as a community, to erect the public buildings and pay the salaries of the proposed new County.[17]

Although Perry's plans had received a severe setback, the passing of the Baldwin Municipal Acts in 1849 opened the way to raise the issue once again. This time, however, two additional elements were added to the struggle. Leading Whitby businessmen had obtained a charter to build a railway from Whitby harbour to Georgian Bay and included the demand for separation with a request for provincial aid in its construction, and a move was begun to separate the northern townships of York and Ontario Counties and to create yet another county, centred in Newmarket. When the ambitions of almost every town to become a county seat was added to this struggle, the possible combinations and re-combinations for political advantage became almost limitless.

The impetus to re-open the issue came once again from Peter Perry in 1850. This time, however, the Whitby merchants found themselves allied with their neighbours and rivals, the merchants of Oshawa. The merchants of Oshawa, however, were uncomfortable allies at best. For though they backed the idea of separation, they did so on their own behalf. Oshawa, the only incorporated village, they argued, must naturally become the seat of government for the projected county.

The first goal of the rival merchants was to get the support of the other residents of Whitby Township both for the separation and for the location of the county seat. The eastern villagers from Oshawa, Columbus, Harmony and Raglan soon found themselves ranged against the western villagers from Whitby, Brooklin and Myrtle. On election days bands from Whitby and Oshawa marched through the villages, while a barrage of handbills, pamphlets and "Facts for Electors" extolled the virtues of the rival centres.[18] In

Original Meeting Place of the Ontario County Council, The Free Church, Whitby

Whitby Historical Society

First County Building, Whitby

Possession of the Author

Sheriff Nelson G. Reynolds
Public Archives of Ontario

James Rowe
Whitby Historical Society

Thomas Nicholson Gibbs
Public Archives of Ontario

Joseph Gould
Possession of the Author

these struggles Whitby village generally managed to obtain a three-two majority in the township council, and thereby obtained the advantage of appearing as the official choice of the electors of Whitby Township.

The main campaign was opened by Perry in northern Ontario County at Chirstmas, 1850, as he attempted to persuade the northern villagers to elect pro-separation township councils. To aid him in his campaign, he took with him Ezra Annis, a well-known Reformer, to advocate separation to the residents of Uxbridge who were Reformers; Captain Rowe, a leading Whitby grain buyer, to influence his Anglo-Irish fellow countrymen in Brock and Thorah; and John Watson, the Whitby warfinger, who had shipped the grain of hundreds of farmers from Whitby harbour, to call upon his friends and acquaintances among the farmers to support Perry's campaign.[19] The main new inducement held out by Perry to residents of northern Ontario County was that Perry and the Whitby businessmen would immediately on separation build a railway through the county, and thereby increase the value of land and reduce the cost of goods for all. This time he had greater success, and a number of townships elected pro-separation councils in order to receive the benefits of the promised railway.

In order to reduce antagonism, the separationists took care to isolate the question of separation from that of the location of the county seat proclaiming that the latter should be decided by a vote of the reeves of the ten townships. In January, the York County (as Home District was now called) Council appointed a seven-member committee comprised of Colonel Cameron (the reeve of Thorah), and Messrs. Howard (Georgina), Gould (Uxbridge), Brabazon (Brock), Hartman (Whitchurch), Ewers (Reach) and Black (Whitby) to study the question.[20] Their report, which was adopted by a vote of 25 to 12, did not go so far as to advocate separation, but contented itself with the statement that all the facilities of York County were overcrowded, that the proposed county possessed both the wealth and population necessary to support separate government, and that it believed that the majority of the residents of the ten townships affected were in favour of the move. It concluded by resolving that

> under these circumstances, and others which might be alluded to if necessary, this Council has no desire or disposition whatever, of throwing any unsurmountable obstacles or impediments in the way of the formation of said proposed County of Ontario.[21]

Opposition to this resolution came from three sources: the reeves from York, Vaughan and the other central townships who saw their influence being diminished by separation, T.N. Gibbs, from Oshawa who saw Whitby's ambitions triumphing over Oshawa's and Howard, the reeve of Georgina who preferred to retain ties with Toronto rather than with Whitby. They were clearly out-voted not only by the reeves from Ontario County, but also by those of Peel County, who were seeking support for separation for that area.

Once the townships had voted to allow separation, the next move came in the Assembly where a motion was presented which created the new boundary lines. This bill, however, had been drawn up with an eye towards achieving the widest possible support, and created four, rather than three counties within the old Home District boundaries. By its terms the following county groupings were to be established: York County, to consist of Scarborough, York, Etobicoke, Vaughan, Markham and King; Peel County, to consist of Toronto Township, Chinguacousy, Caledon, Albion and the Gore of Toronto; Ontario County, to consist of Whitby, Pickering, Reach, Uxbridge, Brock, Thorah, Mara, Rama and Scugog Island; and an unnamed fourth county to be comprised of Whitchurch, Gwillimbury East and North, Georgina and Scott townships.

The Assembly motion brought an immediate response from the York Council. It established a committee to examine the boundary question; that committee brought in a report which strongly rejected the creation of a fourth county. By a vote of twenty-two to nine (the nine were mostly members from the proposed fourth county) the Council proposed that only three counties be created, and that Ontario County should be made up of the townships of Whitby, Pickering, Uxbridge, Scott, Georgina, Reach, Brock, Thorah, Mara, Rama, and Scugog Island.[22] The Assembly accepted the proposal, with the exception that Scugog Island was to be united with Reach Township until such time as its population would reach sufficient numbers to enable it to become a separate municipality.[23] By this Act which came into force on January 1, 1852, Ontario County would be allowed to establish a provisional county council, and be allowed to separate as soon as its county buildings and jail were completed. Because the Act was simply a piece of enabling legislation which could be acted upon only after the local inhabitants had made their will known, there was little basis for opposition to its passing.[24]

With the passing of the enabling legislation, the whole issue once again came to the fore. Now, however, a new set of opponents to the move appeared. Just as the merchants of Whitby and Oshawa believed that the growth of their towns was dependent on the maintenance and expansion of their monopoly over the trade and administration of the area, the merchants, bankers and financiers of Toronto believed also that the creation of a rival municipal centre at Whity or Oshawa would inevitably loosen their control of the northern areas.[25] Thus the local opponents to separation found themselves with valuable allies and ample financing from Toronto in the ensuing contests.

More to the point, however, was the determination of council members from the central townships to get what they could from the separationist townships before the final break. Thus the York County members brought in a series of proposals for enormous and costly county buildings which would have to be paid for by a large increase in local debt and taxation and the equalization rates of local taxation were thus adjusted so that the Ontario County townships were required to pay a much greater proportion of taxation than they had formerly done.[26]

The latter two moves proved to be shortsighted on the part of the York councillors; they ultimately became the primary justification for separation. By the Enabling Act, the reeves of the Ontario County municipalities were allowed to meet together as a Provisional Council to plan for separation and to make such expenditures as might be necessary to bring the proposed county into being. The first meeting of this Provisional Council took place May 3, 1852 in Whitby to discuss the possibility of separation. The reeves and deputy reeves making up the Provisional Council were:

Township[27]	*Reeve*	*Deputy Reeve*
Whitby	James Rowe	James Dryden
Pickering	W. H. Michell	Peter Taylor
Reach and Scugog	Thomas Paxton	A. W. Ewers
Brock	Robert Sproule	A. Carmichael
Uxbridge	Joseph Gould	
Scott	James Galloway	
Georgina	James Bouchier	
Thorah	Charles Robinson	
Mara and Rama	James McPherson	
Oshawa Village	T. N. Gibbs	

The initial meeting was spent in a bitter debate which lasted the better part of the day. Joseph Gould (who on Peter Perry's death had become the leading advocate of separation) opened the discussion with the proposal that "the Council do now proceed to appropriate at once the amount necessary to erect the county buildings, the same to be raised in sums so as to cover a term of twenty years".[28] In a long and eloquent speech Gould laid out the main arguments for separation:

> The accumulating county business, which is now literally choking up every department of our county affairs, in this huge county, has long cried for a division of the county of York, and especially now when other counties, of not half its extent or population, were cheerfully availing themselves of those district divisions which of necessity forced themselves on the Government, and were successfully working out their own local concerns, untrammelled by an overwhelming centralizing influence, such as we have to contend with in the city of Toronto . . . The mainspring of every action is self-interest, and [I trust] that no man present [is] so insensible to the interests of his constituents as to refuse to secure them now by the immediate erection of our county building and a speedy separation. What could we avail by delay? Could we stave off the network of taxation that is now being prepared to be cast over us by the city of Toronto. The county of York is not only erecting a

> court house, . . . but they contemplate further improvements and heavy expenditures, to avoid which is our solemn duty to our constituents. Why did they hurry in this matter? The great and expensive improvements that have been made in the past years render the county buildings sufficiently convenient for years to come, and after our separation, more than sufficient; but York and Peel wish to get a bite out of us first, and the sooner we separate the sooner will we get rid of these debts of their contracting . . . . Let us proceed at once and place ourselves out of danger, and not remain at the further mercy of York and Peel. (Cheers).[29]

The opposition to separation was led by W.H. Michell, reeve of Pickering, and T.N. Gibbs of Oshawa. Both rejected Gould's proposal on the grounds that though York's new county buildings were costly, the erection of local buildings would be even more costly – at least £10,000 for buildings and £3,000 to establish a registry office. Their main demand, however, was that the question be settled, not by the Legislature or Provisional Council, but by a referendum of all the ratepayers. This demand was rejected by Gould and the separationists – a rejection that caused no little amusement among Gould's opponents, who had often been defeated by his ultra-democratic reputation among the farmers. Finally, after hours of furious debate a vote was taken and, to everyone's consternation, it was tied seven to seven. In favour were Whitby's reeve and deputy reeve, James Rowe and James Dryden; Reach and Scugog's reeve and deputy reeve, Thomas Paxton and Abel W. Ewers; the deputy reeve of Pickering, Peter Taylor; Charles Robinson, reeve of Thorah; and Joseph Gould, reeve of Uxbridge. Thus the representatives of four municipalities favoured the separation while one township (Pickering) was divided. In opposition were the representatives of five townships plus the reeve of Pickering, W.H. Michell. Now the decision was up to Joseph Gould who had been elected the provisional warden at the beginning of the meeting. His vote was "yes". Thus by the narrowest of margins it was decided to bring the county into being.[30]

In politics no victory is ever final unless all those involved agree to accept the outcome. No sooner had the vote been given to Gould's separationist forces than his opponents went out to enlist support for continued unity. A protest was entered against Gould's dual vote, and a document was drawn up and signed by six of the protesters stating that they would refuse to attend future meetings of the Provisional Council until a referendum on the question of separation had been completed. Thus when the Provisional Council reconvened on May 10, half of the members were absent, and without a quorum no business could be legally transacted. In spite of this difficulty, a bylaw was passed authorizing the raising of £6,000 and the erection of county buildings.[31] Needless to say this action caused even more anger and controversy among the ratepayers.

From our vantage point it is difficult to imagine the bitterness which went into the separation debate. Even Joseph Gould's biographer, writing thirty-five years after, found it difficult to comprehend the depth of feeling exhibited by the contending factions. As W.H. Higgins reminisced in 1887:

> Looking back now, at this distance of time, at the proceedings in connection with the organization of the new county, one is amazed at the bitterness of feeling displayed, and the tenacity of purpose with which every inch of ground was fought by both sides. The press teemed with letters full of charges and counter charges, impeaching the motives and action of individual members; broad-sheets filled with earnest appeals, and full of forebodings of future ruin, protests and earnest appeals to the ratepayers against separation, were scattered broadcast throughout the country, and public meetings and demonstrations of all kinds were continuously held to keep up the excitement.[32]

But the anti-separationists were not the only ones in the field. There had been a disputed election in Mara and Rama between James McPherson, who was opposed to separation, and Michael McDonagh who favoured the move. The "rump" Provisional Council now proceeded to resolve the dispute in McDonagh's favour, thereby increasing its numbers to a quorum.[33] Moreover, through the exercise of Gould's influence (and, the opposition charged "a consideration") Carmichael, the deputy reeve of Brock, was persuaded to switch sides. Now backed by a majority, Gould called a third meeting of the Provisional Council for June first. At this meeting William Paxton, Junior, was appointed county treasurer, and the bylaw of May 10 to raise £6,000 for building purposes was passed again to ensure it legality. A resolution was also passed requesting the Government to appoint immediately a registrar and county judge.

Gould's opposition watched in helpless rage as decision after decision was made which brought the day of separation ever closer. Suit after suit was undertaken in the courts, but while a few were won by the anti-separationists, none were of great enough significance to halt the creation of the county. Everything then devolved on the results of the township elections in January 1853.

The municipal elections in 1853 were bitter beyond belief. Charges of corruption, dictatorial methods, treason and personal attacks of every description were levelled against opponents. The results were dramatic to say the least: sitting pro-separationists were defeated in Whitby (deputy reeve), Reach and Scugog (reeve and deputy reeve) and in Thorah (reeve), while anti-separationist sitting members were defeated in Brock (reeve and deputy reeve) and Pickering (reeve). As a result, the anti-separationists appeared to have achieved a majority of one (the elected reeve of Mara and Rama, James S. Garnett refused to serve, leaving a thirteen-member Provisional Council). The following men were elected:[34]

Township	*Reeve*	*Deputy Reeve*
Whitby	James Rowe	James Burns
Pickering	John Lumsden	Peter Taylor
Reach and Scugog	James French	P. A. Hurd
Brock	George Brabazon	N. Bolster
Uxbridge	Joseph Gould	
Scott	James Galloway	
Georgina	John Boyd	
Thorah	Donald Cameron	
Mara and Rama	James S. Garnett (refused to serve)	
Oshawa	T. N. Gibbs	

At the first meeting of the Provisional Council, February 10, 1853, T.N. Gibbs was elected provisional warden, but when Gibbs took the chair, his opening remarks so angered the separationists that a sharp quarrel immediately began. Gibbs had stated that his election as warden was a clear indication that the voters of the county were opposed to separation. Since several separationists claimed to have voted for him on the grounds that he was the best man rather than on the issue of separation, Gibbs resigned so that the vote for warden might become a test for separation. James Rowe, reeve of Whitby, was nominated for the chair, and the vote was taken.

While the quarrel went on, James French, reeve of Reach and Scugog and an anti-separationist was persuaded to leave the meeting to dine with a "friend" (who had apparently extended the invitation at the suggestion of the leaders of the separationist cause). Thus when the vote was taken for warden, it produced a six-six tie. As a result, James Rowe, as reeve of the most populous township, cast the deciding vote in his own favour and became provisional warden for 1853.[35] However, it seems that to conciliate both factions, Gould replaced Rowe as provisional warden at the next meeting.

Events might have continued on in this manner indefinitely had not the York County Council, at this point, decided to raise their demands from the ten eastern townships. At the first meeting of the York Council in 1853, the representatives of Peel and York took advantage of the divisions among the members from Ontario County to increase the assessment of that area by no less than £200,000, and to decrease the amount of their own assessment by the same amount. Under the altered "equalization" formula, assessment in Reach was increased by £62,000; Whitby, £56,000; Uxbridge, £13,000; Brock, £20,000, and so on. For T.N. Gibbs, this was the last straw. Recognizing that the senior county representatives were detemined to get as much as they could from the departing townships, Gibbs decided that further delay in separation was pointless. The greed of York County had left him no choice. Thus he now threw his lot in with the separationists. The main battle for the county was over.[36]

Although Gibb's change of position had settled the main issue, a number of smaller, but no less bitter battles remained to be fought. The residents of Georgina Township had never felt much interest in the affairs of Whitby, Oshawa or the southern Ontario County townships. Their trade was centered on Yonge Street and Toronto. They were strongly opposed to the separation of Ontario County and the large expenses involved in the duplication of facilities and services. Thus at the second meeting of the Provisional Council in 1853, John Boyd, the reeve of Georgina, moved "that no further action be taken in the construction of the county buildings", and urged that "it would be conducive to the interests of the townships to remain in connection with the county of York".[37] He was bitterly disappointed when he discovered his oldest and strongest ally, T.N. Gibbs, voting with the separationists.

Boyd's response was immediate and decisive. He returned to Georgina and led a vigorous campaign of petitions, letters and meetings, demanding that Georgina be separated from Ontario County and rejoined to York. Early in March, 1853, a bill to rejoin Georgina to York was presented to the Assembly by Joseph Hartman, the member for the area. Joseph Gould was furious at the defection. In a strong letter to the government leader, Francis Hincks, he protested against Georgina's defection:

> As provisional warden and a county man I protest most solemnly against Georgina being detached; I protest against the bill now before the House, and for the reasons already explained to you, and of which I again beg to remind you - that the whole of the county, except Georgina, are opposed to it. And finally, I beg of you to use your influence as a minister to prevent the passage of the bill.[38]

In spite of Gould's protestations, the Act reuniting Georgina to York County easily passed both Houses, and received Royal assent April 22, 1853.[39]

The introduction of the Enabling Act to allow Georgina's move once again reopened the whole controversy as to where the county seat should be located. Originally, the main claimants were Whitby, Oshawa, Uxbridge, Brooklin and Manchester, although the choice soon narrowed down to the first two villages. The most imaginative proposal was that put forward by Abner Hurd and the merchants of Prince Albert. Because of the small size of Prince Albert, its merchants realized that there was little likelihood of its being chosen as the county seat. In April 1851, however, a plan was hit upon which contained the possibility of success. The merchants of Prince Albert, Borelia and Port Perry got up a petition asking that the three villages be amalgamated into a single incorporated village to be named "Ontario". Not unexpectedly, this proposal was vigorously opposed by the businessmen of both Whitby and Oshawa, and the Government, under this pressure, refused to act on Hurd's request.[40]

The proclamation of the Enabling Act in 1852, which named Whitby as the county town, dashed the hopes of all contenders except Oshawa, whose leaders, T.N. Gibbs, Abraham Farewell and George Grierson, continued to struggle as long as any hope remained. Once the actual construction of the county buildings was begun in 1853, however, they accepted the inevitable and became active members of the Provisional County Council.

The laying of the cornerstone of the new county buildings on June 30, 1853 was an opportunity to heal old wounds and to initiate a new loyalty to the infant county. In order to create the greatest impression on the populace, it was decided to employ the elaborate rituals of the Masonic Order for the occasion. The pomp and ceremony and the feelings of all present are aptly recounted in the newspaper accounts of that period. The Oshawa *Reporter* describes the affair as follows:

> Pursuant to the request of the provisional warden, James Rowe, Esq., and the contractor, James Wallace, Esq., the fraternity of Freemasons began to assemble at an early hour on Thursday, 30th ult. The day was beautiful, and the town of Whitby presented a gay appearance as every avenue leading to it poured in its line of carriages filled with happy faces. Along the east front of the Court House, an area was enclosed, and strong and substantial raised seats at either end erected. In the centre was a raised dais covered with carpet, appropriated to the officers of the Grand Lodge of Freemasons of the Province of Canada, the provisional warden of the county, the provisional council, the members for the county, the bar, the clergy and distinguished strangers. The arch that spanned the opening to the area was surmounted by a large crown, formed of evergreen and roses, and under which was suspended, in letters formed in evergreens the initials of our glorious Sovereign V.R., the whole surmounted by the Union Jack, and from various other points flags were suspended. At about three o'clock the area began to fill up, and at the time of the ceremony the seats presented an interesting appearance, filled as they were with the youth and beauty of the county. The Brooklyn brass band being engaged for the occasion, arrived at an early hour, preceding the brethren of Mount Zion Lodge, Borelia; shortly after which the lodge at Bowmanville arrived, and about two o'clock p.m. the steamer was announced with the officers of the Grand Lodge and brethren from the different lodges in Toronto, accompanied by the city band. The Right Worshipful Grand Master, Sir Allan Napier McNab, was announced to officiate on the occasion but being suddenly attacked with illness, and the Deputy Grand Master, Mr. Ridout, being absent on Railroad business at Quebec, the duties devolved on Bro. Richardson, Grand Secretary. The carriages conveying the grand officers and brethren from the landing having arrived at the lodge rooms of the Composite Lodge, the Provincial Grand Lodge was opened in due and ancient form, after which the brethren, being properly marshalled, proceeded in open lodge to the Court House building. There were represented the –

Cadets of Temperance.
Sons of Temperance.
Bar.
Clergy.
Magistrates.
The Members for Ontario.
Freemasons.

Brethren in proper masonic clothing (i.e., black suit, with the exception of the vest, which is white, white neck-cloth and gloves), and such Aprons and Ornaments as they were entitled to wear:

Two Tylers with Drawn Swords.
Music.
Brethren Members of Various Lodges, Two and Two.
A Cornucopia with Corn, carried by a Master.
Two Ewers with Wine and Oil, carried by Masters.
Grand Steward. Grand Steward.
Grand Pursuivant.
Grand Organist.
Assistant Grand Director of Ceremonies.
Grand Director of Ceremonies.
Grand Superintendent of Works (Architect of the Building)
With the Plans and Inscription Plate.
Past Grand Sword Bearers.
Past Grand Deacons.
Past Grand Secretaries.
Grand Secretary with Book of Constitution on a Cushion.
Grand Registrar, with his Bag.
Grand Treasurer, with Phial containing Coins, etc.
Past Grand Wardens.
Visitors of Distinction.
The Corinthian Light carried by a Master.
The Column of the Junior Grand Warden carried by a Master Mason.
The Junior Grand Warden with the Plumb and Rule.
Banner of the Grand Lodge.
The Doric Light carried by a Master.
The Column of the Senior Grand Warden, carried by a Master Mason.
The Senior Grand Warden with the Level.
The Junior Grand Deacon.

Grand Steward – The Grand Chaplain with Bible on a Cushion-Grand Steward.

The Deputy Grand Master, with the Square.

The Ionic Light, carried by a Past Master.

A Past Grand Warden, with the Mallet.

Grand Sword Bearer.

The Grand Master-Senior Grand Deacon.

Two Grand Stewards.

Grand Tyler.

Having arrived at the Buildings, and the acting Deputy Grand Master, Bro. Richardson, having taken his stand on the platform assigned to him, pursuant to ancient custom addressed the great assembly from all parts of the county in these words: –

Men, women, and children, here assembled to-day to behold this ceremony, know all you, that we be lawful Masons, true to the laws of our country, and established of old with peace and honour, in most countries, to do good to our brethren, to build great buildings, and to fear God, who is the Great Architect of all things. We have among us secrets which may not be revealed, and which no man has discovered, but these secrets are lawful and honourable to know by Masons, who only have the keeping of them to the end of time. Unless our craft were good and our calling honourable, we should not have lasted so many centuries, nor should we have had so many illustrious brothers in our Order, ready to promote our laws and further our interests. To-day we are assembled in the presence of you, to lay the Foundation Stone of Buildings for the public use of this new county, and promote harmony and brotherly love, till the world itself shall end. So mote it be.

A prayer was then offered up by the Grand Chaplain, Rev. Bro. Mayerhoffer, when amidst a strain of music from the band, the Acting Grand Master descended, accompanied by his officers, and approached the north-east corner. The stone being previously raised, the Acting Grand Master placed the deposits underneath. (The deposits were:- Minutes of Provisional Council, Toronto papers of Thursday, June 30th, Scobie's *Almanac*, Ontario *Reporter* and Oshawa *Freeman*, a List of the Executive Government, Members of both branches of the Legislature, of the Judiciary, and other functionaries of the Province, last number of *Canadian Journal*, various silver and copper moneys of the realm, a copy of a letter of Joseph Gould, Esq., concerning the new county.)

The following inscription is engrossed on parchment, and also placed in the bottle, which was carefully embedded in pulverized charcoal in the cavity:—

This
The Chief Corner Stone
Of the Court House and Public Offices
Of the County of Ontario,
was laid on
Thursday, the Thirtieth day of June,
in the year of our Lord one thousand eight hundred and fifty-three.
In the seventeenth year of the Reign
of
Her Most Gracious Majesty Queen Victoria,
The Right Honourable the Earl of Elgin and Kincardine, K.T.,
being
Governor-General of British North America,
by
The Grand Lodge
of
Free and Accepted Masons of Canada West.
On the invitation and in the presence
Of the Municipal Council and the Inhabitants
of the said County.

The Provisional Municipal Council: – James Rowe, Esq., Warden; Thomas N. Gibbs, Reeve of Oshawa; James Burns, Deputy-Reeve of Whitby; John M. Lumsden, Reeve of Pickering; Peter Taylor, Deputy-Reeve of Pickering; Thos. Paxton, Reeve of Reach and Scugog; Abel W. Ewers, Deputy-Reeve of Reach and Scugog; Nathaniel Bolster, Deputy-Reeve of Brock; George Brabazon, Reeve of Brock; James Galloway, Reeve of Scott; Donald Cameron, Reeve of Thorah; Joseph Gould, Reeve of Uxbridge; Michael McDonagh, Reeve of Mara and Rama; William Powson, Clerk; William Paxton, Treasurer.

Cumberland and Storm, Architects.
James Wallace, Contractor.

The mortar being spread, the stone was then slowly lowered to its permanent resting place amidst the solemn and magnificent strains of the National Anthem by both bands. The plumb, square and level were then each respectively handed by the Chief Architect to the Acting Grand Master, who after applying them pronounced the stone "well formed, true and trusty." Three immense cheers were then given for the Queen, and three for the county of Ontario. The silver vessels containing the corn, wine and oil were then presented by the Grand Wardens, and were each successively poured on the stone by the Acting Grand Master, saying: – "May the all-bounteous Author of Nature bless the inhabitants of this place with all the necessaries, conveniences and comforts of life; assist in the erection and completion of this building, protect the workmen against every accident, and long preserve the structure from decay; and grant to us all, in needed supply, the corn of *nourishment*, the wine of *refreshment*, and the oil of *joy*!"

"Amen! So mote it be! Amen!"

The stone was then struck three times with the mallet, and the ceremony was concluded amidst immense cheering from the vast multitude. The procession was then re-formed, and proceeding through the principal streets of Whitby, returned to the lodge room at Scripture's, and the Masonic Lodge was closed.[41]

On January 1, 1854, the Governor-in-Council issued the proclamation separating Ontario County from York. It read:

PROCLAMATION,

Province of Canada. } William Rowan.

Victoria, by the Grace of God, of the United Kingdom of Great Britain and Ireland, Queen, Defender of the Faith, etc., etc., etc.

To all to whom these presents shall come-Greeting:

John Ross, Attorney Genl. } WHEREAS, by an Act of the Parliament of Our Province of Canada, passed in the twelfth year of our Reign, Chaptered Seventy-eight, and intituled, "An Act for Abolishing the Territorial Divisions of Upper Canada into Districts, and for providing for Temporary Unions of Counties for Judicial and other purposes, and for the future dissolution of such Unions as the increase of wealth and population may require," certain provisions are made for the dissolution from time to time of the different Unions of Counties by the Separation of the Several Junior Counties as respects all matters both Judicial and Municipal, and for all other purposes whatsoever, and which provisions are by the said Act made applicable to the dissolution of such Unions in General. And whereas by another Act of Parliament of Our said Province, passed in the Session thereof held in the fourteenth and fifteenth years of Our Reign, intituled, "An Act to make certain Alterations in the Territorial Divisions of Upper Canada," it is amongst other things in effect enacted, that so soon as the Court House and Gaol in any one of the Counties of Elgin, Waterloo, Ontario, Brant, Grey, Lambton, or Welland, shall have been erected and completed at the County Town of such County according to the provisions of the fifteenth section of the said mentioned Act, and the other provisions of the said fifteenth section shall have been compiled with by any of such counties, and so soon as certain appointments mentioned in the seventeenth section of the said first recited Act shall have been thereafter made in any one of the said counties, it shall and may be lawful for the Governor of Our said Province, in Council, to issue a Proclamation dissolving the union between any one of such counties and the county or counties to which it may be united. And whereas, a Court House and Gaol for the said County of Ontario, one of the United Counties of York, Ontario and Peel, in our said Province, have been erected and completed at Whitby, the County Town of the said county, according to the provisions of the said fifteenth section of the said first mentioned Act and the other provisions of the said fifteenth section have been complied with by the said county, and the appointments mentioned in the said seventeenth section of the said Act have been made: And whereas the Provisional Municipal Council of the said county have, thereupon, by their petition to Our Administrator of the Government of Our said Province in Council, Prayed that a Proclamation might be issued by Our said Province in Council, disuniting the said County of Ontario from the said Union: And whereas it hath by Our said Administrator of the Government in Council been, thereupon, thought expedient that such Proclamation shall be accordingly issued, to bear teste on and to declare such separation upon, from and after the thirtieth day of this present month of December: Now, therefore, know ye, that We, taking the premises in Our Royal Consideration and fully approving of the Resolution so come to by Our said Administrator of the Government in Council in that behalf have thought fit to issue this, Our Royal Proclamation for dissolving the said Union. And we do accordingly, in pursuance of the provisions of the said Acts of Parliament, hereby declare that upon, from and after the said Thirtieth day of December instant, the said Union of the said United Counties of York, Peel and Ontario, shall be and the same is herby absolutely dissolved, and that from thenceforth the said County of Ontario shall be disunited from the said Counties of York and Peel, and have a separate and independent organization of its own as to all matters Judicial and Municipal, as well as for all other purposes whatsoever. And we do further declare, that the Provisional Municipal Council of the said County of Ontario shall, upon the day aforesaid, lapse and be absolutely dissolved, and that from thenceforth none of the Courts nor officers of the said Union shall as such have any jurisdiction or authority whatever in or over the said County of Ontario; anything in their respective commissions, or in any Act of Parliament, either of the Province of Canada or late Province of Upper Canada, to the contrary thereof in anywise notwithstanding.

And we do further, in pursuance of the said first mentioned Act of Parliament, hereby further declare, that the said remaining Counties of York and Peel shall, upon, from and after the said Thirtieth day of December instant, constitute and form a Union of Counties under the said Acts, by and under the name and style of the United Counties of York and Peel, and shall continue so to form such last mentioned Union until the same shall be in like manner dissolved in due form of law. And know ye, that we have commanded and ordained, and by these presents do command and ordain that all Magistrates and other Officers holding commissions from us, or by our authority or otherwise howsoever of, in or for the said United Counties of York. Ontario and Peel, except only such of Our Justices of the Peace for the said United Counties as shall be now resident in the County of Ontario, shall, in Our name, or otherwise according to law, continue to exercise the duties of their respective offices in and for the said United Counties of York and Peel as if they had been appointed in and for such last mentioned Union, until our Royal Pleasure shall be further made known therein, or the authority of such officers in that behalf shall be otherwise determined according to law. Of all and singular which premises all Judges, Justices, Sherrifs, Magistrates, Constables and Officers of the said United Counties of York Ontario and Peel, and all Our loving subjects of the said Counties, as well as of all others whom it doth or may in anywise concern, are hereby required to take notice and to govern themselves accordingly.

IN TESTIMONY WHEREOF, we have caused these Our letters to be made Patent, and the Great Seal of Our said Province of Canada to be here unto affixed. Witness Our Trusty and Well beloved William Rowan, Esq., C.B., Administrator of the Government of our said Province, and Lieutenant-General Commanding Our Forces therein, etc., etc., etc., at Quebec, in our said Province, this Thirtieth day of December, in the Year of Our Lord One Thousand Eight Hundred and Fifty-three, and in the seventeenth Year of Our Reign.

By Command,

P.J.O. Chauveau, *Secretary*.[42]

It was not long, however, before the leaders of the new county found that separation of the county brought neither a solution to the problems of the area nor an end to the internal divisions and quarrels. In spite of these failures, few ever regretted separation. While problems and quarrels remained, the increased control over their own affairs allowed by local government vastly outweighed any additional costs involved. The principle of local control which had been fought for by reformers for a quarter of a century would prove its worth many times over in the future.

FARMER AND MASTER CRAFTSMAN, 1851-71

The years 1851-71 were, for most residents of Ontario County, years of great prosperity, change, optimism and self-satisfaction. Almost all of the economic expansion occurred within the first decade, whereas the second ten years were generally static; so pervasive, however was the general optimism and complacency that there was little recognition of this slower growth. It would not be until the rapid inflation of 1872-73 and the severe depression of 1874-76 that serious questions would be asked. By then, unfortunately, the economic and political situation was such that control of the future had slipped out of the hands of the local residents.

Although the 1851-71 period was one which improved the position of many local inhabitants, not everyone enjoyed a better way of life or agreed with all aspects of the changes which were occurring. The drastic alteration of agriculture during the period, the shift of political, social and economic dominance from rural to urban interests, and the rapid growth of the urban labour force all created situations in which certain groups and individuals found their interests and welfare injured, and yet did not enjoy any of the compensating benefits received by the rest of society. In particular, the triumph of a new and pervasive ideology based on economic growth and progress created a situation which attacked and altered social relations in the region. It would not be until the 1880s and 1890s when the majority were subjected to the forces which had injured only the minority previously, that residents would realize that "progress" as it was then defined exacted a price beyond its value. The result of that realization would shake local society to its roots. It was, by then, too late to go back.

Table XXIII
Population in Ontario County, 1840–71[1]

	1840	*1851*	*1861*	*1871*
Whitby E.	3,163*	6,896*	3,665	3,441
Whitby W.			3,546	3,220
Pickering	3,450	6,737	8,002	7,375
Uxbridge	708†	2,289	3,933	4,762
Reach	771	3,897	6,214	6,809
Scugog	—	415	782	880
Brock	1,330	3,518	4,625	5,175
Thorah	514	1,146	1,625	1,965
Scott	†	1,028	2,169	2,775
Mara	215	1,403	1,965	2,697
Rama	14		372	904
Oshawa	1,100*	1,142	2,009	3,185
Whitby T.	750*	1,100*	2,697	2,732

* Estimates by W. H. Smith for 1844 and 1850.
† Scott included in Uxbridge total.

Population in Ontario would continue to grow after 1851, but it would do so at rates much below those of the 1840-51 period. Moreover, as Table XXIII shows, the rate of growth differed sharply from region to region within the area. Most striking, perhaps, is the fact that in the southern areas population growth in the rural districts first slowed sharply between 1851 and 1861, and then declined between 1861 and 1871. This decrease would in later years become general throughout the rural areas, and was symptomatic of the great changes occurring in agriculture. In the northern areas, population would continue to grow, but the rate of growth was generally slower after 1861 than before. For the main urban centres, Whitby and Oshawa, 1851-61 was a decade of great expansion. For Oshawa, this expansion would continue until 1871, while for Whitby, the latter decade would be one of almost complete stagnation.

In spite of the slower rate of population growth in rural areas after 1851, for those who owned land or were capable of acquiring it, the period was one of considerable expansion and consolidation. As Table XXIV shows, not only did the area occupied continue to grow in all regions, but there was a great expansion in the proportion of land actually under cultivation. Thus, while in 1851 most northern farms were only about one-third cultivated, by 1871 most had doubled that proportion. Only Mara (41.7 percent) and Rama (19.0 percent) fell far below the two-thirds level of cultivation.

Table XXIV
Acreages Occupied and Cultivated in Ontario County, 1851–71[2]

	Acres Occupied			*Acres under Cultivation*			*Percent Cultivated*		
	1851	*1861**	*1871*	*1851*	*1861**	*1871*	*1851*	*1861**	*1871*
Whitby E.	61,154	29,873	32,119	40,312	23,454	25,539	65.9	78.5	79.5
Whitby W.		27,849	29,945		19,395	25,022		69.6	83.6
Pickering	64,160	64,889	70,252	38,772	47,298	55,418	60.4	72.9	78.9
Uxbridge	25,983	33,688	43,773	8,980	16,119	28,467	34.6	47.8	65.0
Scott	17,964	33,981	39,244	4,768	15,185	24,757	26.5	44.7	63.1
Reach	42,812	52,376	56,163	18,231	28,300	38,569	42.6	54.0	68.7
Scugog	5,369	180	8,579	1,195	115	5,950	22.3	63.9	69.4
Brock	49,416	60,235	62,417	17,604	31,363	36,767	35.6	52.1	58.9
Thorah	16,436	20,319	22,420	4,846	7,676	16,470	29.5	37.8	73.4
Mara	18,434	22,124	36,591	3,645	9,826	15,255	19.8	44.4	41.7
Rama		8,420	12,166		2,771	2,372		32.9	19.0
Oshawa	1,533	1,317	2,223	1,060	1,022	1,979	69.1	77.6	89.0
Whitby T.	—	3,376	3,855	—	2,829	3,655	—	83.5	94.8

* It should be noted that the 1861 figures were collected on a different basis from those for 1851 and 1871. Whereas the latter figures include all lands actually occupied, the 1861 figures include only those holdings which were actually operated as farms. Because of this practice, townships such as Scugog where most occupants were required to work away from home for most of the year, show sharply decreased figures.

Table XXV
Livestock in Ontario County, 1851–71[3]

	Southern Ontario C. (Whitby and Pickering)			*Northern Ontario C.*		
	1851	*1861*	*1871*	*1851*	*1861*	*1871*
Total Farms (10 Acres and up)	1,362	1,353	1,408	1,872	2,219	2,684
Horses	4,748	5,220	5,139	2,850	5,022	6,677
Milch Cows	5,314	6,858	6,997	4,519	6,998	10,169
Swine	9,154	9,231	9,334	11,676	14,645	16,187
Wool Produced (lbs.)	55,616	71,842	78,474	33,107	70,524	111,872
Sheep	17,168	25,782	16,071	13,389	18,009	25,412
Horses per Farm	3.5	3.9	3.6	1.5	2.3	2.5
Milch Cows per Farm	3.9	5.1	5.0	2.4	3.2	3.8
Swine per Farm	6.7	6.8	6.6	6.2	6.6	6.0
Wool per Farm (lbs.)	40.8	53.1	55.8	17.7	31.8	50.4
Sheep per Farm	12.6	19.1	11.3	7.0	8.1	9.5

The townships of northern Ontario County generally caught up to the southern townships (Pickering and Whitby) not only in the proportion of land cultivated, but also in livestock production. As Table XXV shows, livestock per farm in northern areas was only a little more than one-half that of southern levels in 1851, whereas by 1871 parity had almost been achieved in sheep and swine raising, and the number of horses and cattle had grown to approximately two-thirds of the southern level.

It is clear, however, from the small numbers of livestock owned all through the period that most farmers kept animals primarily for family consumption. Indeed, in 1871, the census reported that an average of only 2.5 cattle per farm was either killed or sold in south Ontario County, while an average of only 2 cattle per farm was killed or sold in the northern townships. Similarly, only 6.0 sheep and 6.8 swine were killed or sold per farm in the south in 1871, and 5.0 sheep and 5.5 swine in the north. Of course, most of the livestock sold went to feed the growing work force in the local towns.

In spite of the slow growth of livestock production, the period – especially the fifteen years from 1851 to 1866 – was one of great prosperity for most local farmers. In particular, the Reciprocity Treaty of 1854, which introduced free trade in agricultural and forestry products between Canada and the United States, greatly benefited the Ontario County region. It increased the demand for locally grown wheat, and the expansion of timber exports provided jobs for labourers in both the woods and sawmills of the area. Moreover, the mills and camps which sprang up provided a ready market for locally grown produce as well. Equally important in the creation of increased prosperity for the area was a world scarcity of wheat caused by the Crimean and American Civil Wars: prices doubled and tripled in some years. As a result of these conditions, Ontario County, which had suffered greatly from a scarcity of capital for half a century, suddenly found itself with a surplus of cash with which to bring its dreams and ambitions to fruition.

Although wheat was the basis of the new prosperity, it proved to be a treacherous foundation upon which to base local agriculture. First, the termination of reciprocity by the United States in 1867 all but cut off one of the best markets for Ontario grain and flour, and secondly, the appearance of the wheat midge in the 1860s drastically cut local yields. Tables XXVI and XXVII show both the great dependence upon wheat in 1851 and 1861, and the reduction in yield and acreage in 1871. From the point of view of the farmer who had depended on wheat as his main crop, the situation was particularly serious. Although wheat yields and prices had both fallen drastically, there was little that could be done to reduce his dependence upon it. There was only a limited market for livestock, and the distance from major markets such as Toronto meant that most produce could not be marketed there profitably.

The one crop that offered a possibility for immediate expansion was barley. Canadian barley was much superior to American-grown barley for beer-

Table XXVI Wheat Acreage in Ontario County, 1851–71[4]

	Acres of Wheat			Wheat as a Percent of Cultivated Area		
	1851	1861	1871	1851	1861	1871
Whitby E.	10,658	7,561	5,130	26.4	32.2	20.9
Whitby W.		4,860	3,985		25.1	15.9
Pickering	9,291	11,403	8,114	24.0	24.1	14.6
Uxbridge	2,203	4,816	3,732	24.5	29.9	13.1
Scott	1,355	4,777	3,868	28.4	31.5	15.7
Reach	4,813	9,962	7,015	26.4	35.2	18.2
Scugog	335	28	980	28.0	24.3	16.5
Brock	5,103	9,923	8,118	29.0	31.6	22.1
Thorah	1,464	2,594	1,965	30.2	33.8	11.9
Mara	1,011	1,425	2,351	27.7	14.5	15.4
Rama		963	257		34.7	10.8
Oshawa	1,017	425	356	96.0	41.6	18.0
Whitby T.	—	875	609	—	30.9	16.7

Table XXVII Wheat Yields in Ontario County, 1851–71[5]

	Bushels of Wheat			Bushels per Acre		
	1851	1861	1871	1851	1861	1871
Whitby E.	210,491	136,133	64,457	19.8	18.0	12.6
Whitby W.		97,663	47,435		20.1	11.9
Pickering	187,414	202,512	91,548	20.2	17.8	11.3
Uxbridge	33,055	88,348	42,389	15.0	18.3	11.4
Scott	23,099	106,736	48,460	17.0	22.3	12.5
Reach	77,780	197,283	88,552	16.2	19.8	12.6
Scugog	6,369	520	11,467	19.0	18.6	11.7
Brock	72,771	183,315	83,307	14.3	18.5	10.3
Thorah	21,544	44,981	20,878	15.0	17.3	10.6
Mara	14,543	33,480	21,988	14.4	23.5	9.3
Rama		20,012	2,548		20.8	9.9
Oshawa	4,524	8,572	4,485	4.4	20.2	12.6
Whitby T.	—	17,519	5,765	—	20.0	9.5

making, and the rapidly-growing American barley market was willing to pay a premium for first grade Canadian malting barley. As Table XXVIII shows, there was little expansion in the growing of oats when wheat failed, but there was an enormous increase in the cultivation of barley. Indeed, in Pickering and Reach, it is clear that the farmers reduced oat acreage severely in order

Table XXVIII
Yields of Oats and Barley in Ontario County, 1851–71[6]

	Bushels of Oats			*Bushels of Barley*		
	1851	*1861*	*1871*	*1851*	*1861*	*1871*
Whitby E.	153,800	77,338	57,161	4,369	14,238	72,025
Whitby W.		74,282	51,280		12,500	51,437
Pickering	167,258	222,555	143,375	5,132	34,195	138,777
Uxbridge	47,497	74,589	84,145	684	2,302	48,385
Scott	22,977	70,502	82,720	338	1,761	38,497
Reach	85,909	170,166	100,600	1,976	2,751	94,436
Scugog	2,560	700	15,060	—	—	11,245
Brock	61,907	118,143	113,878	650	4,526	56,214
Thorah	16,898	32,612	43,906	418	338	14,252
Mara	14,898	29,369	67,884	261	556	9,158
Rama		12,420	5,883		190	436
Oshawa	3,150	2,840	4,950	130	2,105	5,665
Whitby T.	—	13,080	8,285	—	1,640	13,016

to cultivate barley for the export market. With the American and Canadian West's opening, however, barley would soon prove to be unprofitable as well. Thus for the farmers of Ontario County, the late 1860s and 1870s would be troubled times as they searched for crops and agricultural practices that would bring back the prosperity that had been theirs in the 1850s and early 1860s.

The development of improved methods of agriculture in the 1850s and 1860s was based on several factors: increased capital reserves made changes possible; well-to-do British immigrants brought new methods and better bloodlines of livestock with them; and the Provincial Government undertook an active program of support for local agricultural societies, fairs and prizes which encouraged improvement.

In 1851 the Provincial Government began to make annual grants to county agricultural societies which in return were supposed to encourage improvement of agriculture through exhibitions with prizes for grains, livestock, machinery, produce, and the introduction of improved varieties. In 1852, the Ontario County Agricultural Society held its first annual exhibition at Whitby.[7] The Society flourished, and in 1857 reported that it had 189 members, had received $900 in government grants and that "six individual members of the society had, within the preceding year, imported stock from Great Britain . . . two horses, three Durham Bulls, three Durham heifers, twelve Leicester Rams, eighteen Leicester ewes, four Cotswold rams, four Cotswold ewes, two Southdown rams, four Southdown ewes".[8]

In 1857, the Government altered its legislation to permit the establishment

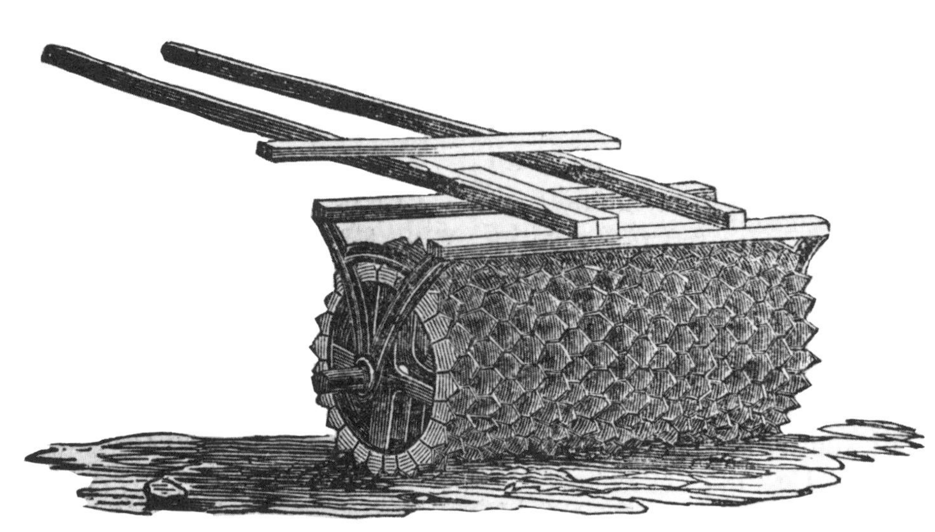

Clod Crusher Roller, 1852

Public Archives of Ontario

Horse-Power Hay Fork, 1855

Public Archives of Ontario

Marsh Harvester, 1866 *Public Archives of Ontario*

Early Steam Engine, c. 1875 *Public Archives of Ontario*

of agricultural societies on the basis of electoral divisions rather than on counties. As a result, on January 1, 1858 new societies for the North and South Ridings of Ontario County were established, and the new North Ontario Agricultural Society held its first exhibition at Prince Albert in September, 1858.[9] In all, about $300 in prizes were given out. In addition, township societies were established, and in 1857 their secretaries reported that Brock had 52 members; Pickering, 187; Reach and Scugog, 187; Whitby, 266, and in 1858 an East Whitby society was formed with 41 members.[10]

The local agricultural societies held township exhibitions and stock sales every three months. Thus the Whitby *Chronicle* of May 6, 1858 noted that spring fairs had been held by the East Whitby Agricultural Society at Columbus on April 23, by the Pickering Society at Claremont on April 28, and by the Whitby Society at Brooklin on April 29. At these fairs horses and cattle were exhibited and prizes awarded, plowing matches held, farm implements demonstrated by the manufacturers, and a sale of livestock conducted.[11] Within five years other local fairs were being held at Manchester, Wick and Uxbridge to serve the northern farmers. Of course, these fairs brought a great deal of business to the towns in which they were held. Thus it was common that merchants competed vigorously in order to have the local fair held at their village. In 1866 the directors of the North Ontario Agricultural Society found that they had received tenders from Manchester, Prince Albert and Port Perry offering cash bonuses if the annual exhibition would be held at their town. Port Perry's tender, the highest, was for $100.[12]

By 1866 the county shows had become large and elaborate affairs. The 1866 North Ontario fair held at Port Perry was described as follows:

> The Fall Show . . . was a decided success as far as the objects of the fair are concerned. The number of articles on exhibition were unusually large and of first rate quality. The Floral hall was all that could be desired. The show of Grain, Roots and Seeds was excellent, and exhibited to great advantage in the large commodious hall in which they were placed. The outside arrangement was not quite so suitable and the pelting drenching rain rendered it very disagreeable indeed.[13]

The prize list showed that there were 30 classes of competition for horses, 13 for cattle, 16 for sheep and 7 for swine. In addition there were 22 classes of grain, roots and seeds, 16 classes for horticulture, 12 for "domestic manufacturers", and 27 in the "Ladies' Department". In addition there were competitions for fine arts, farm implements, manufacturers' cabinet work and 19 other miscellaneous categories.

In addition to fairs, the regular plowing matches held throughout the region under the auspices of the various agricultural societies provided opportunities for farmer education, for the advertising of new and improved agricultural

"Thistle Ha", Residence of John Miller, Brougham *Public Archives of Ontario*

Saint John's Anglican Church, Port Whitby, 1846 *Whitby Historical Society*

implements by local manufacturers, and for a festive occasion for farmers and their families to enjoy. Such occasions, however, were not always attractive to the gentility. In 1868, the Dominion Plowing Match was held at Brooklin, and drew this comment from one editor:

> From early dawn the rumbling of wagons, the rattling of buggies, and the neighing of horses intermingled with the cheerful voices from the well-loaded vehicles might be heard all along the roads leading to the field of action. Notwithstanding the greatest possible dissimularity in every other aspect—from the splendidly caparisoned thousand dollar teams, driven along at 2:40 by some *young bloods*, down to the hacked out nag on his last three legs hobbling along at the rate of ten miles in eleven hours urged by some *canty earle*, who . . . is as happy as a lord, and views with supreme disgust our modern Jehus as they whir past him like a streak of lightening—there is one point on which they all agree, viz: the importance they attach to such matches. . . .
>
> The plowing had got pretty well along when we reached the field, and the whiskey had been doing its work among a certain class of the spectators, if we can call a man who is blind-drunk a spectator. Near to one of the booths there was quite a gathering, and in the centre of the crowd two young men seemed bent on eating each other up. The one commenced chewing the thumb of the other, while the other preferred his neighbours nose . . . A third party was endeavoring to bring the people to time by the powerful argument of the hatchet. In another place two were doing their very best to show that the poet made a sad blunder when he said: "Your little hands were never made to tear each others eyes". Another pair . . . were mercilessly whipping each other (with their tongues), each one boasting of his own pugilistic qualities, and how easily he could annihilate his antagonist.[14]

In spite of the rough behaviour and brawling which were always part of such major public occasions, all agreed that the matches were of significant value to society. As the same editor commented:

> What a splendid sight it was to witness 70 vigorous, intelligent yeomen, contesting the prizes in the large and level field. Our mind was carried back to the palmy days of Greece, when at intervals of four years, her best and bravest sons joined in the public games, and contended with all their might . . . How much more praiseworthy is it in those who come out at a sacrifice of no little time, trouble, and money in order to further the improvement of agriculture.[15]

Over the years, the plowmen of Scott Township became widely known for their success at these matches.[16]

The greater prosperity of the 1850s and the early 1860s, and the new ideas introduced by the agricultural societies and machinery manufacturers brought

Table XXIX
Varieties of Houses in Ontario County, 1851–61[17]

	Log Houses		*Frame Houses*		*Brick Houses*		*Stone Houses*	
	1851	*1861*	*1851*	*1861*	*1851*	*1861*	*1851*	*1861*
Whitby E.	450	70	820	451	53	49	17	21
Whitby W.		104		427		36		14
Pickering	536	374	423	747	19	72	40	83
Uxbridge	262	268	128	382	1	2	2	5
Scott	153	236	13	123	—	1	—	2
Reach	421	246	245	574	5	13	1	9
Scugog	56	73	5	43	—	1	—	1
Brock	456	587	70	234	3	3	—	6
Thorah	156	183	23	67	1	4	2	3
Mara	222	284	3	24	—	—	—	—
Rama		58		9	—	—	—	1
Oshawa	4	11	166	304	14	52	—	—
Whitby T.	—	15	—	372	—	79	—	3

enormous changes to the rural way of life. The most visible mark was the houses and fine large barns built during that period. As Table XXIX shows, new frame, brick and stone houses were particularly noticeable in Whitby, Pickering and Reach townships where there was a sharp reduction in the number of log houses in use. In more northern areas, while many frame and a few brick and stone houses were erected, most new houses were still built of logs – often to replace the rude pioneer shanty of earlier days.

More significant from the farmers' viewpoint, was their utilization of money accumulated during the prosperous era to puchase farm machinery. In the pioneer era, virtually all work was done by hand. Now large amounts of farm machinery were purchased in order to increase productivity. Thus by 1871 the 1,408 farmers of Pickering and Whitby owned 4,167 plows, harrows and cultivators, 1,041 horse rakes, 1,433 fanning mills, 1,071 reapers and mowers,and 165 threshing machines. The 2,684 farmers of North Ontario were not far behind. In 1871 they owned 4,824 ploughs, harrows and cultivators, 952 horse rakes, 2,357 fanning mills, 771 reapers and mowers, and 192 threshing machines.[18]

If the new prosperity brought a greater use of capital goods and machinery in the production of crops, for one class of farmers it brought an immediate problem. Under toiler forms of agriculture, farmers with small acreages could make a living by intensive methods of hand cultivation. As Table XXX shows, in 1851 the great majority of farms contained less than 100 acres, while the most common farm size was between 50 and 100 acres. Significantly, in the whole Ontario County area, only 58 farms contained more than 200 acres.

Table XXX
Acreages and Numbers of Occupiers by Size of Holding in Ontario County, 1851-71[19]

	Under 10 Acres		*10–50 Acres*		*50–100 Acres*		*100–200 Acres*		*200 and Over Acres*		*Average in Acres**	
	1851	*1871*	*1851*	*1871*	*1851*	*1871*	*1851*	*1871*	*1851*	*1871*	*1851*	*1871*
Whitby E.	198	79	208	71	275	126	122	95	23	15	94.6	102.0
Whitby W.		93		72		124		68		21		101.8
Pickering	101	147	287	208	334	320	86	181	13	26	87.8	93.6
Uxbridge	51	57	134	152	158	249	36	68	9	13	75.6	89.6
Scott	1	41	29	51	120	185	22	83	1	17	104.4	115.3
Reach	25	77	194	147	241	258	62	119	—	28	85.6	99.1
Scugog	1	23	24	39	35	38	4	17	—	4	85.1	85.0
Brock	18	4	82	81	283	226	98	179	4	42	105.4	121.3
Thorah	9	22	15	45	97	117	27	36	4	13	114.3	105.2
Mara	25	40	56	88	113	193	22	61	2	15	94.2	101.4
Rama		12		57		60		19		4		86.0
Oshawa	79	27	5	22	5	8	3	5	2	1	49.3	54.4
Whitby T.	—	81	—	18	—	13	—	12	—	2	—	67.7

* Of those holdings 10 acres and over.

The great prosperity which occurred during the Crimean and the American Civil Wars, combined with the depressions of 1857-59 and 1867-69, brought about fundamental changes in the pattern of local agriculture. During periods of prosperity the largest farmers could achieve greater efficiency and productivity through the purchase of better breeds of livestock, improved farm machinery, and additional land; however, in order to keep up, smaller farmers found that it was necessary to go deeply into debt. Thus during periods of prosperity they were burdened with high interest rates, but in periods of depression low sales and low prices forced many into bankruptcy.

As a result of this situation, the years 1851-71 witnessed a consolidation of small holdings and a sharp increase in the number of large farms. This change is most easily shown in long-settled areas such as Whitby and Pickering: the number of farms in the 50-to-100 acre range declined from 500 to 391 as small farmers were forced off the land, while farms of between 100 and 200 acres, and those over 200 acres increased from 211 to 361 and 38 to 65 respectively. As the Oshawa *Vindicator* pointed out:

> The large farmers have bought up the small farms, and the introduction of machinery has decreased the number of laborers. This reduction has gone farther than many are prepared to accept.[20]

Some of the land holdings which were accumulated in this manner were

Cameron Street, Cannington, c. 1860 *Public Archives of Ontario*

Quaker Meeting House, Uxbridge, c. 1820 *Public Archives of Ontario*

large and impressive indeed. The editor of one American farm publication, the *Genessee Farmer*, was so impressed by the holdings of George Miller, Pickering Township's best-known importer of purebred livestock, that he presented the following description to his readers:

> He has 1,100 acres, 300 of which comprise the home farm under his own immediate supervision—the rest being farmed by tenants under his direction. In the first field we entered were seen depasturing some eighty Leicester sheep, mostly ewes with their lambs, and a few Cotswolds. . . . There were some choice imported rams among them, which have been prize-takers both in England and America. . . . In another field, I saw about 100 more sheep, eight of which were Cotswolds, the rest Leicesters. Adjoining it was a ten-acre field just put into Swedes [turnips]. A little further on was another ten-acre field being prepared for Kohl-Rabi. . . . His land is in so high a state of cultivation that he finds little difficulty in keeping down weeds, and his . . . Swedes [average] 1,200 bushels per acre. . . . I will reserve a description of the Short-horns and Galloway cattle for another letter.[21]

Similarly, the farm of W.S. Sexton in Scugog Township, which consisted of 1,000 acres in a block (with 900 acres cleared) was frequently mentioned in the press.[22]

Not only did the destruction of the small farmers help create a class of large landowners, it also brought into being a significant number of tenant farmers as well. Since many of the small farms passed into the hands of banks and others who were not interested in actually farming the land, it became the custom to rent out the lands seized until a suitable price could be obtained for them. Thus by 1871, in Pickering, 267 of the 882 occupiers of land were tenants, while in Whitby East and Whitby Townships, 119 of 386 and 116 of 378 were tenants. In the northern townships, the areas with greatest proportion of tenants were Uxbridge (156 of 539), Reach (174 of 698), and Scott (106 of 377).[23]

Because it was easy for those farmers who survived each round of boom, expansion, depression and failures to explain the bankruptcy of their neighbours on the grounds of inefficiency or shiftlessness, it was a long time before those farmers who remained realized the serious social consequences of this rural depopulation. Moreover, they entirely failed to recognize that the process of agricultural economic centralization was a continuous one in which the weakest survivors of one cycle became the victims of the next. Within a generation, however, with rural population declining and rural social institutions collapsing, the socially catastrophic consequences of these economic changes were finally recognized. Then a whole series of economic and political counter-strategies would be attempted in order to reverse the process. But all would fail. The unfortunate result of introducing economic "progress" to agriculture had the tragic result of progressively destroying rural society. That process continues to the present day.

With the increased prosperity of the early 1850s, there followed a rapid development of rural towns throughout the Ontario County area. Not only did farmers require increased amounts of farm machinery and implements, but they began to demand a wider variety of goods and services than they could previously afford. Because of the peculiarities of local taste and the high cost of transportation owing to bad roads, this increased demand offered new opportunities for the establishment of local merchant shops and the employment of crafts workers to provide manufactured products for the local farmers. Just as Oshawa, Whitby, Duffin's Creek and other centres in the older southern area had grown in response to the needs of the expanding farm communities before 1851, so now did northern centres such as Beaverton, Cannington, Uxbridge, Prince Albert and Port Perry grow and prosper. Moreover, many smaller crossroads hamlets, such as Claremont, Zepher, Leaskdale, Vroomanton, Uptergrove, Brechin and Wick appeared, whose existence was based on a purely local need for a blacksmith shop, general store, church and school. These did not grow beyond a small size, however, because they lacked a central position in a large market area.

But just as bad roads and local peculiarities of taste had made it possible for local crafts workers to establish themselves in the northern towns and to make a good living for themselves, it also made it generally impossible for their manufacturing establishments to grow beyond the size of one- or two-man operations. Thus every successful town contained a variety of boot- and shoemakers, brick makers, cabinetmakers, blacksmiths, carriage makers, tailors and clothiers, sheet metal workers, lime kilns, and so on. In fact, by 1871 in Ontario County there were 39 different kinds of manufacturing being carried on in 513 separate establishments. Moreover, there was an almost equal balance of activity between northern and southern regions. In northern Ontario there were 30 different kinds of manufacturing in 217 separate establishments, while the figures for southern Ontario were 39 and 296 respectively. Table XXXI shows the most common industries in Ontario County. As can be seen, in most cases fewer than five persons, including the owner, worked in the average establishment. The main exception is in cabinet and furniture making where the large business carried on by T.N. Gibbs in Oshawa is included. With the high degree of skills possessed by local crafts workers, a remarkably diversified range of products could be produced. For example, blacksmiths were not simply shoers of horses and repairers of farm machinery, many possessed skills as iron moulders as well. By purchasing the wooden patterns from a machinery manufacturer (usually one who did not sell into the Canadian market) and pouring his own molten iron, local blacksmiths were capable of building such advanced and elaborate farm machines as hay mowers, threshing machines and reapers.

Table XXXI
Most Common Manufacturing Establishments, Employees, Yearly Wages and Output in Dollars in Ontario County, 1871[24]

	Southern Ontario County				Northern Ontario County			
	Number of Establishments	*Number Employed*	*Yearly Wages (Dollars)*	*Value of Products (Dollars)*	*Number of Establishments*	*Number Employed*	*Yearly Wages (Dollars)*	*Value of Products (Dollars)*
Blacksmithing	41	77	21,084	50,020	47	79	20,915	39,598
Boot & Shoe Making	37	76	19,800	56,850	34	71	17,935	53,719
Sawmills	20	44	8,284	35,510	44	409	75,164	304,175
Carriage Making	30	89	28,095	63,317	26	72	20,570	58,765
Flour- & Gristmills	21	65	21,541	950,707	13	38	10,225	249,495
Lime Kilns	10	11	293	935	26	39	654	2,081
Tailors & Clothiers	21	117	25,974	96,178	13	30	6,085	18,826
Cooperages	13	53	12,140	32,355	9	18	2,510	4,735
Saddle & Harness	9	30	6,910	23,150	12	30	7,270	23,560
Shingle Making	3	15	1,403	3,646	14	36	3,051	6,102
Brick & Tile	10	56	7,874	16,450	7	37	4,178	7,450
Cabinet & Furniture	9	217	65,814	191,700	7	18	7,900	15,540
Tin & Sheet Metal	6	20	5,600	18,000	8	15	4,725	14,400
Tanneries	10	77	25,550	160,900	4	14	4,500	26,285
Dress Making & Millinery	7	15	1,837	8,871	3	5	275	1,600
Carpenters & Joiners	6	17	4,575	11,150	10	18	2,842	5,510

Because of the diversity of economic activity each central village, such as Uxbridge, Port Perry, Prince Albert, Cannington, Beaverton, Whitby and Oshawa, enjoyed a great deal of economic autonomy. The villagers manufactured most of the products required by the local farmers, while the farmers supplied the villagers with food, fuel and other agricultural products. In such an economic unit, the only exports were agricultural products, and the only imports were raw materials for manufacturing and luxury goods. For example, Cannington, which in 1870 had only about 500 inhabitants, offered a wide diversity of mercantile and manufacturing establishments. As reported by the Oshawa *Vindicator*, Cannington contained

> four Dry Goods and Grocery stores, two Grocery Stores, one large bakery and Grocery, two Drug stores, one Cabinet Factory, one Stove and Tin shop, two Harness shops, three Tailoring establishments, two Boot and Shoe shops, two Millinery and Dressmaking establishments, one Photography Gallery, and another completed. And in manufacturing there are two Woolen Factories, one large Grist Mill, one Tannery, and one Brewery. In addition to these, there is a Shingle, two

> Planing and Sash and Door Factories in course of erection, which will be soon completed.[25]

When it is considered that these establishments all manufactured goods as well as selling ready-made products, it is clear that for most common goods, Cannington was virtually self-sufficient.

In a similar manner, Brooklin was described as containing a wide variety of manufacturing establishments in spite of its nearness to Whitby and Oshawa:

> The Merchant firms are those of S.M. Thomas and Haywood and Tyler, and their excellent stores are a credit to the village, as are also the factories of Messrs. Phippen and Thomas. The only jeweller's shop is that of W. Hepinstall, Esq. In the manufacture of harness, etc., Messrs. Dale and Maybee do a large and increasing business. The workmen in the blacksmith and carriage shops of Messrs. Hepburn and Roberts, Ketchen and Chamberlain find constant employment, and also in the tanneries of Messrs. Cole and Powell. Near the village are the mills of Messrs. Bickell, Campbell and Francis. The apiary of Mr. John Thomas is very large, and it is probable that his bees, as regards quality and number are the first in the province, if not in the Dominion.[26]

Similarly, in 1869, Port Perry was described as containing

> five Dry Goods Stores, two Drug Stores, two Grocery Stores, a Bakery, four Churches, a first class Grammar and Common School, and a very large Foundry, where all kinds of farming implements are manufactured. The celebrated "Marsh Harvester" is manufactured here. It also contains three Saw Mills, Grist Mills, Stove Factory, a Woolen Factory, two Shingle Factories, and a first class Carriage Factory, also a very large Steam Cabinet Factory, and a branch of the Royal Canadian Bank.[27]

Although Uxbridge had grown slowly in the early part of the 1850s, in the 1860s it flourished during the wheat boom of the American Civil War. In 1871, Uxbridge was described as containing:

> about, 1,500 inhabitants and the number is rapidly increasing. The village contains 2 flour mills, and a third in course of construction, 2 planing mills, 1 woolen factory, 2 saw mills, 2 cabinet factories, 1 small foundry, some 26 stores of different kinds, 8 hotels, 6 churches, Newspaper Office, Bank, Tannery.[28]

Nor were such manufacturing establishments restricted entirely to the larger villages. In 1868, for example, Derryville was described as follows:

> Derryville is a village in embryo, situated on the Centre road on the 11th concession of Brock. Amongst other buildings, it contains a snug little English Church, Mr. Whiteside's thriving store and Post Office, an excellent Blacksmithing establishment, carried on by Mr. J. Allen. Mr. Thomas Allan's prosperous Carriage and Agricultural Implement Factory, and a well-conducted Hotel.[29]

Similarly, Manchester contained

> three first class stores doing an excellent business, two Hotels, two Carriage Factories, several Blacksmith's forges, two boot and shoe Factories, one or two Tailoring Establishments, a Tinware Factory and Stove Shop, and a Grocery, with a Town Hall and a very neat Church, lately erected by the Primitive Methodists.[30]

Similar descriptions might have been written for almost every small village in Ontario County in the late 1860s.

As Table XXXI shows, the only large-scale employers of unskilled and semi-skilled labour in Ontario County were the many sawmills which dotted the northern part of the county. Unlike other forms of manufacturing, the sawmills required large numbers of unskilled workers to perform hard menial labour. Because unskilled labourers were numerous, serious abuses of the workmen were possible. Joseph Bigelow, a leading Port Perry businessman, owner of the foundry and interests in both flour mills and sawmills, paid his workmen on the "truck system", that is, he forced his workmen to buy high-priced goods from a store which he owned rather than pay them in cash. As W.S. Sexton said of Bigelow:

> When he [Sexton] came to the village, workmen had been uniformly paid in truck and traps of one kind and another at the most exorbitant prices and the idea of workmen being paid in money was out of the question. He [Sexton] had come with the idea that men ought to be paid in money when they wrought for it and not in truck and traps. This did not suit Mr. Bigelow's ideas of profit and loss and he did his best to annoy, crush out or ruin him.[31]

The existence of so many local manufacturing establishments, most of which employed relatively highly skilled and well-paid crafts workers, meant that the farmers had an excellent local market for produce. With a local market farming was not so completely dependent upon grain exports as would have been the case if the towns did not exist. Thus until 1871, the process of rural depopulation was slowed by the more diversified farming that was possible so long as the local towns prospered. Once the economy of the local towns was destroyed after 1871, however, the process of rural depopulation and social collapse accelerated.

Not only were there great economic changes in rural areas of Ontario County between 1851 and 1871, but during that period great social changes occurred as well. Thus in religion, education and social welfare new problems appeared. Many of these, while beginning in the 1851-71 period, would not work themselves out until the 1880s or even the 1890s.

The development of religious institutions and the building of churches continued steadily between 1851 and 1871. Although a large number of immigrants continued to arrive in the newer parts of the county, there was no great change in the religious makeup. The county remained predominantly Protestant, with the Anglicans, Presbyterians and Methodists the largest denominations. Roman Catholics continued to constitute a little more than ten percent of the population. The greatest concentration of Catholics was in Mara where, as recent Irish and Scottish settlers, they made up more than half of the population.[32]

The opening of churches and meeting houses would continue to mark both the spread of religious influence among the inhabitants and the growing wealth of the region; however, the greatest impact of religion was in the active attempt by the churches and churchmen to shape society according to their idea of moral order. The churches did not attempt merely to convert others to their views. Rather they undertook to influence legislation in many areas of life so that all members of the community would have to conform to their ideals. Thus, just as Egerton Ryerson had attempted to create a Christian society through his educational legislation, so other churchmen now attempted to enforce Christian ideals through legislation in other areas as well. The influence of the churches was especially felt as they tried to end the sale of alcoholic beverages.

By all accounts drunkenness was a severe problem for pioneer society in Upper Canada. Travellers through the country frequently remarked upon the evil consequences of drinking and gambling among the inhabitants. E.A. Talbot stated in 1824 that:

> The Canadian[s] are very much addicted to drinking; and, on account of the cheapness of liquor, are very frequently under its influence. Card-playing, horse-racing, wrestling, and dancing are their favourite amusements; and as the jingle of a dollar is a rarer sound in the ear of a Canadian, than the voice of liberty is in that of an Algerine [Algerian], their bets are usually made in stock, and are sometimes exceedingly extravagant. The fate of a cow, a yoke of oxen, or a pair of horses is often determined by the colour of a card; and an hour's gambling has deprived many a Canadian farmer of the hard-earned fruits of twenty years' industry.[33]

Susanna Moodie, in 1853, bemoaned both the frequency and the social acceptance of drunkenness:

> Alas! this frightful vice of drinking prevails throughout the colony to an alarming extent. Professional gentlemen are not ashamed of being seen issuing from the bar-room of a tavern early in the morning, or of being caught reeling home from the same sink of iniquity late at night. No sense of shame seems to deter them from the pursuit of their darling sin.[34]

The Reverend F.G. Weir remarked of Ontario County in the same period:

> Whiskey was sold for twenty-five cents a gallon. The pail of whiskey with the tin cup attached was to be found at the back of most stores, and the customer was free to help himself. In the numerous grog shops there was no lack of drink at a penny a glass or five cents a grunt, a grunt being as much as one could swallow in one breath. There was plenty of drink also at most gatherings. . . .
>
> Many a man drank himself off his farm in those days, and there were unprincipled barkeepers who found pleasure in seeing the debts of certain customers pile up, and in anticipating the day when they should be enriched by the possession of another good farm.[35]

As early as the 1820s many leading ministers (particularly among the Methodists) had attempted to reduce the evils of drunkenness through the creation of Temperance Societies.[36] Almost from its founding the *Christian Guardian*, edited by Egerton Ryerson campaigned to create a temperance movement, with the result that the first Temperance Society in Home District was formed at York in 1830.[37]

The temperance movement did not receive immediate or widespread support. In the male-dominated society of Upper Canada, drinking was a key social institution, and although many drank to excess, far more found relief from the toil and boredom of pioneer life in the friendly haven of a bar-room. Indeed, in the early days, so deeply was the use of whiskey ingrained in male social life that attempts by individuals to uphold temperance ideals created a good deal of antagonism among neighbours. Weir reported one such incident:

> Joseph Lee, the founder of Methodism at Greenbank, decided to build a large log barn. Everybody was invited to the raising, and 120 came. It was known that Lee had advanced temperance views, but no one supposed that he would dare to disregard traditional custom. The raising was fixed for a Monday. Soon after the help gathered it was noised around about that no liquor was provided. Lee was coaxed, threatened, etc., but of no use. He would not provide liquor even if the barn was never raised. Despite this the large majority concluded to proceed, as they all had much work at home, but eight of the neighbourhood settlers, some of whom did not care for liquor . . . would not stand for such an innovation, declared the barn should not be raised until liquor

> was provided. As soon as a log was put up those eight and their sympathizers pulled it down, in no case allowing it to remain two logs high. This continued all day Monday and until 5 p.m. Tuesday, yet Lee would not yield. At that hour the eight held a caucus, and as they all had urgent work at home, and personally liked Lee, they decided to yield and so turned in and helped and the barn was raised before they left that Tuesday night.[38]

With the dominance of such pro-whiskey attitudes among male society, it is little wonder that early Temperance Societies were said to consist of "old men and maidens, widows and wives".[39]

The significance of whiskey sales was not restricted to social life. Whiskey sales had an important economic function as well. In early periods when grain was cheap and difficult to transport, whiskey produced from wheat paid for many early farms.[40] Moreover, in an era when travel was slow and difficult, frequent inns were necessary for the comfort and well-being of travellers, and the sale of alcohol was a mainstay of the innkeepers' incomes. Without the sale of whiskey there is little doubt that many, if not most, inns would have been forced to close.[41] Indeed, not only was the latter argument used to defend the sale of whiskey, but in periods of strong temperance agitation the dependency of the public on the inns was exploited to prevent the effective introduction of anti-liquor legislation.

The main reason for the temperance movement's unpopularity, however, was the degree to which temperance was seized upon by a whole spectrum of advocates from all walks of life. While many were sincere, many more used the issue as a means of self-promotion. As R.H. Bonnycastle remarked in 1841:

> It is unfortunately the case, that in a state of society so new as that of Upper Canada, there are never wanting motives to incite obscure individuals to the attainment of a pseudo-celebrity, without the previous acquirements of education, observation, and research. Hence, perhaps, as much evil arises from the meddling of these persons with temperance societies, as the good they achieve. Farragos of voluminous temperance tracts issue in clouds from the press, under the auspices, frequently, of the most inadequate people. . . . Thus you will find, that political quacks, whose sole dependence and livelihood depend on keeping up a scurrilous, agitating, unprincipled newspaper, are generally the firmest and most untiring temperance advocates.[42]

In spite of all the difficulties faced by the temperance movement in Ontario County, it began to take on significant proportions during the early 1850s. In 1853, the Province of Canada passed a law which allowed a modified form of local option, so that each municipality could decide whether or not whiskey could be sold.[43] As a result one issue in almost every township election was temperance. With this impetus, and the strong leadership of Abraham Farewell, a whole series of temperance organizations was formed in Ontario

County. By 1858, there were three in Whitby, two in Oshawa, Brooklin, Greenwood and Brougham; and one in Claremont, Balsam, Prince Albert, Port Perry, Linwood, Beaverton, Manilla, Uxbridge, Columbus, Elm Grove, Vroomanton and Little Britain.[44]

The main methods used to publicize the temperance movement and to recruit new members were demonstrations, picnics and conventions to which famous speakers were invited to speak. One demonstration and picnic held near Oshawa in 1858 was described as follows:

> The turn-out of Sons, Templars, Cadets, members of the O.T. Society and Bank of Hope, was exceedingly imposing. At precisely twelve o'clock the procession formed, containing about 500 members, carrying their banners, and headed by the Oshawa Brass Band. The grove was a very pleasant one, and much thanks are due to the committee for the efficiency of the arrangements. After enjoying a good dinner—every party on its "own hook"—the platform was surrounded by as near as we could compute, 1,500 persons.[45]

Oliver Mowat, a leading reform politician (and later premier of Ontario) was the day's chief speaker. Another winter meeting in Uxbridge consisting of a supper and speeches was attended by 500 adults.

The rhetoric of the temperance movement was given to tales of suffering wives and starving children, and the pages of local newspapers carried sad accounts of men who had drowned or frozen to death while under the influence of whiskey. Particular temperance favourites were sentimental verses which could be recited or sung to familiar tunes. One such poem, entitled "Father's a Drunkard and Mother is Dead", contained the following verse:

> We were so happy till Father drank rum,
> Then all our sorrow and trouble begun;
> Mother grew paler and wept every day,
> Baby and I were too hungry to play.
> Slowly they faded, and one summer's night,
> Found their dear faces all silent and white;
> Then with big tears slowly dropping I said,
> "Father's a drunkard, and Mother is dead.[46]

In spite of the obvious popularity of the temperance movement in the late 1850s, it had little political success in Ontario County. Perhaps the electorate took to heart the results of the passing of a bylaw in Bowmanville in 1859, which prohibited the sale of whiskey by inns and taverns. The Whitby *Chronicle* recounted the bylaw's results:

> The effects of a prohibitory liquor law in Bowmanville are daily becoming more inconvenient, and a subject of public complaint. The Tavern-keepers—prevented from selling that on which alone they derived a profit—keep their premises altogether closed up, their gates locked, and will not open them to travellers or anyone else. This they

> do by way of retaliation for the unjust manner in which they consider they have been treated. The result is that neither food nor a place to rest—for man or horse—can be procured in the Town for love or money.[47]

Meanwhile whiskey, for those addicted to it, was still available within walking distance of the town. When farmers and travellers, complaining of the lack of accommodation for themselves and their horses, began to avoid Bowmanville, the bylaw was hurriedly repealed. After a few such experiences, the movement faded from view until the 1870s.

Although the churchmen and social reformers were unsuccessful in imposing temperance through legislation in the 1850s and 1860s, they were more successful in other areas of moral control. With the rapid increase in population of Whitby and Oshawa in the 1850s, and the building of the Grand Trunk Railway, the two towns became stopping-off points for travelling exhibitions, circuses, fairs and vaudeville shows. Moreover, betting events such as horse and foot racing were promoted from relatively spontaneous events into formalized meets at which the bookies, touts and other denizens of the gambling profession appeared in abundance. Many rural inhabitants and the churchmen were shocked by some of the excesses which accompanied these changes. However, merchants and businessmen in these two villages were on the whole delighted at the crowds these events attracted and the trade which was generated by them.

Moreover, while many of the exhibitions and vaudeville shows were content to present family entertainment in the form of singing, dancing, drama, comedy and animal and gymnastic acts, others aimed at quite a different audience. In these nudity was prevalent and prostitution among the female entertainers was common, as the show owners attempted to maximize their profits. Thus the increased prosperity of the area not only greatly increased the advances of religious observance and church building, but also introduced some of the main enemies against which the churchmen were to direct their legislative prohibitions. Thus it was that in the midst of the controversy over the passing of temperance legislation, the legislative attack upon "immorality" was widened to include horse racing and some forms of vaudeville entertainment.

At the June 1859 meeting of the Ontario County Council, Truman White, reeve of Pickering, and Ezra Gamble, reeve of Scugog, introduced a bylaw to "prevent Horse Racing, posting Indecent Placards and Public Exposure of the Person in an Indecent manner, within the County of Ontario".[48] While no one objected to the prohibition of "indecent placards" or "public exposure of the person", there was strong opposition to the outlawing of horse racing. After considerable debate, an amendment to exclude horse racing from the bylaw was passed on a seven-to-seven tie vote, with the warden, Charles Robinson of Thorah, breaking the tie.[49] The representatives of both the town of Whitby and the village of Oshawa led the opposition to the motion. On the other hand, the bylaw to prohibit "public indecency" passed without recorded opposition. Thus while the proponents of moral legislation were able to triumph against the "newer sins", in areas of traditional activities they were still incapable of changing custom.

The bylaw that passed the Council (no. 65) was a model of brevity:

> *First*—It shall not be lawful for any person to post in any public place within the County any indecent placard, writing or picture, or write any indecent words, or make any indecent drawing or picture on any wall or fence, or other public place within the County.
> *Second*—It shall not be lawful for any person to publicly expose his or her person in or near any public place within the County, in any manner offensive to common decency.[50]

The penalty established for such offences was a fine of from one to twenty dollars, or a jail term not to exceed twenty days.

Six months later, the advocates of "Christian morality" returned once again to the attack. This time, their attention was directed against local prostitution and "houses of ill fame" which flourished in the rising industrial towns. This bylaw, presented by Joshua Wright, reeve of Reach, and Ezra Gamble, reeve of Scugog, read as follows:

> Whereas it is expedient to make provision for the suppression of houses of ill-fame within this Municipality,
> Therefore the Corporation of the County of Ontario, by the Council, enacts as follows:
> That from and after the passing of this By-law, any person or persons keeping a house of ill-fame within the limits of this County, or any persons who shall aid and abet in keeping the same, by his or her attendance at such houses, or otherwise, and any person or persons frequenting the same, shall be liable to a penalty of not less than $5, nor more than $50, together with costs . . . [or for a term] not exceeding 21 days.[51]

This bylaw passed without opposition.

The high point of moral legislation was reached a year later with the passing of bylaw number 85: "A By-law for the prevention of vices, drunkenness and immorality, and for preserving peace and good order throughout the County of Ontario". By now the proponents of moral legislation had learned a number of lessons. Thus, rather than attempting to prohibit traditional habits such as drinking and horse racing, the moralists adopted the stance of "protecting" the public - particularly women and minors - from their influence and consequences. This allowed the male councilmen to demonstrate their public morality without being subjected, themselves, to its terms.

At the January 1861 meeting of Council, James B. Campbell, reeve of Reach, and John Ratcliff, reeve of East Whitby, introduced the bylaw which read:

> 1st. That it shall not be lawful for any Inn-keeper, Saloon-keeper, or any other person, to give or sell to any child, apprentice, or servant within this County, any intoxicating drink, of any kind whatever, without the consent of the parent, master, or legal protector of such child, apprentice, or servant, first had and obtained.
>
> 2nd. That it shall not be lawful for any person to be drunk, or disorderly, or to use any profane, blasphemous, indecent or grossly insulting language in any public street, or public place within this County.
>
> 3rd. That no person shall willfully disturb any religious meeting, or make, or cause to be made any noise, or disturbance, in or near any place or places of worship during Divine Service.
>
> 4th. No person shall utter, employ, or use any profane oath, or indecent language, or make any noise or disturbance upon, or near any street, or public place within this County, whereby any of Her Majesty's subjects may be in any manner annoyed or insulted.
>
> 5th. That each and every person who shall bathe, or wash his or her person, in any water within sight of the public highway, or inhabited houses within this County, shall be subjected [to] penalty. . . .
>
> 6th. That no person shall indecently expose his, or her person, or be guilty of any other indecent, immoral, or scandalous behaviour within this County.
>
> 7th. That no tippling shall be permitted within this County; nor shall any tippling be allowed, or permitted in any Inn, Tavern, or house of public entertainment within this County.
>
> 8th. That no Bowling Alley, kept for hire, shall be permitted to exist within this County. That no gambling Saloons shall be allowed, or permitted within this County; and that it shall be lawful for any constable of the county to take, seize, and destroy all faro banks, rouge et noir, roulette tables, or any other devices for gambling found used therein.
>
> 9th. That no person shall draw, write, or inscribe any indecent words, figures, or pictures, on any building, wall, fence, or other public place within this County.[52]

Sections 10 and 11 prohibited racing on streets and highways and section 12 created a wholly new offence for the area:

> 12th. That it shall not be lawful for any vagrant, or mendicant, to loiter, in, upon, or about, any of the streets, highways, or public places, within this County, and that for the purpose of this By-law, any person found loitering, idle, about the streets without any visible means of living, shall be deemed a vagrant.

Finally, the bylaw prohibited owners from having their stallions service mares in public places. The discussion of the bylaw covered almost three days of the

Council's time, but when it came to a vote, not a single member stood in opposition to it.

Although many of the terms of bylaw 85 might seem either commonplace or trivial today, they represented a distinct departure from previous social ideals. Until that time, it was generally assumed that it was the duty of the "man of the house", not the government, to prevent his children, servants or wife from becoming involved in immoral circumstances. In addition, most legal distinctions previously had been related to the terms of ownership of property and its protection; now women, servants and the young were deemed to be incapable of defending their own virtue as well. More significantly, in those sections prohibiting gambling, games of chance, bowling alleys, and so forth, the long step was taken from a society in which the law was designed to preserve the individual from the illegitimate violence of others, to a society in which the government sought to protect the individual from his own moral weaknesses. Thus the same "Christian" ideals which had caused Egerton Ryerson to require, through legislative changes, moral instruction in the schools, were now extended to require moral legislation in the community.[53]

For the rural residents of Ontario County, the changes in social life, represented by the rise of urban centres such as Whitby and Oshawa and the expansion of the influence of the churches, presented a fundamental dilemma. Society was changing, and almost every change represented an erosion of the ideals of rural independence and self-sufficiency. At every level of their lives – educational, economic, and religious – the pressures on the farmers were away from individualism and co-operation towards centralization and authoritarianism. With the rise of Whitby and Oshawa, with the growing power of their merchants, industrialists and financiers, and the rapidly expanding army of urban workers, the impetus towards centralization would be accelerated.

PROGRESS: THE IDEA AND ITS PROPONENTS

The 1851-71 period brought dramatic changes to the rural society and economy in Ontario County and introduced a number of unprecedented trends. In particular, the rise of several large scale industries in Oshawa and Whitby and the appearance of an entirely new class of entrepreneurs and financiers would have an enormous impact on the area. To these men, Ontario County offered scope for the creation of great enterprises and great fortunes.

In order to persuade the farmers and small businessmen to support these costly enterprises, promises of civic and financial grandeur were circulated widely, while more cautious men were constantly attacked as being ignorant, backward and short-sighted. Moreover, whenever anyone raised the question of who would be the beneficiary of these projects – and who would be required to pay for them – he was immediately attacked as being the creator of divisions within society. The watchword of the rising entrepreneurs was "Progress", and in their hands progress became synonymous with the growth of large capitalist enterprises.

Although the idea of human progress was by no means original to nineteenth-century urban Ontario,[1] nowhere was it embraced with greater enthusiasm. Canada, it was joyously proclaimed, had overthrown the laws of history and the new Society of Progress was being created here:

> THANK HEAVEN! We live in the nineteenth century, in the era of unparalleled improvement in science, in art, in literature, morals and

> religion. Never before did such glorious days as these dawn upon the human race; never were such vistas of fore-shadowed splendor opened up to the view of the contemplative philosopher, as in this enlightened age, when the human mind has burst the fetters of ages, purified from the gross defilement, which overshadowed as with a pall, former ages that have disappeared, and are now almost forgotten. How shall we contrast the darkness of the former ages with the meridian of splendor of modern times.[2]

According to the advocates of progress, it was a law of nature that nations must either advance or decay. As R.B. Sullivan, a leading businessman, argued:

> No country, no community can with safety be stationary. To improve with the improving, to advance with the advancing, to keep pace with the foremost, or to sink into contempt and poverty, or what is worse, into slavery and dependence, seems to be the fate of nations.[3]

In the hands of the rising businessman and entrepreneurs of Ontario County, the idea of progress was purged of its spiritual and idealistic elements. In their hands, progress came to be described almost exclusively in terms of economic growth and business expansion, and its highest form was proclaimed to be capitalism. Nor was it necessary for the capitalist to consider any other than his own best interest to be considered a public benefactor. In an editorial in 1868 one writer argued:

> It can scarcely be denied that the chief—we had almost said the only—subjects which engross the popular attention at the present time are Traction and Extraction. Traction Engines whether on rails or on common roads: and the Extraction of the precious metals from our Mines. . . . The genius of these enterprises point in the same direction, viz: the development of the resources of the country, and consequently those who embark, with reason, in either are public benefactors. We need not be told that many who engage in these enterprises, as in all others, are influenced by the most sordid motives, that they care nothing for the country, and would willingly sink it if by doing so they would forward their own self-aggrandizement. That such is the case no one will attempt to deny; but while many are so moved, very many are influenced by the highest and noblest motives; while wisely seeking their own advancement, the weal of their country is never lost sight of, being always willing to toil, aye, and to risk too, in order to further these ends; and such toil, anxiety and risk as our carpet patriots would not dare to touch even to save the country. But whether willing or not, everyone who aids in the development of the resources of the country is a public benefactor.[4]

As part of the concerted editorial campaign to glorify the wealth and success of local businessmen, newspapers delighted in describing the activities and

"Trafalgar Castle", Residence of N.G. Reynolds, Whitby *Public Archives of Ontario*

acquisitions of the leading entrepreneurs. For example, in 1857 when John Ham Perry built a baronial mansion in Whitby and furnished it lavishly, the Whitby *Chronicle* and Oshawa *Vindicator* described the event in loving detail:

> The building is very spacious—52 x 68 feet, and a wing extending north 50 feet by 20. The height from the foundation to the cornice is 33 feet, and the height to the top of the observatory which surmounts the building is 60 feet. The house contains twenty-two apartments, exclusive of the basement story. . . . The principal entrance is from the south by a magnificent door-way 12 by 7 feet. The doors in front of the building are all of black walnut; some of them and the windows, being those shown as the Provincial Fair at Kingston last year.[5]

The description of Perry's house went on for several newspaper columns and included glowing accounts of its stained glass, carpets and prize-winning furniture. The whole concluded with the comment that Whitby could be proud indeed of the edifice.

In spite of (and perhaps because of) such accounts, the press frequently found it difficult to explain how it was that all inhabitants were bound to benefit from selfishly conducted private enterprises - particularly when the period saw constant attempts to create monopolies and raids on the public purse. To counteract public reaction to revelations of such behaviour, the press created the theory of a great partnership of interest among commerce, industry and agriculture:

> The three great interests of a nation—Agriculture, Manufactures and Commerce—are so intimately connected with and so thoroughly

"Ellesmere Hall," Residence of T.N. Gibbs, Oshawa

Public Archives of Ontario

> dependent, one on another that their relative importance can scarcely be estimated; as the car of enlightenment advances these interests are pushed upwards and onward in a corresponding degree; and the nearer to perfection they rise, the more dependent they become on each other and the difficulty of contrasting their separate values increases. The fact is they are really indispensable to each other and no enlightened community can exist without them all. Hence we have our farms, our factories, our railways and our steamers representative of the great interests; and the prosperous future of that city, town, or village possessing these in sufficient extent and quality is placed beyond all doubt.[6]

Since farming was already the basis of most economic activity throughout Ontario County, this argument was used constantly to justify concessions to industrial and transportation interests.

Nor were these papers at all critical when the manufacturers acted in ways which were clearly opposed to the interests of the other "partners". In 1872, when the carriage- and wagon-makers formed a combine to fix the prices of their goods, the Oshawa *Reformer* excused their actions as being justified:

> About fifty of the carriage and wagon makers and blacksmiths of North and South Ontario met in Manchester, last week, to discuss matters in connection with their business, when it was resolved to raise the prices on wagons, carriages, sleighs, etc., ten per cent, and make a slight advance in all other work. They are forced to do this on account of the rise in prices of materials used by them[7]

Whenever farmers objected to such local "combinations", the press in Ontario County was quick to point out that such actions were justified because manufacturing was the basis of local prosperity:

> In whatever light it may be viewed there is nothing more essential for the upbuilding and healthful maintenance of a community than active, well-conducted manufacturies. These give a permanency and stability to a village or community which no other interest can, and without these the prosperity of any village must be fitful, fluctuating and transitory, hence the greatest benefactors of any community are those who invest their capital, devote their energies and employ their time in establishing, maintaining and increasing manufactures in their midst.[8]

Equally objectionable to the local farmers and craft workers was the entrepreneurs' assumption that the new progressive economics - capitalism - centralized all other activities and that the centralization, as such, was both inevitable and desirable. In discussing Oshawa's prospects in 1871, the *Vindicator* remarked:

> The town has rested its prospects upon its manufactures. This is solid ground if properly cultivated. The tendency of manufactures is to cen-

> tralize and the nucleus already obtained gives us an advantage over other towns.[9]

The innumerable railway schemes which were constantly being advocated by the leading businessmen were especially dear to the hearts of the proponents of progress and centralization. Railways, it was declared, were the chosen instruments of economic rationality which inevitably shaped the future:

> The proposed roads—should they be constructed—would like all others build up some places and utterly prostrate others. This is only what is to be expected; and in many instances, this killing off is no murder; it is not much to be lamented, inasmuch as it only hurries on a result which would have been brought about naturally after a few more years of sickly existence. The inexorable Railway in its decided tones at once solves the problem, "To be or not to be".
>
> Railways have a much more centralizing tendency than common roads. Along our common roads numerous little hamlets and villages from 6 to 8 miles apart manage to limp along with more or less comfort. The Railway grants no such indulgence; from 20 to 30 miles is the shortest distance that it will recognize, so that the first fruits of a new Railway is the building up of a few points, and a general slaughter of the intervening villages and hamlets. The fact is if the Railway could not succeed in accomplishing this, it would itself prove a failure; for it is not the building of the line, but the commanding of the trade which makes the road an institution.[10]

Since farmers depended upon the presence of local villages for both their economic and social existence, the threat of such large-scale destruction of established patterns met with considerable anxiety. Nor was this anxiety felt only by farmers. When railway promoters threatened to bypass established villages, local merchants and crafts workers were quick to recognize that if the proponents of progress were correct, their livelihoods were threatened and their properties would be devalued.

When the farmers, merchants and crafts workers objected to being taxed for the support of the very enterprises which threatened their destruction, their protests were bushed aside by the newspaper editors:

> That dreary doe-faced foggyism which used to hang around wrapped in the impenetrable cloak of some great granny . . . has been very properly driven to the wall, and the car of progress is being pushed with a vigour, and activity proportionate to the youth and resources of this fair province. . . . [An] important feature of these times is the eager desire for increased facilities for communications, we have on the tapis . . . the Toronto and Nipissing and the Scugog and Ontario. The first . . . will open up a large tract of valuable country—open up a new home for a large and industrious population, and running through the north

> and west of this county will give to some back villages, especially Uxbridge and Cannington an importance and position of which few have any conception. [The second], should it succeed in diverting the trade of the upper lakes by way of Scugog [it] will place Port Perry in an enviable position.[11]

When farmers became too restive about the disproportionate benefits received by capitalists in their "harmonious partnership", the editors replied that although the manufacturer and businessman might be richer, his riches were of constant worry and concern to him. By contrast, the farmer's life was pictured as being one which might not bring wealth in worldly terms, but did produce for him happiness and contentment beyond that of other occupations. In 1870, in a week when wheat had fallen to seventy cents a bushel, barley to forty cents, and oats to twenty-eight cents (about thirty to forty percent below the ordinary price), one paper ran the following poem praising the joys of rural life:

The Independent Farmer

Let sailors sing of the windy deep,
    Let soldiers praise their armour,
But in my heart this toast I'll keep,
    The Independent Farmer.
When first the rose, in robe of green,
    Unfolds its crimson lining
And round the cottage porch is seen
    The honeysuckle twining;
When banks of bloom their sweetness yield
    To bees that gather honey,
He drives his team across the field,
    Where skies are soft and sunny.

The blackbird clucks behind the plow,
    The quail pipes proud and clearly,
Yon orchard hides beneath the bows
    The home he loves so dearly.
The grey old barn whose doors enfold
    His ample store in measure,
More rich than heaps of hoarded gold,
    A precious, blessed treasure;
But yonder in the porch there stands
    His wife, the lovely charmer
The sweetest rose on all his lands—
    The Independent Farmer.

To him the spring comes dancingly,
  To him the summer blushes,
The Autumn smiles with mellow ray;
  He sleeps, old Winter hushes.
He cares not how the world may move,
  No doubts nor fears confound him,
His little flocks are linked in love,
  And household angels round him;
He trusts in God and Loves his wife;
  Nor griefs nor ills may harm her;
He's Nature's nobleman in life—
  The Independent Farmer.[12]

Thus, during a period when farmers were beginning to resent their loss of prosperity and the increased pressures to subsidize transportation, commerce and manufacturing through monopoly prices and large-scale grants of public money, the press attempted to reduce their anger by proclaiming that farmers enjoyed the happiest conditions of any group in society.

In their attempts to create the idea of economic harmony, the press found it somewhat more difficult to describe the role played by the working class. Although it was quite clear that capital was incapable of creating either wealth or progress without the employment of labour, it was not at all clear that the labouring class itself was achieving any measure of benefit from the progress that was occurring on all sides. The primary difficulty in bettering the condition of the workers was the general belief that wages were fixed by economic laws which were incapable of any real change. If wages were raised or hours shortened, it was argued, these changes would raise the price of the goods manufactured, and inevitably force up all other wages and prices, with the result that at the end of the cycle (and after a good deal of chaos in the meantime) workers would find themselves right back where they had been at the beginning.

When the workers in local factories began to form unions in the late 1860s and to agitate for a reduction of the work week from 60 to 54 hours (from 10 to 9 hours a day), employers led by George Brown, publisher of the Toronto *Globe*, predicted economic and social disaster would result. Brown's argument, reprinted approvingly by many local papers contains most of the basic arguments which prevailed then, and deserves to be quoted at length:

> "To the Employees of Labour and the Public Generally"
>
> Whereas certain Mechanics and workingmen of the City of Toronto and elsewhere have formed themselves into Trades Unions and Labour Leagues for purposes antagonistic to the interests of their Employers and the public at large—and amongst the rest, for the purpose of shortening the hours of labor from ten to nine hours per day.
>
> And, whereas, it is abundantly proven by existing facts that ten hours

> of work in ordinary manufacturing pursuits is perfectly consistent with the normal conditions of the operative, and shortening the hours of labour would be entirely unsuited to the wants of a young and struggling country like Canada, where skilled labour is comparatively scarce and the production of our own manufacturies are as yet unequal to the supply for home consumption.
>
> Therefore, we firmly believe any attempt to shorten the hours of labour so as to lessen by one-tenth the producing capacity of our manufactories, would proportionately lessen our material advancement as a nation, perhaps permanently divert a portion of our trade from the country, and prove alike injurious to the Employers, the Employees, and the public at large.
>
> To the Employers it would be a serious injury to restrict the use of reproduction power of their limited capital. Capital which in nine cases out of ten is the sole product of their own *extra time, labour*, and energy of character. Any attempt on the part of the Employees to dictate to them in any way, or to what extent they shall lawfully use their own resources, is not only an unwarranted interference with the rights of others, but a very transparent attempt to introduce amongst us the Communistic system of levelling.[13]

The only direct benefits which the press could claim for labour from expansion of the capitalist system were a greater number of jobs and greater stability of income.

To improve the employees' position, it was argued, it was necessary to improve the employee. Thus, a popular response to employee demands for improved wages and working conditions and for shorter hours was the erection of the Mechanics Institutes – libraries and lecture halls – where it was expected that the workers would upgrade their skills and therefore, in the end, would receive higher wages. Thus Mechanics Institutes were erected in several centres in Ontario County to serve as aids to the individual progress of the workers.[14]

In spite of attempts to satisfy workers' demands for increased benefits through projects such as Mechanics Institutes, it was tacitly conceded that general improvement through such methods was unlikely and unrealistic. Ultimately in times of crises in labour, the press fell back on the same methods which had been used to quiet farm antagonism – to counsel peace and contentment with the station allotted by God to each man. The American evangelical minister, Henry Ward Beecher, was a particular favourite of the Uxbridge *Journal* and Oshawa *Reformer*. In 1872 the *Journal* ran the following sermon by Beecher:

> There is a danger that laboring men, in combining for mutual protection, will organize around the core of selfishness. This will be to imitate the very evil that makes corporate wealth dangerous. It will have the

> inherent and essential mischief of the class spirit. . . . If labor is to fight capital by a rivalry in selfishness, then society will be but a carcass lying between two vultures. . . .
>
> Men are in danger of regarding Work as an evil, and Leisure as an end, in itself. Labor is a saleable commodity. To raise the price of it by legimate means is fair and wise. But it will be a supreme folly for poor men to decrease the quantity of labor in the community. While here and there a few men are overworked, the great mass of men do not work enough. . . .
>
> There is a danger, too, that these co-operative associations will set aside the great law of subordination. You cannot by legislation bring all men up to an equality. There are certain great laws which are as inevitable as fate. You can make all men equal to each other politically; you can make all men equal in rights and duties; but you cannot make all men equal in their earning-power. . . . It disregards a distinction which God made, and which will always continue to exist. It takes away the stimulus to development and industry.[15]

The idea of an innately lower class of hired workers was precisely the one which had been advocated by the Colonial Office and William Allan, the Canadian banker, some forty years before, and against which Mackenzie and his followers had struggled.

If one assumes that a portion of society was created by God with fewer talents, and that they must inevitably expect fewer of the world's goods than the more favoured of their fellow men, then acceptance of one's lot must be the essence of good counsel. A little poem aimed at the working poor made the point clearly in 1870:

"If You Should Ever Get Married"

If you should ever get married John,
    I'll tell you what to do
Get a little tenement
    Just big enough for two!
And one spare room for company,
    And one spare bed within it—
And if you'd begin love's life aright,
    You'd better thus begin it.

In furniture be moderate John,
    And let the stuffed chairs wait;
One looking glass will do for both
    Yourself and loving mate;
And Brussels, too, and other things,
    Which make a fine appearance,
If you can better afford it, they
    Will look better a year hence.

Some think they must have pictures, John
Superb and costly too;
Your wife will be a picture, John,
Let that suffice for you.
Remember how the wise man said,
A tent and love within it
Is better than a splendid house
With bickerings every minute. . . .

And now, when you are married, John,
Don't try to ape the rich;
It took them many a toilsome year
To gain their envied niche.
And if you would gain the summit, John,
Look well to your beginning;
And then will all you win repay
The toil and care of winning.[16]

Surrounded as they were by the constant assertion of the wealth, growth and progress of Ontario County, many of the local workers like John were led to demand more in return for their labour than the bare-walled tenements and spartan furnishings recommended by this anonymous author. Thus the rise of large industrial establishments employing many poorly-paid workers brought with it labour unrest as well.

The rise of the capitalists in Ontario County brought with it a series of struggles which were fought along both ideological and practical lines. Out of that struggle would appear the Ontario County with which we are familiar today.

The enterprise which created the most bitter struggle between the various classes and regions of Ontario County, and which had the greatest effect was the building of railways. In one respect the railway issue was merely a continuation of previous attempts by Whitby merchants to maintain and enhance their monopoly over trade in the area; yet they were losing the struggle for control against the more powerful Toronto interests. This loss of local control and autonomy was the major crisis of the 1851-71 period.

No sooner had the newly separated County of Ontario been established than the whole issue of building a railroad from Port Whitby to Lake Huron began to attract public attention. In his original campaign to separate the area from York, Peter Perry had promised to build such a road, but Perry's death and the protracted struggle to bring the County into being diverted men's attention for several years.

In the fall of 1852, however, several leading Whitby businessmen began to raise the question again and were joined in their efforts by Joseph Gould. In order to publicize the project, a preliminary meeting was held in Whitby on

November 13, 1852 which was attended by all the leading businessmen. A committee was established consisting of Dr. Gunn, James Wallace, J.H. Perry, Ezra Annis, Hugh Fraser, Louis Houck, R.H. Lawder, James Rowe and L. Schofield, which immediately called a mass public meeting to rally public support.[17] At that highly successful meeting, attended by "the wealth and intelligence of the township", a series of resolutions was passed which were designed to promote the building of a railroad. The audience was enticed by rhetoric promising that if Whitby were to acquire a direct connection to Lake Huron, it might yet overshadow its rivals, including Toronto, as the trade from half a continent poured through its port. One resolution is significant in this connection:

> Moved by Mr. John H. Perry and seconded by Dr. Foote:
> *Resolved*,—"That the tract of country from Port Whitby, on Lake Ontario, to Sturgeon Bay, on Lake Huron, offers many and important advantages to the construction of a railroad, over all other projected routes between those lakes—viz., while, for instance, the Toronto, Simcoe and Huron Railroad, which stands next in favourableness of route to this proposed line, will lessen the distance between Mackinaw on the west, and New York and Boston on the east, about 310 miles, the Port Whitby and Huron Road by narrows Lake Simcoe, will again decrease the distance some forty miles below the Toronto and Huron route.[18]

After this meeting, an enlarged committee of Whitby merchants carried on a lively campaign of public meetings throughout the county to promote the railway, and two local surveyors A.J. Robinson and John Shier, made a preliminary survey of the route. They concluded that the railway could be built for £4,000 per mile.

In April 1853, a charter was granted by Parliament to the "Port Whitby and Lake Huron Railroad Company".[19] The incorporators named in the charter were Joseph Gould, Peter Taylor, Henry Daniels, James Rowe, William Laing, Ezra Annis, James Wallace, John Shier and R.J. Gunn. Capital was set at £250,00 divided into 25,000 shares of £10 each. At the first meeting of the provisional directors on May 15, Ezra Annis was elected president; W. Laing, vice-president; John Ham Perry, secretary and treasurer; and John Shier, engineer.[20]

The company's management now set about surveying the proposed route and gave every appearance of pushing ahead with the railroad without delay. Everywhere the directors met with the greatest enthusiasm for the project. The northern townships had suffered greatly from bad roads in spring and fall, and the railroad promised to give them greatly improved access to the markets on Lake Ontario. Indeed, Mariposa Township proposed to take £20,000 in stock if the railroad would be deviated eastward from its direct route to pass through that township. Then, in November 1853, it was revealed that the company proposed to build the road only on the condition that the public loan them the money and undertake the risk.

The method proposed to finance the line was as follows: first, the stockholders were to purchase £50,000 ($250,000) worth of stock, of which 10 percent ($25,000) was to be paid into the treasury of the company; second, the Township of Whitby was to purchase stock valued at £50,000; third, the County of Ontario was to guarantee a loan to the company of £100,000 ($500,000), which would be repaid if the railway proved to be profitable.[21] Thus for the small initial sum of $25,000, the promoters proposed to get control of a property valued at $1,000,000. Almost immediately the directors of the railroad signed a contract with a builder whose main details were spelled out in a letter to the directors:

> I am directed by Messrs. J. Sykes & Co. to say that they will build the Port Whitby and Lake Huron Railway in first-class manner, and furnish the required rolling stock and make arrangements for the stock to be taken up in England on the following conditions:
>
> 1st. That municipal aid to the extent of £3,000 sterling per mile be loaned to constitute a first charge upon the road.
>
> 2nd. That sufficient stock be taken within the district to purchase right of way, office (your own) expenses, including Engineer, Solicitor, Secretary, and if any such is appointed, the salary of a paid Director.[22]

The farmers were furious: not only had the Whitby businessmen not been entirely honest in their promises to build a railway if the County were separated and Whitby made the county seat, but now their taxes were to be mortgaged to pay for a road whose profits would go to the promoters, while the farmers guaranteed the risk.

Unlike the farmers, landowners in the small towns along the proposed route were enthusiastic supporters of the project. These men were seized with speculative fever, as visions of huge fortunes to be made by selling lots to newcomers danced before them. As soon as a Mr. Bongard in Utica heard that his village would be along the proposed right-of-way, he divided his land into lots and laid out two streets, Bongard and Broadway, which he dedicated to the township of Reach.[23] Within each township along the route, speculators actively promoted the railway in anticipation of a land boom, while the farmers generally objected to the terms of its financing.

The railway directors, under the influence of Joseph Gould of Uxbridge, a large shareholder, had originally proposed to build the railroad through Claremont and Uxbridge along a western route.[24] This plan had been actively supported by Peter Taylor of Pickering. When the directors from Whitby sat down to calculate the railway's chances of political and financial success, two major considerations caused them to change their minds about the proposed route. First, if the railroad took the longer route through Claremont and Uxbridge bypassing Reach Township and Port Perry, the Reach councillors were almost certain to vote against the loan. Moreover, although Uxbridge represented a likely vote in favour of the loan because of Joseph Gould's influence, Peter Taylor's Pickering electors were much less certain to support so costly a project which would serve only a small part of the township. On the other hand, the future profitability of the road depended upon acquiring the timber export trade of Victoria County. This could be done only if the route met the Lake Scugog-Trent system at Port Perry. In calculating the number of votes from Whitby, Reach, Brock, Thorah, Mara and Rama – the townships which would be directly served by the altered route – nine possible pro-loan votes appeared. Thus it was decided to abandon the Claremont-Uxbridge route and pass through Reach instead. Those who had expected to prosper from land speculation along the original route were furious.

The first hurdle faced by the promoters was persuading the township council of Whitby to purchase £50,000 worth of shares in the railway. This presented little difficulty since both the reeve and deputy reeve were shareholders in the proposed railway, and other members were residents of Brooklin and Myrtle, villages which lay along the new route. The eastern councillors from Columbus and Raglan were strongly opposed to this enormous expenditure which threatened to destroy the economic basis of their little towns, but they were easily outvoted, and the motion was passed.[25] Because all bylaws which required such huge debts had to be submitted to the public, a referendum was required to approve the expenditure. With Whitby's rapidly growing population and the approval of Brooklin and Myrtle, the vote passed easily.

The municipal elections in January 1854 were fought almost entirely on the railway loan issue. To everyone's surprise, Joseph Gould, campaigning on the pro-loan platform, was defeated in Uxbridge by William Hamilton, a farmer opposed to the loan. On the other hand, the change in route had ensured the election of Thomas Paxton and Robert Wells in Reach who were in favour of the loan. Thus, with nine out of the thirteen councillors on the County Council being from townships served by the proposed railway, passage of the bylaw seemed certain. The directors, however, underestimated the degree of opposition from the farm population.

At the first County Council meeting in January 1854, John Ham Perry, reeve of Whitby, moved that the County now loan to the proposed railway an unstated amount of money to aid in its construction. This proposal was immediately attacked by the anti-loan forces led by John Hall Thompson, reeve of Brock, and John Lumsden and Peter Taylor, reeve and deputy reeve of Pickering. The basis for their opposition was similar to that which had defeated aid to the privately-owned toll roads in previous years: why should the farmers and taxpayers use their money and credit to build a railway which would be privately owned and whose profits would remain in the shareholders' hands? The debate was long and furious, and at times bitter.

After innumerable charges and counter-charges, attacks and counter-attacks, the vote was finally taken. As was the case in so many issues of crucial importance, the vote was a tie. Instead of the expected nine votes in favor of the loan, there were only six: John Ham Perry and Abraham Farewell, reeve and deputy reeve of Whitby; Thomas Paxton and Robert Wells, reeve and deputy reeve of Reach; Neil McDougall, reeve of Thorah; and a surprise supporter, James K. Vernon, reeve of Scott. Opposed, as expected, were John M. Lumsden and Peter Taylor, reeve and deputy reeve of Pickering and William Hamilton, reeve of Uxbridge. But to the chagrin of the railway supporters, Lumsden, Taylor and Hamilton were joined in opposition by John Hall Thompson and John Hart, reeve and deputy reeve of Brock, and Thomas McDermott, reeve of Mara and Rama.[26] The railway loan supporters were furious at McDermott's defection: the Whitby *Chronicle* afterwards took every opportunity to refer to him as the "Basswoods Reeve".[27] With the vote tied, T.N. Gibbs, reeve of Oshawa, and warden of the County, was called upon to cast the deciding vote. Gibbs voted against the loan, and the railway project was put aside for the moment.

The whole affair had created a great deal of bitterness in the residents of the eastern half of Whitby Township. With Whitby, Brooklin and Myrtle on their side pro-railway councillors were generally successful in township elections. Thus, the eastern residents petitioned the Government to establish a ward system of local elections in order to ensure themselves of a voice in township council meetings. Their wishes were granted; however because they were outnumbered, they were unable to control the Township council.[28]

Although the Port Whitby and Lake Huron Railway project had received a severe setback by the refusal of the County Council to finance it, the village of Whitby remained in the grip of railway fever. The construction of the Grand Trunk Railway (the present-day Canadian National Railway) from Montreal to Toronto which had begun in 1854, had set off an enormous wave of speculation in the towns along its route, and as construction progressed in 1855 and 1856, the speculative frenzy mounted. Because of the Crimean War, wheat was selling for two dollars a bushel, and with prosperity general throughout the area, Whitby was one of the main centres of land speculation.

In order to maximize the prestige of Whitby, and to gain the greatest degree of autonomy of action, the residents of Whitby in 1854 petitioned the Provincial Assembly to be made a town. Their request was granted and the Town of Whitby came into being on January 1, 1855.[29] The fact that Whitby had been made a town while Oshawa remained a village was seen as a feather in the hats of the leaders of the newest municipality. In the euphoria of this event, the town limits of Whitby incorporated large areas of farm land, town lots were laid out and sold for enormous sums, and enormous and lavish homes were built by leading citizens such as John Ham Perry and Sheriff Nelson G. Reynolds.[30]

When the Grand Trunk was opened between Oshawa and Toronto in August 1856, and between Oshawa and Montreal in October of the same year,[31] the whole question of building the Port Whitby and Lake Huron Railway was again raised. Early in June 1857 the directors of the Port Whitby and Lake Huron Railway held a meeting to reorganize the project. At the meeting, Nelson G. Reynolds, Sheriff of Ontario County, was elected president, and John B. Warren, the influential Oshawa manufacturer, vice-president.[32] The latter appointment was a particularly clever move since it opened the possibility of obtaining Oshawa's support. The proposals for financing the line were equally clever. Because the project was popular in the Town of Whitby, it was proposed that the town should purchase £75,000 ($375,000) in stock. Second, it was proposed that the County Council should purchase £100,000 worth of stock, leaving £25,000 stock to be purchased by the private shareholders. To complete the financing, the company would then issue £235,000 in mortgage bonds on the railway property. In addition it was proposed that other municipalities should buy £20,000 worth of stock, and the County of Simcoe £15,000. Moreover, it was proposed that seven of the thirteen directors of the railroad should be appointed by the various municipalities which had purchased stock.[33]

The last point was made much of by the promoters of the railway. As the Whitby *Chronicle* was fond of pointing out:

> No contact of any kind can be entered into without the consent of the County itself, which will be represented by a majority of the Directors of the Company elected on the Municipal Stock. The Municipal Stock Directors, in other words the County, will not alone have the control of the County Stock, but also of the entire Stock of the company. If proper care be not taken of the County, it will be the fault of the County itself, in the choice of its representatives.[34]

What the *Chronicle* did not say was that even if the municipal stockholders were to elect seven of the thirteen directors, they would be greatly under-represented. The municipalities were to purchase £210,000 worth of stock while the private stockholders purchased only £25,000, yet the municipalities were to elect only a bare majority of the directors. Moreover, with the Town of Whitby holding £75,000 in stock, and the leading businessmen of Whitby being the major stockholders, it was almost certain that the private stockholders would be able to control at least one of the municipal directors. Little wonder then that many of the farmers still viewed the proposals with a good deal of skepticism.

When Whitby had been incoporated as a town, it had included a considerable number of farms within its boundary. Because these farms bore much of the assessment of the town, the farmers were strongly opposed to the huge increase in taxes which would result from the purchase of stock in the railway. Led by William Laing, they fought hard to defeat the measure, but to no avail. The Whitby *Chronicle*, which strongly supported the railway, reported the farmers' efforts as follows:

> On Friday last the Town By-law for taking £75,000 stock in the railroad was passed by the ratepayers. Contrary to our expectation a poll was demanded by the friends and followers of Mr. William Laing. Not apprehending any opposition at the poll, those in favor of a railroad—secure in the passing of the by-law—remained quite passive, and regarded the opening and closing of the poll as a mere matter of form. They little dreamed that a secret combination of the rich Landowners had been entered into, to go to the poll en masse and vote against the by-law. Mr. Laing, on the contrary was hard at work and had his farming friends all well marshalled. . . . Thirty-two votes were immediately polled against the by-law. The friends of the by-law being informed of the coup de main which had been attempted immediately repaired to the Town Hall and polled 114 votes. . . . Nine votes more were polled by the anti-railway men, making the total number of votes against the by-law 41.[35]

Having won the Whitby campaign, the PW & LH directors were now ready for the battle at the county level.

On November 10, 1857 a special meeting of the County Council was called to discuss the railway question. Abraham Farewell, deputy reeve of Whitby Township, and George Currie, reeve of Reach, introduced a motion to commit the County to purchase £100,000 in stock in the PW & LH railway. This motion was immediately opposed by T.N. Gibbs, and a vigorous and bitter debate followed. After more than two days' dispute, the vote was taken. The pro-railway forces scored a decisive win – nine to seven, with only the reeves and deputy reeves of Pickering, Uxbridge, Scott, Brock and Oshawa in opposition.[36] It was now time to take the issue to the electors.

In order to get approval of any proposal to undertake debt, the County Council was required by law to win a special referendum among the citizens. The statute stated that such a financial measure required an absolute majority of electors to pass. Thus non-voters would be counted against the railway proposal. In order to increase their chances of winning the vote, the pro-railway council majority voted to waive the law and to decide the issue by a majority of those who actually voted.[37] Naturally this manipulation of the law made the anti-railway forces more angry than ever.

Now meetings were held in every town and village throughout the County as the pro- and anti-railway forces attempted to rally support. Among the most outspoken advocates of building the PW & LH was Thomas Paxton, sawmill owner, land speculator and railway shareholder of Port Perry. Every afternoon and evening in one village or another, the opponents met to debate the issue. A report of a meeting held at Columbus on December 1, demonstrates the general tone of the meetings held in rural areas:

> The gentlemen from [Reach], who bragged of their success in converting whole droves of their neighbours to the railway principle, found

> the people of East Whitby and Oshawa a little better posed up on the question than to follow their statements, well garnished with easy-flowing words, as they were, without a candid investigation of the truth. If, at a small meeting in the Township of Reach, some of the best supporters of the railway, whose statements were not attempted to be gainsayed, persuaded all but two of the few present, that passing the Bye-law was going to make them independently rich, it must be regarded as something of a triumph that, at the conclusion of the large and influential meeting convened at Columbus, and attended and addressed by the chief organizers and 'big gun' supporters of the Bye-law, nearly every man went away apparently determined to spare no effort to secure the defeat of the measure at the polls.[38]

A resolution passed at the Columbus meeting by a reported majority of ten to one made clear the main point of opposition to purchase of stock by the County:

> Resolved—That the Bye-law passed by the municipal Council of the County of Ontario at its last session, authorizing the Municipality to take £100,000 stock in the P.W. & L.H. R.R., is unjust, inasmuch as the greater portion of the burden will be borne by those . . . which will be least benefitted by the Railway.[39]

The railway promoters cajoled and threatened. If a railway were built, they argued, the greater access to the Toronto market for local cordwood would cause the value of land in Ontario County to rise sufficiently to offset the cost of building the road. If the railway were not built, the farmers would eventually be taxed to improve the privately-owned gravel roads. It was constantly repeated that railroads would inevitably be built in the region. Those towns and townships which supported the railway and which lay along its route would prosper and grow rich. Those by-passed would inevitably grow poor and wither away. Finally, the promoters threatened that if the bylaw was not passed, the merchants and speculators of Whitby and Port Perry would attempt to create a new county which they could control to suit themselves. As the *Chronicle* ominously thundered, "You will see the movement, already set foot, to divide the County, carried out".[40]

The electors of Ontario County, as it transpired, were not intimidated by the *Chronicle*'s warnings, nor were they seduced by the promises of wealth held up to them by the promoters. In one of the most overwhelming expressions of opinion ever recorded in a public vote in the area the bylaw was rejected (see Table XXXII). Only in the Town of Whitby, Reach and Scugog Townships, Mara and Rama was there a majority in favour. In all other municipalities the majority opposed was frequently more than ten to one.

Although the railway proposal was defeated, for the residents of the eastern half of Whitby Township the strong advocacy of the project by their reeve and

Table XXXII
Vote on Railway Bylaw, County of Ontario, December 16, 1857[41]

Areas Opposed	*In Favour*	*Opposed*	*Majority*
Oshawa	5	248	243
Scott	4	177	173
Thorah	43	115	72
Pickering	22	697	675
Uxbridge	29	341	312
Whitby Township	207	529	322
Brock	43	342	299
Totals	353	2,449	2,096
Areas in Favour			
Whitby Town	358	37	321
Reach	340	158	182
Scugog	58	—	58
Mara and Rama	149	43	106
Totals	905	238	667
Grand Total	1,258	2,687	1,429

deputy reeve, James Dryden and Abraham Farewell, was the last straw. The ward system had guaranteed a representation of the views of the farmers and merchants of Columbus and Raglan on the township council, but the larger population of the western half of the township meant that the reeve and deputy reeve invariably represented the pro-railway views of Brooklin, Myrtle and, of course, the Town of Whitby. As a result of their inability to prevent the pro-railway forces from dominating the township council, the eastern residents petitioned the Legislature to have the township divided. This was done, and on January 1, 1858, the Township of East Whitby came into being.[42]

In one respect, the Whitby businessmen had been correct in their analysis of the situation. Because Whitby was primarily a mercantile and administrative centre, its future growth was dependent upon the expansion of either its region of trading dominance or its area of administrative control. With the collapse of the railway proposal, the main strategy to expand Whitby's mercantile empire was defeated. The merchants were not willing to rest quietly nor to be content to remain merely the major businessmen in a small but prosperous trading centre. Both desperation and ambition would continue to drive them towards expansion.

This desperation on the part of many Whitby businessmen stemmed from two causes. First, in the period of speculative fever, many merchants and

Brown & Patterson Manufacturing Company, Whitby

Public Archives of Ontario

tradesmen had come to Whitby expecting to prosper from the great increase in business that would occur once the trade of the Canadian and American Wests began to pour down the PW & LH Railroad. Caught up in the economic mania of the moment, many had mortgaged themselves heavily, and, with the collapse of the railway project, now faced bankruptcy.[43] Moreover, to worsen their condition, the great boom in prices caused by the Crimean War and the building of the Grand Trunk was followed by a severe depression which sharply curtailed business. Thus faced by almost certain ruin, they cast anxiously about looking for some way to bring about further growth for the town.

In those desperate and gloomy days, two strategies appeared which offered some hope of helping Whitby's growth to continue: to expand Whitby's area of market dominance through a large-scale program of road-building, or to enlarge its administrative role by adding more territory to Ontario County. In 1858 both methods would be attempted.

During the spring of 1858, a series of public meetings were held in the Town of Whitby to create support for an ambitious plan to expand the Whitby market area.[44] Singled out for attention were two main roads running north from Whitby: the Centre Line Road from Manchester to Beaverton, and Brock Street (and an extension) which would run from Epsom to Uxbridge and then north through Scott to Georgina. In all, the program of road-building was expected to cost £20,000.

To create public support for the undertaking, meetings were held throughout the County, and petitions were circulated to be presented to the County Council, although, outside the Town of Whitby there was little enthusiasm for the program.[45]

As soon as it became clear that there was little general support for the Town of Whitby's proposals, it was decided to try to enlist the favour of the other areas in the County by expanding the proposals to include the "Brock" or "Centre" Road of Pickering (£9,000) and the Nonquon Road (£6,000). Thus, by the time the proposal reached the County Council at the June meeting, its cost had grown to £36,000. The Whitby strategy very nearly succeeded. By uniting the interests of the towns and the most distant townships against the older rural areas whose taxes would pay for the roads, the proposal very nearly passed the County Council. After a debate which lasted three days, the motion to raise £36,000 for the roads resulted in a tie, and was defeated when the warden, Daniel G. Hewett, the reeve of Mara and Rama, voted against it.[46] In favour were the representatives from the Town of Whitby and the Village of Oshawa and the Townships of Reach, Scott and Thorah. Opposed were Whitby and East Whitby, Uxbridge and Scugog Townships. Pickering and Brock divided their votes.[47]

Encouraged by their near success, the gravel road promoters now expanded their proposals to include roads in every township and region of the County. Included were £6,200 for Simcoe Street from Oshawa to the Ontario-Victoria

County line north of Borelia; £1,200 for roads in Thorah; £12,000 for the Centre Line Road from Manchester to Atherley; £5,500 for roads running north and west from Uxbridge village; and £9,500 for roads in Pickering: all for a total of £34,400. A special meeting of the County Council was called for August to discuss the new proposal, and the fight was on.

Although the new proposals did not appear to guarantee the support of a majority of the County Council, the manoeuvring, once the debate had started, did. In a startling change of strategy, James Hodgson and W.H. Tremayne, the reeve and deputy reeve of the Town of Whitby, moved to cut the grant to Simcoe Street by £3,200 and the Pickering Brock Road-Scott line by £3,000, while increasing the Uxbridge grant by £2,000. This lost them the support of a Pickering and an Oshawa representative, but it caused John Hall Thompson, reeve of Brock to support the proposal, and also won the support of both Uxbridge representatives who had previously been opposed to the proposals. As a result of the money and vote switches, the second reading of the measure passed easily, and it was proposed to raise bonds totalling £30,000.[48]

In order to limit the power of the townships opposed to the road proposals (Whitby, Whitby East and Pickering), a most unusual method of voting was decided upon. Rather than have a general vote for the whole County as was the usual practice on money matters, it was decided to hold elections within each township. The reeve and deputy reeve were bound to vote in accordance with the electorate's decision on the third reading of the roads proposal. Since the representatives of Mara and Rama, Brock, Reach, Scott, Uxbridge and the Town of Whitby favoured the road scheme, it was assumed that passage was assured.[49]

Once again the County was thrown into an uproar over both the roads proposal and the taxation. The mood of the farmers was bitter indeed at this latest manipulation. As one paper reported of the meeting in East Whitby:

> Pursuant to the call of the Reeve in our last issue, about twenty persons assembled . . . at the Town Hall. . . . It was finally decided to open a poll on Saturday next, when everybody wishing to be taxed to build roads for the benefit of the Township of Reach and the Town of Whitby, can have the privilege of voting in favor of the scheme.[30]

The result of the East Whitby poll showed 201 opposed to the road proposal, while only three voted in favour of it.[51]

Nor were the farmers in other areas more favourably disposed. To the astonishment of the representatives of even those townships which were most benefited by the terms of the bylaw, there was a general indignation with the manipulations of the businessmen. When a special meeting of the County Council was called in November 1858 to report on the results of the township votes, it was discovered that only Mara and Rama had voted in favour. Brock (92-53), Pickering (291-1), Scott (34-11), Scugog (37-0), Uxbridge (135-24), and Whitby Township (144-2) had all voted against the proposal,[52] as had East Whitby. Oshawa, Thorah, Reach and the Town of Whitby had not even bothered to hold votes once the voters in other areas had made their anger known. It would be ten years before the Whitby merchants undertook another scheme of this nature.[53]

The gravel road proposals coincided with the attempts of the Whitby merchants to expand the administrative role of their town as well. One of the main reasons for the attempt to extend the gravel road from Uxbridge into Scott was the desire to bring Georgina Township back into Ontario County.[54] Georgina remained so cool to the proposal of amalgamation that no formal steps were taken; an attempt to take over several townships north of Victoria County, however, proved to be more serious.

In May 1858 the Whitby *Chronicle* opened the campaign to acquire the northern townships in an editorial headed, "New Townships - Ontario or Victoria". According to the *Chronicle*, it was entirely in the interest of the new townships to join Ontario County:

> We perceive that Mr. John Cameron, the member for Victoria, has a bill before the Assembly to annex to his County the new Townships of Carden, Draper, Macaulay, etc. Before agreeing to Mr. Cameron's bill we would suggest to the members of the House to examine the map; and they would perceive that the trade and business of these townships must of necessity be directed towards the shores of Lake Simcoe, directly north of this County and that consequently, the *County of Ontario* would be the true County to which it would be for the interest of *some* at least of these new Townships to be annexed. In joining Ontario the inhabitants of the Northern Townships would find County buildings already built.[55]

Of course, Whitby was not alone among lakeshore towns in casting envious eyes on the newly settled area. Bowmanville's leading entrepreneur, manufacturer and politician, the Honourable John Simpson was looking north with plans of his own. As the Whitby *Chronicle* reported:

> The Honourable Mr. Simpson of Bowmanville, has, we are informed, set on foot a Road scheme which he expects to carry out through the assistance of Government. It is to construct a road from Bowmanville to Point Caesarea on Scugog Lake,—bridge the lake from that point to the island, and also construct a second bridge from the island to Port Hoover, and then carry the road through Mariposa and Eldon into the new Township of Carden. . . . Mr. Simpson's object is apparent at a glance—it is evidently to build up the fortunes of Bowmanville.[56]

As it turned out, Mr. Simpson's neighbours were no more eager to impoverish themselves for his benefit, than were the farmers of Ontario County for the benefit of the Whitby merchants. Simpson's road was never built.

Given the impetus of the *Chronicle*'s campaign and the threat of competition from Bowmanville, at the June meeting of the County Council James Hodgson and W.H. Tremayne, the reeve and deputy reeve of the Town of Whitby, introduced a Memorial to the Provincial Government requesting that Carden, Draper and Macaulay be united with the County of Ontario. Surprisingly, five members voted against the proposal - the reeves and deputy reeves of Oshawa, Whitby East and Pickering.[57] The expense to the County of roads into the far north was sufficient to cause their opposition. In the long run the effort to annex the new townships failed. Not even the importunings of the warden could persuade the Government to expand Whitby's power. Eventually most of the new townships were included in the new County of Muskoka.

With the failure of the Whitby merchants and speculators to expand either their area of trading dominance or sphere of administrative control, their fate was sealed. After 1857 Whitby grew hardly at all. In 1861 Whitby had 2,697 residents, and in 1871, 2,732 - a gain of only 35 inhabitants in ten years. Indeed, a constant complaint of its leaders was the number of empty houses and shops. Nor did they receive much sympathy or aid from the other municipalities. Two decades of constant selfishness and sharp dealing had so alienated all the other municipalities that the newspapers of Uxbridge, Bowmanville, Oshawa and Prince Albert took no little delight in Whitby's difficulties.

For generations the residents of Whitby regretted the failure of their great ambitions, and blamed the residents of the other municipalities for the town's stagnation. As W.H. Higgins, editor of the Whitby *Chronicle* remarked:

> This first check to the [railway] enterprise was disastrous in its consequences; . . . by putting back the project [it] gave Port Hope and the railway promoters to the east and west the wished-for opportunity of striking in vigorously and cutting off the trade which properly belonged to, and naturally would flow through the rest of the county town and port of Whitby . . . The great mistake of the county municipalities, in rejecting a proposition which would give them a railway from lake to lake—making the county of Ontario the grand highway for the trade of the west and north—was seized upon by the rival communities to the east and west to extend their railway operations.[58]

Convinced as they were that the expansion of capitalist enterprise was synonymous with progress, and that the private gain of entrepreneurs was actually public benefit, the merchants and businessmen of Whitby staunchly refused either to accept or to forgive the decision of the farmers not to back the railroad. They never understood that the entrepreneurs' promises of greater centralization and economic power concentrated in the hands of a few successful towns and businessmen were exactly opposed to the kind of society that the farmers had struggled to create and were now struggling to preserve. The cleavage which resulted from this polarity of interests and ideals would repeatedly embitter relations between residents of town and country.

In contrast to Whitby, whose economic basis was trade and administration, the foundation of Oshawa's economic life was manufacturing. The failure of Oshawa's merchants, road-owners and harbour company to compete successfully with Whitby, caused Oshawa's businessmen to concentrate their efforts on the expansion of their factories. Like Whitby, the basis of Oshawa's prosperity was the large economic area to its north which was preserved for it by the high cost of transportation from other manufacturing centres. After 1851, however, a number of new circumstances fundamentally changed the main manufacturing activities in Oshawa.

With the great growth in population of the Ontario County market area up to 1851 and the wartime prosperity after that date, a good deal of capital began to accumulate in the hands of Oshawa's businessmen who then began to look around for profitable investment opportunities. At the same time, A.S. Whiting, a successful wholesale distributor of American-made farm implements, concluded that, with the high Canadian tariff and the prosperous and growing market which was developing along the north shore of Lake Ontario, he could make more money manufacturing implements than he could by acting as a wholesale agent for American principals.

In 1852, Whiting approached a number of Whitby, Oshawa and Bowmanville merchants, millers, and prosperous farmers, and persuaded them of the profitability of establishing a small factory in Oshawa which would manufacture scythes, hoes, forks and other agricultural implements. In response to Whiting's proposals, a joint-stock company, the Oshawa Manufacturing Company, was formed with L. Butterfield, Daniel Conant, A. Farewell, Jr., T.N. and W.H. Gibbs, George Gould, J.D. Hoyt, James Morton, A.J. Masson, and John Smith as the major shareholders.[59] The company's subscribed capital was $75,000.

The Oshawa Manufacturing Company represented a distinct departure from previous forms of business in the Whitby-Oshawa area. By utilizing the joint-stock company form of organization for pooling capital, a much larger industrial unit could be created. Whereas most other manufacturers operated what were essentially family concerns, the new company's ownership was in the hands of individuals whose only interest was in the company's profitability, and who otherwise had no direct connection with the business. Finally, the Oshawa Manufacturing Company's production was based almost entirely upon hired labour – and a number of highly skilled New England craftsmen were imported to carry out the tasks requiring the highest skills.

During the great boom of the 1851-57 period, Whiting's business greatly prospered, as did that of other local merchants and manufacturers. Goods manufactured in Oshawa, whether in large-scale enterprises such as the Oshawa Manufacturing Company, or in smaller owner-operated shops such as Bambridge's Carriage Works[60] or Thomas Fuller's furniture factory,[61] soon earned a reputation for excellent design and skilled craftsmanship. A sideboard manufactured by Fuller, which won first prize at the Provincial Fair in Brantford in 1857, was described as follows:

> The bureau is of white oak, and the doors, drawers and sides are ornamented with elaborate carvings representing game, fruits, etc. Between the shelves are two large plate glass mirrors, and the whole is surmounted, at an elevation of nine feet, by a deer's head. The price of this piece of furniture, we understand, is $200, and the remainder of the set is being got up in similar style.[62]

Of course, it was the lavish houses built with the profits made from land speculation and the wealth derived from the Crimean War grain trade that made such costly works of craftsmanship profitable to produce.

It was not long before the growing wealth of the Whitby-Oshawa area drew the attention of businessmen from other areas to the possibility of investment in Ontario County. In 1856, the Honourable John Simpson of Bowmanville was approached by a number of Montreal businessmen connected with the Montreal City and District Savings Bank, concerning the possibility of establishing a bank in the Oshawa-Bowmanville area. As a result of their discussions, the Ontario Bank was chartered, and in 1857 it began business under the direction of its president, the Honourable John Simpson.[63] Directors named for the bank were James Mann, John Burk and Simpson, from Bowmanville, T.N. Gibbs, from Oshawa, James Dryden, from Whitby, and A. Simpson from Montreal.[64]

Although John Simpson had been made president, and all directors except one were from the Whitby-Oshawa-Bowmanville region, ownership of the bank actually lay in Montreal hands. Of shareholders who held more than 125 shares (with a value of $40 each), 16 were from Montreal; 5 were from Bowmanville; 3 were from Oshawa (Abraham Farewell, 200 shares, J.B. Warren, 385 shares and E. Watson, 250 shares); and one each were from Whitby (Chester Draper, 170 shares), Brockville, Rutland (Vermont – the only major American shareholder was the Honourable Solomon Foot who owned 250 shares), and Augusta Township.[65] The presence of the Montreal shareholders was particularly important because through their influence the city of Montreal became the second largest shareholder, purchasing 850 shares for $34,000. The largest shareholder was R.T. Raynes of Montreal who owned 1,000 shares.

It was no accident that a majority of the directors were from the local region. In the nineteenth century, banks had earned a very bad reputation for instability and for exploiting their borrowers. Indeed, a stock character in dramas of that period was the evil banker, eager to foreclose the mortage on the family farm. Thus in starting a new bank it was important to proclaim it as a local institution under the control of businessmen in whom the farmers could trust. So concerned were the shareholders of the Ontario Bank that it appear as a local enterprise, that in the first twenty years of its existence (while its head office was in Bowmanville) it was never admitted in public that the bank was controlled from Montreal. It was always referred to in the local press as "Our Bank".

The directors, recognizing the desperate rivalry among the merchants of Whitby, Oshawa and Bowmanville, hit on a novel scheme to sell stock locally. Because a bank branch was certain to attract business to the town, the Ontario Bank directors proposed to establish a branch in the Ontario County town whose inhabitants purchased the greatest amount of stock. This set off a flurry of local sales promotion which was apparently effective in persuading many local merchants to buy shares in the bank. Oshawa won the contest easily, and in September 1857, a branch was opened in that village. Needless to say, the Whitby merchants were furious, while those in Oshawa were delighted at their victory. In commenting on the victory, the editor of the Oshawa *Vindicator* adopted his favourite tone of calm superiority:

> The *Whitby Chronicle*, indignant at the course pursued by the Directors of the Ontario Bank—after having flown into a terrible passion, is now subsiding into a calm, commonsense view of the question; after talking in his wrath and telling his subscribers that the Whitby stock-holders will sell out their stock and "get up" or "puff up" a Whitby Bank that will truly be an Ontario Bank—now condescends to compare the business of Whitby with that of Oshawa. . . . This is certainly the wisest course for Whitby to pursue; but to brow-beat the Directors—and to spend the overflowing of his bile on Oshawa, because those gentlemen, in the wisdom of their course, saw fit to select this little village as a suitable place for an agency—is at once foolish and absurd.[66]

With the collapse of Whitby's speculative boom in 1858, all thoughts of a second bank were forgotten, and for the next fifteen years the Ontario Bank had no local rivals.

The Ontario Bank was an instant success. At its first annual meeting, held in Bowmanville on June 7, 1858, the directors reported that it was in a "most prosperous condition, the profits for the past six months of its existence being equal to fifteen percent per annum to each shareholder".[67] In 1862, the president could report that in its fifth year of operation the bank had made a net profit of $116,625.41 or nearly 10 percent on its paid-up capital. Of this, $84,832.66 was paid out to shareholders, a dividend of 8 percent.[68] Considering that the total value of all lumber produced by Ontario County's forty-two sawmills was only $141,400,[69] it is clear that the bank's profits had an enormous impact on the local economy. Unfortunately, because most of the bank's shares were owned outside the area, it no doubt had a serious negative effect on Ontario County's ability to accumulate capital.[70]

As the Ontario Bank prospered, its stock became more attractive to investors. Because of the shortage of local capital, virtually all new shares sold went to residents of cities outside the Whitby-Oshawa-Bowmanville region. By 1865 the number of major Montreal shareholders had more than tripled, and large blocks of shares were sold to investors in Quebec City, Toronto, and even Halifax.[71]

Locally, only James Dryden, Chester Draper, T.N. and W.H. Gibbs, Dr. William McGill, J.B. Warren and Enson Watson owned blocks of shares valued at more than $5,000. The Gibbs brothers held the largest block, valued at $34,440. In addition James Mann and the Honourable John Simpson of Bowmanville retained their blocks of shares. As time went on, ownership of the bank became more and more removed from Ontario County, and fewer of its profits returned to the local region to benefit the local economy.

As the Ontario Bank grew, it began to establish branches outside the local area. When these prospered, the bank became less and less dependent on local loyalties for its profits. As a result, in the late 1860s, when the owners' attentions were drawn to the rapidly growing Toronto region, it was decided to move its head office from Bowmanville to Toronto to exploit regional loyalty there and to gain ready access to its potential customers. In 1869 legislation was passed at the bank's request which permitted the change of location.[72] This move infuriated the merchants of Bowmanville and Oshawa who had bought shares in order to obtain the bank. So strongly did they protest the move, and threaten to campaign to have their farmer-customers boycott the bank, that the directors relented, and the head office remained in Bowmanville for another five years.[73]

In spite of the great prosperity of the Ontario Bank, industries such as the Oshawa Manufacturing Company faced grave difficulties in the late 1850s. Not only were such industries selling their goods in a small market which was greatly affected by fluctuations in grain prices, but foreign manufacturers, particularly those in the United States, frequently unloaded their goods at low prices on the Canadian market whenever they found themselves with a surplus inventory.[74]

In 1857, faced with a depressed market, A.S. Whiting sold a part of his implement business to Joseph Hall, an important farm machinery manufacturer in Rochester, New York. Joseph Hall had built his business in the United States on inventions which resulted in improvements in several types of farm machinery. Thus the Hall grain thresher and cleaner, and the Hall mower were well known in the United States. Hall's decision to purchase part of Whiting's business was based on the belief that the growing Canadian market offered an opportunity to expand his operations. The transaction was insufficient to save Whiting's business, and in 1858, in the depth of the depression the Oshawa Manufacturing Company declared bankruptcy.[75]

Whiting's failure was a severe blow to both Whiting and the Oshawa businessmen who had backed him; to a wealthy businessman like Joseph Hall, however, it was no more than a minor set-back in his plans. From Hall's point of view, the current Canadian scene opened up an interesting situation. First, in the depression of 1857-58 many small Canadian businesses had failed, and when prosperity returned, a larger market for goods would open up. Secondly, with many Canadian businessmen failing because foreign manufacturers were dumping surplus inventories in Canada at cut-rate prices, the Conservative Government decided to apply a 20 percent tariff on imported manufactured goods. Finally, with their town's economy threatening to collapse, Oshawa businessmen persuaded the village council to offer Hall a tract of land at a low price, and the remission of taxes for several years, if he would establish a Canadian branch of his business in Oshawa. Ironically then, when a local business failed because of American competition, the Oshawa solution was to subsidize an American businessman to set up a branch plant to take its place.

The Joseph Hall Iron Works, as the new business was called, proved to be a great success for several years. Hall took over Whiting's factory and began to manufacture his patented threshing machines, mowers and plows for the Canadian market. With the return of prosperity and the advent of another boom in the early 1860s caused by the American Civil War, the Hall Iron Works was expanded repeatedly. In 1859, 50 men were employed in the factory, and an average of 69 plows per week were being manufactured. In addition to mowers and other farm machinery, more than 100 threshing machines were reported to have been built.[76] By 1867 the business had expanded to employ 250 men, and the "Champion" mower had become one of the largest selling models in the Dominion.[77] As the Oshawa *Vindicator* explained:

> Year by year as his fields become cleared of stumps and stones, and as the value of manual labour increases the Canadian Farmer feels the desirability of doing as much of his harvest work as possible by machinery. The manufacture of reaping and mowing machines is therefore a very important item in Canadian manufactures. Mr. Glen as the manager of the Hall Agricultural Works here, saw its value and entered into the manufacture. . . . The result has fully justified his expectations, for the present season will find some two thousand of their machines at work in the harvest fields of the country. This year they have under way six hundred and fifty machines.[78]

Not only did the Hall Iron Works prosper during the early 1860s, but other Oshawa factories were prosperous as well. A.S. Whiting, in spite of the failure of his first business, decided to try again. Renting a portion of his old premises from the Joseph Hall Iron Works, Whiting again began to manufacture forks, scythes and other small implements. The recovery in the economy began at the same time, and the new business prospered. By 1862 Whiting had outgrown his premises in the Hall works and was ready to expand. In that year he formed a partnership with two of his brothers and E.C. Tuttle and W.J. Gilbert under the name of the A.S. Whiting Manufacturing Company. The partnership built a large new factory which was known locally as the Cedar Dale works. Soon a village known as Cedar Dale sprang up around the factory, as his employees built cottages near their work.

Thus by 1867, Oshawa presented a distinct contrast to Whitby. Because

Whitby's businessmen had concentrated upon commerce and administration, their prosperity was strictly limited by the small area under their control. Efforts to expand this area had failed with the collapse of the Port Whitby and Lake Huron Railway project, and Whitby had stagnated after 1857. The merchants made a few efforts to make Whitby a manufacturing town, but they were indebted when the speculative boom collapsed, and they had little capital available for new projects.

In contrast to Whitby, Oshawa's businessmen had managed to extend their period of growth and prosperity into the 1860s by subsidizing industry through low land prices and exemption from taxation. Moreover, having persuaded outside capitalists to establish a bank locally, they hoped that the inflow of new capital would provide the basis for large-scale expansion of industry. The great prosperity from 1859 to 1867 convinced the Oshawa businessmen that they had found the key to success, but time would reveal that their hopes had as weak a basis as had those of Whitby. While artificial means could attract capital for a time, absentee owners, in the long run, cared little for the welfare of local residents. Moreover, the high cost of tax exemptions and the outward flow of profits eventually exacted a high cost. After 1867 Oshawa would be forced to pay that cost.

Joseph Hall Manufacturing Company and A.S. Whiting & Company, Oshawa

Public Archives of Ontario

RESPONSES TO URBANIZATION: WELFARE AND EDUCATION

The increase in the working class population in Whitby and Oshawa after 1851 created a number of serious problems for Ontario County. The social ideals which had developed during pioneer days served well enough for rural society, but the problems of poverty, crime and education became crucial issues with the appearance of a large urban population. In particular, the sharp economic depressions which occurred in 1866 and 1874, raised fundamental challenges to established social norms. Since the problems of poverty and crime among the urban poor were insoluble by traditional methods, it gradually became clear that new methods had to be evolved. The debate around these issues and the changing demands for education would reveal much about the transformation of Ontario County.

In rural society the problem of welfare for indigent persons had never seemed difficult to solve. Where most people owned or rented a small acreage, almost everyone, even when employment was scarce, should be able to provide much of his livelihood from his garden and woodlot. As the *Ontario Observer* remarked:

> Everyone knowing anything of the state of the poor in our villages or rural districts knows very well that that there is scarcely an indigent party among us who does not do a very great deal towards his own maintenance, or it is done for him by his friends or relatives. There may

> be an infirm man who can work around a little perhaps to secure him bread for himself and his family and a house; but he may require from the corporation a dollar a week or perhaps even less in order to get fire wood, or perhaps he may require a little for clothing for his family. Or there may be a widow with three or four children, some of whom may be able to care for the others, while the industrious mother is doing something for the support of herself and family. She may by her labor procure food for her family, and the corporation then comes forward and backs her efforts by giving an amount monthly to assist her in paying her rent, etc.[1]

In spite of this rather rosy picture, it should be made clear that welfare was never easy to obtain by those requiring aid.

The key to understanding the limits of welfare laid down by local municipal officials lies in the strong emphasis upon individual initiative and self-reliance which had developed in pioneer rural society. Men who had achieved the status of landowners had little patience with those who had failed to do so. As one newspaper asserted:

> Our emigrants [from England] have nearly all been poor, but of that class of poor whose independence and self-reliance would give them nerve to die by the way side before they would fill the place of a pauper.[2]

This emphasis upon individual self-reliance placed rather strict limits on the distance to which municipalities would go in aiding the poor. One case, brought before Reach Township Council, illustrates the problems which this emphasis created. The Reach minutes, as reported in the *Ontario Observer*, read:

> Mr. Ensign made application in behalf of one Webster, a teamster, who had recently lost one of his horses, and not being able to replace it himself, Mr. Ensign applied to the Council for a grant to assist the party in purchasing another horse.
>
> The Reeve [James Graham] said that no one was more willing to assist the deserving poor than he was, but he had an objection to giving such grants as the one asked for, inasmuch as it would set a dangerous precedent, and would be certain to lead to numerous similar applications, in fact the Council would be inundated with parties having lost horses or cows.
>
> Mr. Ewers moved that the sum of $30 be granted to T. Webster, to assist him in purchasing a horse to replace the one he had lost.
>
> Mr. Ewers said he regarded this as a proper opportunity for exercising the charity of the Corporation, as the party has a large family to support by his team, but he cannot do any thing with one horse, and he is not able himself to supply the one which he has lost, and he regarded it as a much better way of obtaining assistance in coming to

> Council than by applying to private individuals.
>
> Mr. Halman . . . had very grave doubts of the wisdom of any man seeking to make a living by teaming, and he would advise the applicant rather to sell his remaining horse and set about making a living in another way. . . .
>
> Mr. T. Graham said he disliked the principle, as he felt confident that it would lead to a great amount of trouble in the future. Under such circumstances as the present, neighbours and parties knowing the circumstances of the case were the proper parties to apply to.[3]

The motion was defeated, and such a proposal was not made again in the area.

One result of these attitudes was that a practice grew up of "auctioning off" the able-bodied poor who were without families or relatives in the area. When such an individual applied to Council for aid, it became the practice to offer that person to be boarded by the lowest bidder. Since even a very elderly person in good health might be a useful addition in a household where a mother had several young children to care for, it sometimes happened that the poor person might be disposed of for a subsidy of one or two dollars a month. It should be made clear, moreover, that there was no community objection to such an auction. Should the poor individual have objected, all aid would have been immediately withdrawn. Some people in the area became notorious for their treatment of those who fell into their hands through these auctions, but no general condemnation of the system ever developed.

Under the auctioning system, orphaned children suffered the worst abuse. In cases where orphans had no relatives willing or able to care for them, the municipality indentured them (that is, signed them to a binding contract of employment for a fixed number of years) for a period of time – usually seven years or until the age of twenty-one, whichever was longer. Since there were no laws preventing child labour, and no supervision of the conditions under which the child was employed, terrible abuses of these children occurred.

Lists of court cases printed in such newspapers as the Whitby *Chronicle* list frequent charges against employers of assault and non-payment of wages. Notices such as the following were not uncommon:

> RANAWAY
>
> Or left my premises on the 2nd inst., a BOY 12 years of age, small of his age with light hair. I hereby forbid any person or persons harboring him, as he is indentured to me till of age.
>
> Richard Warringer, Borelia.[4]

Clearly, the lot of the poor, even in rural areas, was not a happy one.

The munincipal councils subjected the poor to a careful scrutiny of their economic assets and earning possibilities in the determination of their fate; their moral lives were investigated as well. A long discussion in Brock Township Council concerning the application for aid of J. Mapes in 1868 demonstrates the limits to which municipal officials would go in allowing moral questions to determine just who were the "worthy poor".

> The petition of J. Mapes an indigent party, praying for some assistance from the corporation was . . . presented. The old man was the very picture of want and privation. He stated that his family consisted of nine children, his eldest was a young woman of 20 years who remained at home and found herself from small sums of money which she received from time to time. The next child was a young man of eighteen years who was hired out—the others were home doing nothing. He stated he has resided in the pine woods for upwards of three years, and was quite unable to do anything for himself.
>
> The Reeve [Malcolm Gillespie] said that as guardians of the interests of the corporation the council were very willing to grant assistance to the deserving poor, but there were certain circumstances connected with the present applicant which required at least some consideration.
>
> Mr. Brethour said that while the corporation of Brock was always willing to assist her poor and that the worthy never apply in vain, still as guardians of the funds of the corporation they are bound to see that none but the worthy receive assistance from these funds.[5]

An investigation of Mape's case was ordered by the Brock Council, and no aid was given in subsequent weeks.

The vigilance of township councils in enforcing strict moral standards upon the poor frequently led to injustices. Six months after Mapes had been refused aid, a second case, from Brock, was brought to public attention. The *Ontario Observer* reported the following events:

> A Mrs. Banberry came before the Council and stated that she was in indigent circumstances—that she had herself and five children to provide for, the youngest of whom was five years old, that she had formerly received $1.50 per month from the Council, but for some reason unknown to her, even this small supply has been stopped since April last, and she would like to have Council give their reasons for so doing.
>
> Mr. St. John informed her that the council had heard unfavourable reports of her, and while they were but too glad to be able to assist the worthy poor, they would take care that only the worthy should receive any portion of the public funds; but if she could wipe off the suspicion which has been thrown around her, he for one would be very willing to grant her some assistance. The woman said she was prepared to leave it to any of her neighbours, she said she saw one in the room and she would like the council to call him.
>
> The council asked Mr. Way if he knew anything concerning the applicant, and whether he considered her a proper object of charity?

> Mr. Way replied that he knew nothing against the woman, and he considered that the council, before they stopped the supplies, should have been in possession of facts. The applicant was requested to retire while the council should deliberate. It was finally agreed to continue the grant of $1.50 per month.[6]

Naturally, when municipal officials were so ready to cut off aid on the strength of the least moral excuse or even the rumour thereof, neighbourhood quarrels frequently became the cause of such complaints. For example, one report of Brock Township Council stated that:

> A party whose name we could not learn came before the Council regarding one Mrs. Bramble, who was in receipt of aid from the corporation. Complainant said that this woman is not a fitting object of charity, as she does not conduct herself in a becoming manner, and that as she harbours doubtful characters around her, and they are in the habit of taking his hay, and that the other evening they had opened his (complainant's) stable and taken out his horses and led them down to the swamp and left them there.
>
> Mr. St. John said the Council would look into it and they would give her an overhauling if she came before the Council.[7]

While such righteous indignation was no doubt at times justified, the refusal of aid to the "unworthy" often visited terrible consequences upon their dependents. One such case, that of the mother of an illegitimate child in Whitby, stirred even the Whitby *Chronicle* to protest at the public's calloused attitude. On November 8, 1861, a Coroner's Inquest was held to investigate the cause of death of Eleanor Davis, a child of eighteen months. As the paper reported:

> The body of the child presented a fearfully emaciated appearance, and was a most pitiful spectacle to look upon. It had several marks on the body, called by the doctors "bed sores"; its little arm above the elbow, was bruised and blackened, as if by violence, and a front tooth . . . was missing from the upper jaw.[8]

The mother immediately fell under suspicion of mistreating the child. The Coronor's Inquest, however, uncovered causes of death that were even more shocking.

As the story unfolded, it became clear that the child's mother, a young girl, had been seduced and made pregnant. The girl's family had, apparently, cast her out upon the mercy of the public who in turn rejected such an unworthy and sinful creature. As the *Chronicle* noted indignantly:

> It was given in evidence that the unfortunate outcast mother, having no place to lay her head, slept by fences, on the common, and in out-houses, and wherever she could best obtain a nights shelter for herself and her miserable infant. Undone, and deserted, an outcast and a vagrant—shunned by the virtuous, as a thing too loathsome to be

> touched–she was driven to the terrible alternative of prostitution. Drink, its ever-attendant vice, of course followed, and the natural result was the neglect of the unhappy infant, whose little wants were unattended to, and was unable to take care of itself, ending in its death.[9]

To add to the horror of the situation, the father of the child testified that he had been the individual responsible for the mother becoming a prostitute after the child was born. As a result of the Inquest, the mother was cleared of any direct responsibility for the child's death, which, it was concluded, was due to malnutrition and exposure from sleeping out of doors in November. In pointing out to its readers that "there may be others equally concealed from the eye of society", the *Chronicle* concluded that:

> Apart from the morality of such cases, there is the expense thrown upon the town, of providing burials, etc., and the expense of holding inquests borne by the county.[10]

Cases such as the foregoing demonstrate that there were serious faults with the system of caring for the "able bodied" poor, but the treatment of the bedridden, senile and mentally ill was even less satisfactory. In a society without formal provision for such persons, those without relatives willing to care for them found themselves in an almost helpless situation. In their desperation, many become residents of County jails simply because there was no other place open to them. Dr. Wolfred Nelson described the role of many County jails in 1852:

> The Gaol at present [is] in some sense an asylum for homeless and friendless persons, who from age, decrepitude, blindness, or other infirmity, are unable to maintain themselves. . . . These require nourishment–not punishment; nursing, not hard labour. But again the Gaol is made an Hospital for incurables, who have been discharged from other Hospitals, a lying-in Hospital, and a receptacle for children whose vagrant parents are sent to the House of Correction. The drunkard too, both male and female, instinctively fly to the Gaol for care and treatment, warned by the premonitions of *delirium tremens*. The wretched prostitute artfully turns laws ostensibly made to suppress her vice, into timely and efficient auxiliary to her sad career . . . Lunatics too are frequently found in the Gaol during long periods, thereby rendering their cure less probable, and materially adding to the annual expense.[11]

Those responsible for the Ontario County jail found themselves facing a similar situation. In every report of the County Council's Standing Committee on County Property and Gaol Management the members reported upon the numbers of "lunatics" locked up in jail. No particular treatment was given to mentally ill prisoners, except that in several cases the Standing Committee noted that the jail surgeon had ordered double rations for them. Considering that the total cost of maintenance of prisoners (including food, wood, lights and soap) ranged from eight to sixteen cents per day,[12] even these double rations must have been slim enough. On rare occasions where a person suffering from mental illness had become dangerous or suicidal, they were transferred to the Provincial Lunatic Asylum at Kingston, a difficult and costly process. A typical report of the Standing Committee reads:

> The Standing Committee on County Property and Gaol Management beg leave to report:
>
> 1st. That upon examination of the Gaol and Court House and the management connected therewith, your committee beg to report that they find the same in a very clean and satisfactory condition. . . .
>
> 2nd. That your committee have also examined the prison report of Mr. J.S. Sprowle, Gaoler, and find that during the period from the 1st day of June to the 31st of Dec. last, there had been confined in the Gaol of this county 41 males and 19 females, making a total of 60 prisoners, 11 of whom were lunatics. That on the 31st. Dec. there remained in Gaol 9 males and 2 females. That the aggregate number of days on which prisoners were kept on Gaol allowance during said period is 2376, being an increase over the last year of 396 days, and that the total cost of rations during said time amounts to $258, being at the rate of 10 cents and 8½ mills per day for each prisoner, in addition to which 11 Lunatics and some sick prisoners received (by order of the Gaol Physician) extra allowance. . . .
>
> 3rd. That your committee have had their attention called to a dangerous Lunatic, now in Gaol, named Elizabeth McDougall, of the township of Thorah, who has on several occasions since her commitment attempted to destroy herself. Your committee would therefore recommend that the Warden make immediate application to the Provincial Secretary to have her admitted to the Lunatic Asylum at Kingston.[13]

The lack of facilities to care for the old and invalid patients was an issue which was raised periodically. For example, in 1857, the problem of the indigent poor was raised in the County Council, but no motion was brought forward.[14] Similarly, in 1867, at an inquest into a death from exposure, Sherrif Nelson G. Reynolds reported that the County had no proper place to lodge the destitute and homeless poor.[15] Although many of the helpless and infirm paupers found lodging in the jails and lockups,[16] both the unsuitableness of the surroundings and the expense of their maintenance made County officials anxious to prevent the jail from becoming a residence for the destitute. Thus in 1873, the Standing Committee on County Property and Gaol Management reported that they:

> Regret to find that a helpless invalid old man, named Hazelwood, has been committed to gaol as a dangerous lunatic. That they find no evidence of insanity and recommend that, in the absence of a poor house or hospital for incurables he be returned to the municipality to which he belongs for maintenance.[17]

Upon occasion the building of a Poor House or House of Refuge was proposed as a means of caring for the helpless poor, but this proposal was always rejected on the grounds that the "worthy poor" were already taken care of, and that the erection of a Poor House would involve the County in needless expense. When J.B. Bickell, reeve of Whitby Township, introduced a motion to study the erection of a House of Refuge for the poor, he was roundly attacked by the *Ontario Observer* whose editor declared:

> The poor now with the little help they receive from the municipalities can enjoy all the comfort of which their circumstances are susceptible, and not the least of which is the liberty to pass around among friends and acquaintances, enjoying their society, and performing, it may be, now and then a little service, and receiving a compensation in way of food and raiment, or it may be shelter, in addition to the pleasant smile and encouraging words of friendship. How agreeable is all this compared with the grim confinement of the cold, dreary, naked almshouse and the haughty, overbearing, supercilious, withering frown and stern command of some fat, sleek, over-fed aristocrats who generally care less for the poor than they do for their dogs.[18]

The *Observer* then got to the nub of the matter: a Poor House would raise the cost of welfare from $2-$4 a month to something like $10 a month per person. In the end, the spectre of higher costs proved to be an effective ally to the ideology of self-help and worthiness. In spite of the fact that deaths from malnutrition, exposure and neglect continued to be reported regularly in the local press, no more formal aid to the indigent and helpless would be undertaken for more than thirty years.

Of course, the local municipalities and counties were not the only governmental bodies interested in the welfare and care of the poor and helpless. The growth of large urban centres had created a situation where the fluctuating economy and seasonal unemployment periodically created large pools of surplus labour, and intense suffering among the poorest sectors of the population. To meet this growing problem, the Upper Canadian Government in 1837 passed legislation which permitted the various districts to erect Houses of Refuge at public expense to care for those committed to them, for whatever cause, by the local magistrates.[19] Because the statute was permissive, only those areas with large urban populations appear to have acted upon it.

During the severe depression of 1867-70, faced with large-scale, province-wide unemployment and destitution among the poorer members of the working class, the Province introduced legislation which would have required all Counties to build Houses of Refuge for the poor. The rural press reacted with typical outrage at this latest step towards centralization. As the *Ontario Observer* argued:

> The member for Bothwell argued that if County Councils were not compelled to build those houses, they never would do it. Do the members of the various County Councils not know better what is for the interest of the County they represent than the member for Bothwell does . . . ? The fact is that such houses would never answer the end for which they are designed; and may the day be far distant ere they shall be largely introduced into this county.[20]

As a result of this and similar opposition from other rural areas, the proposal to make the erection of Poor Houses mandatory upon the Counties was dropped.

Although the ideals of self-help for the able-bodied and personal charity for the "worthy poor" had triumphed in the rejection of formalized welfare institutions such as Poor Houses or Houses of Refuge in Ontario County, society was changing and the old ways could no longer serve even the minimal needs of the poor. In particular the growth of industry in Oshawa and the great increase in the urban working-class population meant that inevitably a point would come when the established norms would have to change.

Just as the boom periods of the early 1850s and 60s had been followed with the crashes of 1856-57 and 1867-68, so the period of great expansion from 1870 to 1873 was followed by the crash of 1874 and the depression of 1875-76. Everywhere across the Province men were thrown out of work and in December 1875, the hardest blow fell on Oshawa when the Joseph Hall Agricultural Works, one of the County's largest employers, was thrown into receivership.[21] With no work available in any area, and their wages months in arrears, the unemployed workmen and their families soon found themselves in difficult circumstances. As the Oshawa *Reformer* noted:

> Numbers of people who depend on their earnings from week to week to supply themselves and families with daily food, and find it almost impossible to lay up a penny for a rainy day, are out of work and have nothing to which they can turn their hands. . . .
>
> But sympathy will not fill an empty stomach, nor will the tear of pity supply the lack of bread. The charitably disposed will have many a draft upon their purses in aid of the "deserving poor".[22]

At first, the townspeople responded to the situation by the usual methods of asking for donations and putting on benefit shows for "the Poor".[23] The money raised by such methods, however, fell far short of what was needed, and by mid-January the condition of the poor had become desperate.

The public was generally reluctant to abandon the belief that any able-bodied man who desired work could support himself. As one unemployed workman remarked in a letter to the Oshawa newspaper:

> We have plenty of tavern gossip and street corner parties but that is about all. The vaguest, shallowest and most meaningless rumours will circulate like wildfire, but as for combining for any good purpose and learning the truth we must look elsewhere. Agitation for its own sake I don't want, but the apathetic resignation of Oshawa is intolerable.[24]

In order to dispel the suspicion that the men were unemployed through their own fault, the unemployed workmen got up a petition asking the village Council for employment. The response of the Oshawa *Reformer* revealed the confusion and consternation felt by any society whose favourite beliefs are under attack. After attempting to belittle the petition on the grounds that it had been signed by many "labourers and recent immigrants" the paper went on to ask:

> We cannot see what the Council is expected to do, unless they consider the situation sufficiently grave to call a public meeting. Certainly the village Council is not in a position to give these men employment; neither would it be advisable to make provision for so large a number of men in the way of charity out of public funds. The only course seems to us to be to call a public meeting of the citizens and perhaps appoint persons to canvass the town for subscriptions in aid of those who are really in need. Information is required as to the number of those who are in that condition, and a committee might be appointed at the meeting to find out the true state of affairs and to render assistance to those who are out of work and suffering from want. It is difficult to see what the Council can do in a case of this kind.[25]

Although a special meeting of the Oshawa Village Council was called, no practical means of solving the problem could be found.

The little aid that did materialize came from quite another source. The receivers appointed to manage the affairs of the bankrupt Hall Agricultural Works decided that the creditors could best realize their debts by selling the business as a going concern. To do so, it was necessary to retain the work force who were drifting away to seek employment elsewhere. Thus J.H. McClellan and Jonathan Porter, two of the receivers (and later partners in the firm that purchased the business) hit upon a clever method of retaining the work force. As the Oshawa *Reformer* explained:

> They announced their willingness to advance to any of the late employees of the Hall Works, a sum amounting to not more than one-third of their claims against the estate . . . The men were to pay eight per cent per annum on the amounts loaned. This was a happy thought, and . . . about $1,600 has been paid out on these terms during the present week.[26]

While eight percent hardly represented the highest form of charity, and the loans to the men were secured by their claims against the company, still the advances against their wage claims did much to relieve their financial distress. Those who were unemployed for reasons other than the Hall Works bankruptcy were left almost entirely to their own resources. Of the more than one hundred families who needed help, the Oshawa *Reformer* reported that about seventy had received aid to the extent of a total of $300 for the winter (or about 25 cents per family per week). In addition "some relief has been afforded . . . in the way of a loan from the Reeve and other private individuals".[27]

With the reopening of the Hall Works in April 1876, and the increase in employment in the summer months, the problems created by urban unemployment were temporarily relieved. Given time to contemplate the situation, the Oshawa Village Council began to prepare for the unemployment which would occur during the coming winter. The answer arrived at went some small way towards providing municipal aid to the unemployed while still satisfying the idea of self-help and "worthiness". As the Oshawa *Reformer* reported in February 1877:

> A number of men out of employment have been working at breaking stones in the Drill shed this week. The sound is not unlike a busy shooting gallery. There are about 23 cords of stone in the shed, and men are employed to break them at $3 per cord. A man who breaks a quarter cord in a day does a good day's work.[28]

Although 50 or 75 cents for a day's hard labour scarcely constituted generous wages, it did provide the unemployed with a "respectable" way to provide for their hungry families. This modest adjustment to the problem of urban unemployment was the most that the leaders of the time were capable of making.

Just as the need to provide welfare for the poor revealed the fundamental changes taking place in society in Ontario County, so too, did the development of the school system after 1850 reveal the fundamental social conflicts which were occurring between a growing urban population and the original rural residents. These differences would be revealed most sharply with three issues: "free" public schools, compulsory attendance of children and the creation of a universal high school system.

The development and public acceptance of a general system of tax-supported "free" schools would occasion a struggle that would last for more than twenty years. When Egerton Ryerson first introduced the legislation in 1850 calling for the establishment of local public schools which would be supported by real estate taxation, he did so with full knowledge of the strong hostility that the proposal would create. By the terms of the Education Act of 1850, the Boards of Trustees of the common schools in towns and cities were permitted to decide whether to establish free schools; in rural school districts, the annual township meeting was required to decide each year whether or not

Henry Street School, Whitby, c. 1854 — *Whitby Historical Society*

Saint Thomas Rectory, Cannington — *Cannington Historical Society*

a rate-bill (i.e., attendance fees) would be demanded from the parents of children attending school.

As soon as Ryerson introduced these changes he was confronted by two quite distinct kinds of opponents: the independent-minded farmers and craftsmen who rejected such a state-run system as being "socialistic and communistic" and unsuitable for a society where children were required to learn "practical" skills from their parents; and the rich property-owners, urban and rural, who objected to being taxed for the support of schools for the children of the working class.

The opposition of many of the farmers and crafts workers was based on the conviction that the individual must be entirely self-sufficient. As Dr. John Roaf reported to the *Globe* of one township vote on free schools in 1852:

> I am happy to inform you that school section No. 1, Township of York, including the village of Yorkville, have this day negatived a proposal to have a free school, preferring to give the teacher £60 from the Public funds, and a right to charge 1s. 3d. per month for every child attending the School. The mechanics and labourers here have thus discharged the power, for there cannot be any such right, so wrongfully given them by the School Act, to educate their own children at the expense of their more wealthy neighbours.[29]

In a further letter, Roaf, a Congregationalist minister, argued that free schools would have the inevitable result of creating a heartless bureaucracy:

> The free system divests the teacher of all proprietary and personal interest in his school, and will speedily render him syncophantic and servile to his trustees, but haughty and negligent towards his pupils and friends. . . . It will destroy all the confidence and love felt towards the teacher as the employee and friend of the child's parents, and substitute for them a cold respect due to the public official. It will render school attendance desultory and variable, because unpaid for, and always, to be had for the asking. Instead of the soft, familiar, and refined circle in which wise parents like to place their children, it will drive gentle youths and sensitive girls into the large herds of children with all the regimental strictness and coldness and coarseness by which such bodies must be marked, and thus while the child asks bread you will give him a stone.[30]

Ryerson was quick to defend himself against such attacks. In reply to those who charged that tax-supported schools were the first step towards socialism, Ryerson objected that they were intended to have quite the opposite effect:

> I have observed that the question of Free Schools is of late engaging more than an ordinary degree of attention . . . and its introduction has been greeted in one or two instances by the cry of "Socialism", and

> "Communism":—words, which, in this instance, are but the symbols of selfishness and reaction. In no Countries is private property held more sacred, and more effectually protected than in the Countries of Free Schools,—Prussia, Switzerland, and the New England States of America. Socialist Newspapers do not exist in any Free School State of America; they only exist in States where the system of Free Schools has not yet formed and developed the popular mind.[31]

Indeed, although Ryerson was quite willing to condemn his free school opposition as "wealthy selfishness and hatred of the education of the poor and labouring classes",[32] he was perfectly willing to appeal to the same "wealthy selfishness" in support of his cause. Education, Ryerson argued, was a primary source of national wealth:

> The question of Free Schools,—whether the property of all should be made liable for the education of all,—has been thoroughly discussed, and it has been decided with unprecedented unanimity that each man should contribute to the education of all the youth of the land according to the property which he possesses and which is protected in the land, and made valuable by the joint labour, intelligence and enterprise of all the people.[33]

The degree to which Ryerson promoted the "Idea of Progress" in the field of education, and rejected the anti-industrialization, anti-urban attitudes of rural society was shown in his explanation of the amendments that he proposed to the Education Act in 1870:

> I . . . direct attention to one of the great objects of the Bill, namely to make our Common Schools more directly and effectively subservient to the interests of Agriculture, Manufacturers and Mechanics. . . . When we consider the network of Railroads, which are . . . extending from one end to the other of our Country, the various important Manufacturers which are springing up in our Cities, Towns and Villages, and the Mines which are beginning to be worked, and which admit of infinite development, provision should undoubtedly be made for educating our own Mechanical and Civil Engineers, and chief workers in Mechanics and Mines; but here I speak of the more elementary part of this work of practical education. . . . Something more is required to give our education a more decidedly practical character, especially in reference to the Agricultural and Mechanical Classes of the Community, which comprise the great bulk of the population, and constitute the principle means of our wealth and prosperity.[34]

The Toronto *Globe*, in supporting Ryerson's proposals put the matter more clearly, if less delicately: "Public money employed in educating the masses is a most profitable investment".

Ontario County offered little concerted resistance to the implementation of a free-school system. While a number of school sections fluctuated in their willingness to accept tax-supported common schools, most school districts immediately adopted the free-school system. Indeed, as early as 1853 Ryerson reported that only one school section in the County had rejected free schools.[36] In that year the annual County Common School Convention passed a motion confirming the County's support of the free-school idea:

> Resolved—That this meeting recognizes the principle that the wealth of a Country should be chargeable with the education of the youth of that Country, and looks forward with satisfaction to the time when such principle shall obtain generally in Canada, and be introduced in our school law.[37]

This early enthusiasm for free schools was dampened by the failure of parents to send their children regularly to school and the increased taxes. Thus in 1859 and 1860 free schools were retained in Whitby only after a vigorous campaign by the *Chronicle*.[38] In the rural areas the reaction against free schools was even more extreme. By 1861 some 31 of the 102 county schools were again charging tuition.[39]

Egerton Ryerson, however, never relented in his campaign to create a universal system of tax-supported primary education. Just as he had believed that religious education was a social necessity, it was his belief that free schools were a social necessity. In both cases, if society failed to recognize its duty, then it became necessary, as soon as practicable, to enforce that duty by legislation. As Ryerson stated in 1852:

> I have been assured by the most experienced and judicious men that it is impossible to have good Schools under the present system of Rate Bills. I think the substitute I propose will remedy the evil. I know of none who will object to it but some of the rich, and of the childless and the selfish. Education is a public good; ignorance is a public evil. What effects the public ought to be binding upon each individual composing it. . . . In every good government, and in every good system, the interests of the whole society are obligatory upon each member of it.[40]

By 1868 Ryerson was convinced that the principle of tax-supported schools had received a sufficiently wide acceptance that he could now introduce compulsory tax support. As he said in his *Annual Report* in that year:

> I have also to suggest the important question of declaring the Common Schools Free throughout Ontario. . . . With us the Legislature, by the School Act of 1850, invested each School Division, or section, with power to decide the question annually for itself. . . . As the Ratepayers themselves have made more than four-fifths of the Schools Free, the question now is, whether the Legislature should not declare them all Free.[41]

In 1871 the Ontario Legislature finally amended the Education Act to require that all common schools be free to students and supported by property taxation.

While the local newspapers strongly approved the idea of free schools, they vehemently objected to this additional step towards authoritarianism and centralization. As the editor of the *Ontario Observer* bitterly observed:

> A few years ago the ratepayers of each School Section could, by a majority of votes, at the commencement of each year say whether the School for the coming year should be free or have a rate-bill. This was all that could be desired, the people had the best right to know which of the two ways suited them best. . . . The Schools were passing on quietly and comfortably and the working of the system improved year by year; but the aristocratic school law tinkerer preferred a change and obtaining the ear of the legislature got the law so amended that the people were left no choice but that the schools must always be free.[42]

Thus, the autonomy won by the rural society in the Baldwin Acts of 1849-50 was again eroded in a significant way.

Although Ryerson had, over a period of twenty years, achieved his goal of making all common schools free to all children, he was much less successful in forcing all children to attend them. The number of children between the ages of 5 and 16 who received no schooling declined from 2,184 in 1853 to 857 in 1861, but that number increased between 1861 and 1870 to 1,335.[43] Moreover, almost two-thirds of all children outside Whitby and Oshawa, were absent from school on an average day, and more than half of those resident in the main centres were absent. With such absenteeism it was impossible for most children to obtain more than the rudiments of education. Thus, as Table XXXIII shows, Ryerson's hopes that his free-school plan would bring about a modern education for the masses was largely frustrated.

The reasons for non-attendance, particularly among rural children, were both economic and social. The economic reasons were much the same as they had been two generations before – the children were needed at home to help with the farm work. As the Reverend James Dowling reported of the situation in Uxbridge:

> The people of the County sections do not seem sufficiently awakened to a sense of the importance of regular attendance on the part of their children; hence, when corn or potatoes are to be hoed or berries to be picked, the school is neglected and the future forgotten. Several of the teachers have expressed to me their great discouragement from this source, and I cannot wonder at it.[44]

Yet while such economic reasons were important, almost every observer agreed that the main reason for non-attendance was that the parents placed a low

Table XXXIII
Common School Attendance in Ontario County, 1861 and 1870[45]

	1861			*1870*		
	Ontario County	*Whitby*	*Oshawa*	*Ontario County*	*Whitby*	*Oshawa*
Total Children 5–16 years	10,634	720	440	12,470	820	740
Total Pupils 5–16 years	9,132	677	343	11,135	676	725
Pupils — other ages	777	58	18	778	19	1
Boys — pupils	5,412	409	182	6,770	392	391
Girls — pupils	4,497	326	179	5,143	303	335
Attendance						
— less than 20 days	1,036	24	9	1,247	43	55
— 20 – 50 days	1,913	114	45	2,307	104	108
— 50 – 100 days	2,454	136	81	3,287	138	165
— 100 – 150 days	1,954	217	72	2,464	156	187
— 150 – 200 days	1,546	130	102	1,718	147	155
— 200 or more days	942	104	52	761	107	56
No Report	64	10	—	—	—	—
Average Daily Attendance	3,785	367	196	4,487	366	368
Per cent Daily Attendance	35.6	51.0	44.5	36.0	44.6	49.7

value on formal education for their children. As the *Ontario Observer* explained:

> The inestimable blessing of Free Education is not valued sufficiently high or improved as it ought to be, otherwise the large discrepancy between the number on our school rolls and the average daily attendance would not exist. When we consider that the average attendance at our Schools, in all parts of the country, is little more than one-third of the number of the children at School age we are forced to ask why it is so. Of course every one at all acquainted with the frequent necessity that there exists for keeping boys, aye of girls too, at home, will admit that this has considerable to do with it. . . . It is not of those kept at home by their parents for some useful purpose that we complain, but it is of those children who are allowed to run about our streets instead of being in school.[46]

It was not simply the failure of parents to provide for the future of their children, however, that brought the issue of compulsory attendance to the fore in the 1860s. The growth of urban centres with their masses of poorly-paid labour, and periodic unemployment and the lack of an organized system of welfare created an increase of poverty and crime which soon began to reach crisis proportions. In particular, the rise of vagrancy and crime among the children of the very poor drew the attention of the authorities. For example, Justice Hagarty of Toronto stated to a Grand Jury in 1860 that

> the streets of Toronto, like those of too many other towns still present the miserable spectacle of idle, untaught children, male and female—a crop too rapidly ripening for the Dram-shop, the Homes of Vice and the Prison. . . . Any person acquainted with the lowest classes of our poor is aware of the extreme difficulty in inducing them to let their children attend School. They will keep them from School, to gather wood for fuel, to beg from door to door, in short, do anything in preference to sending them to school. . . . Now, as has been frequently repeated, it is from this class that our young criminals spring,—it is this class that we are chiefly interested in humanizing by education.[47]

Ryerson, always ready to seize the legislative initiative whenever public sentiment would allow greater centralization of educational control, began to agitate for compulsory school attendance as a means of preventing juvenile vagrancy and adult crime. As early as 1857 he argued:

> If ignorance is an evil to society, voluntary ignorance is a crime against society. And if society is invested with power to relieve all from the evil of ignorance of all, the safety and interests of society, no less than the mission of its existence, require that it should be able to suppress and prevent the crime of voluntary ignorance by punishing its Authors. If idle mendicancy is a crime in a Man of thirty years of age, why is not idle vagrancy a crime in a Boy of ten years of age? The latter is the Parent of the former. Why is not crime prevented by being punished and suppressed in its commencement, rather than being allowed to advance to the completion of manhood—ignorance, mendicancy and even theft—before being punished?[48]

Newspapers in Ontario County expressed deep concern about the problem of absenteeism, but they objected both to the elements of centralization and compulsion, and to the economic difficulties that mandatory school attendance would create for farm families. When Ryerson first introduced an amendment to the Education Act which made school attendance compulsory, the *Ontario Observer* objected to its terms:

> Section 16 [of the new school bill] provides that each child between the ages of 7 and 12 years shall attend some school at least six months during every year. Failing to do so a penalty is attached by the 17th section.
>
> We consider that the 16th section would have answered the end much better had the compulsory attendance been from 7 years of age, six months of every year, until the pupil had acquired sufficient education to enable him to pass a board of examiners appointed for the

> purpose. There are parties who cannot well spare their children 6 months in the year after they are ten years old. Were this examination clause inserted in the Bill in place of the words "12 years old", parties desirous of having full control of their children's time after they reach the age of 9 or 10 years would be careful to see that they get along with their education.[49]

Although innumerable objections and suggestions such as these were made by rural sections of the province, compulsory attendance was included in the amendments to the Educational Act in 1871.[50] Again, the economic and social needs of the new industrial society took precedence over the preferences and interests of the older agrarian society.

In spite of the fact that Egerton Ryerson was strongly opposed to the creation of separate common schools for Roman Catholic children, and although the separate school issue was one of the longest and bitterest religious and political debates in Canada's history, the creation of a separate school system in Ontario County was brought about without serious local dispute. The basis of Ryerson's opposition to the creation of separate Catholic schools (and, for that matter, of other types of separate schools as well) appears to have stemmed from two sources: first, the duplication of school facilities threatened to weaken an already weak school system; and secondly, sectarian and social fragmentation caused by religious warfare had to be avoided at all costs. This did not mean that Ryerson favoured a purely secular education. He was always careful to make it clear that the inculcation of "Christian Principles" was the only proper basis for education. As he said in his first report upon assuming the office of Chief Superintendent of Education in 1846:

> By education, I mean not the mere acquisition of certain arts, or of certain branches of knowledge, but that instruction and discipline which qualify and dispose the subjects of it for their appropriate duties and employments of life, as Christians, as persons of business and also as members of the civil community in which they live.[51]

It was Ryerson's belief that certain basic truths underlay Christianity which could be taught to children without offence or injury to any religious body. He disapproved of the teaching of beliefs and attitudes to children that resulted in the creation of divisions and conflicts within the body of the "Christian" community. This position he made clear in 1847:

> To be zealous for a sect and to be conscientious in morals are widely different. To inculcate the peculiarities of a sect, and to teach the fundamental principles of religion and morality, are equally different. . . .
>
> Such teaching may, as it has done, raise up an army of pugilists and persecutors, but it is not the way to create a community of Christians. To teach a child the dogmas and spirit of a sect, before he is taught the essential principles of religion and morality, is to invert the pyra-

> mid,—to reverse the order of nature,—to feed with the bones of controversy instead of with the nourishing milk of truth and charity.[52]

Ironically, it was the complete agreement by Catholics regarding the significance of religion as a basis for all true learning that drove Catholics to demand their own religious schools.

The basis for the demand by Catholics to have separate schools stemmed from their belief concerning the uniqueness of Catholicism among Christian religions. As the Toronto *Mirror*, a Catholic newspaper, explained the Catholic position:

> Theirs is not a difference of opinion from the Protestant population, but a difference of *faith*—a difference in the belief of certain dogmas which they are taught to regard as of the greatest importance, while any deviation from this belief would be attended with future punishments.[53]

One correspondent of the *Mirror* put the problem in even plainer terms:

> An education which excludes religion and the relations of man to society . . . rushes forth under the hideous guise of Socialism and Pantheism, threatening to demolish all order, and the divine fabric of Christianity. . . . I am no advocate of mixed education. It is a natural result of Protestantism with its thousand and one creeds. . . . Every parent has a natural right to superintend the education of his child; he is bound under pain of damnation to give his child a moral, a religious education, hence arises the necessity of Separate Schools. Where is the religious and moral parent that would be willing to send his child to a *nothingarian* school in which he must naturally imbibe infidelity from his intercourse with others who believe in clashing and jarring creeds.[54]

It should be made clear, however, that the main antagonism to separate schools came not from Egerton Ryerson, but from the Orange Order and George Brown of the Toronto *Globe*. It would be difficult indeed to invent attacks more violent than those mounted by the anti-Catholic press. In 1855 the *Globe*, in denouncing the existence of separate schools, argued:

> Romish and Puseyite [Anglican] priestcraft cannot stand against the enlightenment fast spreading over the land by means of our Common Schools—almost its last hope is to strangle them.[55]

While the Toronto *Examiner* used such invectives as:

> The idolatrous Church of Rome, which has so overlaid the Gospel with doctrines of Human Invention that it has scarcely the semblance of Christianity, that wicked and persecuting Church, which is drunk with the blood of Saints, and which is clearly denounced for utter destruction by the word of God.[56]

In comparison to public voices such as these, the voice of Ryerson was that of moderation and good sense. Indeed, it must be pointed out that while he never agreed with the principle of separate schools, he always administered the law with impartiality.

After more than a decade of bitter and often acrimonious debate, the Separate School Act of 1855 finally laid down the general outline under which separate schools in Ontario exist to the present day. The act made possible the establishment of a Roman Catholic separate school in any school section or ward of a town or city on petition of ten Roman Catholic ratepayers and gave Catholics a separate school board with their own superintendent in towns and cities. Where a Catholic school was established, Catholic ratepayers were relieved from all municipal taxes for common school purposes, and were to receive from the Province a proportionate share of the common school grant.

The Catholics of Oshawa and Whitby were quick to take advantage of the terms of the 1855 Separate School Act. In that year Father J.P. Proulx established the first separate school in the county, conducting it in the Oshawa Sons of Temperance Hall, where it was taught by a Mr. Cullen. In1858, at the request of Father Proulx, the Sisters of St. Joseph, of Toronto, formed a new mission house in Oshawa and took charge of the school. Because of expanding attendance, the school, now conducted by two nuns, Reverend Mother Francis McCarthy and Sister Aloysius Tuite, was moved first to the Sacristy of St. Gregory the Great, Roman Catholic Church, and then to the main body of the church as the school continued to grow. In 1859 a one-story separate school was built to house the expanding school population.

The first separate school in Whitby was established in 1860, and moved into its own building in 1861. Like the Oshawa school, its attendance grew rapidly. In 1861 the Superintendent of Education reported that 97 pupils attended the Oshawa separate school, while 111 attended the school in Whitby.[58] Both schools were conducted twelve months of the year, and each had only one teacher. In the late 1860s (the first mention locally is 1869) a third separate school was founded in Mara. It remained very small, however, because the scattered population and poor roads made attendance difficult.[59] In spite of the controversy surrounding their establishment, and the fears expressed by men such as Ryerson that the existence of separate schools would deepen religious strife, these schools in Ontario County soon became an accepted part of the educational system.

Although the creation of a tax-supported compulsory public school system revealed several significant aspects of the social changes that were occurring in Ontario County, the creation of the modern high school system from the old district grammar schools was even more revealing of the social transformations that were taking place. Here Egerton Ryerson found opposition not only from those objecting to the increased centralization and great costs attendant in providing a higher education which rural people found both useless and destructive of local values, but he also found himself in opposition to the old

Tory elite for whom the grammar schools had provided classical education suitable for a governing class.

In 1807, well before government aid was extended to the common schools, an Act was passed[60] creating in each district a grammar school whose master was to be paid £100 per year from government funds. The grammar schools were intended to be classical schools, teaching Greek and Latin, in order to prepare the children of the wealthy for government, university and the professions. While a few scholarships were offered to poor children, the extremely high fees charged to pupils effectively prevented the children of even fairly prosperous individuals from attending. Moreover, the grammar schools offered not only the higher grades, but completely duplicated the offerings of the common schools from primary grades to the "sixth form".

From 1807 to 1853 the grammar schools were entirely in the hands of the Family Compact: the District Trustees were appointed by the Lieutenant Governor, and because these appointments were effectively for life, there was absolutely no control by either government or local citizens over the operation of the grammar schools. This, then, was the situation when the Whitby Grammar School was founded in 1846.

Ryerson's method of getting control of the grammar schools and changing them to fit into his long-term design for the Canadian education system was accomplished in two stages: first, he gave control of the grammar schools to the County Councils, and then gradually centralized that control into the Province's hands through a series of changes in the Education Acts. As might be expected, he met opposition every step of the way.

To get public support for the removal of grammar school control from the hands of those appointed by the Family Compact, Ryerson opened a campaign in 1849 and 1850 to discredit the Compact's management of the grammar schools, and to argue that the grammar schools, as then constituted, operated against the interests of the general population. Thus, in the Chief Superintendent's Report for 1850, Ryerson argued that:

> As at present established [the grammar schools] form no part of a general System of Public Instruction; and the manner in which public money is expended for their support, is unjust to the larger portion of the community. . . . It injures the Common Schools in the neighbourhood of the Grammar Schools, as the elementary branches which are taught in the former are also taught in the latter. Thus are Pupils who ought to be learning the elements of Reading, Writing, Arithmetic, and Geography in the Common School, introduced into the Grammar School; and a teacher, who receives £100 per annum as a Teacher of a Classical School, is largely occupied in Teaching the A.B.C. of Common School instruction, to the injury of the Common School, and to the still greater injury of the real and proper objects of the Grammar School. . . . Pupils who are learning the first elements of an English Education, are sent and admitted to the Grammar School because it

> is thought to be more respectable than the Common School, and especially when Grammar School fees are made comparatively high to gratify this feeling, and to place the Grammar School beyond the reach of the multitude.[61]

It is clear that the Whitby Grammar School fell into this pattern because in 1853, of the 75 pupils enrolled, only 10 had progressed to the point of studying the classics.[62]

In Ryerson's plans, the function of the grammar schools was to be changed from that of a training ground of a social and economic elite to that of an intermediate link between the common school and the university. As he said in explaining the purpose of the Grammar School Act in 1853:

> Each Grammar School is intended to fulfil the double office of a English High School and an elementary Classical and Mathematical School,—a School into which pupils will be admitted from the higher classes of the Common Schools, and receive such an Education as will fit them for mercantile and manufacturing pursuits, and the higher employments of Mechanical and Agricultural Industry . . . a School also forming a connecting link between the Common School and a University College, in which youth may be thoroughly trained in the elementary Classics, Mathematics, and Physical Sciences, for admission to the University, and entrance upon professional studies.[63]

In the Grammar School Act of 1853 Ryerson took the first steps towards establishing intermediate schools free from the control of the old elite. A major step towards this end was a clause that required County Councils to appoint Boards of Trustees for each grammar school. In order to establish a degree of central control over the schools, the Chief Superintendent (Ryerson) was given the right and duty to report annually to the Government on the condition of the grammar schools, while the Council of Public Instruction which Ryerson controlled was given the power of selecting books, preparing courses, and appointing a special inspector of grammar schools.

In order to finance the new grammar schools, the annual payment of £100 from the provincial Grammar School Fund was reserved for payment of the master of the senior county school, while any surplus from the fund was to be divided among the counties on the basis of population. In addition, the County Councils were authorized to levy and collect whatever sums were required to support the grammar schools, while the trustees were empowered to use rate bills on the parents of students to meet expenses. Finally, counties were empowered to establish new grammar schools as soon as £50 per year was available from the Grammar School Fund for support of its master.[64] In 1854 Ryerson took the further step of allowing the union of common and grammar schools. This union allowed the trustees to levy local taxes to support the grammar schools as well as the common schools when the township ratepayers approved the step at the annual meeting.[65]

Almost immediately after the changes in the Grammar School Act, steps were taken in Ontario County to create grammar schools in other villages. Thus the Uxbridge Grammar School was established in 1855, and others were authorized in Oshawa and Borelia in June 1857.[66] The organization of the new grammar schools, however, did not come about without considerable difficulty. As the Standing Committee on Education reported to the County Council in January 1858, neither the Uxbridge nor Borelia grammar school had, as yet, managed to get under way.[67] It was not until May 1858 that the Whitby *Chronicle* could report that

> the Uxbridge Grammar School was opened on Tuesday last, 11th inst., under very pleasing auspices. Mr. Strachan, late head master of the Grammar School, at Consecon, is Principal.[68]

In spite of continued prodding by the County Council, the Borelia Grammar School project had to be abandoned for lack of local support.

Moreover, even the Oshawa Grammar School had a good deal of difficulty getting established. Although it operated between 1857 and 1860, it was apparently forced to close in 1860. It reopened in 1863, united with the common school and flourished from that time on, reporting a total of 92 pupils in 1864.[69]

In June 1864 two new grammar schools were authorized by County Council for Beaverton and Manilla.[70] While the Beaverton Grammar School was unable to get sufficient support to open, that at Manilla remained in operation until 1874 when it was moved to Cannington.[71] In 1868 another grammar school was opened at Port Perry, the last to be established in the county for many years.[72]

Table XXXIV
Grammar School Attendance in Ontario County, 1853–69[73]

	1853	*1861*	*1869*
Whitby	75	52	136
Oshawa	—	—	104
Uxbridge	—	23	60
Manilla	—	—	40
Port Perry	—	—	70

Ryerson's enforcement of minimum entrance standards for admission to grammar school greatly reduced enrollment in schools such as that at Whitby. As Table XXXIV shows, in spite of the rapid growth of population in Whitby between 1853 and 1861, there was a sharp drop in grammar school attendance when the higher standards were enforced. The figures for 1869 show the results of the increase in population in the northern area as well as the changing attitude towards education.[74]

In spite of Ryerson's attempts to raise the standards of education in the grammar schools, many schools continued to admit students who were not capable of following courses at the upper school level. In order to force grammar schools to offer classical studies, in 1865 the Council of Public Instruction issued a revised "Programme of Studies" which included a system of "Regulations for the Government of Grammar Schools". These regulations required that no school be entitled to receive any portion of the Grammar School Fund unless it had an average daily attendance of at least ten pupils studying Latin and Greek. More significantly, the grant was henceforth to be distributed, not on the basis of population, but on the basis of school attendance. As it turned out, this last regulation set off a long debate which had lasting significance.

During the early nineteenth century it had been the custom to send both boys and girls to common schools, but to retain the grammar schools for the education of boys only. So long as grants to grammar schools were tied to population rather than attendance, there was little impetus to encourage the schoolmasters to accept female students. In spite of this drawback, in August 1859, well ahead of most grammar schools in the Province, the Oshawa Grammar School trustees voted to accept female pupils. The Oshawa *Vindicator* reported:

> In another column will be found an announcement relating to the next term of the Grammar School, with the name of T.S. Russell, A.M., attached as master. What will more particularly strike the attention is the low rate (Classical Pupils, \$3 per term, non-classical pupils, \$2 per term) hereafter to be charged for tuition—about one-half the amount heretofore demanded for the privilege of becoming a pupil—and the throwing the doors of the institution open to female as well as male students.—Both these we consider very commendable features.[55]

Following Oshawa's example, other grammar schools in Ontario County began to admit female students. By 1866, girls actually outnumbered boys in the highest educational departments in Ontario County grammar schools – as the Chief Superintendent of Education reported, this was a most unusual situation.[76] Once payment of the Grammar School Fund was made contingent upon attendance, most other grammar schools followed Ontario County's example, and began to admit girls to the study of classics.

The appearance of so many female students in the grammar schools after 1865 upset Ryerson's budget calculations, and apparently offended his sense of propriety. The mixing of the sexes in grammar school, he argued, would inevitably lead to immorality. As the Reverend G.P. Young, Chief Inspector of Grammar Schools, argued in 1867 and Ryerson reiterated in 1868:

> The risk of moral injury resulting in carelessly conducted schools, from the co-education of the sexes, though it may be easily exaggerated, is an element that cannot be neglected. . . . It is not so much, however,

> any gross and palpable departure from the ordinary moralities, that is to be feared in mixed schools, as the loss of higher moral refinements. I can hardly describe what I wish to indicate; but every one will understand it, who has been accustomed to associate with cultivated women:—an ever present delicacy, married to an intelligence which at once strengthens it and liberates it from constraint. That the atmosphere of the generality of our mixed Grammar Schools is favourable to the growth of this, the flower of all female accomplishments, I do not believe.[77]

In order to discourage the admission of girls to the grammar schools, the Education Department reduced the apportionment made for female students by half in 1866 and eliminated entirely payment for female students in grammar schools in 1867.[78]

To Ryerson's astonishment, there was an almost universal rejection of his stance on female grammar school education. One Board of Grammar School Trustees (Clinton) made the pointed argument that:

> If any evils result from allowing Boys and Girls of the age of those commonly attending Grammar Schools to be taught together, these evils will not be diminished; but rather increased, by excluding Girls from those Schools. Upon such exclusion, the Girls will be placed in the first, or highest, class [of the common schools]. The Boys in this class will ordinarily be of about the same age as the Boys in the Grammar School . . . To send back the Girls from the Grammar to the Common School would, therefore, necessarily lead to the inference that the Department of Public Instruction is only anxious about the character and demeanour of the Pupils in Grammar Schools.[79]

Dr. William McGill, the provincial member for Ontario South Riding also strongly supported the admission of female students to the grammar schools on the grounds that if girls should be excluded, they would, to a large extent, be practically excluded from the superior education which they were now enjoying.[80] The new urban industrial and mercantile elite of the growing towns clearly expected that its female members would play a much more active role in society than that played by the wives and daughters of the old Tory compact. Faced with such strong opposition, Ryerson was forced to retreat, and girls continued to attend the grammar schools.

The Grammar School Act of 1871 went a long way toward fulfilling Ryerson's ambitions to upgrade upper school education in Ontario. This Act abolished the term "Grammar School" with its elitist connotations and substituted the title "High School". Strict standards of admission were established, and all incoming students were required to pass an entrance examination. Henceforth, every high school was required to employ at least two teachers, and adequate provision had to be made so that all schools were capable of providing the elements of an advanced English education, including natural sciences and commercial subjects. The study of Greek, Latin and modern languages was made optional upon the decision of the parents or guardians of the pupils.

In addition, a completely new kind of high school, the "Collegiate Institute" was created. In order to acquire the status of a collegiate institute (and its attendant special grant of $750 per year), a high school was required to employ at least four teachers, and to have at least sixty boys studying Latin and Greek. Such a large high school was beyond the ability of most towns, however, and a dozen years after the passing of the 1871 Act, only Whitby High School had acquired the status of a collegiate institute.[81]

In spite of the growth of student attendance in the grammar schools in the 1860s, the enthusiasm for higher education was not shared by rural inhabitants. The rural press made all the usual objections to the new Grammar School Act of 1871 which gave greatly increased powers over textbooks, examinations and school administration to the provincial education authorities,[82] but the strongest opposition was directed against an attempt to force the rural areas to become part of grammar school districts and thereby assume a major part of responsibility for their support.

Until 1871, grammar school districts were coincidental with the limits of the towns in which they were established. Thus, as the towns moved more and more toward municipal taxation in support of grammar schools, and the elimination of grammar school fees, town residents often found themselves being taxed to pay for the education of non-resident pupils who lived either just outside the town line or who were boarding in the town in order to attend school. Some towns such as Whitby solved this problem by charging fees to non-residents while admitting children of residents free. The growing unhappiness of many town residents appeared to give Egerton Ryerson an opportunity to make the grammar school taxation universal just as had been done with common schools. Thus, as was his usual practice, Ryerson included in the Grammar School Act of 1871 a provision that made it possible for County Councils to divide the whole county into grammar school districts without regard to municipal boundaries, with the intention of making it mandatory after people had become accustomed to the change.

No one objected to a provision that increased the latitude of power enjoyed by the County Councils. Indeed, when Uxbridge village was incorporated in June 1872, thereby greatly reducing the area served by the local grammar school, the Ontario County Council availed itself of its new powers to pass a bylaw re-uniting Uxbridge township and village for grammar school purposes.[83] When Port Perry attempted to force Reach and Scugog to support its grammar school, however, the move was vigorously rejected by the local press.[84]

In November 1872, the provincial education authorities moved to complete their upper school design by making it mandatory that County Councils divide the counties into high school districts in order to force all area residents to pay taxes in support of higher education. This move enraged the rural press to a degree greater than any other action yet taken by the education department. As the *Ontario Observer* objected:

> The law as it now stands as to the boundaries of High School Districts is all that could be desired. The legislature knew that it would be a piece of the most unvarnished tyranny to force those who received no benefit from High Schools to pay as much for them as those who receive all the benefit, so they wisely left it in the hands of Counties Councils to determine the boundaries of High School Districts . . . and no section need have a High School unless they please. . . .
>
> [Now] our local legislature would look well in coming down to Counties Councils and commanding them to do this or that as if they were puppets. We hope that our Counties Councils are made of sterner stuff than to allow even the local legislature (should they attempt to do so) to ride them around the ring with blinders on . . . Why don't they move to do away with Counties Councils altogether? Better far to do away with them than seek to make a burlesque of them.[85]

The main opposition to extending the high school districts was economic. As the reports of the education department showed, provincial support for high school students averaged about twenty dollars per year per student, while that for common school children averaged only about one dollar per year. Since almost all high school students were from the towns, this meant that urban students already received far more provincial support than did their rural counterparts. To tax rural residents to support urban students to an even greater extent seemed to the rural press not only the height of injustice, but a clear example of legislation enacted in favour of the rising urban elite. With the rural economy already in considerable difficulty, every cent taken to support urban high school students had the effect of reducing the farmer's ability to support the local common school system. The rural-oriented *Ontario Observer* rejected the changed high school boundaries for precisely these reasons:

> The friends of class education, those who wish to rob our Public Schools and hand over the funds to pamper our so called High Schools, those who seek to deprive the children of the sons of toil of the benefits of a good education in order that the chicks of our pinfeathered aristocracy may get all the change that is going, those who would starve the intelligence and dwarf the intellects of our country's hope—the offspring of the toiling multitude—in order to pamper and satiate the enfeebled intellects of our future codfish aristocracy are stirring heaven and earth with a view to accomplish their design, and they appear to long for the time when the educational funds of Canada shall be distributed on principles similar to those of the midnight of the dark ages when

> the would-be better class received all the educational loaves and fishes while the poor were denied even the crumbs . . . The young aristocrats must have all the educational luxuries, but the fathers of those children who get only these scraps must pay for the luxuries to these others.[86]

In spite of such outcries and protests, when the interests of the urban elite were in conflict with established rural values, the urban interests triumphed.

Although the rural residents of Ontario County failed to hold back the changes, they continued to oppose the creation of an elaborate and costly system of public supported high school and university education. Like William Lyon Mackenzie, they viewed anything that removed the young from the role of a direct producer of wealth to be socially dangerous, if not an actual social evil. As the Cannington *Gleaner* observed in 1897:

> Our high schools are robbing Ontario of her brightest and best. Go through the towns and cities of the United States and you find bright young Canadians everywhere. What sent them there? My answer is: Our high school system. Go through Canadian towns and cities and you find them filled with starving doctors, lawyers, pedagogues, and civil engineers. Who took all those from the plough, the bench, the machine, and the counter and sent them out to be consumers of wealth instead of producers? I am fain to return the same answer.[87]

THE BUILDING OF THE RAILWAYS

If the years 1851-71 had been generally a period of economic expansion for Ontario County, they had also been a period of phenomenal growth for the City of Toronto.[1] Not only had Toronto's population and trade been greatly expanded through the building of railroads and the establishment of a great wholesale trade that covered central Ontario, but it had become a dominant banking centre as well. Until the late 1860s none of these developments posed any great threat to the mercantile trade or manufacturing activities of Ontario County. The relatively small scale of Toronto manufacturing and the high cost of shipment of many goods meant that the merchants and crafts workers of Ontario County could offer effective competition.

But just as Whitby's merchants had struggled long and hard to increase their trade and wealth through the improvement and expansion of their transportation system, so too did the merchants of Toronto constantly look for ways to increase their area of dominance. Although the building of the Northern Railway in the early 1850s had captured for Toronto the Georgian Bay and Upper Lakes trade that had so attracted the envy of Whitby, the failure of that trade to develop at anything like the expected rate soon turned Toronto's attention to closer opportunities. Thus it was that in 1867 a group of Toronto financiers and entrepreneurs decided to explore the possibility of building railways from Toronto to the northwest and northeast into territories that previously had been under the dominance of Hamilton and Guelph on the one hand and Whitby and Port Hope on the other. The result of those explorations was the Toronto, Grey and Bruce and the Toronto and Nipissing Railways, both chartered on March 4, 1868.[2]

The dream of building a railroad to Lake Huron, thereby making Whitby a great international lake port, had never quite died among Whitby's merchants, but the expansionary plans of the Toronto entrepreneurs altered the matter. Now a railroad was no longer a question of expansion, but rather one of defending the trade that Whitby already possessed. As long as no rival metropolis built a railroad into the back areas of Ontario County, the well-travelled Centre Line road effectively captured the trade of the area for Whitby. But if Toronto built a railroad into the area, Whitby's trade was doomed unless its merchants could respond in kind. From 1866 on, when rumours of the Toronto plans began to circulate in the area, and meetings of various leading merchants and businessmen began to be held in towns along the projected route of the Toronto and Nipissing Railway, Whitby's leading businessmen became increasingly anxious to build a railway of their own.

There were, however, two serious drawbacks relating to the building and ownership of railways in the 1860s: first, while the trade that a railway generated was extremely profitable to the merchants, manufacturers and wholesalers at its terminus, the operation of railways themselves had proved to be, almost universally, a money-losing proposition; secondly, railways were extremely expensive to build, and since the crash of 1857, Whitby had remained a relatively poor town compared to other local centres.[3] Any hopes that Whitby had of building a railway depended on persuading residents of other centres, or the various municipal and provincial authorities, to pay for the local railroad.

Finally, one other problem would be constantly present. Because such large projects entailed the expenditure of large sums of money, there were always innumerable entrepreneurs anxious to use the project for their own enrichment by fair means or foul. Indeed, the history of railway building in Canada is replete with stories of the milking of railway contracts by men who possessed the public's confidence.[4] In this respect, the Whitby railway project would follow the national example.

The chain of events which would result in the building the Port Whitby and Port Perry Railway began innocently enough. Over the previous decade (since the collapse of the rather grandiose Port Whitby and Lake Huron scheme), local residents had become inured to the blandishments of a series of promoters who, carpetbag in hand, would stop at the best hotels, dine with the leading businessmen, call a series of public meetings to promote a railway scheme and, when the local citizenry did not rush forward with their savings in their hands, would disappear never to be seen again. Thus the arrival of John Fowler, Esq., of Port Hope, in August 1866, caused little local enthusiasm.

There were, however, a number of local businessmen to whom a railway offered decided advantages. Chief among these men were Chester Draper, merchant of Whitby, and in 1864, purchaser of the Port Whitby harbour, and Thomas Paxton, lumber mill operator and owner of most of the land in Port Perry. If a railway were to be built which offered the possibility of tapping the rapidly expanding lumber industry of Victoria County, both men would prosper enormously. For this reason, when Fowler arrived looking for local support, Draper and Paxton offered enthusiastic backing for the project. Thus at a series of meetings held in the villages throughout the area to "talk up" a railway, it was Chester Draper or Thomas Paxton who introduced Fowler and who offered the strongest support for the proposed railroad.

Because the Toronto and Nipissing Railroad project had not yet been started, the basis for argument in favour of the local railroad was the same as it had been a decade before: Whitby was the natural outlet of the northern trade, and the building of a railway would ensure stability and prosperity for the area. The *Ontario Observer* explained the benefits to be gained by building a railroad:

> It is no secret, that the business of this County was very materially affected by the opening of the Port Hope and Lindsay Railway. The trade which found its way through this County (as the most natural route) has been diverted into other channels. The great and rapidly increasing trade of the North has passed, or is passing into other hands. The business, which should be done at Whitby or Oshawa, is now transacted at Port Hope, We may congratulate ourselves as heartily as we please on our local trade and prosperity, we may boast of the many superior advantages we enjoy, yet there is nothing plainer than the fact, that nothing will so certainly insure us a healthy and permanent prosperity, nothing will be so conducive to our material advancement, as the construction of a railway to connect Lake Scugog with Ontario.[5]

The main problem was who would pay for the project – and who would benefit.

By Confederation, knowledgeable railway promoters were aware of the cost of building railroads under the conditions of Canadian terrain and climate. In Ontario, the average cost of 1,407 miles of railway was $75,344 per mile, while less ambitious projects on smoother ground in New Brunswick cost $30,771 per mile.[6] The latter figure would be the generally accepted minimum cost of the cheapest broad-gauge line, including rolling stock, which could be built under Canadian conditions. Thus, a realistic estimate for an eighteen-mile railroad from Port Whitby to Port Perry would have been $550,000. When Fowler, Paxton and Dryden pointed out that Reach township alone would be required to purchase $100,000 worth of stock (at a required annual tax cost of 115 mills per dollar of local assessment for 20 years)[7] whatever local enthusiasm there might have been quickly evaporated, and the local railway boom subsided once again.

In the winter of 1867 a group of Toronto businessmen led by William Gooderham, president of the great grain wholesale and brewing concern of Gooderham and Worts, and A.M. Smith, president of the Royal Canadian Bank, began to investigate the possibility of building a railroad through Ontario and Simcoe Counties to tap the timber trade of Muskoka and Haliburton, as well as the local farming trade. To lead the campaign to gather public support, the Toronto businessmen hired George Laidlaw, a talented public speaker and pamphleteer.

The Toronto campaign, as it was thought out by Laidlaw, was a stroke of genius. By 1867 almost everyone had long since concluded that railroads, because of their high cost and small traffic, must be money-losing endeavours. Laidlaw proposed to overcome this problem by building a "narrow-gauge" railway (i.e., with three feet, six inches between the rails) instead of the "standard gauge" (five feet, six inch) railway. By so doing, Laidlaw argued, the cost per mile of railway construction could be reduced to $15,000, thereby making the railroad a profitable venture.[8] Even more spectacular, on Laidlaw's part, was his campaign designed to appeal to the humanitarian instincts of the citizens. In the previous decade as industrialization grew, Toronto had developed a large population of very poor workers who huddled in ghetto areas such as "Cabbagetown" just west of the Don River. Laidlaw proposed to ease their hardships through a drastic reduction in the cost of firewood. Both the Toronto, Grey and Bruce, and the Toronto and Nipissing, he promised, would guarantee in their charters to carry cordwood from the farmers to the city for a rate of not more than two and one-half cents per cord per mile.[9] With cordwood currently selling in Toronto at rates up to six dollars per cord, this promised to reduce the price of firewood by fifty percent or more.

To complicate the railway picture in the northern part of Ontario County, the Port Hope and Lindsay Railway began once again to make motions toward extending its line from the terminus at Lindsay to Beaverton. This proposal, however, met with a certain amount of skepticism locally since the Beaverton extension project had been causing little flurries of excitement around Beaverton for more than a decade, and nothing had ever come of it except the usual meetings and optimistic speeches.[10]

By the first week of April 1867, the Toronto and Nipissing propagandists were beginning the long process of "talking up" their railroad. Among the first centres to be approached was Beaverton, where the T. & N. representatives received a warm welcome. The businessmen of Beaverton had long regarded their position on the edge of the lake as one that must inevitably make it a major centre of transportation and commerce. Thus when the T. & N. representative arrived it appeared that at last their dreams were about to be realized. At a well-attended public meeting, held on April 5, 1867, the following motions, which were indicative of Beaverton's hopes for the Toronto and Nipissing project and their disillusionment at the many broken promises of the owners of the Port Hope and Lindsay Railway, were passed:

> It was moved by Duncan Calder, Esq., seconded by A. Cameron Esq.—That this meeting learns with pleasure of the proposition to construct a Railway from Toronto to Lake Nipissing via Gull River. . . . We would express it as our opinion that the commercial prosperity of the road would depend in a great measure upon the securing of the vast and rapidly increasing trade of Lake Simcoe . . . and that Beaverton is the best point for such connecting. . . .
>
> D. Ross moved, seconded by Mr. R.N. McTaggart, that the failure of the Port Hope, Lindsay and Beaverton Railway Company to extend their road to Beaverton, as at first intended in order to reach the Lake Simcoe trade . . . justified us in offering our support to any other Railway that may be the first to profit by that trade.[11]

Throughout the summer and fall of 1867 meetings in support of the Toronto and Nipissing Railway continued to be held. A typical meeting in Markham village on December 31, 1867 is described below:

> A most influential meeting, with a view to the furtherance of this proposed work, was held at the village of Markham—Scarboro, Uxbridge, and other Townships were well represented at said meeting. The deputation from Toronto consisted of over twenty of the most influential, enterprising businessmen in the city. Business was commenced by a public dinner in honour of the occasion, in which over one hundred and fifty of the leading men in the various townships took part.[12]

Such lavish affairs, of course, cost a great deal of money, but they were not acts of simple generosity on the part of the Toronto railway entrepreneurs. Railways cost enormous sums to build, and just as the Whitby promoters had hoped in their campaign to build the Port Whitby and Lake Huron Railway at public expense, it was the intention of the Toronto promoters to persuade the local residents to subsidize a large part of the cost of the Toronto and Nipissing. Unfortunately for the T. & N. promoters, the local citizenry had been bitten far too often for them to allow themselves to be easily persuaded. It was this delay that permitted the Whitby businessmen to begin a campaign in favour of their own route.

During the summer and fall of 1867, while the Toronto entrepreneurs were busily promoting their line, the Whitby leaders dithered and hesitated and were unable to reach a decision. The local newspapers brought out all the old ideas from the need for better gravel roads, to the desirability of the Huron and Ontario Ship Canal, but none of these would serve to preserve Whitby's dominance over its hinterland should the Toronto and Nipissing be built. Among the more imaginative new ideas put forth was a proposal to establish a freight line hauled by steam traction engines on the Whitby and Scugog gravel road.[13] After a time it became clear that Whitby's choice was either to attempt to build its own railroad, or to abandon hope of ever becoming a major metropolis. Putting the best face possible on their decision, the

Whitby businessmen called in John Fowler once again to start the process of whipping up enthusiasm for a local railroad. As a first step, the local business communities of Whitby and Port Perry applied to the Ontario Legislature for a charter. Ironically, it was granted on March 4, 1868,[14] the same day that the charter of the Toronto and Nipissing was granted. The preliminaries were over, and the battle to extract the finances from the farming community had begun.

The campaign of the Toronto and Nipissing promoters was much the more professional and well-managed of the two. First, the northern part of the country had always chafed under the Whitby mercantile monopoly; therefore, the Toronto interests could rely on the tenets of *laissez-faire* economics and the ideals of competition to help justify their enterprise; second, Joseph Gould became one of the first major shareholders in the Toronto and Nipissing and his local prestige removed the stigma of the project's Toronto control.

As soon as the T. & N. charter was approved, the Toronto forces were ready to swing into action. Meetings were scheduled in all the villages in townships along the proposed line. Chief among the speakers at each meeting were the leading political, mercantile and manufacturing men of Toronto, led, in most cases by A.M. Smith, president of the Royal Canadian Bank and, in 1867, mayor of Toronto. Typical of the arguments used was that put forth by Smith at a meeting at Greenbank:

> Railroad building, he said, is a matter of money and muscle; and the delegation are passing round in order to find out what the people are willing to do in way of assistance in order to obtain so important a work. . . . The speaker dwelt upon the advantages that the people of Reach, especially the northern portion of it, should derive from the proposed work, as it would enable them to sell their grain at the Toronto Market.—The best buyers, he said, always attend the largest market, and there the highest prices are always paid. The gentleman next referred to the advantages that Toronto would offer as a market for cordwood, and showed the advantage it would be to farmers to sell their cordwood there.[15]

The T. & N. promoters were always careful never to raise the anger of local residents by overt attacks on Ontario County businessmen. Rather they adopted a rather patronizing attitude toward their local rivals. As George Laidlaw remarked at the Greenbank meeting:

> We have no doubt but the influence of the wealthy men of Toronto would cause the bonds of this road to sell well in the British market. The Toronto merchants are determined to build this road. . . . Reach has almost no trade with Toronto, and it cannot be denied that Toronto is the best market for the farmer to sell his grain. Whitby, is doubtless a good market, and its merchants honourable men, but there is not that competition amongst buyers which is found in Toronto. . . .
>
> We wish all manner of success to the Whitby and Port Perry Road;

> but it is a common saying among the people that "the big fish eat the little ones", and I sincerely hope that the Toronto and Nipissing scheme may eat up the Whitby and Port Perry scheme (laughter).[16]

Similar speeches were made at Uxbridge, Cannington, and other villages along the proposed route.

When the promoters returned to Toronto, they adopted rather a different tone. In Toronto the emphasis was on the profits to be reaped by Toronto businessmen if they could capture the northern timber trade. As one influential editorialist pointed out:

> The grain and passenger traffic to be secured by this road to Lake Nipissing will not, it is considered, exceed half that of the Northern [the railway running from Toronto to Barrie], but the practically inexhaustible supplies of pine and other kinds of timber will afford a business durable and profitable.[17]

As the same editor remarked, the Toronto and Nipissing was simply another method of expanding the Toronto sphere of mercantile dominance:

> The object which Toronto has at heart, and which is worth every legitimate effort she can put forth, is to attract to herself a perpetuity of the traffic of the districts which these lines are designed to serve and in a secondary sense to do this with the least possible burden to herself.[18]

Persuading local municipalities to tax themselves in order to build the road clearly came under the latter heading.

Since the laws regarding the procedure by which local municipalities might undertake public debt were very elaborately framed in order to protect the ratepayers, it required a great deal of time from the start of such a campaign until the point when the money would be available to the railway. By law it was required that bylaws to borrow money had to be printed in the local press for four weeks, and then voted on in a municipal referendum. Those residents who rented property could vote only if their leases ran as long as the term of the municipal debentures.[19] The amounts demanded by the Toronto and Nipissing promoters from the Ontario County municipalities totalled $165,000 (Reach, $30,000; Brock, $65,000; Uxbridge, $50,000; and Scott $20,000). All the other municipalities along the route were expected to contribute to the railway as well. The City of Toronto was asked for $150,000.[20]

From the schedule of meetings set up to discuss the bonus bylaws, and the timing of the meetings, it is clear that the T. & N. directors considered Thorah and Brock to be the key areas upon which the whole proposal would stand or fall. Thus the first meetings were held at Beaverton and Brechin on June 16, 1868; Cannington, June 17; and Oakwood on June 18. Almost immediately the Toronto proposal received a severe setback.

When the Brock Township Council met to discuss the proposed railway bylaw, two immediate objections were made: first, the sum of $65,000 was more than the township could afford; and second, that the bylaw as it stood offered no protection whatsoever to the local citizens. As the deputy reeve, Henry Brethour pointed out:

> Not one of the other municipalities on the route has yet attempted to call a meeting for the purpose of passing the bylaw, and who knows whether they will submit the bylaws or not. Supposing that we should pass a bylaw to grant a certain amount, and that bylaw be carried by the people, the corporation would then give its bonds for the amount; and it might be that no other municipality would grant a dollar, but according to the conditions of the charter the company might go on and spend our money while we might not get a foot of railroad.[21]

After a long discussion, the Brock Council moved to reject the T. & N. bylaw, but left open the possibility of a further bylaw offering better terms:

> Moved by Mr. Brethour, seconded by Mr. Amey, that this Council, having carefully examined the Bylaw submitted by the Directors of the Toronto and Nipissing Railway company for a bonus to aid in the construction of said road, have come to the conclusion not to submit said By-law to the rate-payers until certain alterations are made therein with certain conditions, viz: That after the said company shall have expended a specific sum in making a road through this municipality; the Council will—on said By-law receiving the approval of a majority of the rate-payers advance the bonds of this corporation in due proportion—as the work proceeds, the last installment being given on the completion of the road through this township.[22]

It appears that the rejection by Brock of the open terms of the T. & N. bonus forced the T. & N. directors to make a thorough reappraisal of the project's financial possibilities, for nothing more of the project was heard in the area for the next three months. The problem facing the directors was this: assuming that in fact a narrow gauge railway could be built for $15,000 per mile (a doubtful assumption at best) and that the railway promoters could raise bonds on sections of the railway as they were finished, equal to one-third of the total cost of that section, then the promoters would be required to lay out something like $450,000 in cash to cover the first thirty-mile section from the Grand Trunk junction in Scarborough to Uxbridge village before anything substantial could be collected on the bonuses or borrowed on the bonds of the railway. Whereas, if their first bylaw had been approved, they could have used the bonus money from the whole railroad on the first section, and then borrowed against that to extend the line. Only when the line neared completion, and freight was running on the first section would any personal outlay have been required. It was a clever net that had been cast by the Toronto entrepreneurs, but the Brock councillors had escaped its meshes. Now the promoters would have to reach into their own pockets at the outset. Little wonder then, at the long pause in activities.

Moreoever, during the long pause for reconsideration, the T. & N. promoters received a second blow. While the Toronto and Nipissing leaders debated among themselves the merits of going ahead with their railroad, the owners of the Port Hope and Lindsay Railroad were acting to preserve their interests which had been threatened. After a powerful campaign in Port Hope, that town's residents were persuaded to grant to the Port Hope and Lindsay Railway a bonus of $40,000 to expand that line from Lindsay to Beaverton.[23] The goal of the bonus was to capture the trade of northern Ontario and Simcoe Counties.

The Port Hope and Lindsay quickly followed up its advantage by calling a meeting in Beaverton in order to persuade Thorah Township also to grant a bonus in aid of the construction. With the Toronto and Nippissing apparently stalled, Thorah's residents decided that the renamed Port Hope, Lindsay and Beaverton promised the only hope for expanded prosperity, and voted it $50,000 as a bonus.[24] Only a mile or so of right-of-way was cleared in 1868, but the Lindsay-Beaverton section was pushed ahead rapidly in the spring of 1869 – so much so that a flood of newcomers to Beaverton used the intervening period before the actual opening of the railroad to build houses and business blocks. The *Ontario Observer* reported:

> That this village is at the dawn of a prosperous future, we think is beyond denial. Situated as it is on the eastern shore of Lake Simcoe . . . it affords one of the most pleasant resorts for those in quest of a healthy retreat in summer from the din and bustle of city life. . . .
>
> The extension of the Railway from Lindsay is being rapidly pushed forward. Gangs of men are busy at the work daily, and this fall [1869] will see all the grading . . . completed and the spring of 1870 will witness the entry of the iron horse into Beaverton. . . .
>
> In view of the extension, property has advanced and is beginning to change hands. Those contemplating coming here had better secure lots now, ere they reach a price that will render them *non combatibus*. . . . already the dullness which has pervaded the village for years is being succeeded by the noise of the mason's trowel and the carpenter's hammer. . . . Every old shanty that for years has been tenantless has been taken possession of, and to-day not a store or dwelling can be had in the village.[25]

After twenty years of waiting, it appeared to Beaverton's residents that boom times had come at last.

In the face of the Port Hope, Lindsay and Beaverton decision to go ahead with the extension to Beaverton, and signs of renewed activity on the part of the Whitby businessmen, the T. & N. promoters decided to make another attempt to secure bonuses for their project. This time, rather than opting to begin with the most difficult township, it was decided to begin with Uxbridge where Joseph Gould's influence could be put to best effect. A series of meetings were called, but this time the Whitby businessmen were better prepared for battle. In a series of face-to-face debates between the two groups of promoters, at which the Whitby men promised to build a branch line from Port Perry to Uxbridge Village, the Toronto forces scored a clear victory. As the Oshawa *Vindicator* reported:

> At the Uxbridge Railway meeting, directors of both Nipissing and Port Perry roads were present. The motion in favour of the Nipissing was carried almost unanimously, an amendment to the effect, pledging the farmers to vote against the $50,000 bonus, scarcely getting a vote.[26]

The Uxbridge Township Council now introduced a bylaw to grant the Toronto and Nipissing a bonus of $50,000, and a referendum on the bylaw was called for September 19, 1868. The affair now took on the dimensions of a general election. The *Vindicator* gave this lively description of the campaign:

> The contest in Uxbridge was sharp. Prominent railroad men from Toronto assisted by the local supporters on the one side, and the leading supporters and directors of the Port Whitby and Port Perry road were on the other. The township was canvassed as in a close election, both sides for a time feeling confident of victory.[27]

The lines of battle were drawn between the rural and village sections of the township, with the residents of Goodwood and Uxbridge village being the bylaw's chief supporters. When it was reported that the bonus proposal had triumphed by a majority of fifty-two, "Great rejoicings took place . . . , bonfires were lighted, the band played, and the people of the village [of Uxbridge] were in high glee over their success".[28] Like the businessmen of Beaverton, the Uxbridge village residents believed that they had taken the first great step to perpetual prosperity.

The Toronto and Nipissing promoters followed up their Uxbridge success with an even greater triumph in Toronto. In concert with the promoters of the Toronto, Grey and Bruce Railway (while the T. & N. and the T.G. & B. had many directors in common, the two projects were not identical in ownership) the T. & N. directors had persuaded "a large and influential audience" at Toronto's St. Lawrence Hall to support a motion requesting the City of Toronto to grant the two railway projects a total of $400,000 in bonuses: $250,000 to go to the T.G. & B., and $150,000 to the Toronto and Nipissing.[29] Thus encouraged, the T. & N. promoters began to canvass the country in earnest.

Once again the Toronto enterpreneurs had bylaws printed for each of the townships in the area. This time the amounts demanded were Scarborough, $10,000; Markham, $30,000; Whitchurch, $15,000; Scott, $20,000; Brock, $58,000; Eldon, $44,000; Bexley, $15,000; Laxton, Digby and Longford Townships, $25,000; and the Toronto suburb of Summerville, $15,000. With promises of $200,000 already safely in their pockets, the T. & N. directors were

Joseph Bigelow
Public Archives of Ontario

George Laidlaw
Public Archives of Ontario

Thomas Paxton
Public Archives of Ontario

James Holden
Whitby Historical Society

now prepared to take a much stronger line with townships that failed to exhibit the same enthusiasm already demonstrated by Uxbridge and Toronto. In order to focus their efforts, the directors decided to concentrate first on Scott, Brock, Whitchurch, Markham, Summerville, and the referendum in Toronto. It was the intention of the promoters that all these bylaws would be passed by December 31, 1868. The bylaw campaign received an almost immediate check, however, when both Whitchurch and Scott municipal councils refused to send the bonus bylaws to a referendum.[30]

The most difficult campaign was fought in Brock. At the special township Council meeting called to consider the bonus bylaw, the proceedings started as though there would be no great difficulty. The reeve, Malcolm Gillespie, announced that the Council had come to a unanimous decision to submit a motion for a $50,000 bonus rather than the $58,000 demanded by the railway promoters. One by one the councillors rose in turn to support the motion in favour of a $50,000 bonus, each in turn arguing that they would not present a bylaw for the $58,000 requested unless the railwaymen would pay the expenses of the referendum should it lose. Finally, several of the councillors expressed doubt that the railway company was giving sufficient guarantees to ensure the completion of the railway through the township. Having expressed these sentiments the Brock Council then invited the Toronto representatives to reply.

George Laidlaw, who spoke for the promoters, was alternately scathing, angry and condescending. Toronto, he said, had done its share – indeed, had done more than its share – to ensure the success of the venture. The *Ontario Observer* reported Laidlaw's answer:

> The Reeve had spoken of the bonus of $150,000 which the people of Toronto were prepared to grant but he could tell the meeting that the sum referred to is only a portion of the grant which the citizens are prepared to give. The privileges of the harbor alone will be worth $80,000, besides the right of way which the city is prepared to grant free . . . with regard to the $50,000 proposed by the council, it is entirely out of the question, and he had no authority to make such an arrangement, and [for the township] to attempt to enforce it would be equivalent to saying that this road was not wanted. The $58,000 asked from Brock is an equitable proportion with what is sought for from other municipalities and sooner than change it, he for one would prefer to throw up the whole thing . . . With regard to paying the expenses connected with the election, let the council submit the $58,000, and if no one else would pay the expense, he will do it himself if the by-law is voted down . . . The whole won't exceed $70 or $80, and that is no great matter.[31]

Having delivered himself of this charge, Laidlaw then went on to extol the great benefits that the Brock farmers would receive when Toronto became a market for their potatoes, pork, dairy products and course grains. The whole speech was a virtuoso performance, and made clear why Laidlaw had been hired by the Toronto businessmen to lead the campaign. Overwhelmed by Laidlaw's rhetoric, the Brock Council introduced the bylaw for $58,000 as requested,[32] and the referendum was set for December 4, 1868. Other votes scheduled for the same week were in Toronto, Markham, and Eldon.

Meanwhile, as the various campaigns were being waged by the Toronto and Nipissing supporters, the opponents to the venture in Uxbridge had sought legal counsel. To the chagrin of the pro-railway forces, when Edward Blake, one of Ontario's leading legal experts, was consulted on the Uxbridge bonus bylaw, he gave it as his opinion that the bylaw was illegal.[33] Moreover, when the railway promoters submitted the question to their legal experts, they were informed that not only was the Uxbridge bylaw illegal, but so were all the bylaws now in the process of being voted upon.[34] In spite of the illegalities (most were of a purely technical nature, such as Brock's omission of a place of voting) it was decided to go ahead with the voting.

The various railway referenda in the early part of December produced but one surprise. Toronto approved the $150,000 bonus by a vote of 790 to 119; Markham approved a $30,000 bonus by 315 to 125; and Eldon carried a $44,000 bonus by "a handsome majority"; however, the Brock voters defeated the $58,000 bonus bylaw by a majority of 28.[35] The *Ontario Observer*, which had been one of the strongest supporters of the Brock bylaw commented sourly:

> This result was altogether unexpected, and must have taken even the majority by surprise, as the inhabitants of Brock must all be aware that railway communication in these times of progress, is a *sine qua non* to rapid advancement; and the further from the best markets the more necessity is there for railway communications.[36]

It is not recorded whether or not Laidlaw offered to pay the cost of the vote.

In spite of the setback in Brock, the Toronto and Nipissing directors continued their campaign elsewhere, and on December 30, 1868, they could report that the village of Summerville had ratified a bonus of $15,000. The matter of the illegal bylaws, however, provided a rather more difficult puzzle. No one was completely certain whether the bylaws, if they were re-submitted to the electorate in a corrected form, would be passed when the voters had had an opportunity for second thoughts. In the end, the solution was found in the Ontario Legislature. On January 23, 1869, the charter of the Toronto and Nipissing was amended to legalize all bylaws granting bouses to the railway, no matter what the cause of the illegality.[37] This move caused no little anger among the railway's opponents.

Having settled the difficulty of the illegal bylaws, the T. & N. promoters turned once again to the attack in Scott and Brock. This time, they dropped the facade of high principle and presented bylaws which seemed likely to pass – for $10,000 in Scott, and $50,000 in Brock. This time, all went smoothly in

Scott, and on April 7, 1869, the directors reported that the Scott bylaw had passed with a majority of 52 votes.[38] The struggle in Brock, however, proved to be much more difficult.

When the charter of the Toronto and Nipissing Railway had been amended in January 1869, it had included a new clause which allowed its owners to extend a branch to Lindsay if they so desired. The T. & N. directors were not, however the only people interested in the branch line manoeuver. At the same time that the T. & N. charter was amended, the Port Whitby and Port Perry Railway directors had obtained an amendment which allowed them to extend its line to Beaverton, and to build a branch line to Uxbridge.[39] Thus when the T. & N. directors renewed their efforts in Brock, they found themselves confronted by a group of Whitby businessmen intent upon defeating the Toronto railway in favour of their own.

This example of Whitby's anti-Toronto "selfishness" drew forth from the northern press one of the most violent anti-Whitby attacks ever seen in Ontario County. The whole purpose of Whitby's interest in the Brock vote, it was argued, was a vicious attempt to keep the residents of Brock forever enslaved under the oppression of its mercantile dominance and governmental control. As one spokesman proclaimed, it was time to end both ties forever:

> The more than necessary share of attention paid to Brock and her private concerns by the liberal minded gentry of the town of Whitby, and a few of the disinterestedly generous people of [Port Perry] ought not to be allowed to pass unnoticed, lest these unselfish individuals may add the sin of ingratitude to the already too extensive catalogue of vices which they have trumped up against us unfortunate Brockites. . . . These gents find their craft in danger, and forseeing, with a clearness which none but selfish men can, that should our railway go on, that that unnatural connection which has apparently been already too long in existence would be cut short, and such a division of the county take place as both nature and justice demand, came hurrying back to Brock in feverish haste, and aweful earnestness determined, if possible, to upset our hated plans, and frustrate our designs. . . .
>
> The townships of North Ontario have, I should judge, been nearly long enough under the whip of a few wire pullers whose only ambition is to fill their own coffers at the expense of the rest of the county; and the day may come when . . . a permanent cure is obtained.[40]

The strong anti-Whitby campaign which was run by the T. & N. promoters and the Cannington businessmen had the desired effect. On March 9, 1869 the electors of Brock voted 287-to-123 in favour of the $50,000 bonus for the Toronto and Nipissing Railway. Of the three polls, only the rural area around Barker's School opposed the bonus by a 68-to-20 vote, while Cannington and Vroomanton which had been promised stations on the line voted strongly in favour (Cannington by 165-to-23 and Vroomanton by 102-to-32).[41]

In analysing the triumph of the Toronto railway project, at least one writer believed that a desire to escape Whitby's mercantile dominance had been the main factor:

> We have fought and conquered, and the Nipissing may be regarded as *un fait accompli*. We are much indebted to the missionaries from the town of Whitby and Port Perry for the splendid victory which the friends of the scheme have been able to achieve. The very *disinterested* opposition of these gentlemen roused the indifferent, confirmed the wavering, and brought the merits of the road more prominently to the foreground, and showed the people of Brock how very anxious these gentry are to retain Brock in her old relation to the front, that of lion's provider.[42]

Needless to say, the businessmen of Cannington, who expected that they would prosper as Cannington escaped from Whitby's dominance and became a great metropolitan centre in its own right, were overjoyed at the results of the vote. As the *Ontario Observer* reported:

> There was a big time in Cannington over the result. The victory was celebrated by a grand supper in Ward's Hotel. . . . After supper there was a grand torchlight procession which marched through the streets headed by a Brass Band. Bonfires were lighted . . . and speeches made.[43]

Again, as with the leaders of Uxbridge and Beaverton, the businessmen of Cannington believed that their fortunes had been made.

With the last of the major bonus campaigns out of the way, the Toronto and Nipissing promoters were now ready to issue shares in the company. The prospectus made it clear, however, that the Toronto businessmen were most reluctant to invest their own money in the venture. Whereas the charter of the company had allowed a total capitalization of $3,000,000, and this figure had been used constantly to demonstrate both the seriousness and generosity of the promoters, in fact, before the final vote in Brock, not a single share had been sold or a single dollar invested that had not come from, or been guaranteed by, a taxpayer. As one director had pointed out when asked about the failure of the promoters to pledge their own money to the project:

> The company had determined not to open the books until after the bonuses were granted, after which there would be no difficulty in getting all the stock taken up . . . when one-third of the stock had been provided for in bonuses.[44]

As events developed it became clear that even this statement was a great exaggeration of the actual willingness of the promoters to back the venture. The prospectus which was issued on April 9, 1869 covered only the eighty-five miles from Toronto to Coboconk. Of the $1,275,000 required to build this section, $399,000 had already been voted as bonuses, while an additional $476,000 was to be obtained by company bonds. This arrangement left

$400,000 to be taken up by the shareholders.[45] Even this amount failed to find takers, and when the first meeting of directors was called to formally set the project in motion, it was discovered that only $180,300 had been subscribed by 221 shareholders. So little confidence had been displayed by the originators of the railway that only William Gooderham held shares of more than $10,000 par value, while only eight others had bought more than $5,000 worth of shares.[46] Considering that the first call on the shareholders was for only 10 percent of the face value of the shares taken, this meant that the Toronto railway enterpreneurs had gotten control of the whole project, bonuses and all, for an initial investment of just over $5,000.

The promoters of the T. & N. now undertook the last campaign of the affair – to sell stock in the railway to the merchants and farmers of the hinterland. Again they were accompanied by all the fanfare and glowing praise which the local newspapers could muster. The *Ontario Observer*, in particular, outdid itself in its efforts to persuade the population to take stock in the T. & N. One aspect of this promotion was the following "history" of the efforts of the T. & N. promoters:

> Notwithstanding the vast amount of personal inconvenience, and no small pecuniary sacrifice that such a campaign would necessitate a company of the most busily employed men in the city left all behind, set off on their mission of progress and did not return until they had listed under their banner a large proportion of the life and vigor of the several townships through which the road was expected to pass. . . . The friends of progress . . . achieved a handsome victory, and a charter was secured for the road. But a charter is only an authority to build. Cash must be raised before another step can be taken. The municipalities along the proposed route must now be approached, and the city of Toronto, now being sensible of the vast importance of the undertaking, places $150,000 to the credit of the enterprise. . . . This was the Bonus Era of the enterprise. The next is the stock Era, equally important and no less hazardous. Again the city of Toronto has acted in the most handsome manner, no sooner were the Stock Books opened than a few of her merchants and leading men came down with the handsome sum of $150,000 subscribed stock; and again the party is out on its third and last campaign soliciting subscriptions for stock throughout the municipalities. . . . The next will be a pleasant and to many a profitable era— we mean the building era. Business then will get an impetus in these localities which will continue till the opening of the road, the trade of which will guarantee future progress.[47]

Although by all accounts the local farmers and merchants had little ready cash to invest in the project, the little they had was soon swept up in the whirlwind campaign. Thus, on August 18, 1869, after more than two years of rumours, campaigns, votes and promises, the Toronto and Nipissing directors announced that tenders were being called and that surveying had begun.[48] At last, the much hoped-for Toronto and Nipissing was about to come into being.

While the Port Hope, Lindsay and Beaverton and the Toronto and Nipissing Railway campaigns were being waged to successful conclusions in north Ontario, an equally controversial campaign was being carried on in the southern townships on behalf of the Port Whitby and Port Perry Railway. Because the P.W. & P.P. ran through only two townships and covered a projected distance of only eighteen miles, the details of its promotion were much less complex. In the first public meetings held after the Port Whitby and Port Perry Railway had received its charter on March 4, 1868, it promoters informed the public that the whole project would cost about $500,000 and that in order to carry out the project, municipal bonuses of at least $100,000 would be required.[49] Later meetings revealed that this total was broken down to require bonuses of $50,000 from the Town of Whitby; $15,000 from Whitby Township; $30,000 from Reach, and $4,000 from Scugog. An additional $10,000 was requested from Reach should the P.W. & P.P. undertake a branch line via Manchester to Uxbridge.

The primary theme of the Whitby and Port Perry business men was that they were the innocent victims of voracious capitalists from Toronto and Port Hope, and that they were forced to build the P.W. & P.P. for purely defensive reasons. At a meeting at Jewett's Hotel in Borelia, held on March 31, 1868, Captain James Rowe, wharfinger and grain merchant of Whitby, made this appeal:

> This scheme, he said, is a necessity, it is no matter of choice. It is absolutely necessary to our existence as a county.... [I look] upon the scheme as a simple matter of self-defence, we are being cut off on the right and left, and if something is not done we will be entirely cut off.[50]

Other leading spokesmen adopted a much more aggressive tone. At the Borelia meeting John Ham Perry issued this strongly-worded call to battle for the glory of progress and the Port Whitby and Port Perry line:

> Reach must take stock in proportion to that of Whitby, and at least as much; and why, he would ask, should Reach expect to get out of contributing her just proportion; does she not wish to maintain her position in the march of progress? Can she afford to be wiped off the map? By constructing this road we will not only secure and consolidate the trade we now have but we will encroach upon the territory of those who have so long encroached upon us, and absorbed so much of our legitimate trade. We in our turn would invade their territory and draw a large amount of their trade through this country.[51]

One of the favourite pro-railway arguments used in the northern campaigns could not be used in the south. The northern railway promoters could make much of the cheaper costs which railway transportation offered to the farmers, but in the case of the P.W. & P.P. there was little validity to this argument. Since most local farmers in Whitby and Reach townships moved their grain in the winter months when their time was free anyway, only grain from the northern township would benefit from a railway running from Whitby to Port Perry. It was this factor that had caused the *Monetary Times*, in 1868, to remark that, "The first 25 miles of a railway out of a city, as is well known, are unproductive of local traffic."[52]

The great difficulty created by the lack of a significant economic argument which would appeal to the farmers was shown in the pro-P.W. & P.P. editorials written in the Prince Albert *Ontario Observer*. On one occasion when the *Observer*'s editor attempted to demonstrate the manner in which all the economic groups and classes in Reach would benefit by the railway project, he found it relatively easy to show why groups other than farmers should support the railway. In the case of the labouring class, he argued, the benefits of having a railroad were clear. Since the labourer owned no property, he would pay nothing, or almost nothing, of the railway's cost, while

> it would open up to him an inexhaustible field of highly remunerative labour (selfish people would say, O! that would be a damage to the township, for when private parties require a labourer they will have to pay him more) hence all day labourers will wish success to the enterprise.[53]

The crafts workers would also benefit, the editor explained, because they would only pay a little of the cost, and the resulting growth would open up jobs for carpenters, masons, painters, cabinet makers, tinsmiths, stove dealers, shoemakers and tailors. Moreover, a strong demand for such skilled workmen would inevitably make wages rise.

To the merchants and manufacturers, the benefits were clear. While they would have to pay a large proportion of the railway bonus in their taxes, their benefits would be larger still:

> They will supply the materials for building and furnishing the houses, and for feeding and clothing the inhabitants—in fact nearly all the money coming into the hands of the labourer and the mechanic will pass into the hands of the merchant, and through his into those of the manufacturer, leaving a profit in the hands of each.[54]

Moreover, a second happy result of the increase in money in circulation, he believed, would be the end of the local credit trade.

As for the farmers, however, the editor found himself without a ready answer:

> Now for the largest and most important class—the farmer. This class must pay the larger portion of the tax. The profit which they will derive from it cannot be so easily pointed out—at least by us—as that of the

> other classes. We believe, however, that they will gain more by it than it will cost them.[55]

After a few rather vague references to the benefits that might be obtained locally from off-season shipment of grain, and, perhaps the opening up of the Toronto market for local dairy products, the editor concluded, "Many other benefits will doubtless present themselves of which we cannot now speak. A large majority of the farmers will, there is little doubt, sustain the By-law".[56]

Although the railroad offered no direct transportation benefits to the local farmers, the economic health of the nearby villages was of real concern to them. A large portion of their cash income came from the sale of produce to the labourers and craftsworkers employed in the local merchants' shops and manufacturing establishments. With the collapse of the wheat trade in 1867, and the depression which began the same year, the farmers were desperate to preserve the one good market that remained to them. Arguments such as the one made in April, 1868 by Thomas Paxton had a profound effect upon their outlook:

> Reach, he knew, was the highest assessed township in the Province, and withall she was not progressing. Why was it, he would ask, that land won't sell for as much as it had years ago? The reason is that we are not progressing, but we have lain still and allowed others to come in and carry away out trade, and should we continue this practice any longer we are bound to retrograde if not go down entirely. We all know that the villages of this township pay one-fourth of the taxes but this will not continue; for the villages will go down unless the present opportunity is seized upon, and the farmers must see that as the villages go down their taxes will increase in an equal ratio; the merchant may pick up his goods, the manufacturer his machinery, the mechanic his tools and remove to some other place where business is prospering, but the farmer must remain; he can't move his lands. He must stay and bear the burden.[57]

The only major objection to Paxton's argument was raised by Adam Gordon of Manchester who asked how the farmers could know that the P.W. & P.P. was not designed simply to create a huge land speculation boom in Port Perry which would enrich the main promoters of the railway, but would leave the farmers carrying a greatly increased tax burden. In a long letter to the *Ontario Observer* Gordon made these points:

> When the Railway is completed, a town will undoubtedly spring up at the Port Perry terminus, and the ratable property of that *special locality* will be greatly increased; but this will not lessen the taxes of the *Township* ratepayers, as the probability is, that the Port Perry people will at once apply to be set off from the township, and set up a separate municipality, . . . The great property holders at Port Perry such as

> Messrs. Paxton, Bigelow, Sexton and Perry, will have but light taxes, while at the same time reaping a harvest of profit, caused by the rapid growth of the town and the consequent enhancement of the value of their extensive real estate.[58]

In spite of Gordon's concern, the P.W. & P.P. bonus votes were held with little of the bitterness which characterized the battles in north Ontario. The Town of Whitby passed it on June 13; Reach, August 19, and Whitby Township on September 19. The only setback was the vote in Scugog Township which was held on October 13. There the bonus bylaw for $4,000 was defeated by "a large majority".[59] The loss in Scugog, because of the small amount involved, was more an embarrassment than a hindrance. With $95,000 in the till (and the promise of an additional $10,000 from Reach should the Uxbridge branch be built), the directors of the P.W. & P.P. decided to go ahead with the railway, and on October 14, 1868 announced that they were calling tenders for the contract immediately.[60] Thus while the Toronto and Nipissing was still deeply involved in its struggle to persuade local municipal councils to submit its bonus bylaws to the people, and two months before it had received the $150,000 vote in Toronto, the Whitby endeavour was ready to begin.

It did not take the Port Whitby and Port Perry directors long to discover that it was one thing to persuade the voters to back a bonus bylaw but quite another to sell them stock in the railway. At the time when the directors were advertising for tenders on the project, it was reported that not a single share had as yet been sold.[61] Moreover, in spite of a strong push by the P.W. & P.P. enterpreneurs during the month of October 1868, it is clear that little stock was taken, even by the promoters and merchants who stood to gain the most by the railway's construction. As was the case of the Toronto enterpreneurs, the Whitby and Port Perry businessmen were much freer with the taxpayers' money than with their own.

In spite of the slow rate in which the stock was taken up, the directors on November 10 were able to announce that they had signed an extremely favourable contract with the Toronto firm of Kestevan and Starrat to build the road on a broad gauge (5 feet, 6 inches) basis, and equip it for a total of $330,000. To obtain the contract, Kestevan and Starrat agreed to take $40,000 stock themselves, and to accept bonds in the railroad for a sum of $140,000. Thus, besides the $95,000 in bonuses already voted by the municipalities, the promoters were required to raise only $75,000 from the sale of stock in order to make up the remaining $55,000 on the contract and to raise $20,000 in order to purchase the right-of-way.[62] In spite of this favourable start, a month later the directors were forced to admit that the stock was still not selling "as readily as is desirable".[63]

Meanwhile the contractors had started work as soon as the contract was signed, hiring subcontractors and a large number of labourers to begin clearing the right-of-way. But as time dragged on and no stock was sold, the

Port Perry Railway Station, c. 1872 *Public Archives of Ontario*

contractors soon found themselves in a difficult situation with payments coming due and, as yet, nothing received of the cash promised by the directors of the P.W. & P.P. Even more troubling was the fact that unless the P.W. & P.P. immediately sold a large portion of its stock, no bank or financier would buy or lend money against the railway's bonds. With bills and debts overdue and piling up, and several thousand dollars of its own money tied up on the construction, the construction firm of Kestevan and Starrat were forced to close down operations, leaving unpaid many of those who had undertaken subcontracts or who had advanced supplies and building materials to them. Commenting on the losses, the editor of the *Ontario Observer* remarked:

> This Company has passed through some rather odd phases. In the first instance a couple of contractors undertook to work and went on and expended several thousand dollars of their own money, and a good deal belonging to other people ... but when pay day came the poor contractors and their creditors found to their loss that they had been dealing with shadows.... The result was that the contractors got only experience for their pay, and the creditors had to take part of it.[64]

In spite of a court battle which lasted several years Kestevan and Starrat never managed to collect from the perpetually financially embarassed P.W. & P.P., and eventually the contracting firm was forced to declare itself bankrupt because of its P.W. & P.P. losses.[6]

On the grounds, presumably, that when the public refuses to risk their money on the shares of a short railway, they might be persuaded to take stock in a longer one, the Port Whitby and Port Perry promoters now applied to the legislature for an extension of their line to Beaverton and the right to build a branch line to Uxbridge.[66]

In spite of the failure of Kestevan and Starrat, and the difficulties experienced in selling shares, the village of Port Perry began to experience a rapid expansion as businessmen, crafts workers and labourers rushed in to take advantage of the expected economic boom once the P.W. & P.P. railway was completed. It was significant that already some of the businesses and professional men from nearby towns had already begun to publish notices of their impending moves to Port Perry.[67] The *Ontario Observer* described the local changes in this way:

> We have Manchester, the natural, the legal, and the grain centre of the municipality. We have Prince Albert, the commercial centre, and Port Perry, the manufacturing centre. It is not to be expected that this state of things can continue long. About the commencement of the present year our enterprising neighbours at Port Perry determined by one grand united effort to give that village such a push as would drive it ahead of its competitors and secure for it a more prominent position in the township.[68]

The editorialist then went on to point out that in the past six months in Port Perry a grammar school had been established, a "somewhat expensive" Anglican church and a "handsome" Presbyterian church were built, a carriage factory was established, and two new commercial buildings had been erected – one a frame building containing two stores owned by Mr. Allison and the second, a brick block building owned by Joseph Bigelow, one of the P.W. & P.P. promoters.[69] Thus within a short period after the railway had been proposed, Port Perry surpassed in population its two older and larger rivals, Prince Albert and Manchester.

Except for obtaining the amendment to the P.W. & P.P. charter, and for their ill-fated venture into the railway wars of Brock in February, 1869, the railway scene in south Ontario remained generally quiet all winter. Since the company could not legally come into being until $100,000 worth of stock had been subscribed for, and a first payment of 10 percent paid thereon, the collapse of Kestevan and Starrat, who had agreed to take up $40,000 worth of shares, had left the railway promoters far short of the necessary total. Indeed, by July 2, 1869, it was reliably reported that no more than $60,000 of the necessary $100,000 had been subscribed.[70]

In July, however, the P.W. & P.P. directors unveiled a number of new plans intended to raise the necessary money to begin legal operations. The first effort, to persuade the Reach Township Council to divert the $10,000 voted for an Uxbridge branch from that extension to the main line, brought the first major intervention of the Toronto and Nipissing into P.W. & P.P. affairs. In order to persuade the Reach council to make this change, the P.W. & P.P. promised a route change so that rather than following an extreme easterly route by-passing both Manchester and Prince Albert, it would now follow a more central route, passing between the two villages, thereby preserving their grain and mercantile trade.[71] This move certainly pleased the residents of Manchester and Prince Albert, and the Reach Council quickly voted to send the changed bylaw to a municipal referendum. It was at this point that George Laidlaw of the T. & N. entered the picture.

In a strongly worded letter printed in the *Ontario Observer*, Laidlaw pointed out that although the Toronto and Nipissing route crossed the northwest corner of Reach Township, the T. & N. had neither asked for nor received a bonus from Reach. Condemning the attempt by the P.W. & P.P. to get possession of the $10,000 voted originally in aid of the Uxbridge branch, Laidlaw demanded that justice be done, and the $10,000 be given to his line. Having stated his case, Laidlaw warned:

> The Toronto and Nipissing have claimed from Reach an equitable share of support. That claim will have to be met by direct measures on behalf of the Township, or the Toronto and Nipissing Company will have to collect it by *indirect means*, on the passengers and traffic of Reach.[72]

Apparently fed up with the constant demands and attempts of railway promoters to extort more money from them, the ratepayers of Reach defeated the bonus amendment by 322 to 192. Fully 150 of the 192 votes in favour of the change came from Port Perry.[73]

The second method hit upon by the P.W. & P.P. enterpreneurs was an attempt to persuade the local municipalities to buy stock in the railway, in addition to the bonuses already voted. Under this plan, the Town of Whitby, Whitby Township and Reach were each to purchase $10,000 of stock. Although the Whitby Town Council (which was controlled by the P.W. & P.P. directors) quickly approved the purchase of $10,000 worth of stock, the other municipalities clearly had had enough. Both the Whitby Township and Reach Councils rejected the stock-purchase request out of hand.[74] Finally, after a short campaign, the P.W. & P.P. directors persuaded the Scugog ratepayers to vote the railway a $2,000 bonus.[75] Thus with stock subscribed for a total of $70,000 and bonuses promised of $97,000, the Port Whitby and Port Perry directors once again set out to find a contractor for the railway.

The question as to whether the P.W. & P.P. directors found the next contractor – or whether it was he that found them – would long be debated in Ontario County. On September 1, 1869, the railway directors announced that the contract had been awarded to J.H. Dumble, an experienced railway contractor and operator from Cobourg. Dumble, they said, had agreed to build the road and to equip it for a total of $350,000, and, in order to make the railway a legal entity, he had promised to accept a total of $30,000 in shares as part of his pay. Dumble was to begin work on September 15, 1869, and complete the project by August 31, 1870.[76] Thus, in spite of all the problems and delays, the P.W. & P.P. was to begin construction less than three weeks later than the Toronto and Nipissing.

In order to give the P.W. & P.P. a glorious send-off (and, perhaps, to encourage the sale of shares) His Royal Highness Prince Arthur, who was touring Canada, was invited to turn the first sod. To everyone's surprise and joy, the Prince accepted, and the date for the official opening was set for October 6, 1869. The event was a gala affair. As W.H. Higgins remembered the scene:

> No fewer than about one hundred carriages and many equestrians waited at the station, and accompanied the procession thence to the town. The town-bells rang out, cannon belched forth, the bands played martial airs, and the Prince's party received a right royal and hearty greeting from the loyal people of the Town of Whitby. Everywhere arches and decorations were visible, and flags, banners and streamers fluttered in the breeze.[77]

Innumerable speeches were made and addresses presented, after which His Royal Highness, the Governor-General, Joseph Bigelow and J.H. Dumble descended from the platform to go through the ceremonial sod-turning:

> A handsome silver spade, and a bird'e-eye maple wheelbarrow, specially prepared for the occasion . . . were brought into requisition, and the Prince, with much ease and deliberation, performed the ceremony "of turning the first sod" of the Whitby and Port Perry Railway amidst ringing shouts of applause.[78]

As Higgins noted, however, "The auspicious proceedings with which the turning of the first sod was inaugurated did not help the road along".[79]

Although the first few week after the official inauguration brought bits of encouraging news about the progress being made on the P.W. & P.P., it soon became clear that there was much more involved in the Dumble contract than had immediately met the eye. Several of the directors, particularly Dr. Gunn and James Holden, began to complain that they were not informed of meetings of the board of directors, and rumours of illegal actions on the part of the contractor and directors soon began to circulate.[80] Indeed, before long it became public knowledge that far from being the substantial businessman that had been portrayed, Dumble was little more than a swindler, bent upon looting the treasury of the P.W. & P.P. through false certificates of performance, and inflated subcontract agreements. Moreover, all this was being carried out apparently with the active cooperation and mutual profit of Joseph Bigelow, the president of the railway. Several other directors (particularly those who stood to profit most from land speculation in Port Perry) were also suspected of being deeply implicated.[81] The Bigelow-Dumble coalition was particularly notorious. As the *Ontario Observer* explained the arrangement:

> We are told, for instance, that the Directors presented the Contractor with a gratuity of $30,000 worth of Stock, and that he in return agreed to allow the President of the Company to furnish the fencing stuff at

> a price which would allow the President to pocket a pretty handsome amount. But the contractor is not responsible to the people for this. What man would refuse $30,000 if he were offered it and could obtain it by giving a *quid pro quo* to the extent of five or six thousand dollars.[82]

As a later accounting revealed, Dumble had through a variety of devices received a total of $105,000, made up for $63,000 in P.W. & P.P. bonds, $12,000 in stocks, and $30,000 in cash. The total value of work performed by Dumble never exceeded $50,000.[83]

Having exhausted the P.W. & P.P. treasury, Dumble, Bigelow and the other implicated directors now fell to quarelling among themselves, and began suing each other.[84] Dumble, seeing that no more could be extracted from the line, sold his "interest" to a Toronto contractor named English, and left the scene. It was left to the *Ontario Observer* to have the last word concerning Dumble's short but profitable career:

> The poor contractors [Kestevan and Starrat] being buried, the traps were again set, and it was not long ere another contractor is caught. This one—the trappers pronounced as "no fool" (we guess that they have found that to their sorrow.) The trappers pronounced him to be as rich "as Croesus and as sharp as a brier", and in fact the mention of the name of Mr. Dumble put them into ecstacies, and his word was law with the majority of the Board. They presented him with all the stock he wished. . . . Taking and giving were the order of the day, and if the funds had been inexhaustible, there is no saying how long this honeymoon would have continued; but like all other subluminary enterprises, this delectable state of things was liable to change; and when the means of taking ceased, the work of giving became irksome. . . . Mr. Dumble finding, however, that his late admirers began to cool, and latterly to fail in coming to time, was accordingly proclaimed, and the contractor applied to the courts in order to bring his quondam friends to their senses, and here the matter rests.[85]

Mr. English, the new contractor, under the impression that the railway company was still solvent, brought in a large gang of railway workers, and for a short time during the early summer of 1871, made rapid progress on the construction work. But finding that no money was forthcoming when he presented his certificates of performance, Mr. English abandoned the work and entered suit against both Dumble and the P.W. & P.P. management. Eventually, English would collect $13,500 from Dumble and $46,000 from the P.W. & P.P. for his injuries.[86] On August 3, 1871, the *Ontario Observer* reported that:

> From all appearances affairs seem to be in a frightful plight, the poor miserable road lies curved and twisted like a serpent, forsaken and deserted. The workmen, poor fellows, were starved off to a man, and now the concert lies waiting the next shuffle of the cards.[87]

While the Oshawa *Vindicator* remarked:

> The road is about as far from completion as ever. It is said the iron [rails] at the harbour belongs to the bank, the solitary locomotive to private individuals, and the stations to the men who built them. If the directors only hold out long enough the interest on the debentures will build the road. The municipalities have learned a lesson about aiding railroads.[88]

Their reputations in tatters, and faced with major losses in their land speculations and mercantile interests should the P.W. & P.P. be thrown into outright bankruptcy, a group of directors led by Joseph Bigelow and Chester Draper, owner of the Whitby Harbour Company, now decided it was necessary to gain complete control of the railroad before outside interests took it over for default. In particular, the Dominion Bank interests, led by James Holden (a director of both the P.W. & P.P. and the Dominion Bank who had opposed the Dumble-Paxton-Draper group from the beginning) now threatened to take control and to institute one of their number as president. Faced with such a threat, Bigelow now lent the railway some $20,000 so that work could proceed. Since no contractor would become involved in such a problematic situation, the directors appointed Edward Major as superintendent, and gave him authority to complete the route.[89]

The board's decision to carry on construction themselves led to a comic opera confrontation between English and Edward Major's recruits. The Oshawa *Vindicator* reported the incident as follows:

> Mr. Major, who was appointed supervisor, placed men on the road. The contractor [English] assembled a body of his workmen to drive off those sent by the Company, but a collision was prevented by constables who were placed along the line to preserve the peace. The contractor then arraigned a number of persons belonging to the Company before the Mayor of Whitby for trespass, but the case fell through. He next departed for Toronto to obtain a Chancery injunction against the Company.[90]

Since the matter was already before the courts the injunction was refused, and the board of directors was allowed to proceed.

Under Major's direction, the construction work progressed rapidly, although the controversy did not end. In order to complete the line as cheaply as possible, the directors decided to lay the track on a narrow gauge (4 feet, 8 inches between the rails) instead of a broad gauge (5 feet, 6 inches) which had been specified in some of the municipal bonus bylaws.[91] While the use of the narrow gauge did not affect the price of transportation of goods destined to be shipped from Whitby harbour, it did make it necessary to trans-ship all goods destined for Toronto and points along the Grand Trunk. Since the only direct economic advantage which the farmers could receive from the road had been the opening of the Toronto market to their dairy products and garden crops, this great increase in the cost of transportation, when rail cars from the P.W. & P.P. could no longer run over the Grand Trunk tracks directly to Toronto, was bitterly resented. As a result, both Reach and Scugog withheld the final installments of their bonuses to the railway on the grounds that the P.W. & P.P. had broken their agreement. In return, the P.W. & P.P. directors once again solved the problems created by their illegal behaviour by persuading the Ontario Legislature to pass an amendment to their charter which required all the municipalities to pay up their bonuses even though the terms for the bonuses had not been fulfilled.[92]

In spite of the constant upheaval which this and similar problems created, the construction work progressed to the point that although the line was, as yet, unfit for regular traffic, a train was able to reach Port Perry for an "official opening" ceremony on November 15, 1871. Regular scheduled service did not begin until June 1, 1872, when the line began to carry the mails between Whitby and Port Perry.[93]

In spite of the best efforts of Joseph Bigelow, Chester Draper and the other directors, the P.W. & P.P. was so badly constructed and under-capitalized that it never achieved either a profit or even an assured schedule. Eventually, in the spring of 1873, with the wages of their employees months in arrears,[94] and the interest on both debentures and floating loans unpaid, the directors decided to sell the road to the highest bidder. Once again it was James Holden and his associates in the Dominion Bank who entered the scene. Holden's interest in the railway had a simple economic basis: as one of the original large shareholders, he had been forced to watch his stocks deteriorate to less than one-seventh of their value in just two years. If the railroad could be rescued and put on a paying basis, there was still the possibility that he could recover his losses.[95]

The agreement drawn up between the Dominion Bank group and the directors of the Port Whitby and Port Perry railway was most revealing. Although a total of $448,208 had been poured into construction, an independent evaluator placed the actual worth of work completed at only $165,000, leaving more than $280,000 to be accounted for through fraud and mismanagement. At the same time it was estimated that it would require an additional $81,000 to put the rail line in good working order on the narrow gauge principle.[96] Once the sale of the railroad's assets was completed, James Austin, President of the Dominion Bank, became president of the P.W. & P.P. as well, while James Holden and Chester Draper remained on the board of directors to represent the few shareholders from Ontario County who retained their interest in the road.

It was the intention of the Dominion Bank group to extend the Port Whitby and Port Perry line of communications inland to Victoria County to acquire the northern timber trade, in competition with the Port Hope and Lindsay and Beaverton railway and the Toronto and Nipissing line. In spite of expending a large amount of money on the construction of extensive docks at Port Perry and the purchase of the steamboat *Victoria* to run three times a week each way between Port Perry and Lindsay, the P.W. & P.P. never managed to make substantial profits. The high cost of trans-shipment of goods from boat to train, and the slow speed of passenger travel by water gave both the T. & N. and the P.H., L. & B. an advantage over the Whitby line.

In 1876 the Port Whitby and Port Perry railway (now renamed the Whitby, Port Perry and Lindsay Railway Company) was extended to Lindsay, and in 1881 it was amalgamated with other local lines into the Midland Railway system.[97] Ironically, as one amalgamation followed another and new bonds were issued to replace old bonds, the P.W. & P.P. debts incurred under Joseph Bigelow eventually became part of the debt of the Canadian National Railway. As a result, although the track of the original P.W. & P.P. line has long been torn up and the right-of-way abandoned, Ontario County's citizens continue to be taxed to pay the interest on its debts.

Beaverton's experiences with the owners of the Port Hope, Lindsay and Beaverton Railway were almost as unhappy as those of the southern residents with the P.W. & P.P. line. No sooner had the P.H., L. & B. been assured of the $50,000 bonus from Thorah to complete its line to a terminus at Beaverton, than the owners of the road applied to the Ontario Legislature for the right to extend its line from Beaverton to Orillia and then to Georgian Bay. The residents of Thorah who had voted for the bonus in the belief that Beaverton would become the terminus of the railway and thus a major inland port were furious to find that they were about to be relegated to the status of a way-station along its route. At a public meeting called to oppose the extension, a motion was passed detailing the townspeople's grievances:

> Resolved: That whereas the Municipality of Thorah voted the large sum of $50,000 to aid the Port Hope, Lindsay and Beaverton as the proposed terminus, and whereas the same company are now . . . engaged in making arrangements to extend their road to Penetanguishene, or Lake St. John, thereby breaking faith with the ratepayers of Thorah, and depriving the Municipality of the increase of taxable property which would result from Beaverton being made the terminus . . . Therefore the council of Thorah are hereby respectfully requested to submit the whole arrangement with the Company to some high and legal authority.[98]

In spite of numerous protests such as this, on December 24, 1869, the Port Hope, Lindsay and Beaverton received permission from the Ontario Legislature to extend its line to Georgian Bay, and to change its name to the Midland Railway.[99] In spite of the controversy surrounding the extension, the Midland moved ahead quickly with its extension to Beaverton, the first trains reaching that town on December 23, 1870. On July 8, 1871, a regular daily Port Hope-Beaverton passenger and freight service was begun.[100] Just as Beaverton's residents had feared, however, the track was continued on to Orillia, and Beaverton's railway boom quickly subsided.

In contrast to the constant controversy and the charges of dishonesty and broken faith which had surrounded the promotion and building of the Port Whitby and Port Perry, and the Port Hope, Lindsay and Beaverton railways, the actual construction of the Toronto and Nipissing, once begun, proceeded smoothly. On September 9, 1869, tenders were called for clearing, grading and bridging along the Scarborough-Uxbridge section of the route, and on October 28, it was announced that the contract had been let to Mr. Ginty. Work began immediately.[101]

The lack of controversy concerning the Toronto and Nippissing, however, did not mean that there were not serious problems. The most serious problem was the slow sale of stock in the enterprise. On September 23, 1869 the first "call" on the subscribed stock (that is, a demand that those who had signed for stock should now pay ten percent of its face value) was made.[102] The results were disappointing; only $18,000 was produced.[103] Considering that this first thirty-mile section would cost a minimum of $450,000 to build and unless further stock was sold, the railway's funds would be exhausted by the time it was completed.[104] The directors, therefore, undertook an extensive campaign throughout the municipalities along the proposed route in an attempt to sell further shares.

Just as the P.W. & P.P. has used a gala opening ceremony to start its sales campaign, so the T. & N. also utilized a spectacular sod-turning to begin its push on stock sales. The T. & N. was unable to discover so glamorous a figure as Prince Arthur; however, the Honourable John Sandfield Macdonald, premier of Ontario, was willing to take part. The sod-turning ceremony at

The "John Shedden", locomotive on the Toronto and Nipissing Railway

Public Archives of Ontario

The Soil Turning Ceremony of the Toronto and Nipissing Railway, Cannington

Cannington Historical Society

Cannington on October 16, 1869 was described as follows by the Prince Albert *Ontario Observer*:

> Shortly after noon on Friday . . . a large number of carriages set out for Beaverton, on purpose to meet the Premier, the Provincial Secretary [Malcolm Cameron, a large shareholder in the T. & N.] and other members of the Government, the President and Directors of the Railway Company and others who had come from Toronto by way of Beaverton . . . The arches were all complete by noon on Friday. They were got up in excellent style and many of them at considerable expense. The mottoes on all of them were most appropriate: such as— "Welcome to the Premier", "Welcome to the Provincial Secretary", "Gooderham and Worts, the Friends of Progress", and others of a similar kind."[105]

The paper went on to describe in loving detail the sod-turning ceremony, the shovel used (with a handle of "polished maple with silver bands" and a blade "of steel plated with silver"), and the speeches and banquet which followed the event.

The Premier, John Sandfield Macdonald, took the opportunity to put pressure on local businessmen and municipal authorities to purchase shares and (in Brock Township's case) to hand over the bonus money before the construction of the railway was complete. He spoke, he said, as a strong supporter of the promoters of the Toronto and Nipissing "in whose interests we had met on the present occasion".

> He attributed a large share of the marked prosperity of the country during the past fifteen years to the greatly increased facilities for business offered by our railways; and he felt certain from the extraordinary energy put forth by the directors of the Toronto and Nipissing Railway that its success is beyond a doubt . . . This railway, he believed, would be a great benefit to the country at large and especially to that section of it through which it may pass. He would at least claim fair play for the promoters of this scheme; the efforts they had put forth had merited encouragement . . . and in view of the vast advantages to be derived from the undertaking, is it too much for the company to ask for a small amount to assist in the realization of those benefits, benefits which shall descend to their children, who shall bless them for bringing those advantages within their grasp.[108]

In spite of such a strong appeal by the Premier, little stock was sold in the rural areas. A year later, the directors reported that less than $200,000 of the total authorized stock had been taken up.[107]

The Toronto and Nipissing, like so many railways of the period, was finally financed almost entirely by the municipal bonuses and bonded debt. The reason that even the main promoters preferred to buy bonds rather than to subscribe to a large amount of shares was simple: if an enterprise lost money, the bondholders were still guaranteed their interest and if the bond interest should be defaulted, the bondholders could take over ownership of the railway, but the stockholders would lose their investment. Thus promoters preferred to purchase only enough stock to retain control of the board of directors, and then to sell the balance of shares to the public. The importance of retaining control of the railway's board of directors (at least during the construction period) was shown by an interesting transaction carried out by the directors of the Toronto and Nipissing in September 1870.

At a special meeting held in Toronto, the board of directors voted to sell to William Gooderham, the largest shareholder, bonds having a face value of $150,000. These bonds were discounted by $15,000 (that is sold to Gooderham for $135,000), thereby returning to Gooderham in a single transaction a sum far larger than the total purchase price of his shares. For their trouble, the directors voted themselves a commission on the bond sale of eight percent ($10,800), an amount sufficient to cover most of the cost of their own shares. Thus in one transaction the directors had recovered most of the capital that they had risked in promoting the railway. The real losers were the other shareholders who were not directors and the municipal taxpayers who had voted bonuses in the belief that all the money in the railway's treasury would be used in the actual construction of the work.[108] As the editor of the *Ontario Observer* commented, "This Commission is a stinger and takes the cream off the whole concern".[109]

While transactions concerning bonds, contracts, and stock manipulations provided opportunities for profiteering for promoters, the largest profits gained by the Toronto and Nipissing directors came from land speculation in the villages along its route. Here control of the route and placement of stations was crucial. In 1856 Joseph Gould had purchased a large property (about 280 acres consisting of the east half of lot 31 and lot 32, concession VI, in Uxbridge) just at the northern edge of the village. Thus, when the route of the T. & N. was being surveyed, Gould, as a director, was assured that the line would pass through his property on the north side of the village rather than taking the slightly more direct route to the south. Gould's biographer noted that after selling 30 acres of village lots (in the area around the T. & N. station) he had 250 acres left, free and clear, with the whole of the purchase money paid, "and $2,000 over, from this bold and lucky venture".[110]

In contrast to Gould, who was able to enhance the value of property that he already owned through the placement of the Uxbridge railway station, George Laidlaw's speculations in Cannington were based entirely on his prior knowledge of where the railway would run. Early in 1869, long before local residents had any knowledge of the proposed route of the T. & N., Laidlaw had purchased the Davidson property which lay just outside the little village of Cannington, and had fifty acres of it laid out in town lots. As soon as the T. & N. directors announced that the contract had been let to build the

Residence of Joseph Gould, Uxbridge *Public Archives of Ontario*

Interior of Mullen's Store, Cannington *Cannington Historical Society*

The Laidlaw Block, Cannington, c. 1875 *Cannington Historical Society*

Dobson's Woolen Mill, Cannington, c. 1878 *Cannington Historical Society*

railroad through Cannington, the two main roads bordering Laidlaw's lots were widened and named Cameron Street (after Matthew Crooks Cameron, a director of the T. & N.) and Laidlaw Street (after the promoter). All this was done with a good deal of pomp and ceremony.[111]

As railway construction approached Cannington, dozens of businessmen scrambled to buy lots in anticipation of the boom which would follow the arrival of the railway. The price of land skyrocketed, and, as Laidlaw had foreseen, the central location of his land made him the chief beneficiary of the boom. The Oshawa *Vindicator* reported one sale of lots in September 1870:

> If any one has an idea that speculation in lots has died out, we hope he will visit Cannington. On the 16th, at the sale of the Laidlaw farm which has been cut up into lots, a fifth of an acre was sold at $455. The price a short time ago was about $50 per acre.[112]

With profits of over 800 percent, there is little wonder that successful railway promoters became wealthy men.

Meanwhile, as the directors and promoters pursued their private interests, the construction of the railway continued. Because money was so scarce, construction proceeded slowly, requiring eighteen months to complete the first 30 mile section from Scarborough to Uxbridge. Finally, on April 17, 1871, the first train, loaded with Toronto dignitaries, arrived at the Uxbridge depot for the opening of the line. As the Uxbridge *Reformer* said of the event, "joy was unconfined", and the day and night were given over to revelries as the population greeted the prosperity that was sure to follow the arrival of the iron horse.[113]

Having completed the line to Uxbridge, the contractor refused to proceed further, and construction was continued under the direction of the chief engineer of the T. & N., Edmond Wragge. By November 1 track had reached Sunderland (which had recently changed its name from Jones' Corners in honour of the event) and by the end of the month trains were running to Cannington. Finally, a year later, the line was completed to Coboconk.[114] Thus, in spite of everything that the merchants of Whitby could do, and although the residents of the southern part of the country had made great financial sacrifices to preserve Whitby's control over the inland trade of Ontario County, the south's mercantile dominance of the north was broken forever. Unfortunately, as the northern residents soon discovered, the economic changes which accompanied the arrival of the railways quickly destroyed whatever advantages might have been gained by breaking Whitby's monopoly of northern trade.

SOCIAL CRISIS: ORGANIZATION FOR REFORM, 1871-75

The period 1851-71 had brought about a fundamental alteration of life in Ontario County; pioneer methods and social relations were swept aside by the introduction of mechanized agriculture, the rise of the inland villages, the industrialization of Oshawa (and to a much lesser degree, Whitby), the building of railroads, and the creation of new educational and moral systems. The next decade (1871-81) would see not only the confirmation of these but the destruction of much of the remaining economic autonomy. Until 1871 Whitby and Oshawa had managed to maintain a central position in the economy of Ontario County, but after that date they were gradually reduced to the status of economic satellites of Toronto. This reduced status, and the greater economic vulnerability which accompanied it, forced local leaders to develop new responses as they struggled to retain their position.

Although the rural inhabitants had complained long and bitterly before 1870 about the changes that were occurring – without questioning the basic social relations that caused them – after that date both farmers and labourers began to question the very existence of the capitalist system that was developing in Ontario County, and to introduce new organizational methods to combat its effects upon them. As a result of their efforts, the years 1870-75 would mark the end of an era, and would foreshadow many of the major social trends of modern times.

The immediate effect of the railways, as their promoters had promised, was the displacement of local trade from towns not on the lines to towns which had acquired a station. Nowhere was this more apparent than in Prince Albert and Port Perry. Until 1869 Prince Albert had been the largest village and the mercantile centre of Reach Township. As soon as the Port Whitby and Port Perry Railway contract was let, however, businessmen in Prince Albert, Manchester and Borelia began to look for suitable locations in Port Perry in the belief that farmers would inevitably transfer their mercantile business there as a by-product of their use of the Port Perry station. Thus even before the railway was begun in ernest, Port Perry began to demonstrate signs of growth. In 1870, the *Ontario Observer* noted that while nothing new was being built in Prince Albert,

> the Port Perry of 1869 is not the Port Perry of today. It has effectively burst the bonds which then confined it and it is stretching out its arms to the west, north and south with a giant's grasp. Buildings are springing up in groups, all of them respectable and many of them handsome.[1]

Within a year, well before the completion of the railway, the merchant shops and houses of Prince Albert began to stand empty as their owners scrambled to reap the expected wealth which they were sure the railway would bring to Port Perry. As one Reach Township councillor explained the process, in March 1872:

Queen Street, Port Perry, before 1884 — *Public Archives of Ontario*

Baldwin and Mill Streets, Brooklin, 1878 *Whitby Historical Society*

Claremont, early 1900s *Public Archives of Ontario*

> Port Perry was being rapidly built up and drawing away trade from the rest of the township. . . . The trade of the township instead of being divided among three or four villages, was being concentrated at one point, and hundreds of thousands of dollars worth of property are being moved into Port Perry from Prince Albert and other parts of the township.[2]

Of course, those businessmen who remained behind were distressed to see their neighbours abandoning the outlying villages, because of the likelihood that their customers would follow them to their new location. As local business declined, more were tempted to follow, with the result that by 1873 the advertising columns of the *Ontario Observer* were filled with notices of stores for rent in Prince Albert.[3] The editor of that newspaper, watching his fellow townsmen disappearing in droves, did his best to rally local loyalty and civic pride by praising those who remained. A long editorial about one such local businessman, Joshua Wright, was typical of his efforts:

> For many years Mr. Wright has been one of the chief props of this village. Besides running his tannery he has been engaged extensively in the manufacture of boots and shoes, thus employing a large number of hands, and through them expending thousands of dollars annually in the village. Mr. Wright as a businessman has always been active prompt and honourable. A few such men in any village would entirely expunge from its vocabulary that imbecile phrase: "going down", or render it harmless. Let only a dozen men, men who have made their fortunes in Prince Albert, take a leaf out of Mr. Wright's book and the tables will soon be turned. Should a dozen men of some means invest in manufactures, singly or more or less collectively in our midst, the happy effects would speedily follow: no longer would the inhabitants of this, one of the finest, villages in the province be found packing up their traps, hanging their harps on the willows, putting their fingers in their mouths, and setting out weeping, on a mournful, dreary pilgrimage to the land of the stranger in a neighbouring municipality.[4]

His efforts were in vain. In advertisements under such headlines as "With the Stream" or "Following the Cars", business after business announced its departure. Even the much-praised Joshua Wright moved his retail outlet to Port Perry although Wright's "Beaver Meadow Tannery" continued to operate in Prince Albert for several years.[5] Finally, facing bankruptcy, the *Ontario Observer* was forced to follow suit, and on August 28, 1873, announced that it too was moving to Port Perry. The editor's explanation of the move was simple and to the point:

> This [change of headquarters] is rendered necessary from the altered condition of our village, owing to the concentration of the greater part of the business of the township in the village of Port Perry; and a newspaper above all things, in order to be profitable to its proprietors and

> convenient to its patrons must have it headquarters as near as possible to the business centre of the locality in which it is published.[6]

Similar scenes of the removal of businesses from outlying towns to railway centres were played out over and over again throughout the County. Uxbridge doubled its population between 1864 and 1871 (from 600 to 1,200 residents), and between May and August, 1871, added another 300 inhabitants. The cost of this growth, however, was the destruction of towns such as Leaskdale, Sandford, Roseville and Epsom. The effect of the railways was not so much to create new retail trade as it was to concentrate that which already existed. The price of this concentration was disastrous for those who had, through hard work, built up the village trade of places such as Prince Albert or Leaskdale. What the railway promoters had brought (at least as far as local retail trade was concerned) was not progress but change: changes costly to retailers and citizens who lived in the by-passed villages, but immensely profitable to those such as John Ham Perry, James Dryden, Joseph Bigelow, Joseph Gould and George Laidlaw who owned land around the newly-erected railway stations.

One immediate by-product of the movement of population to Port Perry and Uxbridge was the incorporation of those two villages. The first to seek incorporation was Port Perry. On June 9, 1871, a motion to incorporate Port Perry was introduced to the Ontario County Council by William Sexton, reeve of Scugog seconded by James Holman, deputy reeve of Reach. It passed unanimously.[7] However, the question of the division of Reach Township's debt for the P.W. & P.P. bonus was not so harmoniously settled. This dispute finally went to arbitration, and in the end the debt was divided on the basis of assessment as of January 1, 1871. On that date, the village of Port Perry came into being.

The decision to incorporate Uxbridge proved to be much more controversial. Because of Uxbridge's rapid expansion from 1869 to 1871, it quickly outstripped its roads, sidewalks and other services. Since any expenditure for these created a general charge on the township, there was a natural reluctance for the farmers to tax themselves for the benefit of the village residents. Thus for local inhabitants to obtain these services quickly, it was necessary to separate from the township, and to incorporate Uxbridge village as a separate municipality.

No sooner had the movement for incorporation begun, however, than it became clear that the residents of the village were sharply divided on the question. On the one side were the largest property-holders led by Joseph Gould and his son Isaac, J.C. Fawcett, J. Plank and Edmund Wheler, while on the other were most of the residents who were anxious to obtain better municipal services. The issue, of course, was taxation. As long as the village was part of the township, the large property-holders who were opposed to extended services (because they would be required to pay most of the taxes) had natural allies among the farmers. Once separation occurred, however, they could easily be outvoted.[8]

In order to settle the issue, a public meeting was held on January 20, 1872. As discussion developed, it became clear that the farmers were as anxious as most of the residents to see Uxbridge incorporated. From the farmers' viewpoint, as long as Uxbridge village required services, they were in danger of being forced to pay for them – particularly since the village's growth promised that eventually its population would outnumber the rural residents. Faced with almost certain defeat, Gould and Wheler now changed their tack – arguing that the residents could incorporate if they liked, but that their mills and other property should be left in the township. As Joseph Gould argued:

> He thought that he and other large property-holders in the village should have been consulted. . . . He maintained that the boundary as described was one-sided and partial—that they had gone out of the way to take in a mill of his, and that he thought that the proper [thing] to do was to tear up the present petition and appoint a committee of five of the principal property-holders . . . to take in the propriety of incorporating and [to investigate the location of] the boundary of the proposed Corporation.[9]

Edmund Wheler, of course, supported Gould's arguments, and went on to say that at the time of the railway bonus vote, both he and Joseph Gould had promised the farmers that the railway's arrival would not bring about incorporation of the village.

In response to Gould's and Wheler's arguments, one merchant (Mr. Weeks) angrily stated that "he felt satisfied that Mr. Gould and Mr. Wheler would not for one moment expect the rate-payers of the village to sacrifice their interests to suit the views of one or two large property-holders".[10] The meeting then disintegrated into a general row. As the Uxbridge *Journal* reported:

> Mr. Gould took the floor and stated that he would speak until Sunday morning rather than the motion [to incorporate] would pass. . . . Mr. Keller . . . claimed that he had a right to state to the meeting that if Mr. Gould persisted in preventing the motion being put to the meeting, he (Keller) would say to the meeting that those in favor . . . would have the kindness to rise and leave the hall. Upon which, nearly every one . . . left the hall to Mr. Gould and about half a dozen more, including his sons, after which Mr. Gould admitted he was fairly beaten.[11]

Thus on June 5, 1872 the motion to incorporate the village was moved and seconded by Anson Button and Samuel Widdifield, the reeve and deputy reeve of Uxbridge Township, and was passed unanimously by the Ontario County Council. The new village of Uxbridge came into being on January 1, 1873.[12]

In spite of the golden promises made to local residents when the railroads were being promoted, once the first spurt of growth in the railway towns was over, it soon became clear that no further prosperity was to follow. By 1873, with both Port Perry and Uxbridge having grown to about 1,800 inhabitants, expansion stopped, and by 1881 no further growth had occurred.[13] In Whitby's case, the change was even more dramatic. Growth there had slowed drastically after 1861, and after 1871 there was a sharp decline in population, from 3,732 in 1871 to 3,140 in 1881.[14] The loss of the northern trade to Toronto and Port Hope had clearly undermined it economic base. In the long run then, the railways had brought little over-all or lasting prosperity to the villages.

The railway failed to reverse the economic tendencies that were creating such hardships for the poorer farmers. As Table XXXV shows, after 1871, the population of the rural areas continued to decline, particularly in the oldest settled areas. Only in the northern townships such as Thorah, Mara and Rama where new settlers were still clearing farms and acquiring further acreage did rural population increase. The cause of this decline throughout the County was the continuation of the process of mechanization which made small holdings economically non-viable. In the older townships in particular, while the number of farms declined sharply (see Table XXXVI), there was a slight increase in the total acreage occupied – resulting in an increase of more than ten percent in average farm size. Even in the still-expanding northern townships of Mara and Rama, the number of small farms (under 50 acres) declined from 88 and 57 in 1871 to 80 and 50 in 1881. Thus the extension of railways into the area had little effect on the tendencies of farm occupancy which had been established after 1861.

Table XXXV Ontario County, Census by Municipality, 1871–91[15]

	1871	*1881*	*1891*
Whitby E.	3,441	3,417	3,080
Oshawa V.	3,185	3,992	4,066
Whitby W.	3,220	2,946	2,551
Whitby T.	3,732	3,140	2,786
Pickering	7,375	6,883	5,998
Uxbridge	4,375	4,081	3,461
Uxbridge V.	—	1,824	2,023
Scott	2,775	2,563	2,342
Reach	5,252	4,949	4,190
Port Perry	1,557*	1,800	1,698
Scugog	880	768	662
Brock	5,175	4,378	4,071
Cannington	—	922	1,050
Thorah	1,965	2,542	1,623
Beaverton	—	—	850
Mara	2,697	3,237	3,152
Rama	904	1,370	1,752

* Report of census of the village at incorporation.[16]

Table XXXVI
Ontario County: Number of Farms, Acres Occupied, and Average Size by Municipality, 1871–81[17]

	*Farms**		*Acres Occupied*		*Average Acres*	
	1871	*1881*	*1871*	*1881*	*1871*	*1881*
Whitby E.	301	286	32,119	31,996	102.0	111.8
Oshawa V.	36	33	2,223	3,126	54.4	94.7
Whitby W.	285	266	29,945	31,178	101.8	117.2
Whitby T.	45	44	3,855	3,029	67.7	68.8
Pickering	735	666	70,252	66,505	93.6	100.0
Uxbridge	526	494	43,773	46,765	89.6	94.7
Uxbridge V.	—	15	—	1,806	—	120.4
Scott	360	341	39,244	43,723	115.3	109.7
Reach	552	548	56,163	57,000	99.1	104.0
Port Perry V.	—	22	—	3,678	—	167.2
Scugog	95	87	8,579	9,548	85.0	109.7
Brock	528	516	62,417	64,007	121.3	124.0
Cannington V.	—	15	—	998	—	66.5
Thorah	211	233	22,420	26,735	105.2	114.7
Mara	357	401	36,591	46,674	101.4	116.4
Rama	140	163	12,166	15,510	86.0	95.7

* Ten acres and over.

The pattern of agricultural activity in the area was unchanged by the railways. As table XXXVII illustrates, the proportion of land under cultivation continued to increase, although there was no great change in the proportion of land planted to wheat or in the number of animals owned by each farmer. Surprisingly, in spite of the fact that the railroad promoters had promised that Toronto would be a good market for locally grown produce and livestock, it would appear that few Ontario County farmers had been able to send produce there. Since neither butter nor other perishable food-stuffs were capable of being marketed profitably in Toronto, the number of milk cows per farm declined in the southern townships, although they continued to rise in the north, while swine, mutton and wool production declined in both areas. In all cases, however, changes were relatively small. In fact, the most significant change in crop production appeared to be the return of wheat planting in the northern townships to the 1861 levels. No doubt the burden of high taxation brought about by the railway debts made the decline of local agricultural prosperity that much more difficult to bear.

The greatest disillusionment awaiting local farmers came not from the failure of the railways to expand the produce market, but from their monopolization of the cordwood trade. In their original charter proposals and bonus

Table XXXVII
Ontario County: Agricultural Production, 1871–81[18]

	Whitby and Pickering		Northern Ontario	
	1871	1881	1871	1881
Total farms	1,408	1,295	2,684	2,835
Total acres occupied	138,394	140,664	281,353	323,214
Total acres cultivated	111,623	121,176	168,597	211,858
Percent cultivated	80.7	91.9	59.9	65.6
Total acres wheat	18,194	18,803	28,286	50,986
Percent wheat of cultivated land	16.3	15.5	16.8	24.1
Horses	5,139	5,589	6,677	8,788
Milch cows	6,997	6,116	10,169	11,342
Swine	9,334	6,914	16,187	15,132
Sheep	16,071	12,022	25,412	23,620
Wool produced (lbs.)	78,474	61,042	111,872	107,465
Horses per farm	3.6	4.3	2.5	3.1
Milch cows per farm	5.0	4.7	3.8	4.0
Swine per farm	6.6	5.3	6.0	5.3
Sheep per farm	11.3	9.3	9.5	8.2
Pounds of wool per farm	55.8	47.1	50.4	37.9

promises, the railway promoters (in particular those of the Toronto and Nipissing) had justified the introduction of the narrow-gauge principle on the grounds that it would have the effect of greatly lowering transportation costs of fuel wood to the benefit of both the poor in Toronto and the farmers in Ontario County. Moreover, the charter of the Toronto and Nipissing had established a fixed price for the freight charges on cordwood being shipped to Toronto. Since cordwood was a major producer of railway revenues, it was not long before the directors of the T. & N. found a way to evade the limitations imposed by their charter.

Early in 1873, a number of residents of Reach, Brock and Uxbridge began to complain publicly that the Toronto and Nipissing Railway was showing favouritism in transporting cordwood to Toronto. At a meeting held in Manchester on February 5 to discuss the question, one local farmer, a Mr. Campbell, complained:

> Parties connected with the companies have purchased all the cheap wood-lands accessible to the roads, and the poor ratepayers who gave their votes for bonuses on the strength of the bright prospects held out by those who canvassed for these bonuses . . . are being deceived as they find that they cannot sell wood except to the company and at the company's price; of course the company never says that they won't take

> it, but they never can supply cars to take away the poor settlers' cordwood.[19]

Campbell's charges were substantiated by a Mr. Chambers who appeared before the Brock Township Council meeting on February 7, 1873, to complain about the behaviour of the T. & N.:

> He had laid 400 cords at the Wick station and applied for cars again and again to get the wood forwarded, but he has only succeeded in obtaining three cars since the commencement of the season. If he sells to parties connected with the Company they have no trouble in getting it taken away.[20]

The Brock Council decided to write to the T. & N. management demanding an explanation and asking for an immediate change in their policies.

Not only was there agitation and concern in Ontario County about the "cordwood question", but in Toronto there was a growing anger at the monopoly practices of the railroads and fuel dealers, which had resulted in rising prices. It was E.D. Dodds, editor of the Toronto *Sun*, who brought matters to a head. In a series of articles denouncing the "cordwood ring" Dodd demanded a public accounting by the railroads and pointed his finger at William Gooderham as the chief protagonist of the price-fixing group.[21]

Within a week of Dodd's exposure of the situation, a huge indignation meeting was held in Toronto's St. Lawrence Hall which was attended by citizens of Toronto and by representatives of the townships along the railway line. At this meeting a number of resolutions were passed condemning the railway directors and fuelyard owners for their monopoly practices, and an investigating committee was established to look into the whole situation.[22]

The most ingenious answer to the problem of fuel monopolies was that put forward by the Toronto labour newspaper, the *Ontario Workman*. Instead of constantly exposing oneself to the mercies of the middlemen in trade, the *Workman* argued, why not form fuel cooperatives? "Every householder wants wood; let a number of them organize co-operative fuel associations - ten, twenty or thirty households together". By purchasing directly from the farmer, monopolies would be made impossible.[23] In the face of the constant public outcry and such proposals, the T. & N. abandoned its selective practices, and the price of fuel in Toronto dropped immediately. But while the issue soon died down, it did much to cause both farmers and workmen to question the morality of both businessmen and the capitalist system.

Although the railways appear to have had little direct effect upon local agricultural production, they did have an immediate effect on the nature and content of local manufacturing. Before the widespread building of railways, the northern villages had grown up around mercantile and industrial establishments. Because markets were small and transportation was expensive, most goods were made by self-employed craft workers. But with the building of the railroads, transportation of manufactured commodities became cheap enough for mass-produced goods from Toronto and other major manufacturing centres to compete locally.

Table XXXVIII
North Ontario County: Industrial Employment and Production, 1871–81[24]

	Number of Establishments		*Number of Employees*		*Total Wages Paid (Dollars)*		*Total Value of Production (Dollars)*	
	1871	*1881*	*1871*	*1881*	*1871*	*1881*	*1871*	*1881*
Blacksmiths	47	71	79	105	20,915	26,410	39,598	71,397
Boot & Shoe	34	22	71	46	17,935	13,135	53,719	40,009
Sawmills	44	37	409	428	75,164	96,149	304,175	495,170
Carriage Works	26	27	72	71	20,570	21,172	58,765	60,650
Flour and Gristmills	13	22	38	58	10,225	17,680	249,495	469,090
Lime Kilns	26	9	39	24	654	460	2,081	913
Tailor & Clothiers	13	12	30	54	6,085	9,935	18,826	31,315
Cooperages	9	7	18	11	2,510	2,695	4,735	7,217
Saddle & Harness	12	15	30	28	7,270	9,931	25,560	34,250
Shingle Making	14	3	36	18	3,051	5,050	6,102	14,500
Brick & Tile	7	3	37	17	4,173	2,800	7,450	9,350
Cabinet and Furniture	7	11	18	38	7,900	16,800	15,540	35,050
Tin and Sheet Metal	8	8	15	19	4,725	5,920	14,400	18,900
Tanneries	4	4	14	15	4,500	6,200	26,285	48,000
Dress & Millinery	3	12	5	43	275	6,050	1,600	28,630
Carpenters and Joiners	10	4	18	5	2,842	880	5,510	1,530
Agricultural Implements	2	3	28	12	6,750	4,200	10,900	7,000
Foundry and Machinery	2	4	61	58	23,000	19,600	70,500	69,500
Woolen Cloth	3	16	29	36	5,100	5,156	37,000	17,912
Total	284	290	1,047	1,086	223,649	270,223	952,241	1,460,383

As Table XXXVIII shows, the effect of this competition was to injure specific trades such as boot and shoe-making and agricultural implement manufacturing first, but more importantly, to restrict generally the normal increase in manufacturing that would have occurred under previous conditions. While activities directly related to farming, such as blacksmithing and grist milling, continued to increase as settlement spread into Thorah, Mara and Rama, no new manufacturing centres were started to serve the recent immigrants. Thus while the population of the northern area increased by 2,854 between 1871 and 1881 (from 25,580 to 28,434), manufacturing employment in the main industries increased by only 39 (from 1,047 to 1,086). As a result, the proportion of manufacturing employees in the northern townships declined from 4.0 percent to 3.1 percent of the population.

The largest employer in north Ontario County (using forty percent of the men and producing more than one-third of the value of goods) was the lumber industry. Large steam sawmills at Port Perry, Atherley and on Lake St. John in Rama produced millions of board feet of lumber and barrel staves for the Toronto and American markets. This trade would be temporary, and after 1881 would decline rapidly.

In contrast to the north, the southern townships, especially the village of Oshawa, would respond to improved transportation and the resulting enlargement of the industrial market area by a move from crafts production to more highly specialized forms of mass produced goods - particularly those that employed large numbers of female workers, such as dressmaking and millinery. Also noticeable is the disappearance of many of the primitive agriculturally-oriented activities such as lime kilns, shingle-making, blacksmithing and small local sawmills. The largest employers were relatively sophisticated manufacturing establishments such as cabinet and furniture makers (particularly the large factory in Oshawa owned by T.N. and W.H. Gibbs), agricultural implements manufacturers (especially the Cedar Dale works of the A.S. Whiting and Company) and foundry and machinery manufacturers (in particular, the Joseph Hall Works in Oshawa, and Brown and Patterson in Whitby). Several of these employed more than fifty men, and one, the Joseph Hall Works, occasionally employed more than one hundred and fifty men. As a result, while Whitby declined as a mercantile centre and experienced a sharp drop in population, Oshawa flourished, and local manufacturing employment in southern Ontario County increased from 1,413 to 1,612 (an increase from 7.1 percent of the population in 1871 to 7.9 percent in 1881). Thus the spread of railways had the effect of destroying craft production but of enhancing the growth of large-scale establishments. In the long run the same advantages that had encouraged the growth of Oshawa at the expense of manufacturing in the hinterland towns, would see many of Oshawa's industries collapse after 1881 because of competition from Toronto and Hamilton.

The growth of large manufacturing companies created more problems for crafts workers than simply their loss of independence. As transportation improved and competition increased on a world-wide basis, businessmen found themselves under pressure to replace highly skilled, highly paid crafts workers with low-paid, low-skilled labourers in order to meet competition. Although there was little indication that this process reached Oshawa's industries in the 1860s, by 1870 many people were concerned that local practices

Table XXXIX
South Ontario County: Industrial Employment and Production, 1871–81[25]

	Number of Establishments		Number of Employees		Total Wages Paid (Dollars)		Total Value of Production (Dollars)	
	1871	1881	1871	1881	1871	1881	1871	1881
Blacksmiths	41	36	77	56	21,084	10,656	50,020	34,875
Boot & Shoe	37	31	76	50	19,800	10,361	56,850	44,050
Sawmills	20	13	44	27	8,284	6,575	35,510	29,900
Carriage Works	30	22	89	71	28,095	18,300	63,317	50,000
Flour and Gristmills	21	24	65	66	21,541	19,715	950,707	757,475
Lime Kilns	10	1	11	1	293	10	935	125
Tailor & Clothiers	21	12	117	99	25,974	18,617	96,178	71,600
Cooperages	13	12	53	30	12,140	5,715	32,355	24,581
Saddle & Harness	9	11	30	24	6,910	4,740	23,150	19,040
Shingle Making	3	—	15	—	1,403	—	3,646	—
Brick & Tile	10	7	56	31	7,874	3,180	16,450	9,300
Cabinet and Furniture	9	6	219	202	65,814	59,620	191,700	178,760
Tin and Sheet Metal	6	8	20	63	5,600	10,390	18,000	41,200
Tanneries	10	5	77	96	25,550	36,000	160,900	264,000
Dress & Millinery	7	18	15	81	1,837	7,405	8,871	26,000
Carpenters and Joiners	6	8	17	33	4,575	9,240	11,150	54,040
Agricultural Implements	3	6	56	405	28,775	149,600	101,500	602,500
Foundry and Machinery	4	5	290	212	150,300	61,000	360,500	205,100
Woolen Cloth	3	3	86	65	16,900	14,050	134,000	95,500
Total	263	228	1,413	1,612	452,749	445,174	2,315,739	2,508,046

would soon follow the international example. The close local attention paid to a tailors' strike in Cork, Ireland, and the extensive local agitation on the "Chinese Question", showed the deep concern felt by local residents, particularly the rural community, about these social and economic transformations.

The first news that the Cork tailors had struck for better conditions was carried in the *Ontario Observer* on June 30, 1870. The reason for the strike was the reduction of wages by the employers; when the tailors resisted that reduction, low-wage German labour was imported to replace them. A riot resulted, and a large number of people were injured before the police restored order.[26]

The reaction of the *Ontario Observer* was most significant. Before this event all local papers had unanimously supported the quick suppression of social disorder without regard to cause; now for the first time since William Lyon Mackenzie's *Colonial Advocate* had argued the rights and duties of citizens to rebel against tyranny, a local voice again raised the question. The oppression discussed was not the tyranny of a Family Compact, but that of the conjunction of economic and political power. The degree to which the *Ontario Observer*'s editor was shaken by the Cork incidents was revealed in his news reports. This, for example, was his examination of the events of the third day of the Cork strike:

> The Cork tailors little daunted at their indifferent success on the two previous days, attacked the police and troops on Sunday and gave some of them some rather ugly knocks; many of the rioters fight at considerable distance, they get to the house tops and hurl down stones on the heads of their enemies. The cause of the oppressor against the oppressed is clustering round its friends and its foes, the troops and the police take the side of the petty tyrants while the working population join hands with the oppressed, and the consequence is that the strike is becoming general. Labourers in all departments are leaving, or threatening to. The steamship works are abandoned. Foundrymen have left work; even work-women stay at home and newsboys refuse to sell papers.[27]

The basis of the editor's concern was made clear in a long lead editorial published the same day, examining the relations of capital and labour on an international scale, and referring in particular to the lesson to be learned in Canada from the Irish strike:

> The constant aim of many unprincipled employers is to test to its very utmost the productive powers of the workman by the worst phases of the sweating system, and paying him in the inverse ratio of his production. . . . A case in point is now before us in the city of Cork, Ireland, there the sweating master tailors sought to screw their workmen down beneath the living point, the men remonstrated, and the haughty sweaters turn round, lock them out and send to Germany for hands to fill their places, and thus the trickly employers find willing tools and get one class of workmen to work against another, until the other is starved into obedience.[28]

The problem, as the editor pointed out, was much closer to home than Cork, Ireland. There were many employers in California who had begun to import indentured Chinese labourers to displace white workers, and there was beginning to be agitation in Canada by employers to import Chinese workers here as well. In the editor's words:

> Again look at our cousins across the lakes, what more despicable means could be employed than they are adopting to reduce the workman to

> a state no better than slavery . . . The money loving employers are doing their best to bring the . . . China-man into competition on the labour market with the American workman. . . . If the American workmen are willing to allow the continuance amongst them of a system more fraught with mischief and blacker than even slavery itself, they may do so; but if they do they will get time and opportunity to lament it when it is too late. Let a stand be taken at once, put a veto on the accursed system of sweating one class by another, and thus reduce the labouring portions of the community to the condition of paupers, and that is worse than slavery.[29]

Considering that for almost twenty years the equation of progress with the development of capitalist forms of production had gone unchallenged, this was a strong statement indeed.

Nor did the debate concerning the proper relationship between ownership and production end here. The following spring, a four-way newpaper debate broke out among the Whitby *Chronicle*, the Prince Albert *Ontario Observer*, the Oshawa *Vindicator* and the Uxbridge *Journal* concerning the revolt of the Paris Commune. The contrasting sympathies of the newspapers in the debate are illustrated in the descriptions of the *Communards'* decision to tear down a famous Paris landmark, the column in the Place Vendôme. In the words of the *Ontario Observer*:

> This emblem of spoliation and plunder is threatened with destruction. It is proposed that each National Guard in Paris, his wife and children should be presented with bronze medals in token of their "heroism" in defending Paris.[30]

In contrast the Uxbridge *Journal* denounced the decision:

> The destruction of the Vendôme Column by the Communists is perfectly in keeping with their past proceedings and could not have been perpetrated except by men lost to all sense of decency and patriotism. The memories that clung to this monument of triumph were full of pride and glory for France. . . . But the column must go down before the fury of the Communists as a souvenir of Monarchical rule. The decree for its destruction was couched in this language, 'The column of the Place Vendôme is a negation of fraternity and therefore let it be destroyed'.[31]

While events so distant from Ontario County as the revolt of the Paris Commune might seem a peculiar issue to engage so much local attention, its prominence was symptomatic of the questioning of social values that was occurring in the area.

To complicate matters, the Franco-Prussian War of 1870 had set off a wave of uncontrolled speculation and inflation. By the end of 1871 its effects had helped to create the first major socialist American labour organization, the American Workingmen's Association. The creation of this new form of worker organization was welcomed by the *Ontario Observer*:

> Measures are being perfected for an American Working Men's Association, with branches all over the United States and Canada. One part of the programme is a general strike to take place early next Spring, with a view of bettering the condition of working men, by securing them a fair share of the profits of their own labour, and shortening somewhat the hours of labour. The day has gone by when the sons of toil will be satisfied with working ten or twelve hours per day and at the same time receive such a pittance as puts it out of their power to maintain their family with any degree of comfort.[32]

The first trade union in Ontario County had come in 1866 with the establishment of an Assembly of the Iron Workers International Union by the journeymen moulders at the Joseph Hall Works.[33] So little importance had been attached to this event that no local newspaper made reference to the creation of local no. 136 IWIU, although occasional references were made after that date to social events such as the IWIU annual ball. This neglect should not be surprising. At this time unions were generally social organizations concerned almost entirely with welfare, death benefits, and employment opportunities for its members. Wages were fixed largely by custom, and only fully qualified craftsmen (that is journeymen who had completed a four-year apprenticeship) were eligible to join. Moreover, in Canada there was no sound legal basis for trade unions to bargain effectively for wages or conditions of labour. Strikes were illegal (they contravened laws against conspiracy and restraint of trade) and punishment by the courts had always been most severe. Thus the appearance of a large international labour organization which promised to organize all workers, whether fully-skilled craftsmen or not, and to bring about a general strike, threatened the businessmen, as well as the privileged position of the higher paid skilled workers.[34]

At first the organization of the American Workingmen's Association created little local anxiety, but the rapid spread and evident popularity of one of the Association's offshoots, the Nine Hours League, soon unsettled local businessmen. In a period when men, women and children laboured up to twelve hours per day, seventy-two hours per week, the demand for a nine-hour day, fifty-four hour week, appeared to many to be the first step toward a socialist revolution. The organization of a chapter of the movement in Oshawa on March 8, 1872 threw the local business community into a panic.[35]

The Oshawa *Reformer*, reporting the formation of the local branch of the Nine Hours League, launched an immediate counter-attack. Such organizations, it declared, served only to divide society. What was needed was a method by which the working man could help himself to achieve the ownership of property and a respectable position in society. This could be done, the editor asserted, by the creation of a home-building association whereby a man could save one or two dollars a week towards the purchase of a house for himself. The benefits of such an organization were many:

> The advantages of such action, too, would not cease merely with the securing of house and home, great as is that blessing. The man or boy who has saved money for a year or two, and bought something with it, has more than that, acquired the habit of saving and accumulation, is strengthened in the consciousness of the possession of property, begins to experience the self-reliance and prudence of the capitalist and land-owners. . . .
>
> Here is something better than the [communist] International, because it builds instead of tearing down—because it organizes for society instead of against it—because it aims to make every man a capitalist instead of robbing those who are; and the capital that it offers, too, is not merely the aggregation of moneys—it is the solid capital of health, content, and happiness.[36]

In contrast to the Oshawa *Reformer*, the *Ontario Observer* favoured the Nine Hours Movement, and spoke glowingly of the communist International:

> Of all the great and interesting movements of the nineteenth century the organization and development of the International society is one of the most significant and certainly the most important, an organization destined to revolutionize the labour mart and ultimately to raise the sons of sweat and toil to that position of comfort and importance of which they have hitherto been deprived and to which on every principle of right and justice, they have a legitimate claim. Under various names such as National Labour Leagues, Trades unions, etc., etc., the organization is rapidly spreading over all lands where the great body of workmen are sufficiently intelligent to realize the necessity for the organization and forsee the benefits certain to arise from it. . . .
>
> One of the first permanent steps towards [their] elevation is the short hour movement. . . . cheap philanthropy has long talked of the elevation of the working population as something of much importance, but it most likely would never have gone further than talk had the men themselves not inaugurated a scheme by which this desirable end might be made possible, the diminishing the hours of labour, and thus securing the necessary time for the proper cultivation of the mind by lessening the hours of labour and increasing the hours of study.[37]

The structure of the working class in Ontario County, however, soon proved a stumbling block for any widespread local militancy.

The division of the employees of the main industries in Oshawa between the well-paid highly skilled craftsmen (some of whom made up the membership of the local trade unions[38]), and the unskilled day labourers was a serious hindrance to any unified local action. The editor of the *Ontario Observer* had recognized this problem when he argued that "the better paid classes of workmen cared little for those whose labour did not command so high wages",[39] but expressed the hope that the current attempts by businessmen to reduce the craftsmen's status would overcome this problem and create unity in labour's ranks. As the first meeting of the Oshawa Nine Hours League demonstrated, he was doomed to be disappointed.

By the time that the first meeting of the Oshawa Nine Hours League was called on March 27, 1872, events elsewhere had already moved to the point of collision between workmen supporting the Nine Hours Movement and businessmen opposing it. Already strikes had broken out in Hamilton (among the machinists), Montreal (among the boot and shoemakers) and Toronto (among the printers and bookbinders). Efforts were being made on a province-wide basis to boycott the Toronto *Globe* whose publisher, George Brown, was the leader of the anti-nine hours forces - in Oshawa, for example, the *Reformer* reported that "about fifty of the Oshawa workingmen gave up taking the *Globe* last week on account of the stand it had taken against the 'nine hour' movement".[40]

In spite of growing bitterness elsewhere, and the presence of delegates from the striking organizations in Toronto and Hamilton, the Oshawa meeting took quite a different direction. The president of the local league, Mr. D. Porteous, set the tone of the meeting with his opening remarks.

> Mr. Porteous stated the object of the meeting—to support the 'nine hours' movement. He considered the request of the workingmen reasonable, and was not in favor of rash means being used to obtain it; but that the men should be moderate and secure it by arguments. He was opposed to strikes, although he believed they were the means of a great deal of good as well as harm; and concluded by advising the men not to strike but be moderate, and not to use angry words, as it would do them more harm than good.[41]

Porteous (and the other members of his committee) belonged to the group of well-off workmen that the *Ontario Observer* had referred to earlier, and being relatively well-paid, he was interested, above all, in appearing to be "respectable" in the eyes of the town's leading citizens. This the committee managed to do, for, as the Oshawa *Reformer* commented, "It would be useless for us to attempt to give the speeches made on the occasion - speeches that, had they come from professionals and not from working men, would be considered good.[42]

Unfortunately, logic and a respectable presentation by the workmen of the "facts" produced few results. In spite of a considerable degree of success in other towns in winning the nine-hour day, in Oshawa with such "respectable" leadership little improvement occurred. For a few months several local businessmen closed their factories one hour early on Satudays, but once local agitation died down, even that concession was taken back.[43] In spite of such limited local gains by labour, the newspapers in Ontario County continued to be dominated for months afterwards with news about the national and international struggles between capital and labour, and sharp local debates about the wages, working conditions and labour practices in local factories.[44]

Perhaps the most significant long term effect of the local labour unrest and the bitter debate regarding the relations between capital and labour was the keen attention paid to the local "labour vote" after that period. In the federal election of 1872, Truman P. White, the wealthy owner of the large woollen and grist mills at Whitevale in Pickering, ran as the "workingman's candidate", opposed to T.N. Gibbs whom he characterized as an "aristocrat". White's pre-election propaganda was most explicit:

> There are some of Mr. Gibbs' snobbish supporters who affect to sneer at Mr. White's pretensions, because he is a working man. This class of gentry (always more ornamental than useful) will be greatly shocked to learn that Mr. White is not only a working man, but that he is actually proud of the fact that he is a good mechanic. . . . Truman P. White is one of the men of the people; a man who does not believe in those broad distinctions between what are called the upper and lower class in the old country. He believes in the dignity of the Nine-hours system, and of giving the workingman a fair reward for daily toil.[45]

Although White himself was pro-labour, the Liberal Party was lead by George Brown who was the strongest anti-union figure in the country. On the other hand, John A. Macdonald, the Conservative leader, had promised to legalize trade unions. Thus although local labour sentiment leaned toward Truman White, to get favourable labour legislation it was necessary to vote for T.N. Gibbs, the Conservative. With no little bitterness (for Gibbs was notorious for his personal antagonism to labour) the Oshawa workmen voted for Gibbs, and he was elected.[46]

Even more important than the anxiety of political figures to cater to the "labour vote" was the first movement by workingmen to enter the political arena themselves. The first time a workman actually stood for public office in Ontario County was in the Port Perry municipal election in December 1871. Mr. Sheehey told a general meeting of ratepayers that he was running to put an end to both the railway scandals and the vicious political infighting that accompanied them. Moreover, he said, he was a representative of a class which did not have one of its members in the halls of power:

> He said he stood before them as a working man, a son of toil, a labouring man. . . . He would rather be out of it, but feels confident that he will be elected by a large majority, the working men will put him in, the working men of Port Perry will give him their support. We as working [men] are not dependent on the rich men of Port Perry, he is independent of them and don't expect their support.[47]

He was, however, a reluctant candidate, and when a pro-retrenchment merchant decided to run, Sheehey withdrew.

The following year, another labourer decided to contest the municipal elections in Oshawa. This time, however, Michael Quigley, an abrasive Irishman, was determined to fight to the end. The Oshawa *Reformer* gave the results:

> The contest here was very slow till about half-past two when Messrs. Thornton, Quigley and Luke were at the head of the polls, Messrs. Gibbs and Wall seeing that their chances for re-election were looking slim, sent for their "missionaries" to drum up votes and got a lot of slips printed with the name "Gibbs and Wall" on them. These were slung around the factory men and others, who came up to the hall, slip in hand, and *voted as directed*—for Gibbs and Wall. By this means these two gentlemen were elected with Mr. R.H. Thornton.[48]

Because there was no secret ballot (each voter was required to step up to the municipal clerk and announce his vote before the crowd) it was relatively easy, if illegal, to put pressure on employees to vote for the candidate of the employer's choice. James Brown "Heather Jock" described this process at work in the Oshawa municipal election:

> Here in the Cabinet Factory [owned by the Gibbs brothers], the president generally at election time requests the voters of the factory, as a personal favour, to vote for his "ticket". If he don't suceed, the manager next visits them, and, as was the case at the last general election, he will tell anyone who might be inclined to vote against the boss that "*It is no use voting against power, because power can retaliate*"—that generally fetches them.
>
> In the Joseph Hall Works, on occasion, the president [F.W. Glen], if he cannot succeed in getting the voters in his establishment to vote as he wants, he will request them not to vote at all, or, as I am informed was the case at an election of School Trustees some time ago, he told a man that he "would mind him" for voting contrary to his wishes. The man referred to had his wages cut a York shilling a day shortly afterwards; but of course, his voting against the boss had nothing to do with it—oh no.[49]

In the face of such problems, little wonder that Brown felt encouraged by the 170 votes received by Quigley. As Brown commented on the election:

> It may seem a small matter to record, but to those who know how workingmen in the Oshawa Cabinet Factory and Joseph Hall Works are in general importuned at elections, the fact that so many of the men in those establishments voted for one of their own number, gives us reason to hope that they will do better next time.[50]

Brown was over-optimistic, however. The constant opposition of leaders of social institutions (church, school, and on most occasions, the newspapers), their own embarrassment over their lack of learning, and the powerful economic opposition they faced, meant that it would be many decades before the labourers began to play a significant political role. Meanwhile, they had become a factor with which political and social leaders would have to reckon.

Just as the changes in the local economy had caused labourers and their supporters first to question the social and economic relations that were developing and then to attempt to change them through organizations such as the Nine Hours League, so too the farmers began to seek ways to organize against the growing economic power of bankers, merchants and manufacturers. For men who were as independent and as deeply committed to the myth of individual self-sufficiency as the farmers, creating such a cooperative movement was extremely difficult.

Their first steps towards formal economic cooperation was the establishment of a number of cheese factories in the early 1870s. The first step in the area to establish a cheese factory took place in Uxbridge and Scott in May, 1871. At a meeting held in the schoolhouse, in school section no. 2, Uxbridge, Ira Chapman, a master cheesemaker outlined the manner of operation of such an enterprise:

> All milk brought to the factory shall be weighed and booked to the party supplying it during the season; in case a party wishes to dispose of his milk, he [Chapman] was prepared to purchase it at nine cents per gallon, in which case it shall be booked to him. At the end of the season the gross amount of milk is ascertained, as also the whole amount of the cheese made therefrom. Each party gets the full amount of cheese which his milk makes, the proprieter charging two cents per pound for making and curing.[51]

Under the direction of a committee consisting of Chapman, William Kidd and E.H. Hilborn, the Uxbridge Cheese Factory accepted 132,824 pounds of milk from 31 patrons, and made 12,932 pounds of cheese during the summer of 1871.[52] Encouraged by this success, cheese factories were built at Udora and Sunderland in 1872,[53] and a fourth was built on lot 1, concession II, Pickering, in 1873.[54] Unfortunately, with the American border closed to cheese exports and, as yet, no well-developed marketing system for European exports, the growth of cheesemaking after its initial surge was very slow. In 1881 only three cheese factories were operating in Ontario County, one in Pickering and two in the north. The total value of cheese made was $2,000 in Pickering and $5,600 in the north. Dairying was still a poor alternative for farmers interested in diversifying production.

Although from an economic standpoint the cheese factory cooperatives had been only moderately successful, the cooperative principle was soon expanded. In February 1874 a number of farm families in East Whitby Township formed a farmers' club which was designed to operate generally along the lines of the Mechanics' Institutes. Calling themselves the "Foley Farm Club" (although they met at other centres such as Courtice, Taunton and Columbus), the group established a program of discussions on topics which were of special interest to "practical" farmers. The first four subjects were: February 20, "Has the importation of foreign-bred stock been beneficial to the country"; March 4, "What is the best breed of stock for this country"; April 27, "Country life is preferable to city life" (a debate); and May 11, "Practical working of the farm".[55]

The mode of operation of the farm club's meetings was an interesting attempt to prevent the opinion of "experts" from intruding upon the sound experience of such practical folk as themselves. Instead of bringing in speakers to address the meetings (as was the practice of the Mechanics' Institutes), the farmers relied on themselves. The May 11 meeting was described by the Oshawa *Reformer*:

> The evening was devoted to asking and answering questions pertaining to the practical workings of the farm. A committee being appointed at previous meetings to ask what questions they thought would be of importance in the practical pursuit of agriculture, and refer them to any member of the club they saw fit, the member to whom the question was referred was expected to give the club the benefit of his views thereon, and then to refer it to another until the subject was fully ventilated. By this means a large amount of practical experience is obtained, ideas of which perhaps many never before entertained are brought forward, many of them of a highly interesting and valuable character.[56]

Once the farmers began to discuss the practical problems that they faced, it was not long before they began to concentrate on their economic difficulties. With wheat prices dropping (from $1.23 per bushel for fall wheat in June 1873 to $0.94 in February, 1875[57]) the farmers found themselves in a serious cost-price squeeze, and began to look for methods of cutting costs. The Grange movement developing in the United States caught their attention.

The Grange, a secret society of farmers and their wives, had been founded in the United States in 1867. Its aims were to further the moral, social and economic interests of its members through their united action. Among its many professed objectives were:

> To foster mutual understanding and cooperation.
>
> To maintain inviolate our laws, and to emulate each other to hasten the good time coming.
>
> To reduce our expenses, both individual and corporate.
>
> To buy less and produce more, in order to make our farms self-sustaining.
>
> The discontinuance of the credit system, the mortgage system, the fashion system, and every other system tending to prodigality and bankruptcy.

> We propose meeting together, talking together, working together, buying together, selling together, and in general acting together for our mutual protection and advancement as occasion may require.
>
> For our business interests we desire to bring producers and consumers, farmers and manufacturers, into the most direct and friendly relation possible. Hence we must dispense with a surplus of middlemen; not that we are unfriendly to them, but we do not need them. Their surplus and the exactions diminish our profits.
>
> We are opposed to excessive salaries, high rates of interest, and exorbitant percent profits in trade. They greatly increase our burdens, and do not bear a proper proportion to the profit of producers.
>
> We emphatically and sincerely assert the off repeated truth, taught in our organic law, that the Grange is not a political or party organization.[58]

The Grange's motto was: "In essentials, Unity; in non-essentials, Liberty; in all things, Charity".

The Grange entered Canada in 1872 when Mr. Eben Thompson brought the order to Quebec. It grew slowly, and by the spring of 1874 only fifteen local units ("Subordinate Granges" as they were called) had been organized.[59] Almost from its organization the Foley Farm Club had been interested in the Grange movement,[60] but it was not until April 13, 1875 that they decided to organize themselves into a local "Subordinate Grange". Within six months other Subordinate Granges were established in Oshawa, Columbus, Pickering, Shirley and Cannington, and within a year others were organized at Uxbridge, Whitby, Scugog, Ashworth, Whitevale, Brougham, Kinsale, Manilla, Mount Zion (Balsam), Victoria Corners, Wilfred, Utica, Altona, Reach, Port Perry, Saintfield, Duffin's Creek, Myrtle, Claremont, Greenbank, Brooklin, and Zephyr.[61]

At first the local newspapers welcomed the appearance of the Grange movement in the area. As the Oshawa *Reformer* put it:

> To elevate the calling of the farmer—to improve his social condition, and to educate him as to his rights, duties, and interests, are all of great moment, not only to farmers, but to the whole community, and if the Grange is the means of accomplishing the tithe of its objects and aims, it will not have lived in vain.[62]

This approving attitude quickly disappeared, however, when the farmers began to use their organization to improve their economic position.

No sooner had the first local Granges been organized, than the members began to use their bargaining power to get lower prices from Oshawa merchants. The Oshawa *Reformer* reported:

> A Committee of grangers called at nearly all the stores in the village this week, and made the request that all members of the local granges

> be furnished goods at ten percent advance on invoice prices. Some of the storekeepers replied that they would be willing to treat for large quantities of goods at reduced rates, but they could not sell cheaper to one customer than another merely because he happened to be a member of a particular society.[63]

Within the week, however, when the grangers threatened to take their trade elsewhere, the storekeepers capitulated and "very satisfactory arrangements were entered into with the committee by some of the oldest and largest and most reliable houses in Town, in reference to the supply of goods".[64]

The newspapers, always on the alert to anything that might reduce the extent and profitability of local mercantile trade, now opposed the Grange. The Oshawa *Reformer* which had so recently supported the movement's social activities, now attacked its attempts to further the economic interests of its members:

> The Grangers are upon us. Two or three preliminary meetings have been held here, and merchants and mechanics are preparing to do business without profit. The terror inspired by the "tater bug" is nothing compared to this visitation of the head Grangers. Farmers are going into it because it is only to cost $5 and they are to get tea, tobacco, coats, cottons, implements, organs, pianos, and everything else for about half or less.[65]

On other occasions the *Reformer* denounced the movement for "the attempts now being made to . . . annihilate tradesmen, or – as they call them – middlemen".[66]

The Grange movement would, over the next decade, greatly expand its operations to include its own mutual fire insurance company, trust company, wholesale supply company, and factories to manufacture salt and soda.[67] At its peak, the movement in Ontario consisted of 821 Subordinate Granges, with a membership of tens of thousands.[68] For a group of men as individualistic as the farmers, it was a profound break with the past, and the first concrete recognition that their once-paramount position as the shapers of society was no more.

The century after 1870 would see the farmers undertake innumerable other organizations and strategies in the hope of at least slowing the inexhorable changes that were destroying the society and way of life that they had created. All would be in vain. The reins of political and economic power had passed into other hands, and henceforth the farmers would remain little more than reluctant passengers as the much-praised "car of progress" was driven forward.

It is difficult indeed to communicate the bitterness felt by rural residents about the changes that had occurred and continued to occur as time went on. In 1897 the editor of the Cannington *Gleaner* would look back over the previous decades and comment angrily upon them:

> The department stores have brought ruin to merchants in many of the small towns and villages within a hundred miles of Toronto and caused to be tenantless and unproductive many of the finest business buildings . . . because of the power of capital to centralize so much control and interest in these establishments. The provincial government has centralized all control over education, liquor licenses, appointments to municipal as well as provincial offices, and every petty kind of patronage that it can grasp. . . . The rights of the people to self-government are totally disregarded and they are imposed upon and robbed [by taxes] to appease the hungry maws of favourites of the ministry. . . . It acts on the same lines as the big trusts, monopolies, combines and political rings across the border and is as destructive of good government and local self-respect among the people.[69]

The first eighty years of white settlement in Ontario County had been eventful ones indeed. For the first two generations, with settlement sparse and capital almost non-existent, life was a constant struggle for all members of every family to wring a poor existence out of the reluctant frontier. The hardship and struggle forged a unique society which had its own visions, dreams and ideas. In particular these people, because of their own experiences, developed the belief that it was the men who tilled the soil or laboured in the workshops who were the real creators of wealth and the fundamental unit of society. It was inevitable that such a society had to come into conflict with an aristocratic government and a mercantile system based upon high-cost credit and monopoly relations.

After three decades of social and political struggle, those who agreed with the independent commodity producers' view of society achieved a constitutional system based on the principles of subsidiarity and the decentralization of political power. But hardly had that triumph been incorporated into the Baldwin municipal and educational reforms, than the social chaos caused by the processes of urbanization and industrialization began to push society toward greater social and moral regulation and the centralization that such controls require.

From 1850 to 1870, the dimensions of Ontario County coincided closely with the economic region centered around Whitby and Oshawa. The merchants and manufacturers of those two villages, however, were incapable of maintaining their economic dominance of the area once their competitors in Toronto decided to annex the northern part of the region. The railways, however, did far more than merely detach the northern townships. They first centralized the northern mercantile trade in the villages of Port Perry, Uxbridge and Cannington, and at the same time destroyed other villages which had been by-passed by the rail lines. Finally, they subjected the local independent crafts producers to competition from the large factories in urban centres, with the result that even those towns which had benefited initially by the railway soon stopped growing.

By 1870 the rise of industrial centres, the centralization of educational and social institutions and the growing concentration of economic and political power, led to the first major questioning of social relations since the days of the Clear Grits. The Nine Hours Movement and the Grange were significant for their political and economic effects and because they exemplified the marked decline of independence of both the crafts workers and the farmers. By 1875 the process of integration of local society into the larger Toronto-based economic and social region was established. Ontario County's story over the next century would, above all, consist of the diminishment of local institutions and values, and their replacement by those generated by and appropriate to that dominant metropolitan centre. The century-long struggle of local society to adjust to the new reality would be as complex and as difficult as that of the previous eighty years.

NOTES

Chapter 1
The Native Peoples

1. Reuben Gold Thwaites, ed., *Jesuit Relations and Allied Documents* (hereafter abbreviated *JRAD*) Cleveland, 1896-1901), VIII, p. 115; George T. Hunt, *The Wars of the Iroquois* (University of Wisconsin Press, 1967), p. 67.
2. *JRAD*, XIII, p. 239; XV, p. 155; Hunt, p. 59.
3. Hunt, pp. 56-59.
4. Hunt, p. 62.
5. *JRAD*, X, pp. 223, 225.
6. Hunt, p. 41.
7. *JRAD*, XLII, p. 265.
8. For instance, among the Six Nation Mohawks, the ancient and honoured name "Hiawatha" is still passed on in this way.
9. *JRAD*, XLII, pp. 55-57.
10. H.P. Biggar, ed., *The Works of Samuel Champlain* (Toronto, 1929), II, p. 24.
11. Biggar, III, p. 156.
12. *JRAD*, XVIII, p. 17.
13. *JRAD*, LI, p. 139.
14. *JRAD*, XXXVIII, p. 245.
15. *JRAD*, XVII, p. 141.
16. Biggar, III, p. 122.

17. Wilfrid and Elsie Jury, "Saint Louis, Huron Indian Village and Jesuit Mission Site", University of Western Ontario Museum Bulletin, no. 10 (n.d.).
18. Ibid., p. 8.
19. *JRAD*, VIII, p. 107.
20. Father Gabriel Sagard, *The Long Journey To The Country of the Huron* (Toronto, 1939), pp. 94-95.
21. *JRAD*, XVIII, pp. 13-15.
22. *JRAD*, XLIII, p. 139.
23. *JRAD*, XXXVIII, p. 257.
24. For an excellent analysis of the development of native peoples from contact to colonial dependency see E. Palmer Patterson II, *The Canadian Indian, a History Since 1500* (Don Mills, 1972), Section I, "The Colonial Parallel: A View of Canadian Indian History".
25. There is some confusion among historians as to which nation actually inhabited the villages. For instance, Morris Bishop in *Champlain* (Toronto, 1964) p. 36, stated that the Stadaconans were Huron while Gustav Lanctot in *History of Canada* (Toronto, 1963) I, pp. 104-5, argues that the Stadaconans were Iroquois who were held in vassallage by the Hurons of Hochelaga.
26. Lanctot, I, p. 59.
27. Lanctot, I, pp. 104-5.
28. See Bishop, pp. 201-210 for an account of the expedition.
29. Bruce G. Trigger, "The French Presence in Huronia: The Structure of Franco-Huron Relations in the First Half of the Seventeenth Century", *Canadian Historical Review* (hereafter abbreviated *CHR*), XLIX (1968), no. 2, pp. 107-41; *JRAD*, XX, p. 19.
30. Trigger, p. 120; Sagard, I, p. 42.
31. Peter G. LeBlanc, S.J., "Indian Missionary Contact in Huronia, 1615-1649", *Ontario History* LX (1968) no. 3, p. 137. See also *JRAD*, VII, p. 15.
32. Trigger, p. 127.
33. *JRAD*, XXVII, p. 65.
34. Trigger, p. 128; *JRAD*, XIX, p. 223.
35. LeBlanc, p. 144.
36. *JRAD*, XXVIII, p. 57.
37. *JRAD*, X, p. 13; XIII, p. 171; Trigger, p. 137.
38. Trigger, pp. 133-34; *JRAD*, XIX, p. 191.
39. *JRAD*, XXXII, p. 179; Trigger, p. 134.
40. Trigger, pp. 135-39.
41. Hunt, pp. 101-2.
42. Percy J. Robinson, *Toronto During the French Regime, 1615-1793* (Toronto, 1965), pp. 15-16.
43. Robinson, p. 53.
44. Wm. A. MacKay, *The Pickering Story* (Township of Pickering, 1961), p. 10.
45. Robinson, pp. 21-22.
46. E.B. O'Callaghan, *Documents Relative to the Colonial History of the State of New York* (Albany, 1853-1887), IX, p. 30.
47. W. Vernon Kinietz, *The Indians of the Great Lakes* (Ann Arbour, 1940), p. 319.
48. For an interesting traditional view of the wars between the Council of the Three Fires and the Iroquois, see George Copway, *The Traditional History and Characteristic Sketches of the Ojibway Nation* (Boston, 1851).
49. A detailed (if biased) account of the French-Iroquois wars is given in Lanctot, II, pp. 100-131.
50. O'Callaghan, IV, p. 694. See also Robinson, p. 476.
51. O'Callaghan, IX, p. 889.
52. Diamond Jenness, *The Indians of Canada* (Ottawa, 1967), p. 279.
53. Ibid., pp.277-78.
54. For a description of Sahgimah, see H.G. Tucker, "A Warrior of the Odawahs", *Ontario Historical Society Papers and Records* (hereafter abbreviated *OHSPR*), XVIII (1920), pp. 32-35.

Chapter 2
Preparing for Settlement: Treaties and Surveys

1. Cited in Gilbert C. Paterson, "Land Settlement in Upper Canada, 1783-1840", Sixteenth Report of the Public Archives . . . of Ontario (Toronto, 1921), p. 220.
2. Robert Mathews to Lieutenant Colonel Mason Bolton, Haldimand Papers, B 104, p. 125. P.A.C. Cited in Florence B. Murray, *Muskoka and Haliburton 1615-1875* (Toronto, Champlain Society, 1963), p. 9.
3. Printed in Murray, pp. 10-14. The anonymous journal is discussed by Dr. Percy J. Robinson in "The Toronto Carrying Place", *Ontario History*, XXXIX, no. 1 (March, 1947), p. 42.
4. Quoted in Murray, p. 97.
5. Ibid., p. 99.
6. J.L. Morris, *Indians of Ontario* (Toronto, 1943), p. 9.
7. "Statement by Alexander McKee", June 10, 1795, Ministry of Natural Resources of Ontario, Williams Treaty File 2 (19388) (copy).
8. Paterson, p. 220.
9. Verschoyle Blake, *The Humber Valley Report*, Ontario Department of Planning and Development (Toronto, 1952) pp. 28-29.
10. Edith Firth, *The Town of York, 1793-1815* (Toronto, 1962), p. xxxiii. For a copy of these treaties see Government of Canada, *Indian Treaties and Surrenders* (Ottawa, 1891), I, pp. 32-36.
11. See Aitkin's letter dated September 15, 1788 printed in Percy Robinson, *Toronto During the French Regime, 1615-1793* (Toronto, 1965), pp. 166-67.
12. "Captain Anderson's Evidence", *Report of the Special Commissioners . . . to Investigate Indian Affairs in Canada* (Toronto, 1858), appendix 29, pp. 87-88.
13. This confusion is discussed in Paterson, p. 233.
14. This map is printed in Province of Canada, Legislative Council, *Sessional Papers*, 1847, no. I. vol. 6.
15. See the "Report of the Commissioners, A.S. Williams, R.V. Sinclair, and Uriah McFadden, to the Honourable James Lyons, Minister of Lands and Forests of Ontario, October 10, 1923", Williams Treaty File 2 (copy).
16. "Captain Anderson's Evidence", pp. 87-88.
17. Government of Canada, *Indian Treaties and Surrenders*, vol. I, Treaty no. 19, pp. 47-48.
18. Ibid., Treaty no. 61, p. 149.
19. "Report of the Commissioners . . . 1923".
20. R.V. Sinclair to E.L. Newcombe, Deputy Minister of Justice for Canada, November 23, 1916, in Williams Treaty File 2 (copy).
21. For a thorough discussion of the British Columbia Land Claims, and similar issues, see E. Palmer Patterson II, *The Canadian Indian, A History Since 1500* (Toronto, 1972), pp. 145-91.
22. See statement by Hon. Charles Stewart, July 8, 1924, Canada, House of Commons, *Debates*, V, pp. 4173-74.
23. See the discussion in Peter A. Cummings and Neil H. Mickenberg, eds., *Native Rights in Canada* (Toronto, 1972), pp. 115-17.
24. R.V. Sinclair to B.L. Newcombe, November 23, 1916, Williams Treaty File 2 (copy).
25. D.C. Scott to W.E. Raney, December 5, 1821, Williams Treaty File 1 (copy).
26. Deputy Minister [of Lands and Forests of Ontario] to Daley, Deputy Attorney General, December 20, 1921, Williams Treaty File 2 (copy).
27. "Memorandum of Agreement between the Government of the Dominion of Canada . . . and the Government of the Province of Ontario", April, 1923. Williams Treaty File 2 (copy).
28. Ibid.
29. See Williams Treaty File 2 for copies of these letters.
30. See the series of Letters no. 217130, Indian Affairs, Red Series, R.G. 10, P.A.C. On this reserve there are several instances of wills being altered or voided and estates being distributed according to the wishes of the Indian Agent rather than those of the deceased person.

31. Speech of July 8, 1924, Dominion of Canada, House of Commons, *Debates*, CLXIV, vol. 5, p. 4173.
32. Between September 12 and 23, 1923, the commissioners visited reserves at Georgina Island, Christian Island, Rama, Rice Lake, Mud Lake, Lake Scugog and Alderville. See "Report of the Commissioners . . . 1923".
33. Ibid.
34. Ibid.
35. Ibid.
36. Ibid.
37. Ibid.
38. Ibid.
39. See Honourable James Lyons, Minister of Lands and Forests of Ontario, to the Honourable Charles Stewart, Superintendent General of Indian Affairs, November 6, 1923, in Williams Treaty File 2 (copy).
40. A.S. Williams, R.V. Sinclair and Uriah McFadden to the Honourable James Lyons, October 18, 1923, Williams Treaty File 2 (copy).
41. A copy of the Ontario Order-in-Council of October 31, 1923 is included in the Williams Treaty File 2.
42. Dates are from the Williams Treaty itself.
43. Canada, Parliament, *Sessional Papers*, vol. LXI, no. 1, part 1, paper 1, pp. 82 ff.
44. In an internal review of the situation in 1930, F.E. Titus, a solicitor for the Ontario Department of Lands and Forests, noted to Mr. Cain, Deputy Minister of the Lands Branch, that the second part of the treaty had been suppressed in 1924. See Titus to Cain, August 29, 1930, in Williams Treaty File 2. On personal inquiry at the Information Canada offices on Yonge Street in Toronto, it was learned that copies of the Williams Treaty are not available to the public except by special permission of the Department of Indian Affairs.
45. For a discussion of survey practices see R. Louis Gentilcore, "Lines on the Land", *Ontario History*, vol. LXI, no. 2 (June, 1969), pp. 57-73.
46. J.E. Farewell, *County of Ontario: Short Notes as to Early Settlement and Progress of the County* (Whitby Gazette-Chronicle Press, 1907), p. 11.
47. John Graves Simcoe to Henry Dundas, *The Correspondence of Lieutenant Governor John Graves Simcoe*, ed. E.A. Cruikshank (Toronto, 1924), II, pp. 51-52.
48. See the Constitutional Act printed in Adam Shortt and Arthur G. Doughty, eds., *Documents Relating to the Constitutional History of Canada, 1759-1791* (Ottawa, 1918), pp. 1044-46.
49. Henry Dundas to John Graves Simcoe, May 2, 1793, *Simcoe Papers*, I, p. 32, shows the great emphasis the British Government placed on this point.

Chapter 3
Land Grants and Early Settlement, 1790-1820

1. Gerald Craig, *Upper Canada: the Formative Years, 1784-1841* (Toronto, 1963), p. 5.
2. Ibid., p. 12.
3. Smith's patent covered Concession I, lots, 1, 3, 4, 6, 7, 9, 10, 12, 13, 14; Con. II, lots 1, 2, 4, 5, 7, 8, 10, 11, 13, 14, 15; and the Broken Front, lots 1, 3, 4, 6, 7, 9, 10, 12, 13, 14, all in Pickering Township. See *Land Books of Upper Canada, Lands Patented to 1850,* (microfilm) P.A.O.
4. J.G. Simcoe to Henry Dundas, November 6, 1792, *Simcoe Papers*, V., p. 115.
5. "Minutes of Council, Land and State", p. 49, cited in Gilbert Paterson, p. 42.
6. Paterson, p. 43.

7. Ibid.
8. Advertisement from the *Mohawk Mercury*, Schenectady, New York, Aug. 25, 1795, Clipping in "Miscellaneous, 1795", P.A.O.
9. E.B. Littlehales to D.W. Smith, Jan. 6, 1796, *Simcoe Papers*, IV, pp. 169-70.
10. "Proclamation, May 25, 1896", *Simcoe Papers*, IV, p. 276.
11. *Upper Canada Land Book C, 1797-1802*, p. 106, P.A.C.
12. "Lands Patented to 1850", (microfilm) P.A.O. The Willcocks family received the following grants of land in Whitby Township:

	Concession	Lots	Date	Acres
W. Willcocks, Sr.	Br. Front	29, 30	March 14, 1798	1,000
(father)	I	29, 30		
	II	28, 29		
Eugenia Willcocks	II	21, 22, 25	Sept. 4, 1800	1,200
(daughter)	III	27		
	V	19, 20		
Maria Willcocks	II	19	Sept. 11, 1800	1,200
(daughter)	III	19, 20		
	IV	21, 22, 23		
Charles Willcocks	III	26, 27, 30	May 17, 1802	1,200
(son)		32, 33, 35		
Phoebe Willcocks	I	19, 20, 21	Nov. 25, 1802	1,200
(wife)		23, 24		
	II	23		
Phoebe Willcocks	IV	25, 26, 31	March 15, 1804	1,200
Baldwin (daughter)		32, 34, 35		

13. For a detailed account of the Emigrés see Lucy A. Textor, "A Colony of Emigrés in Canada, 1798-1816", *University of Toronto Studies in History and Economics*, vol. III, no. 1 (1905).
14. Paterson, p. 187.
15. Ibid., p. 188.
16. Chevalier de Marseul to de Puisaye, August 27, 1799, "Puisaye Papers", trans. Lucy Textor, p. 80. P.A.O.
17. The following emigrés received grants in Ontario County in 1807 and 1808 in compensation:

Le Chevalier de Marseul: Whitby — Con. VII, Lot 17
Scott — Con. V, Lots 22, 23
Scott — Con. VI, Lots 28, 29
Uxbridge — Con. I, Lots 25, 26, 28, 29, 37

Lieut. Col. Augustin Boiten: Scott — Con. I, Lot 27
Scott — Con. III, Lots 26, 27
Uxbridge — Con. IV, Lot S½ 10
Uxbridge — Con. VI, Lots 9, 10

René Augustin Comte de Charles: Scott — Con. VI, Lots 18, 19, 25

Jean Louis Vicomte de Charles: Scott — Con. IV, Lot 22
Scott — Con. VI, Lots 21, 22, 23
Uxbridge — Con. II, Lots 16, 17, 18

18. See Farewell, pp. 6-7 and pp. 18-19; also a clipping from the Oshawa *Times-Gazette* (n.d.) in the "Grafton Scrapbook", P.A.O., for a description of Wilson's settlement.
19. Ibid.

20. "Proclamation, Feb. 7, 1792", *Simcoe Papers*, I, pp. 108-9.

21. "Petitions read July 4, 1796", *Simcoe Papers*, V, p. 243.

22. Henry Scadding, *Toronto of Old* (Toronto, 1873), pp. 414-15.

23. "Lands Patented to 1850", Whitby Township, (microfilm) P.A.O.

24. Ibid. Pickering and Whitby Townships. The annual total of lands patented, 1795-1799, as follows:

	Pickering	*Whitby*	*Total Ontario Co.*
1795	4,800	—	4,800
1796	3,600	5,500	9,100
1797	—	—	—
1798	15,200	6,600	21,800
1799	4,800	3,100	7,900
	28,400	15,200	43,600

25. Ibid. The annual total of lands patented, 1800-1804, breaks down as follows:

	Pickering	*Whitby*	*Uxbridge*	*Total*
1800	1,200	3,600	—	4,800
1801	1,900	8,200	—	10,100
1802	2,800	12,150	—	14,950
1803	1,400	200	—	1,600
1804	1,000	1,630	3,000	5,630
	8,300	25,780	3,000	37,080

26. Ibid.

27. All these men are listed as being township officials either by Farewell, p. 3, or in the Ontario Archives, *Report*, 1932 (Toronto, 1933), p. 15.

28. Ibid., pp. 31, 44, 57 and 71.

29. "Provincial Secretary's Papers", R.G. 5, B 26, Vol. I, P.A.O.

30. Farewell, p. 13.

31. "Lands Patented to 1850". The annual total of lands patented, 1805-1809, breaks down as follows:

	Pickering	*Whitby*	*Uxbridge*	*Scott*	*Total*
1805	200	800	6,600	—	7,600
1806	200	—	9,200	—	9,400
1807	1,000	2,640	15,612	6,000	25,252
1808	1,000	420	2,400	12,700	16,340
1809	200	1,240	—	4,540	5,980
	2,600	5,100	33,812	23,240	64,572

32. Ibid. The annual total of lands patented, 1810-1814, breaks down as follows:

	Pickering	*Whitby*	*Uxbridge*	*Scott*	*Reach*	*Total*
1810	—	520	—	8,300	—	8,820
1811	450	400	—	650	36,300	37,800
1812	472	—	—	1,500	6,520	9,492
1813	200	—	—	—	—	200
1814	—	—	—	—	—	—
	1,122	920	—	10,450	43,820	56,312

33. By 1812 the detrimental results of the lavish land grants to "official" grantees were obvious:

	Lands Patented	*Percent Patented of lands available*	*Acres in hands of settlers, 1812*	*Acres Cultivated, 1812*	*Number Assessed*
Pickering	40,222	80.2%	10,359	819	53
Whitby	47,000	98.1%	8,422	660	47
Uxbridge	36,812	100.0%	*	*	—
Scott	33,690	95.9%	none	none	none
Reach	43,820	97.7%	none	none	none

* In 1812 Uxbridge was united with Whitchurch for the purposes of local government. Some idea of the rate of progress in Uxbridge can be gained by examining the totals for 1827, the second year that Uxbridge and Whitchurch were separated (no figures are available for 1826). In that year, of the 36,812 acres patented only 4,307 acres were in the hands of farmers, and of this only 1,137 acres were cultivated. Uxbridge's population in 1827 was 238, made up of 67 men, 67 women and 104 children. It is notable that it was in Pickering Township, the area with the lowest percentage of land granted, that settlement had progressed at the greatest rate. See "Provincial Secretary's Papers", R.C. 5, P.A.C.

34. The following lots were patented by the Quaker settlers:

Grantee	*Lot*	*Concession*	*Date Patented*
William Gold	31	V	April 13, 1804
Dr. Christopher Beswick	30	V	Sept. 19, 1805
Elijah Collins	21	V	Sept. 19, 1805
Robert Wilson	29	VI	Sept. 19, 1805
Joseph Collins	34	V	Sept. 19, 1805
James Hughs	22	V	Oct. 11, 1805
George Webb	23	V	Oct. 11, 1805

35. For a more detailed analysis of the effects of land policies upon settlement and social development see Leo A. Johnson, "Land Policy, Population Growth and Social Structure in Home District, 1793-1851", *Ontario History*, LXIII, no. 1 (March, 1971), pp. 41-60.
36. Upper Canada, Legislative Assembly, *Journals*, 1818, pp. 133-34, and appendix, p. 41.
37. Farewell, p. 33.
38. Lillian F. Gates, *Land Policies of Upper Canada* (Toronto, 1968), pp. 86 and 325.
39. See "Persons Receiving Military Grants under Order of June 18, 1817", P.A.O.
40. Gates, p. 92.
41. "Persons Receiving Military Grants . . . ", P.A.O.
42. Farewell, pp. 51-52; Prince Albert *North Ontario Observer*, September 24, 1874.

Chapter 4
Pioneer Society, 1790-1820

1. Population figures are from "Provincial Secretary's Papers", R.G. V, B 26, vols. I and VII, P.A.C.
2. Ibid., vol. VII.
3. Ibid.
4. Ibid. Calculations are my own.
5. Ibid.
6. Province of Canada, *Census of 1851-52,* vol. I, appendix II, pp. 36-39. Calculations are my own.
7. In 1824 William Lyon Mackenzie attacked the high fees because of the hardship they imposed on poor immigrants who were prevented from acquiring lands. See *Colonial Advocate*, July 29, 1824.
8. "Provincial Secretary's Papers", vols. I and VII.
9. See Farewell, pp. 12, 20 and 21.
10. Of note are an early tavern kept by Hawkins Woodruff in Pickering in 1805, and those kept by Jabez Lynde and Moody Farewell in Whitby Township in 1811. Early mills include that of Dr. Beswick (later completed by Joseph Collins) in Uxbridge in 1806 and that of Timothy Rogers at the mouth of Duffin's Creek in 1810. See Farewell, p. 12 and p. 45, and W.H. Higgins, *The Life and Times of Joseph Gould* (Toronto, 1887), pp. 67-68.
11. For a detailed description of pioneer life, see the many works by Edwin C. Guillet, particularly his *The Pioneer Farmer and Backwoodsman*, 2 vol. (Toronto, 1963).
12. David Gibson, "Conditions in York County a Century Ago", *OHSPR*, XXIV (1927), pp. 359-60.
13. These ashes were leached in "potasheries" and the resulting solution was boiled down in order to obtain their potassium content – a chemical used in the glass-making, textile and fertilizer industries.

14. Guillet, *Pioneer Farmer*, vol. I, p. 312.
15. Edwin C. Guillet, *Pioneer Life in the County of York* (Toronto, 1960), p. 29.
16. Ibid., p. 277.
17. John Howison, "The Pioneer Society of Upper Canada After the War of 1812", *Early Travellers in the Canadas*, ed. G. Craig (Toronto, 1955), p. 64.
18. Ibid.
19. W.H. Smith, *Canada: Past, Present and Future* (Toronto, 1851), I, p. 283.
20. Patrick Sherriff, "A Critical View of Upper Canada in the 1830's", in Craig, *Early Travellers*, p. 118.
21. Isaac Fidler, "The Advantages of Upper Canada Over the American States", in Craig, *Early Travellers*, p. 91.
22. Quoted in the Oshawa *Reformer*, March 9, 1877, *Oshawa Times* library holdings.
23. Ibid.
24. Higgins, p. 69.
25. Port Perry *North Ontario Observer*, September 24, 1874.
26. The works of Edwin C. Guillet provide rich details of pioneer technology and technique, as do many local histories.
27. William Thompson, *A Tradesman's Travels in the United States and Canada in the Years 1840, 41* & 42 (Edinburgh, 1842), pp. 104-5.
28. Thomas Hamilton, *Men and Manners in America*, cited in Guillet, *Pioneer Farmers*, II, p. 279.
29. "Journal of Mary Gapper O'Brien", Journal no. 12, February 21, 1829, P.A.O.
30. The best published study of the many boundary changes of the districts is G. W. Spragge, "The Districts of Upper Canada 1788-1849", *OHSPR*, XXXIX (1947), pp. 91-100.
31. J.M. McEvoy, "The Ontario Township", *University of Toronto in Political Science*, vol. I (1889), no. 1, p. 21.
32. C.R.W. Biggar, *Municipal Manual* (Toronto, 1901), p. 5.
33. Adam Shortt, "Municipal Government in Ontario", *University of Toronto Studies in History and Economics*, vol. II (1903), no. 2, p. 5.
34. Ibid. The first townships surveyed for the Loyalists along the St. Lawrence were numbered in this way.
35. *Journals and Proceedings of the House of Assembly of Upper Canada*, 1792, Q. vol. 279-81, pp. 87 f. P.A.C.
36. Ibid.
37. 33 George III, cap. 2.
38. 34 George III, cap. 8.
39. Farewell, p. 12.
40. Ontario Archives *Report*, 1921, pp. 15, 31, 44, 57, 71.
41. Farewell, p. 12.
42. "Provincial Secretary's Papers", vol. VII.
43. Ibid. In 1820 the rate of local taxation was one penny per pound for district purposes and 1/18th penny per pound for the salary of the member of the Legislative Assembly. In 1826 when the first separate assessment of Uxbridge was made the taxes amounted to £15.15s. 5½d.
44. 47 George III, cap. 6.
45. 4 George IV, Session 2, cap. 8.
46. See Robinson to Hillier, Jan. 12, 1824, "Upper Canada Sundries," P.A.O.; J.H. Aitchison, "The Development of Local Government in Upper Canada, 1783-1850", (Ph.D. Thesis, University of Toronto, 1953), p. 722.
47. The members of the Home District Board of Education were Grant Powell, William Allan, Alexander Wood, Peter Robinson and the Reverend John Strachan, all either members of the Family Compact or closely associated with them. For a more detailed description of the various school Acts see Aitchison, pp. 700 ff.
48. Higgins, p. 39.

49. Higgins, p. 133.
50. It is significant that many of these learned to write, or at least to sign their names, as adults. Many later records show signatures being used by those who had previously used crosses.
51. Uxbridge *Journal*, June 8, 1870.
52. Farewell, p. 21.
53. Farewell, p. 23. In 1875 the veterans of 1812-15 met in Toronto to commemorate their service. Of all those who had bravely defended Canada just seventy remained, including five from Ontario County. The latter included Thomas Henry, Moses Martin, David Bedford, Samuel Cochrane and a Mr. Fisher (whose first name was not given). For a brief description of their service see the Oshawa *Reformer*, October 8, 1875.

Chapter 5
Immigration and Settlement, 1820-40

1. For a more detailed analysis of these problems see Johnson, "Land Policy, Population Growth and Social Structure", pp. 55-56.
2. Craig, *Upper Canada*, pp. 188-209.
3. Statement by W. Allan and R.A. Tucker, Upper Canada, "State Papers", vol. 24.
4. Goderich to Aylmer, November 21, 1831, Province of Canada, *Journals of the Legislative Assembly*, 1852-1853, appendix U.U., no. 69.
5. Goderich to Aylmer, January 1, 1833, Ibid., no. 109.
6. See Craig, *Upper Canada*, pp. 134-38.
7. Lillian F. Gates, *Land Policies of Upper Canada* (Toronto, 1968), p. 169.
8. That is, one-seventh of all of Ontario County except Rama Township and the King's College endowment.
9. Mary Gapper O'Brien, "Diary", Journal X, February 6, 1829, P.A.O.
10. "Lands Patented to 1850". Calculations are my own. In addition to the 8,374 acres which were given to King's College in Pickering, Whitby and Uxbridge, the College received 200 acres from each of Reach and Brock, and 167 acres in Thorah.
11. Ibid.
12. Ibid.
13. Gates, pp. 136-38.
14. *Colonial Advocate*, 29 July 1824, cited in Margaret Fairley, *The Selected Writings of William Lyon Mackenzie, 1824-1837* (Toronto, 1960), pp. 18-19.
15. Fairley, p. 224.
16. Paterson, pp. 65-66.
17. For the best discussion of the Clergy Reserves see Alan Wilson, *The Clergy Reserves of Upper Canada: A Canadian Mortmain* (Toronto, 1967).
18. All data on Clergy Reserves is calculated from "Minutes of Clergy Corporation, Upper Canada", (microfilm) P.A.O.
19. According to the minutes of the Clergy Corporation the totals leased up to 1833 were: Pickering, 5,400; Whitby; 6,800; Uxbridge, 1,000; Reach, 3,200; Brock, 2,500; Thorah, 1,400; Scott, 400; and Mara, 1,000 – a total of 22,700 acres.
20. "Provincial Secretary's Papers", vols. I to VII; Upper Canada, *Journals of the Legislative Council*, 1828 to 1840, appendices.
21. For a comparison of development, see the maps in Johnson, "Land Settlement, Population Growth".
22. Higgins, p. 146; "Lands Patented to 1850", P.A.O.
23. The fullest account of the Thorah Cameron settlement is in Norman Macdonald, *Canada, 1763-1841: Immigration and Settlement* (Toronto, 1939), pp. 181 ff.
24. Gates, p. 95.
25. Macdonald, p. 182.
26. Upper Canada, *Land Book E*, p. 281, June 9, 1849; cited in Macdonald, p. 183.

27. "Persons Receiving Military Grants", P.A.O.
28. Higgins, p. 147; Farewell, p. 55.
29. Macdonald, p. 185.
30. Higgins, p. 147.
31. Ibid., pp. 150-51.
32. Ibid., p. 152. Benjamin Yarnold, Henry Fry and William Frederick Hill Rouke (Rooke) were among those whose lands were sold by the Bank of Upper Canada. Yarnold owned 691 acres; Fry, 713 acres; and Rouke, 461 acres almost all of which was along the Lake Couchiching front. See "Lands Patented to 1850".
33. Farewell, pp. 13-14.
34. "Canada West Census, 1842", (microfilm no. 1344) P.A.C. Calculations are my own.
35. Ibid.
36. Upper Canada, *Journals of the Legislative Assembly, 1840*, p. 146, "A Return of the Religious Denominations of Home District for the Year 1839".
37. Canada, *Census, 1860-61* (Quebec, 1963), vol. I.
38. "Canada West Census, 1842" in "Provincial Secretary's Papers", vol. VII; *Journals of the Legislative Assembly of Upper Canada*, appropriate years.
39. Ibid.
40. Ibid.
41. Capital in this sense, of course, did not refer merely to money, but to the accumulation of all assets such as cleared fields, buildings, livestock, tools and machinery. For a contemporary discussion, see Edward Gibbon Wakefield, *England and America*, 2 vols. (London, 1833), and also his *Statement of the Principles and Objectives of a proposed National Society for the Cure and Prevention of Pauperism by means of Systematic Colonization* (London, 1830).
42. George Walton, *City of Toronto and Home District Registry, 1837* (Toronto, 1837), places two Dows in Whitby Township: William Dow, Jr., Concession V, Lot 19, and Peter Dow, Concession II, Lot 23. Since the anonymous writer places his Mr. Dow in Concession III, it is probably Peter Dow he visited.
43. "Memorandum Book on Places and Things, A Tour of Upper Canada in 1837", P.A.O., p. 7.
44. Because "pleasure vehicles" were taxed so highly they offer a useful index of the relative degree of personal wealth in an area. For example, four-wheeled closed carriages were assessed at £100 which would make the minimum annual taxation £5. With the average annual labouring wage in Whitby 2s.6d. per day in 1842, the tax on such a carriage equalled 40 days wages for a working man. In 1830 there were 1 four-wheeled covered carriage and 8 "pleasure wagons" in Whitby. No other townships show any taxable vehicles. In 1840 there were 1 covered four-wheeled carriage, 4 open four-wheeled carriages, 4 two-wheeled gigs, and 26 pleasure wagons. The only other taxable vehicles in Ontario were 4 two-wheeled gigs and 5 pleasure wagons in Pickering.
45. Calculated from the population and assessment figures in "Provincial Secretary's Papers", and Upper Canada, *Journals of the Legislative Assembly*, appropriate years.

Chapter 6
The Developing Agrarian Society, 1820-40

1. "Grafton Scrapbook", P.A.O.
2. For example, see Walton; page 40 gives the following table of statutory labour:
Every person inserted on the Assessment Roll is, in proportion to the estimate of his property, held liable to work on the highways or roads in every year as follows:

Property Rating	*Days*
£25	2
£25 to 50	3
£50 to 75	4

Property Rating	*Days*
£75 to 100	5
£100 to 150	6
£150 to 200	7
£200 to 250	8
£250 to 300	9
£300 to 350	10
£350 to 400	11
£400 to 500	12 etc.

3. Peter Russell to the Duke of Portland, June 19, 1799, reproduced in Edith Firth, *The Town of York, 1793-1815* (Toronto, 1962), p. 146.
4. Paterson, p. 84.
5. Department of Public Records and Archives of Ontario, *Report*, 1932 (Toronto, 1933), p. 45.
6. Ibid., p. 147.
7. Farewell, p. 12.
8. Aitchison, p. 440.
9. J.J. Talman, "Travel in Ontario before the Coming of the Railway", *OHSPR*, XXIX (1933), p. 89.
10. Ibid.
11. Ibid.
12. *Colonial Advocate*, December 7, 1826.
13. "Minutes, Inspection of the Newcastle District Made by Mr. John Smith, Junior Deputy Provincial Surveyor at the Request of Mr. Galt", in E.C. Guillet. *The Valley of the Trent* (Toronto, 1957), pp. 29-36.
14. Farewell, pp. 40-41.
15. Ibid., p. 41.
16. *Pickering News*, Feb. 10, 1882.
17. Higgins, p. 49.
18. Farewell, p. 46.
19. One of the earliest boats to ply the route from Beaverton to Holland landing was a small packet owned by Colonel Donald Cameron of Thorah. As an aid to his settlers he charged rates so low it was regarded as "misguided altruism". See Macdonald, p. 181.
20. See the statement by the enumerator on the manuscript Census of 1842, (microfilm) P.A.O.
21. Aitchison, pp. 497-98.
22. Windsor (Whitby) Harbour was named as a port of entry on May 12, 1831 although Tincombe was not appointed until September. See F.H. Armstrong, *Handbook of Upper Canadian Chronology and Territorial Legislation* (London, Ontario, 1967), p. 224.
23. *Letters of Sir John A. Macdonald, 1836-1857*, ed. J.K. Johnson (Public Archives, Ottawa, 1968), p. 122, note 2.
24. Aitchison, p. 531 and fn. 5.
25. One proposal for a major road project in 1822, had it been acted upon, might have completely changed the economic development of North Ontario. Because of the fears of another American invasion, Lord Bathurst suggested to Sir Peregrine Maitland, the Lieutenant-Governor, that an inland line of communication should be built. In 1823, Thomas Ridout, the Surveyor General, suggested that such a route could be built from Lake Simcoe through Georgina, Brock, Mariposa, Ops, Emily, Smith, Douro, Dummer, Belmont, Marmora, Madoc, Elzevir, Kaladar, Kennebec, Olden and Oso, "connecting with the Military Road by the way of Perth and Richmond to Ottawa". See Thomas Ridout to George Hillier, May 30, 1823, Ontario, Department of Lands and Forests, Surveyor General's office, "Letters Written", vol. 26, pp. 36-37, cited in Florence B. Murray, *Muskoka and Haliburton, 1615-1875* (Toronto, 1963), p. lxxvi.
26. "Provincial Secretary's Papers", vol. VII; Farewell, p. 23.
27. Farewell, p. 23.
28. Compiled from "Provincial Secretary's Papers", vols. I-VII, and *Journals of the Legislative Assembly*, appendices. According to Joseph Gould, there was a small store in Uxbridge from 1830 on kept by

Carleton Lynde. It does not show in the assessment figures. See Higgins, p. 67.

29. The Oshawa *Vindicator*, April 6, 1870, dated Cameron's venture at 1830, while Farewell, p. 89, dated it at 1833.
30. Farewell, p. 51. No date was given.
31. Higgins, p. 86.
32. *Colonial Advocate*, March 8, 1827.
33. Ibid., May 18, 1824, reprinted in Fairley, pp. 109-110.
34. These problems are discussed in detail in contemporary works such as Robert Gourlay, *General Introduction to Statistical Account of Upper Canada* (Yorkshire, 1966), and Charles Lindsay, *The Life and Times of William Lyon Mackenzie* (Toronto, 1862). See also S.D. Clarke, *Movements of Political Protest in Canada 1640-1840* (Toronto, 1959).
35. Compiled from "Provincial Secretary's Papers", vols. I-VII, and *Journals of the Legislative Assembly of Upper Canada*.
36. See Chapter 4.
37. *Colonial Advocate*, March 1, 1827.
38. Ibid., May 13, 1831.
39. Farewell, p. 75.
40. "Returns for the information of His Excellency, the Lieutenant-Governor, in reply to his circular letter dated 18 March 1829 from the Honourable Simeon Washburn", "Provincial Secretary's Papers", R.G. 5., P.A.C.
41. Farewell, p. 21.
42. Higgins, p. 70.

Chapter 7
Social Crisis: Conflict and Rebellion, 1820-40

1. Letter, John Strachan to the Right Hon. Thomas Franklin Lewis, in J.L.H. Henderson, ed., *John Strachan: Documents and Opinions* (Toronto, 1969), p. 10.
2. Kingston *Chronicle*, letter, February 11, 1820.
3. Ibid., editorial, January 7, 1820.
4. Ibid., editorial, June 4, 1820. I am indebted to Tom Kolin for these quotes from the Kingston *Chronicle*.
5. Ibid., letter, February 19, 1819.
6. Susanna Moodie, *Roughing it in the Bush*, 6 rev. ed. (Toronto, 1913), pp. 245-50.
7. Letter to the editor signed "Oxygen", Kingston *Chronicle*, August 4, 1818.
8. Editorial, *Upper Canada Gazette*, February 13, 1823.
9. Strachan to John Macaulay, November 18, 1821, "Macauley Papers", P.A.O.
10. Strachan, Speech to the Legislative-Council, reported in the Kingston *Chronicle*, March 30, 1821.
11. Strachan to Hargrave, March 18, 1833, "John Strachan Letterbook, 1824-1840", p. 214, P.A.O.
12. *Colonial Advocate*, January 3, 1828.
13. *Constitution*, May 24, 1837.
14. *Constitution*, January 4, 1837. For a good discussion of William Lyon Mackenzie's ideas and policies see R.A. MacKay, "The Political Ideas of William Lyon Mackenzie", *CJEPS*, III (Feb., 1937), pp. 1-22; and Lillian F. Gates, "The Decided Policy of William Lyon Mackenzie", *CHR*, XL, no. 3 (September, 1959), pp. 185-208.
15. *Correspondent and Advocate*, July 23, 1835.
16. Upper Canada, House of Assembly, *First Report of the Select Committee Apointed to inquire into the state of Trade and Commerce of Upper Canada*, 1835, pp. 9-11.
17. *Constitution*, October 26, 1836, cited in F.H. Armstrong, "Reformer as Capitalist: W.L. Mackenzie and the Printers' Strike of 1836", *Ontario History*, LIX, no. 3 (September, 1967), p. 194.
18. *Colonial Advocate*, January 3, 1828.
19. *Constitution*, November 27, 1837.

20. Gates, *Land Policies*, pp. 119-21, provides an excellent discussion of this issue.
21. *Colonial Advocate*, March 22, 1827.
22. Ibid., May 14, 1827.
23. Ibid., A Mr. Callum or Collum (Mackenzie was not sure which) was named Justice of the Peace in Warren's place.
24. Craig, *Upper Canada*, pp. 121-22.
25. From 1792 to 1828 the following members of the Legislative Council represented the inhabitants of Ontario County:

    1792 — Nathaniel Pettitt
    1797 — Richard Beasley
    1800 — Justice Henry Allcock (unseated)
    Angus Macdonell (July 30, 1801, seated).
    1804 — Angus Macdonell (died in the wreck of *Speedy*).
    William Weekes (killed in a duel, 1806).
    Robert Thorpe
    1808 — Thomas B. Gough
    1812 — Thomas Ridout
    1816 — Peter Robinson
    1820 — Peter Robinson; William W. Baldwin
    1824 — William Thompson; Eli Playter

    See Frederick H. Armstrong, *Handbook of Upper Canadian Chronology and Territorial Legislation* (London, Ont., 1967), pp. 81, 101-2.
26. "A Copy of the Proceedings of a Public Meeting in Brock", *Colonial Advocate*, July 22, 1828.
27. Gourlay, *Statistical Account*, I, p. 458.
28. *Colonial Advocate*, July 24 and 31, 1828.
29. This period is discussed in Craig, *Upper Canada*, pp. 196-97, and in Aileen Dunham, *Political Unrest in Upper Canada 1815-1836* (Toronto, 1963), pp. 124-27.
30. *Colonial Advocate*, March 10, 1831.
31. *Colonial Advocate*, June 23, 1831. The petition was dated June 8, 1831.
32. A number of petitions with attached signatures were reprinted in the *Colonial Advocate* during June and July, 1831.
33. See the list of proposed meetings, *Colonial Advocate*, July 14, 1831.
34. *Colonial Advocate*, July 14, 1831.
35. *Colonial Advocate*, August 11, 1831. In all, some 24,500 persons signed the petitions. See Charles Lindsay, *The Life and Times of William Lyon Mackenzie* (Toronto, 1862), pp. 203-4.
36. *Colonial Advocate*, August 4, 1831.
37. *Colonial Advocate*, November 24, 1831.
38. Lindsay, p. 223. For a drawing of the medal see Lindsay, pp. 203-4.
39. Lindsay, p. 223.
40. The list of those who voted is printed in the *Colonial Advocate*, February 23, 1832.
41. Quoted in Lindsay, p. 250.
42. Ibid.
43. See Lindsay, pp. 244-52 for descriptions of this and other events of violence in 1832.
44. *Colonial Advocate*, January 11, 1834.
45. Ibid.
46. *Christian Guardian*, October 30, 1833.
47. Lindsay, p. 286. These words were written by Mackenzie on April 15, 1833.
48. Children of six or seven years of age were commonly employed in British mills in this period.
49. It was common practice in the nineteenth century to fine workers for infractions of the rigid company rules of the time. Fines (i.e., pay deductions) might result from tardiness, singing at work, insufficient

production, etc. Since there were no laws whatsoever to protect the workers, they were completely at the mercy of their employers. See the extensive literature by such authors as E.P. Thompson, E.J. Hobsbaun, and contemporary authors such as Charles Dickens for descriptions of the conditions of the British working classes.

50. *Colonial Advocate*, January 17, 1833, Letter 24.
51. See the Upper Canada, *Journals of the Legislative Assembly* 1839-40, appendix, pp. 233-34.
52. Carol L. Vaughan, "The Bank of Upper Canada in Politics", *Ontario History*, LX, no. 4 (December, 1968), pp. 196-99.
53. *Arthur Papers*, ed. Charles R. Sanderson (Toronto, 1943), Part I, p. 160.
54. *Colonial Advocate*, January 11, 1834.
55. Ibid.
56. *Colonial Advocate*, March 6, 1834.
57. *Colonial Advocate*, June 13, 1833.
58. 3 William IV, cap. 15.
59. John Charles Dent, *The Story of The Upper Canadian Rebellion* (Toronto, 1885), I, p. 280.
60. Clark, p. 488.
61. For example in 1838 Lieutenant-Governor Sir George Arthur wrote, "There is a numerous and very troublesomely disposed class of Persons in this Province – Orangemen". *Arthur Papers*, Part I, p. 198.
62. "The Memorial of John Elliot to Durham, Toronto, July 17, 1838", "Durham Papers", sect. VI, vol. I, p. 854, quoted in S.D. Clark, pp. 488-89.
63. Arthur to Colbourne, Toronto, July 11, 1839, *Arthur Papers*, Part III, p. 192.
64. *Constitution*, November 29, 1837.
65. Clark, p. 489.
66. See testimony of James Carey, April 12, 1838, Trial of Doctor James Hunter, in "John Beverley Robinson's Trial Notes", P.A.O. I am indebted to Dr. John S. Moir for a copy of these notes..
67. Quoted in Craig, *Upper Canada*, p. 244.
68. Vaughan, p. 200.
69. *Constitution*, May 24, 1837.
70. *Constitution*, August 2, 1837.
71. *Constitution*, November 15, 1837.
72. Dent, I, p. 369.
73. Lindsay, II, p. 47.
74. *Mackenzie's Gazette*, May 12, 1838, quoted in Clark, p. 387.
75. Ibid.
76. The account of the Pickering rebels in taken from Dent, II, pp. 144-47.
77. C.P. Stacey, "The Crisis of 1837 in a Back Township of Upper Canada", *CHR*, XI, no. 3 (September, 1930), p. 226. The rebel names are reconstructed from Lindsay, appendix I, and Walton's *Directory*.
78. Higgins, pp. 106-7.
79. Ibid., p. 107.
80. Ibid., pp. 107-8.
81. Testimony of John Carey, Noah Hawkins, James Dryden and others, "John B. Robinson's Trial Notes".
82. See Hunter's letter in the *Constitution*, October 18, 1837, which condemned Mackenzie for his attacks on the other reform groups which were splitting the reformers.
83. Testimony of Abner Hurd, "John B. Robinson's Trial Notes".
84. Stacey, "Crisis", pp. 226-28.
85. Ibid., p. 228.
86. R.C. Watt, "The Political Prisoners in Upper Canada, 1837-38", *English Historical Review*, XL, no. 1 (1926), p. 528.

87. Testimony of John Leslie, "John B. Robinson's Trial Notes".
88. Draper to Joseph, March 14, 1828, cited in Watt, p. 529.
89. Higgins, p. 109.
90. Lindsay, Appendix 1, and the "Home District Gaol Register", P.A.O. From these records it appears that a total of 449 persons were jailed in Home District, of whom 411 were residents of the area. In addition, true bills of high treason were returned against 29 residents of Home District who had fled the province to escape arrest. Among the latter, only Landon Wurtz of Brock appears to have been from the Ontario County area.
91. Watt, p. 530.
92. Sir George Arthur to Lord Glenely, April 14, 1838, quoted in Watt, p. 532.
93. Walton's *Directory* places Matthews on Lot 18, Concession VI, Pickering (the northeast corner of Brougham).
94. Edwin C. Guillet, *The Lives and Times of the Patriots* (Toronto, 1968), p. 270. This description was written by W.L. Mackenzie.
95. Dent, II, pp. 249-50.
96. Quoted in Watt, p. 535.
97. Quoted in Guillet, *Lives and Times*, p. 122.
98. Watt, pp. 537-39.
99. This list is arrived at by comparing the various lists of prisoners with Walton's *Directory* and land records, as well as casual mentions made of places of residence in the "Lindsay-Mackenzie Papers", P.A.O. and "Upper Canada Sundries", P.A.O.
100. R.S. Longley, "Emigration and the Crisis of 1837 in Upper Canada", *CHR*, XVII, no. 1 (1936), p. 31.
101. Quoted in Longley, p. 30.
102. Wm. Gordon to G.B. Brand, July 14, 1838, "Gordon Papers", P.A.O.
103. Wm. Cox to Arthur, September 5, 1838, *Arthur Papers*, Part I, p. 268.
104. Colborne to Arthur, September 28, 1838, Ibid, p. 286.

Chapter 8
Mercantile Development: Villages and Roads, 1840-51

1. Canada, *Census*, appropriate years; R.G. 5, B 26, vol. 7, P.A.C.
2. "Canada West Census, 1842", (microfilm) P.A.C.; Canada, *Census*, 1851-52. Calculations are my own. The total for 1842 and 1851 for each country of origin were:

	1842	*1851*
England	1,102	4,376
Ireland	936	3,877
Scotland	1,516	3,331
Canada — not French	8,209	16,352
Canada — French	326	93
United States	1,688	1,199
Other	172	343
	13,949	29,571

3. F.G. Weir, *Scugog and Its Environs* (Port Perry, 1927), p. 13.
4. "Petition of William Purdy, Ops Township, and Report of A. McDonnell, 1837", in E.C. Guillet, *Valley of the Trent* (Toronto, 1957), pp. 260-61, also in Weir, pp. 14-15.
5. Weir, pp. 14-18.
6. See the *Nineteenth Annual Report of the Canadian Conference, Missionary Society of the Methodist Episcopal Church*, 1844, p. xi, in the Archives of Victoria College.
7. Higgins believed that the first settler in Scugog was Charles Nesbitt, while Farewell and Weir name

Graxton. Because of Weir's superior research it would appear that Joseph Graxton was probably the first settler. See Higgins, p. 142; Farewell, p. 44; and Weir, p. 20.

8. See the lists in Higgins, Farewell and Weir.
9. "Provincial Secretary's Papers"; R.G. 5, B 26, vol. 7; Canada, *Census*, 1851, Vol. II, Table VI.
10. W.H. Smith, *Gazeteer* (Toronto, 1844), p. 222; W.H. Smith, *Canada Past, Present and Future* (Toronto, 1852), I, pp. 24-26.
11. Smith, *Canada*, I, p. 26.
12. Jacob Spelt, *Urbanization In South-Central Ontario* (Assen, Netherlands, 1955), p. 64.
13. Ibid.
14. Smith, *Gazetteer*, p. 221.
15. Ibid., p. 222.
16. Smith, *Canada*, I, pp. 23-24.
17. Smith, *Gazetteer*, p. 136.
18. Ibid., p. 63.
19. Ibid., p. 136.
20. M. McIntyre Hood, *Oshawa* (Oshawa, 1967), pp. 42-43. The Harbour Company was formally incorporated September 18, 1841, 4-5 Victoria, cap. LXI.
21. Smith, *Gazetteer*, p. 136; Smith, *Canada*, I, pp. 25-26.
22. Smith, *Canada*, I, p. 25. The 1851 census put Oshawa's population at 1142.
23. The Baldwin Municipal Act, 12 Victoria, cap. 81, named three cities, fifteen towns, and six villages. In the latter group Oshawa was listed along with Chippewa, Galt, Paris, Richmond, and Thorold.
24. R.G. 5, B 26, vol. 7; Smith, *Canada*, II, p. 47.
25. Smith, *Gazetteer*, p. 48.
26. Smith, *Canada*, I, p. 22.
27. Higgins, p. 139; Farewell, p. 15.
28. *Pickering News*, December 2, 1881.
29. Smith, *Gazetteer*, p. 38.
30. Smith, *Canada*, I, p. 30.
31. Farewell, pp. 26-27.
32. Smith, *Canada*, I, p. 32.
33. *Uxbridge Journal*, July 20, 1870.
34. *Uxbridge Journal*, July 27, 1870.
35. Ibid.
36. Smith, *Canada*, I, p. 35.
37. Abner Hurd to Robert Baldwin, February 5, 1845, "Baldwin (R.) Papers", 53/33, Metropolitan Toronto Reference Library.
38. Smith, *Gazetteer*, p. 153.
39. Smith, *Canada* I, p. 30.
40. Prince Albert *Ontario Observer*, May 28, 1859.
41. Farewell, p. 43.
42. In 1837, Mackenzie explained Perry's refusal to join him in his attacks on the banks by pointing to Perry's speculations in Loyalist lands with money borrowed from the Bank of Kingston. With characteristic vehemence Mackenzie said of Perry: "His legislative independence is in his grave, the bank has dug the hole. True he appears as usual as a patriot on the ballot, clergy lands and questions which effect not the monied monster to whom he is slave – but the sepulchre is a whited one – within all is corruption and rottenness". (*Constitution*, May 24, 1837). Also see *Ontario Observer*, May 26, 1859.
43. Prince Albert *Ontario Observer*, May 26, 1859; Higgins, p. 164.
44. Prince Albert *Ontario Observer*, May 26, 1859; Farewell, p. 83.
45. Farewell, p. 83; Smith, *Canada*, I, p. 31.

46. Smith, *Canada*, I, pp. 30-31.
47. Ibid., Prince Albert *Ontario Observer*, October 15, 1874.
48. Prince Albert *Ontario Observer*, May 26 and June 2, 1859.
49. Smith, *Canada*, I, p. 33.
50. L. Davidson to Robert Baldwin, May 16, 1849, "Baldwin (R.) Papers", 41/40.
51. Smith, *Canada*, I. p. 32.
52. 9 Victoria, cap. 37.
53. Weir, p. 9.
54. See for example J.R. Thompson to Robert Baldwin, January 6, 1845 and "Petition of the inhabitants of Brock Township", January 25, 1845, "Baldwin (R.) Papers", 74/79.
55. J.R. Thompson to Robert Baldwin, May 5, 1845, "Baldwin (R.) Papers", 74/83.
56. For example, the Robert Baldwin papers contain several petitions from Reach, Brock and Mariposa Townships, as well as letters from local dignitaries and businessmen. See volume 53, numbers 36, 37 and 38, and volume 74, numbers 85, 86, 88 and 90.
57. Ibid.
58. See J.R. Thompson (Brock), to Robert Baldwin, June 7, 1847, "Baldwin (R.) Papers", 74/90.
59. Abner Hurd (Reach), to Robert Baldwin, June 6, 1846, "Baldwin (R.) Papers", 53/38.
60. Canada, Province, *Sessional Papers*, XIX (1861), vol. IV, paper no. 33.
61. For a description of the Centre Line road, see the anonymous note on the original census book for Brock Township for 1851. According to the writer, the Nonquon Swamp could not be crossed even in summer. The original census is in the P.A.C.
62. 4-5 Victoria, cap. 10.
63. 12 Victoria, cap 5; Toronto *Globe*, August 22, 1850.
64. See Smith, *Canada*, I, pp. 44-45; *Minutes of the Municipal Council of the County of York*, 1852 (Toronto, 1852), pp. 28-30; Canada, Province, *Sessional Papers* XIX (1861), vol. IV, paper no. 33.
65. Canada, Province, *Sessional Papers*, XI (1852-53), pp. 383 ff.
66. Prince Albert *Ontario Observer*, June 2, 1859; Farewell, p. 41.
67. *Minutes of the Municipal Council of the United Counties of York, Ontario and Peel*, 1853, meeting of June 31, 1853, p. 39.
68. Ibid.
69. There are innumerable letters in the Robert Baldwin Papers and in the records of the Department of Public Works on this road.
70. Canada, Dominion, *Sessional Papers*, 1867-68, vol. I, part 5, no. 8.
71. *24th Annual Report of the Wesleyan Methodist Missionary Society* (Toronto, 1849), p. xxiii; "Enumerator's Remarks", Individual Census, 1851-52, Reel 973C, P.A.C.

Chapter 9
Conflicting Visions: Education and Religion, 1840-51

1. Canada, *Census*, 1851-52, appendix II, pp. 136.
2. In 1861, when the census included only active farmers, few 10-acre holdings were noted. It would appear, therefore, that these holdings were simply large-size town or dwelling lots.
3. Town and dwelling lots were omitted from the calculations. It was assumed that they averaged 10 acres each.
4. Canada, *Census*, 1851-52. Calculations are my own.
5. H. Claire Pentland, "Labour and the Development of Industrial Capitalism in Canada" (Ph.D. Thesis, University of Toronto, 1960), p. 269, fn. 74.
6. "Emigration, 1843", Report by A. McPherson, Esq. to Chief Secretary, Emigration Service, Kingston, R.G. 5, B 21, vol. 3, P.A.C.

7. "Statement by R.B. Sullivan and Robert Baldwin", "Upper Canada State Papers", vol. 24, P.A.C.
8. "Emigration, 1843".
9. Ibid., Report by Francis Leys.
10. E.A. Talbot, *Five Years' Residence in the Canadas* . . . (London, 1824), II, p. 119.
11. Ibid., p. 116.
12. *Views of Canada and the Colonists, By a Four Years' Resident* (Edinburgh, 1844), pp. 55-56.
13. *Colonial Advocate*, August 14, 1828.
14. Ibid., December 6, 1837.
15. "Report Upon the Subject of Education", February 24, 1836, quoted in J. George Hodgins, *Historical and Other Papers and Documents . . . of the Education System of Ontario* (Toronto, 1911), I, p. 70.
16. Strachan, "Speech to the Legislative Council on the Clergy Reserves", *Upper Canada Gazette*, May 17, 1828.
17. Ibid., May 10, 1828.
18. Strachan to The Lord Bishop, February 26, 1821, *The John Strachan Letter Book: 1812-1834*, ed. George Spragge, (Toronto, 1946), p. 212.
19. Strachan to the Bishop of Quebec, September 30, 1816, "Strachan Letterbook 1812-1823", P.A.O.
20. Quoted in George W. Spragge, "Elementary Education in Upper Canada, 1820-1840", *Ontario History*, XLIII (1951), p. 121.
21. See, for example, the comments by Susan F. Houston, "Politics, Schools, and Social Change in Upper Canada", *CHR*, LIII (1972), no. 3, pp. 252-53.
22. Farewell, p. 41.
23. Ibid., p. 88.
24. Canada, Province, *Journals of the Legislative Council*, 1836, appendix 35, p. 57.
25. Ibid., p. 60.
26. Robert Murray to Alex McMillan, April 12, 1843, "Education Office, Canada West", Letter Book A, pp. 251-52. Also cited in Huston, p. 261.
27. "Report of a System of Public Elementary Instruction For Upper Canada, 1846", Hodgins, III, p. 143.
28. Ibid., p. 146.
29. Ibid., p. 145.
30. See 4-5 Victoria, cap. XVIII, and 7 Victoria, cap. XXIX.
31. Farewell, p. 41.
32. Smith, *Canada*, I, pp. 43-44.
33. Hodgins, "Papers on the School System of Upper Canada, 1852", III, p. 273.
34. Ibid., "Papers Illustrative of the State of Popular Education in Upper Canada, 1853", V, pp. 164-65.
35. Ibid., "Papers on the School System of Upper Canada, 1852", III, p. 271.
36. J. Harold Putnam, *Egerton Ryerson and Education in Upper Canada* (Toronto, 1912), pp. 130-31.
37. 9 Victoria, cap. XX.
38. Putnam, p. 131.
39. Ibid., p. 138.
40. Higgins, p. 258, and Farewell, p. 66, give 1846 as the date for the Ontario County Grammar School at Whitby. J. George Hodgins, *The Establishment of Schools and Colleges in Ontario, 1792-1910* (Toronto, 1910), I, p. 278, gives the date as 1849.
41. 47 George III, cap. VI.
42. Putnam, p. 206.
43. Farewell, p. 66.
44. Farewell, p. 44.
45. Strachan to Brown, October 3, 1803, quoted in J.L.H. Henderson, *John Strachan*, p. 25.
46. J.J. Bigsby, *The Shoe and Canoe* . . . (London, 1850), I, p. 28.

47. J.F. Sanderson, *The First Century of Methodism in Canada* (Toronto, 1908), I, pp. 43-45.
48. Ibid., p. 58.
49. Ibid., p. 112.
50. Ibid., p. 123 ff.
51. J. Carroll, *Case and His Contemporaries* (Toronto, 1867), I, pp. 114-15.
52. See several quotes to this effect in S.D. Clark, *The Social Development of Canada* (Toronto, 1942), pp. 284 ff.
53. Strachan to Brown, July 13, 1806, Henderson, p. 25.
54. "Ecclesiastical Chart of the Province of Upper Canada", "Minutes of the Clergy Corporation", (microfilm) P.A.O.
55. W. Bell, *Hints to Emigrants, in a Series of Letters From Upper Canada* (Edinburgh, 1824), p. 89.
56. *Views of Canada and the Colonists*, p. 244.
57. See Table VII chapter 5.
58. Farewell, p. 42.
59. Hood, p. 195.
60. *By-laws of the Council of the Corporation of the County of Ontario*, 1907, pp. 234 ff.; Farewell, p. 35.
61. Farewell, p. 63; Hood, p. 189.
62. Farewell, p. 79.
63. J. Douglas Ross, *Education in Oshawa* (Oshawa, 1970), pp. 160-61.
64. Smith, *Canada*, II, p. 22.
65. Farewell, 56.
66. Ibid., p. 42.
67. "Highland Settlement in Canada", P.A.O., p. 6.
68. *21st Annual Report of the Missionary Society of the Wesleyan Methodist Church* (Toronto, 1846), p. xxiii, Victoria College Archives, Toronto.
69. Canada, *Census*, 1851-52, vol. I, appendix 15.
70. This and subsequent information about the Mormons is taken from *A History of the Mormon Church in Canada* (Lethbridge, 1968), Chapter I, unless otherwise noted.
71. Ibid.
72. Hood, p. 187.
73. "Gordon Papers", Notes by Christiana Gordon Ross, Monday, May 28, 1816, P.A.O. The *History of the Mormon Church*, notes that this body of Mormons left for the trek west in August, 1838.
74. Over the next several decades the Mormons were vigorously persecuted for their beliefs. Joseph Smith and his brother Hyrum were lynched in 1844 while awaiting trial.
75. Thomas Conant, *Upper Canada Sketches* (Toronto, 1898), pp. 92-96, quoted in John S. Moir, ed., *The Cross in Canada* (Toronto, 1966), pp. 128-29.
76. Hood, p. 187.
77. Hodgins, *Historical . . . Papers*, I, pp. 82-83.
78. Letter by Judge Kingsmill, Chairman of the Board of School Trustees in Niagara, 1859, quoted in Ibid., III, pp. 26-27.
79. Ibid., III, pp. 270-71; Putnam, pp. 110 ff.
80. Rev. Egerton Ryerson, *Report on a System of Public and Elementary Instruction for Upper Canada* (Montreal, 1847), p. 23, quoted in Franklin A. Walker, *Catholic Education and Politics in Upper Canada* (Toronto, 1855), p. 60.
81. Speech by the Honourable John Elmsley, *The Banner*, December 10, 1847.
82. Hood, p. 235.

Chapter 10
The Creation of Ontario County

1. C.P. Lucas, ed., *Lord Durham's Report on the Affairs of British North America* (Oxford, 1912), p. 238.
2. See 4-5 Victoria, cap. 10.
3. By far the best study of local government is Aitchison's Ph.D. Thesis, cited previously.
4. *Act for Better Internal Government*, 4-5 Victoria, cap. 10.
5. Ibid.
6. Farewell, pp. 48-49.
7. 9 Victoria, cap. 40.
8. Biggar, *Municipal Manual*, p. 4.
9. Ibid., pp. 4-5.
10. Ibid., p. 8.
11. 12 Victoria, cap. 81. There were slight modifications in the 1849 version.
12. 12 Victoria, cap. 78.
13. See I.A.E. Irving to Robert Baldwin, September 5, 1842, "Baldwin (R.) Papers", 53/74.
14. 7 William IV, cap. 32.
15. See Joseph Gould to Robert Baldwin, January 30, 1849, "Baldwin (R.) Papers", 47/60, and especially the Oshawa *Vindicator*, May 6, 1868, which contains several reprinted articles from the Oshawa *Literary News Letter and Friendly Moralist*, no. XLVI and XLVII, (February, 1849).
16. Ibid., also Joseph Gould to Robert Baldwin, January 29, 1849, and John R. Thompson to Robert Baldwin, January 6, 1849, "Baldwin (R.) Papers", 46/60 and 74/96.
17. "Minutes of the Municipal Council of Home District", January 25, 1849, cited in *Minutes of the Municipal Council of the County of York*, 1st Session, January 31, 1851.
18. Farewell, p. 32.
19. Ibid., p. 25.
20. *Minutes of. . . the County of York*, January, 31, 1851.
21. Ibid.
22. *Minutes of. . . the County of York*, June 19, 1851.
23. 14-15 Victoria, cap. V.
24. Weir, p. 5.
25. Higgins, p. 173.
26. Ibid., pp. 167-71.
27. "*Minutes of the Provisional Council of the County of Ontario*", May 3, 1852.
28. Ibid.
29. Quoted in Higgins, pp. 167-68.
30. Ibid., pp. 169-73.
31. *Minutes of the Provisional Council of the County of Ontario*, May 10, 1852.
32. Higgins, p. 179.
33. McPherson appealed to the courts and McDonagh was later unseated, but by then all the important decisions had been made. Higgins, p. 176.
34. Ibid., p. 178.
35. Ibid., pp. 178-79.
36. Ibid., pp. 179-80.
37. Ibid., p. 180.
38. Joseph Gould to Francis Hincks, March 11, 1853, quoted in Higgins, p. 180.
39. Canada, Province, *Journals of the Legislative Council*, XI, 1852-53, pp. 330 ff.

40. See Abner Hurd to Robert Baldwin, May 10, 1851 and June 12, 1851, "Baldwin (R.) Papers", 53/47 and 53/48.
41. Higgins, pp. 181-86.
42. Ibid, pp. 188-90.

Chapter 11
Farmer and Master Craftsman, 1851-71

1. These figures are compiled census data and Smith, *Canada*, I. Calculations are my own.
2. Canada, *Census*, 1851, 1861 and 1871. Calculations are my own.
3. Ibid.
4. Ibid.
5. Ibid.
6. Ibid.
7. Whitby *Chronicle*, September 24, 1857; Oshawa *Vindicator*, September 29, 1858.
8. Oshawa *Vindicator*, January 12, 1859.
9. Oshawa *Vindicator*, September 29, 1858.
10. Oshawa *Vindicator*, January 12, 1859.
11. Whitby *Chronicle*, May 6, 1858.
12. Prince Albert *Ontario Observer*, July 12, 1866.
13. Ibid., October 11, 1866.
14. Ibid., May 28, 1868.
15. Ibid.
16. Farewell, p. 50.
17. Canada, *Census*, 1851 and 1861.
18. Canada, *Census*, 1871.
19. Canada, *Census*, 1851 and 1861. Calculations are my own.
20. Oshawa *Vindicator*, May 10, 1871.
21. Printed in the Whitby *Chronicle*, August 18, 1860.
22. For a description of Sexton's farm see the Port Perry *North Ontario Observer*, September 25, 1873.
23. Canada, *Census*, 1861, "Occupiers of Land".
24. Canada, *Census*, 1871, "Manufacturing", Tables XXIX ff.
25. Oshawa *Vindicator*, February 23, 1870.
26. Ibid., November 27, 1867.
27. Prince Albert *Ontario Observer*, March 17, 1869, from an advertisement offering a house for rent at six dollars per month.
28. Uxbridge *Journal*, August 31, 1871.
29. Prince Albert *Ontario Observer*, May 21, 1868.
30. Ibid., November 7, 1867.
31. Ibid., December 28, 1871.
32. Canada, *Census*, 1871.
33. Talbot, II, pp. 57-58.
34. Moodie, pp. 63-64.
35. Weir, pp. 116-17.
36. Anson Green stated that the Canadian societies were influenced by those established in New England. Green, p. 112.
37. Edith Firth, *The Town of York* (Toronto, 1966), II, pp. 342-43, fn. 43.
38. Weir, p. 116.
39. Firth, II, pp. 342-43, fn. 43.

40. See several letters in the Alexander Wood Correspondence, Toronto Reference Library, where transactions of this sort are described.
41. Edwin C. Guillet, *The Pioneer Farmer and Backwoodsman* (Toronto, 1963), vol. I, chapter XI, provides an excellent description of pioneer inns. His five-volume work *Pioneer Inns and Taverns*, of course, provides innumerable examples of tavern life in the early history of Canada.
42. R.H. Bonnycastle, *The Canadas in 1841* (London, 1841), I, pp. 128-29.
43. J.M.S. Careless, *The Union of the Canadas* (Toronto, 1967), p. 174.
44. Oshawa *Vindicator*, August 11 and September 15, 1858.
45. Ibid., September 15, 1858.
46. Quoted in Graeme Decarie, "Something Old, Something New ... Aspects of Prohibitionism in Ontario in the 1890s", *Oliver Mowat's Ontario*, ed. Donald Swainson (Toronto, 1972), p. 159. The verse dates from the 1870s.
47. Whitby *Chronicle*, May 13, 1859.
48. *Minutes of . . . the County of Ontario*, June 11, 1859, p. 19.
49. Ibid., p. 20.
50. Ibid., pp. 51-52, By-law no. 65.
51. Ibid., January 27, 1860, pp. 65; By-law no. 72.
52. Ibid., June, 1861, By-law no. 85.
53. Over the next twenty years, other levels of government became involved in moral legislation as well. By 1879 sufficient laws had been passed by the Provincial and Federal Governments, that the County bylaws were redundant. They were repealed by By-law no. 315.

Chapter 12
Progress: The Idea and Its Proponents

1. For an excellent background to the rise of the idea of progress, see R.V. Sampson, *Progress In the Age of Reason*. Cambridge, Mass., 1956. For a useful study of the idea's background in Upper Canada see L.S. Fallis, "The Idea of Progress in the Province of Canada: 1841-1867" (Ph.D. Thesis, U. of Michigan, 1966).
2. *Literary Garland*, vol. II (1840), cited in Fallis, pp. 5-6.
3. R.B. Sullivan, *On the Connection between the Agriculture and Manufactures of Canada* (Hamilton, 1848), pp. 4-5, cited in Fallis, p. 7.
4. Prince Albert *Ontario Observer*, March 12, 1868.
5. Oshawa *Vindicator*, October 7, 1857.
6. Port Perry *North Ontario Observer*, October 23, 1873.
7. Oshawa *Reformer*, April 5, 1872.
8. Port Perry *North Ontario Observer*, August 26, 1875.
9. Oshawa *Vindicator*, May 3, 1871
10. Prince Albert *Ontario Observer*, February 27, 1868.
11. Prince Albert *Ontario Observer*, February 6, 1868.
12. Ibid., February 10, 1870.
13. Toronto *Globe*, April 8, 1872.
14. Mechanics' Institutes were established in Whitby, Oshawa, Port Perry and Uxbridge.
15. Uxbridge *Journal*, June 13, 1872.
16. Port Perry *North Ontario Observer*, February 10, 1870.
17. Higgins, pp. 194-95.
18. Ibid., pp. 195-96.
19. Canada, Province, *Journals of the Legislative Council*, XI (1853), p. 383.

20. Higgins, p. 197.
21. Whitby *Chronicle*, June 18, 1857.
22. Higgins, pp. 198-99.
23. In later years, Bongard would regret his enthusiasm for speculation. When the directors changed their minds about the proposed route, Bongard was unable to sell his lots, with the result that his land was now fragmented and he was a good deal poorer for his efforts. Eventually he petitioned the Reach Township Council for the return of the streets, but when other residents objected, his request was refused. Prince Albert *Ontario Observer*, January 21, 1869.
24. Uxbridge *Journal*, July 27, 1874.
25. Farewell, p. 32, notes the divisive effects of this action on the township.
26. *Minutes of . . . the County of Ontario*, 1854.
27. Higgins, p. 151.
28. Farewell, p. 32.
29. Ibid., p. 62.
30. Farewell, pp. 62-63; Higgins, p. 157.
31. Canada, Province, *Sessional Papers*, XX (1862), vol. 3, part 16.
32. Whitby *Chronicle*, June 18, 1857.
33. Ibid., June 18, 1857.
34. Ibid., June 25, 1857.
35. Ibid., September 17, 1857.
36. Higgins, p. 201; Whitby *Chronicle*, November 18, 1857.
37. Whitby *Chronicle*, November 18, 1857.
38. Oshawa *Vindicator*, December 2, 1857.
39. Ibid.
40. Whitby *Chronicle*, December 10, 1857.
41. *Minutes . . . of the County of Ontario*, 1857, Report of the Clerk to Special Sessions, December 21, 1857; Oshawa *Vindicator*, December 26, 1857.
42. Farewell, p. 32.
43. Higgins, pp. 157-58.
44. Whitby *Chronicle*, May 13, 1858.
45. See the list of petitions presented to County Council, June 2, 1858, *Minutes . . . of the County of Ontario*. In all, nine petitions containing 1,134 names were presented. The petition from the Town of Whitby contained 506 (or almost half) of the names.
46. *Minutes . . . of the County of Ontario*, 1858.
47. Ibid., June 10th.
48. Ibid., August, Special Meeting.
49. Ibid., p. 88.
50. Oshawa *Vindicator*, October 20, 1858.
51. Ibid.
52. *Minutes . . . of the County of Ontario*, 1858.
53. In 1860, the County Council voted $20,000 for improvements to the main county roads. This was divided as follows: Simcoe Street, $2,000; Centre Line Road north of Manchester, $8,000; and Brock Road in Pickering, $5,000. The balance was spent on various bridges and road improvements. See Higgins, p. 241.
54. Whitby *Chronicle*, May 6, 1858.
55. Ibid., May 13, 1858.
56. Whitby *Chronicle*, May 13, 1858.
57. *Minutes . . . of the County of Ontario*, 1858.
58. Higgins, pp. 200-202.

59. Hood, p. 59; Farewell, p. 77; "Pedlar Papers", clipping from the Oshawa *Vindicator*, October 3, 1894, P.A.O.
60. Established in 1846 by an English immigrant, Martin Bambridge. Hood, p. 74.
61. Thomas Fuller and his four sons came to Oshawa in 1837 and set up a small chair and bedstead factory. Hood, p. 75.
62. Oshawa *Vindicator*, October 7, 1857.
63. For a list of shareholders and the numbers of shares held by each, see Canada, Province, *Sessional Papers*, no. 5, 1860.
64. Oshawa *Vindicator*, June 23, 1858.
65. Canada, Province, *Sessional Papers*, 1860.
66. Oshawa *Vindicator*, October 7, 1857.
67. "Minutes of the First Annual Meeting of the Ontario Bank", printed in Oshawa *Vindicator*, June 23, 1858.
68. Prince Albert *Ontario Observer*, June 26, 1862.
69. Canada, *Census*, 1860-61, vol. 2, Table 13.
70. The question of just how serious this drain was is difficult to answer. It is clear, however, that it represented a serious charge against locally created wealth. For example, the total wheat crop in Ontario County in 1861-62 was 1,137,074 bushels, valued at approximately $1,100,000. Even if it is assumed that farmers realized a twenty percent net profit on growing wheat, the bank's profits represented fifty percent as much as that created by the main economic activity of Ontario County.
71. Canada, Province, *Sessional Papers*, 28 Victoria, cap. 9, 1865.
72. 34 Victoria, cap. XXVII.
73. A. St. L. Trigge, *A History of the Canadian Bank of Commerce* (Toronto, 1920-34), III, p. 297, fn. 1.
74. See especially the agitation for tariff protection of manufacturing discussed in Peter B. Waite, *Canada, 1874-1896*, (Toronto, 1971), pp. 80-85.
75. Hood, p. 79; Toronto *Mail*, April 8, 1872; Pedlar Papers, P.A.O.
76. Prince Albert *Ontario Observer*, July 14, 1859.
77. Oshawa *Vindicator*, December 18, 1867.
78. Ibid., June 5, 1867.

Chapter 13
Responses to Urbanization: Welfare and Education

1. Prince Albert *Ontario Observer*, March 5, 1868.
2. Toronto *Ontario Workman*, August 14, 1873.
3. Prince Albert *Ontario Observer*, September 22, 1870, "Minutes of the meeting of Reach Township Council, September 17, 1870".
4. Advertisement dated August 9, 1869 in the Prince Albert *Ontario Observer*, August 12, 1869.
5. Prince Albert *Ontario Observer*, April 23, 1868.
6. Ibid., December 17, 1868.
7. Ibid., April 21, 1870.
8. Whitby *Chronicle*, November 14, 1861.
9. Ibid.
10. Ibid.
11. Prince Albert *Ontario Observer*, April 23, 1868.
12. See *Minutes of . . . Ontario County*, Reports, June, 1859 and January, 1877.
13. Ibid., January, 1869.
14. Farewell, p. 70.

15. Whitby *Chronicle*, December 19, 1867.
16. For example, in the first six weeks of winter in 1875-76, some 69 persons were provided with temporary quarters in the Oshawa lock-up.
17. *Minutes of . . . the Ontario County Council*, June, 1873.
18. Prince Albert *Ontario Observer*, June 20, 1872.
19. Passed March 4, 1837.
20. Prince Albert *Ontario Observer*, March 5, 1868.
21. Oshawa *Reformer*, December 10, 1875.
22. Ibid., December 17, 1875.
23. Ibid.
24. Ibid., January 14, 1876.
25. Ibid.
26. Ibid., March 31, 1876.
27. Ibid., March 24, 1876.
28. Ibid., February 2, 1877.
29. Letter of Dr. John Roaf to the editor, Toronto *Globe*, January 31, 1852.
30. Roaf to *Globe*, February 5, 1852.
31. Ryerson, "Papers by the Chief Superintendent of Education, 1852", J.G. Hodgins, ed., *Historical . . . Papers*, V, p. 155.
32. Putnam, p. 145.
33. Ryerson, "Suggestions for the Further Improvement of Public Instruction in Ontario, 1868", Hodgins, *Historical . . . Papers*, IV, p. 89.
34. Hodgins, *Historical . . . Papers*, IV, p. 195.
35. Toronto *Globe*, January 30, 1851.
36. "Report of the Chief Superintendent . . . 1853", Hodgins, *Historical . . . Papers*, V, p. 164.
37. Hodgins, *Historical . . . Papers*, III, p. 281.
38. See the Whitby *Chronicle*, January 3, 1860, and November 29, 1860.
39. Canada, *Sessional Papers*, 1862, vol. 4., pt. 34.
40. Ryerson, "Papers on the School System of Upper Canada, 1852", Hodgins, *Historical . . . Papers*, III, p. 273.
41. "Report of the Chief Superintendent . . . 1868", Hodgins, *Historical . . . Papers*, IV, p. 89.
42. Prince Albert *Ontario Observer*, February 27, 1873.
43. Hodgins, *Historical . . . Papers*, V, p. 164; Canada, *Sessional Papers*, 1862, vol. V, pt. 34; Ontario, *Sessional Papers*, 1870-71, vol. I, no. 4.
44. "Report of the Reverend James T. Dowling, Uxbridge", Canada, *Sessional Papers*, 1865, vol. I, no. 5.
45. Hodgins, *Historical . . . Papers*, V, p. 164; Canada, *Sessional Papers*, 1862, vol. V, pt. 34; Ontario, *Sessional Papers*, 1870-71, vol. I, no. 4.
46. Prince Albert *Ontario Observer*, January 30, 1868.
47. "Justice Hagarty's charge to the Toronto Grand Jury, 1860", Hodgins, *Historical . . . Papers*, III, pp. 26-27.
48. "Report of the Chief Superintendent . . . 1857", Hodgins, *Historical . . . Papers*, V, p. 240.
49. Prince Albert *Ontario Observer*, February 11, 1869.
50. For a short discussion on the debate on the 1871 Education Act, see C.B. Sissons, *Egerton Ryerson, His Life and Letters* (Toronto, 1847), pp. 582-87.
51. Quoted in Franklin A. Walker, *Catholic Education and Politics in Upper Canada* (Toronto, 1955), p. 59.
52. Ibid., p. 60.
53. Toronto *Mirror*, August 15, 1851.
54. Letter from "A Catholic" to the editor, Ibid., March 7, 1851; also quoted in Walker, p. 98.
55. Toronto *Globe*, June 25, 1855.

56. J. George Hodgins, *The Establishment of Schools and Colleges in Ontario* (Toronto, 1910), II, pp. 166-67; also J. Douglas Ross, *Education in Oshawa* (n.p., 1970), p. 161, and Hood, p. 215.
57. Ross, pp. 160-61.
58. Hodgins, *The Establishment of Schools* . . . II, p. 167; Canada, *Sessional Papers*, 1862, no. 34.
59. Prince Albert *Ontario Observer*, July 15, 1869.
60. 47 George III, cap. 6.
61. "Report of the Chief Superintendent . . . 1850", Hodgins, *Historical . . . Papers*, V, p. 104.
62. *Journals of the Legislative Assembly of Canada*, 1854, appendix B, Table G.
63. Hodgins, *Historical . . . Papers*, V, pp. 159-60.
64. 16 Victoria, cap. 186.
65. Putnam, p. 211.
66. *By-laws of . . . Ontario County*, pp. 235, 238.
67. "Report of the Standing Committee on Education", *Minutes . . . of the County of Ontario*, January, 1858.
68. Whitby *Chronicle*, May 13, 1858.
69. Canada, *Sessional Papers*, 1861, 1863, 1864. There is no report of a grammar school in Oshawa in the Chief Superintendent's report in either 1861 or 1863.
70. *By-laws of . . . Ontario County*, By-law no. 122 passed June, 1864.
71. *By-laws of . . . the County of Ontario*, By-law no. 244, and *Minutes*, January, 1874, pp. 10-11.
72. Higgins, p. 259.
73. Canada, Province, *Journals of the Legislative Assembly*, 1854, appendix B: Canada, *Sessional Papers*, 1862, no. 34; Ontario, *Sessional Papers*, 1870-71, no. 4.
74. It is interesting to note that in 1887 Higgins reported that little further growth in grammar school attendance had occurred. In that year he reports that there were 164 students at Oshawa High School; 161 at Whitby; 101 at Uxbridge; and 114 at Port Perry, for a total of 540 students.
75. Oshawa *Vindicator*, August 3, 1859.
76. The Chief Superintendent reported that in the study of classics, girls outnumbered boys in Oshawa by 28-26; in Whitby, by 37-23; and in Uxbridge, by 11-7. Canada, *Sessional Papers*, 1867, no. 9.
77. Canada, *Sessional Papers*, 1867, no. 9; Hodgins, *Historical . . . Papers*, VI, pp. 124-27.
78. Hodgins, *Historical . . . Papers*, IV, pp. 78-80.
79. Letter, H. Hale, Chairman, Board of Clinton, Grammar School Trustees, to Egerton Ryerson, December 23, 1867; Hodgins, *Historical . . . Papers*, IV, pp. 79-80.
80. Hodgins, *Historical . . . Papers*, IV, p. 78.
81. Ontario, *Sessional Papers*, 1883, no. 5.
82. Putnam, pp. 225-26.
83. By-law no. 232, passed January, 1873.
84. Prince Albert *Ontario Observer*, May 9, 1872.
85. Ibid., November 28, 1872.
86. Prince Albert *Ontario Observer*, February 27, 1873.
87. Cannington *Gleaner*, July 29, 1897.

Chapter 14
The Building of the Railways

1. For an effective description of the 1850-90 period in Toronto see D.C. Masters, *The Rise of Toronto* (Toronto, 1947).
2. Ontario, 31 Victoria, cap. 41, March 4, 1868.
3. One indication of the availability of liquid wealth in the lakeshore towns (Whitby, Oshawa and Bowmanville) is shown in the amounts of bank stocks possessed by local residents in 1860 and 1870. Since only two stocks were held locally to any extent, these are shown for comparative purposes.

	Ontario Bank[a]		*Bank of Toronto*[b]	
	1860	*1870*	*1860*	*1870*
Whitby	644	499	5	5
Oshawa	2,450	1,031	93	23
Bowmanville	3,975	3,408	12	—

[a] Shares valued at $40 each.
[b] Shares valued at $100 each.

Canada, *Sessional Papers*, 1860 and 1870.

4. For an examination of the best-known of these railway frauds see Gustavus Myers, *A History of Canadian Wealth* (Toronto, 1972 [reprint], originally printed in 1913).
5. Prince Albert *Ontario Observer*, August 9, 1866.
6. J.M. and Edward Trout, *The Railways of Canada* (Toronto, 1871), p. 46. As Trout notes (p. 96) the Galt and Guelph Railway, completed in 1857 over terrain very similar to that to be covered by the P.W. & P.P. railway, cost approximately $28,400 per mile without rolling stock.
7. Prince Albert *Ontario Observer*, September 6, 1866.
8. George Laidlaw, *Cheap Railways, A Letter to the People of Bruce and Grey . . . With an Appendix Addressed to the People of Ontario and Victoria* (Pamphlet, Toronto, 1867), P.A.O.
9. Ibid.
10. Prince Albert *Ontario Observer*, January 3, 1867.
11. Ibid., April 18, 1867.
12. Ibid., January 9, 1868.
13. Ibid., November 7, 1867.
14. Ontario, 31 Victoria, cap. 42.
15. Prince Albert *Ontario Observer*, April 9, 1868.
16. Ibid.
17. Toronto *Monetary Times*, November 9, 1868.
18. Ibid.
19. Prince Albert *Ontario Observer*, June 18, 1868.
20. Ibid., October 15, 1868.
21. Ibid., July 2, 1868.
22. Ibid.
23. Ibid., September 17, 1868.
24. Ibid., September 23, 1869.
25. Ibid., May 13, 1869.
26. Oshawa *Vindicator*, September 16, 1868.
27. Ibid., September 22, 1868.
28. Ibid.
29. Prince Albert *Ontario Observer*, October 15, 1868.
30. Oshawa *Vindicator*, October 28, 1868.
31. Prince Albert *Ontario Observer*, October 22, 1868.
32. Ibid.
33. Oshawa *Vindicator*, October 14, 1868.
34. Prince Albert *Ontario Observer*, November 26, 1868.
35. Ibid., December 10, 1868.
36. Ibid.
37. Ibid., January 28, 1869.
38. Oshawa *Vindicator*, April 7, 1869.
39. Ontario, 32 Victoria, cap. LX.
40. Letter to the editor from "A Prudent Ratepayer", Prince Albert *Ontario Observer*, February 28, 1869.

41. Ibid., March 11, 1869.
42. Letter to the editor from "Nipissing", Prince Albert *Ontario Observer*, March 11, 1869.
43. Prince Albert *Ontario Observer*, March 11, 1869.
44. Ibid., March 4, 1869.
45. The final total of bonuses voted was $399,000 made up of Toronto, $150,000; Scarborough, $10,000; Markham, $30,000; Uxbridge, $50,000; Scott, $10,000; Brock, $50,000; Eldon, $44,000; Bexley, $15,000; Laxton, Digby and Longford, $25,000; and Summerville, $15,000.
46. G.R. Stevens, *Canadian National Railways* (Toronto, 1960), I, p. 451.
47. Prince Albert *Ontario Observer*, June 10, 1869.
48. Uxbridge *Journal*, August 18, 1869.
49. Prince Albert *Ontario Observer*, April 2, 1868.
50. Ibid.
51. Ibid.
52. Toronto *Monetary Times*, November 19, 1868.
53. Prince Albert *Ontario Observer*, August 13, 1868.
54. Ibid.
55. Ibid.
56. Ibid.
57. Ibid., May 7, 1868.
58. Ibid., August 6, 1868.
59. Oshawa *Vindicator*, July 13 and September 22, 1868; Prince Albert *Ontario Observer*, August 20 and October 15, 1868.
60. Oshawa *Vindicator*, October 14, 1868.
61. Ibid.
62. Ibid., November 18, 1868.
63. Ibid., December 9, 1868.
64. For details of the Kestevan and Starrat contract see the Prince Albert *Ontario Observer*, February 2, 1871.
65. Ibid., October 7, 1869 and February 2, 1871.
66. *Ontario*, 32 Victoria, cap. LX, January 23, 1869.
67. For example, see the advertisement by Dr. Jones, dentist, in the Prince Albert *Ontario Observer*, December 31, 1868. Others quickly followed Jones' example in succeeding weeks.
68. Ibid.
69. Ibid.
70. Oshawa *Vindicator*, July 7, 1869.
71. Ibid., July 28, 1869.
72. Prince Albert *Ontario Observer*, August 26, 1869.
73. Ibid., September 9, 1869.
74. Ibid., August 5, 1869.
75. Oshawa *Vindicator*, September 1 and September 22, 1869.
76. Prince Albert *Ontario Observer*, September 2, 1869.
77. Higgins, p. 215.
78. Ibid., p. 221.
79. Ibid.
80. For example, see the report of a general meeting of ratepayers in the Town of Whitby, November 8, 1869, in the Prince Albert *Ontario Observer*, November 11, 1869.
81. Most of the details of this scandal are spelled out in the Prince Albert *Ontario Observer*, November 11, 1869, February 2, and December 28, 1871.
82. Ibid., October 6, 1870.

83. Ibid., December 28, 1871.
84. Details of some of the suits are given in the Prince Albert *Ontario Observer*, October 12, 1870.
85. Ibid., February 2, 1871.
86. See C. Draper to F. Shanly, July 29, 1871, and Shanly to James Austin, May 7, 1873, *Shanly Papers*, Box 73, P.A.O.
87. Prince Albert *Ontario Observer*, August 3, 1871.
88. Oshawa *Vindicator*, August 30, 1871.
89. Bigelow's security was $40,000 worth of bonds in the P.W. & P.P. Railway. Oshawa *Vindicator*, September 13, 1871.
90. Ibid.
91. The 5-foot, 6-inch width, for example, had been made a specific condition of the Scugog bonus bylaw, as well as of the original P.W. & P.P. charter. See Prince Albert *Ontario Observer*, February 22, 1872.
92. Ontario, 35 Victoria, cap. LVI, March 2, 1872.
93. From local newspaper reports it would appear that G.R. Steven's date (p. 445) of July, 1871, for the opening of the P.W. & P.P. is in error. See Prince Albert *Ontario Observer*, November 23, 1871 and July 4, 1872, and Toronto *Mail*, May 29, 1872.
94. See Prince Albert *Ontario Observer*, April 3, 1873, for details of the treatment of the employees who were fired when they asked for some of their back wages.
95. Francis Shanly, for example, reported in 1873 that $35,000 worth of shares could be bought from their holders for $5,000. See Shanly to James Austin, May 7, 1873, *Shanly Papers*, Box 73, P.A.O.
96. Ibid., and Prince Albert *Ontario Observer*, May 29, 1873.
97. Stevens, pp. 446-47.
98. Prince Albert *Ontario Observer*, September 23, 1869.
99. Ontario, 33 Victoria, cap. XXXI, December 24, 1869.
100. Oshawa *Vindicator*, July 28, 1871.
101. Prince Albert *Ontario Observer*, September 9 and October 28, 1869.
102. Ibid., September 23, 1869.
103. Although the Uxbridge *Journal*, October 13, 1869 stated that $200,000 worth of stock had been subscribed, the Prince Albert *Ontario Observer*, December 16, 1869 stated that only $185,000 had been taken up. Whichever statement was closer to being correct, the total fell far short of the $3,000,000 capital which had been authorized by the railway's charter.
104. The Uxbridge *Journal*, October 13, 1869 calculated that the section would require the bonuses from Toronto, Scarborough, Markham, Uxbridge and Scott (totaling $250,000) as well as one hundred percent of the total subscribed stock of $200,000.
105. Prince Albert *Ontario Observer*, October 21, 1869.
106. Ibid.
107. Uxbridge *Journal*, September 21, 1870.
108. See Prince Albert *Ontario Observer*, July 21 and September 1, 1870; Uxbridge *Journal*, September 21, 1870.
109. Prince Albert *Ontario Observer*, September 1, 1870.
110. Higgins, p. 291.
111. Oshawa *Vindicator*, August 18, 1869; Prince Albert *Ontario Observer*, August 12, 1869.
112. Oshawa *Vindicator*, September 21, 1870.
113. Uxbridge *Reformer*, April 20, 1841. A second "official" ceremony was held on September 15, 1871.
114. Prince Albert *Ontario Observer*, November 16, 1871, and Stevens, I, p. 451.

Chapter 15
Organization for Reform, 1871-75

1. Prince Albert *Ontario Observer*, December 29, 1870.
2. Mr. Holman, quoted in Prince Albert *Ontario Observer*, March 28, 1872.
3. Ibid., January 23, 1873.
4. Ibid., April 18, 1872.
5. Ibid., August 28, 1873.
6. Ibid.
7. *Minutes . . . of the County of Ontario,* June 9, 1871, and By-law no. 216.
8. Uxbridge *Journal*, January 18 and January 25, 1872.
9. Ibid., January 25, 1872.
10. Ibid.
11. Ibid.
12. *Minutes . . . of the County of Ontario,* June 5, 1872, and By-law no. 226.
13. In 1881 Port Perry's population was 1800, while that of Uxbridge was 1824. Canada, *Census*, 1881.
14. Canada, *Census*, 1871 and 1881.
15. Canada, *Census*, 1871, 1881, and 1891.
16. Prince Albert *Ontario Observer*, June 1, 1871.
17. Canada, *Census*, 1871 and 1881.
18. Ibid. Calculations are my own.
19. Prince Albert *Ontario Observer*, February 13, 1873.
20. Ibid., February 13, 1873.
21. Toronto *Ontario Workman*, February 7, 20 and 27, 1873.
22. Ibid., February 27, 1873.
23. Ibid.
24. Canada, *Census*, 1871 and 1881. Calculations are my own. This table includes all municipalities north of Pickering and Whitby.
25. Ibid. This table includes Pickering, Whitby and Whitby E. Townships and the towns of Whitby and Oshawa.
26. Prince Albert *Ontario Observer*, June 30, 1870.
27. Ibid., July 7, 1870.
28. Ibid.
29. Ibid.
30. Ibid., May 18, 1871.
31. Uxbridge *Journal*, May 25, 1871.
32. Prince Albert *Ontario Observer*, September 28, 1871.
33. "Minutes of the 8th Annual Session of the Iron Workers International Union". Philadelphia, 1867, p. 5, (microfilm) P.A.C.
34. The basic antagonism between the skilled crafts workers and mass organizations of unskilled workers would be demonstrated more clearly with the rise of the Knights of Labour in the 1880s. See especially Charles Lipton, *The Trade Union Movement in Canada, 1827-1959* (Montreal, 1968), pp. 68-72.
35. Oshawa *Reformer*, March 15, 1872.
36. Ibid.
37. Prince Albert *Ontario Observer*, March 29, 1872.
38. A second local union, the Machinists' and Blacksmiths' International Union, no. 3, was organized on February 19, 1872. It was purely a mutual benefit and welfare society. Oshawa *Reformer*, March 1, 1872.
39. Prince Albert *Ontario Observer*, March 29, 1872.

40. Oshawa *Reformer*, March 23, 1872.
41. Ibid., March 29, 1872.
42. Ibid.
43. Oshawa *Reformer*, April 12, June 28, and November 1, 1872.
44. See especially a long series of letters and replies in the Oshawa *Reformer* and the Toronto *Ontario Workman* by "Heather Jock", the pseudonym of James Brown, an Oshawa labourer. Brown was bitterly opposed to the conciliatory attitude of Porteous and the leadership of the Oshawa Nine Hours League whom he often attacked for "selling out" the interests of the ordinary workman.
45. Oshawa *Reformer*, June 21, 1872.
46. In particular see the debate between James Brown ("Heather Jock") and the editor of the Toronto *Ontario Workman* on this point. *Ontario Workman*, July 11, August 1, November 21 and December 12, 1872.
47. Prince Albert *Ontario Observer*, December 28, 1871.
48. Oshawa *Reformer*, January 10, 1873.
49. Toronto *Ontario Workman*, January 16, 1873.
50. Ibid.
51. Uxbridge *Journal*, May 2, 1871.
52. Ibid., April 11, 1872.
53. Ibid., March 28, 1872.
54. Whitby *Chronicle*, March 20, 1873.
55. Oshawa *Reformer*, February 20, and May 7, 1874.
56. Ibid., May 15, 1874.
57. Prince Albert *Ontario Observer*, June 19, 1873; Port Perry *North Ontario Observer*, February 11, 1875.
58. H. Michell, "The Grange in Canada", *Bulletin of the Department of History and Political and Economic Science in Queen's University*, no. 13 (October, 1914), pp. 3-4. These rules and several others were printed in the Oshawa Reformer, July 2, 1875.
59. Ibid., p. 6.
60. Oshawa *Reformer*, May 15, 1874.
61. Oshawa *Reformer*, July 2 and 9, and December 24, 1875, January 14, 1876, and February 8, 1878.
62. Ibid., July 2, 1875.
63. Ibid.
64. Letter to the editor from "One of the Committee", Oshawa *Reformer*, July 9, 1875.
65. Ibid., December 17, 1875.
66. Ibid., December 24, 1875.
67. Michell, pp. 12-13.
68. Ibid., p. 9.
69. Cannington *Gleaner*, September 16, 1897.

INDEX